The International Series in
Guidance
and
Counseling

Consulting Editor
R. WRAY STROWIG
Department of Counselor Education
University of Wisconsin

Professional Problems in
School Counseling
Practice

Professional Problems in School Counseling Practice

Edited by

RICHARD S. DUNLOP

University of Missouri at Kansas City

INTERNATIONAL TEXTBOOK COMPANY

Scranton, Pennsylvania

830,001

Dedication

It is customary to dedicate books. The purposes behind this folk-way are obscure, but one flaunts tradition—especially if he is an educator—at peril of professional life and specialized limb. So, since one must, let this book stand dedicated: to school guidance workers who have problems in the practice of their profession; who seek to alter conditions for the benefit of their clientele; and who need aid, comfort, and sustenance while coping with the world of a changing counselor.

Referral

This book evolved from a collection of readings which were gathered for the use of advanced students of school counseling at the School of Education, University of Missouri at Kansas City. The UMKC seminars and the book are focused upon some of the more vexing problems faced by practitioners in the school setting who are trying to professionalize: (1) counselor role and function; (2) training, certification, and admission to practice; (3) competence, autonomy, and professionalism of the practitioner; and (4) the varied and complex matters of ethics.

The readings, and the seminar discussions evolving from them, have proved to be so productive of action and renewed commitment among students that it has seemed desirable to offer them to broader audiences. To be sure, most of the papers are already available to the profession, having been published during the past few years in diverse journals; but the utility of having a variety of opinions—most of them generously contributed by some of the outstanding leaders in school counseling today—on a rather narrow but important area of professional concern, within the limits of a single text, appears to have had distinct advantages.

There are probably three major audiences at whom the symposium is directed. The first of these would include formally organized groups of post-masters' students who have engaged themselves in university-level study of selected professional problems in counseling. This group, consisting entirely of practicing school counselors, is the one for which the collection of readings was originally compiled.

Another audience might include students of counseling who are in advanced stages of preparation, perhaps at the Practicum level, and who might well be introduced to some of the concerns which occupy substantial attention among their professional seniors.

A third audience, and perhaps the broadest, is composed of practitioners who for some reason are not continuing with university work, but who, possibly through their local guidance associations, are turning their attention to the problems discussed herein.

The book is not designed for the beginning student of counseling, although exposure to its contents would surely not harm him. The beginning student would be well advised to familiarize himself first with a variety of other professional problems in school counseling practice: the several counseling theories, methodological approaches, developmental characteristics of persons, sociological considerations in education, deviant personality, community pressures affecting educational practice, the mechanics of guidance office organization and administration, tools and techniques of specific guidance and counseling applications, learning theory, tests and measurements, and a multitude of philosophical concerns. It is better to be thoroughly competent at one's occupation before becoming too concerned with making that occupation a profession.

It is to the advanced student, and to the competent practitioner, that this collection of readings is addressed.

A number of ways suggest themselves for using any book as an instructional tool. Probably the best use of this text is as a stimulator. Its function is less one of instruction than of motivation to discussion and, hopefully, to action—"boat rocking," if you will. But the tool by itself is a lame thing without serious efforts toward interchange of the many ideas it may prompt, be they basically of agreement or of dissent. It is recommended that the reader concern himself with those articles in the book which are to occupy class attention, then respond in writing to each of the numerous points raised at the conclusion of each part of the book in the section labeled "Catharsis."

"Catharsis" items typically take issue with points raised by authors of the several papers. Many reflect questions and comments which have been raised by professional counselors who have used these materials in postmasters' seminars at the University of Missouri at Kansas City. Some represent the editor's efforts to stir things up. All, it is hoped, are pertinent.

Student responses might be typed in such a fashion that they occupy only the left half of those sheets of paper on which reactions are presented. The student's paper, once completed, might be passed on to another class member, whose responsibility it would become to comment on the original student's remarks in the space available on the typed sheet. The paper might next be given to still a second reviewer, who would read the materials and comment again. The whole package could then be routed to the professor for *his* comments, and get back, ultimately, to the student who initiated the procedure.

The numbering of the "Catharsis" items has been arranged so that each one can be easily identified. The articles are numbered consecutively throughout the book. The first Catharsis item for the first article is labeled 1A; the second item for the first article is 1B. Following this system, 28C refers to the third Catharsis item for Article 28.

The system could be used in various ways: permitting written responses to *single* "Catharsis" items; asking for responses to items *grouped by parts* of the book; perhaps the professor might want to select particular items for response; or a free choice system could be introduced. The important thing is that serious professional interaction be generated, by whatever means.

Counseling is either an evolving profession with the school application as a specialty, or is, itself, a specialty within the profession of education. This is a difficult and significant question, and it is dealt with at some length in the book which follows. Whatever school counseling is, though, it is clearly in the throes of evolution and is trying to aim somewhere. Those of us in counselor education, training, or professional practice who are concerned with its growth must increasingly turn our attention to some basic questions, many of which are related to issues treated here. It is hoped that the readings, referred herein to the profession, will contribute to discussion, reasoned controversy, and the ultimate kinds of action which are basic to professional growth. Such growth must, in the editor's bias, precede the full opportunity for school counselors to do the work for which they are trained; and to do it ethically and well, without irrelevant interference, and in the best interests of the students whom they serve.

If this collection of papers contributes in some measure to the attainment of the goals suggested, its purposes will have been well served.

RICHARD S. DUNLOP

Kansas City, Missouri
May, 1968

Contents

Professional Problems in
School Counseling
Practice

part I

The Counselor's Role and Function

PRESENTING PROBLEM

The role of the school counselor can be stated simply. He is the specialist on the school staff who is uniquely qualified to help students work out increasingly complex problems of vocational choice, help them plan and carry through meaningful and appropriate educational programs, and help them identify more satsifactory solutions to personal-social problems which may be having an adverse effect upon their lives. To this definition of responsibility could be added other areas of the counselor's particular expertise. These might include specialized competence in psychology and psychometry, child and adolescent growth and development, mental health, group procedures, broad personal knowledge of the school, and so on.

But the role which any counselor plays may not always be related as closely as we would like to the lengthy training which he has experienced. Too often his position in the school and the duties which he is expected to perform there are related less to his particular professional competencies than to the semi-skilled job which an administrator has in mind for him. Such a job, as defined by too many administrators, may include such diverse and inappropriate duties as: proctoring group tests; performing routine clerical, filing, and low-grade secretarial tasks; obtaining homework assignments for absent students; carrying out the school's disciplinary policies; translating student course requests into code numbers for data processing equipment; checking up on truants; making out class schedules; computing grade point averages; selling dance tickets, patrolling the halls, following up on overdue books; and whatnot.

Super Clerk is needed in the school—there is much for Super Clerk to do. But the counselor is not properly involved in the performance of Super Clerk's duties. That's for someone else to do. Nonetheless, it is probably safe to say that thousands of school counselors are forced by local job demands into positions where avoidance of Super Clerk's responsibilities in favor of conducting a professional counseling practice is held as being tantamount to treason. Fears can be raised, quite realistically, over the safety with which any counselor can protest limitations imposed upon him by those who have specialized in school administration. Nevertheless (and putting aside for the moment the question of who on the

school staff should define limits of the counseling practitioner's autonomy),
it seems desirable to look closely at this question of counselor role as it has
been treated by a number of persons who have contributed to our professional literature on this subject in recent years.

In the first article, broad treatment is afforded the question of counselor
role by Dr. Gail Farwell, of the University of Wisconsin. The relationship
which exists between the practicing counselor in the school setting and
the pressures which may be exerted by his several publics is examined by
Purdue University's Drs. Bruce Shertzer and Shelley C. Stone. Dr. Buford
Stefflre and the editor of this volume have both been concerned with the
way in which some of these "publics" view the counselor, and papers
from both are included. Particular attention to the elementary school
counselor's role is provided by Mrs. Edna Harrison of Wichita, Kansas.
Psychiatrist I. N. Berlin looks at the counselor as one who has a unique
mental health function; and Dr. Dan C. Lortie, of the University of
Chicago, raises questions related to whether the counselor is properly conceived of as being some sort of administrator, an advocate of policy, or a
therapist. Toward the end of the section Dr. C. C. Dunsmoor calls upon
counselors to get busy in establishing their professional identity. A study
by Dr. William D. Dannenmaier reports data relating to the question of
full- or part-time counselor employment. The relationship between time
availability and job demands is treated by Dr. W. Wesley Tenneyson.

As the reader studies the articles presented, there are a number of
thoughts which he might bear in mind as he prepares to contend with
"Catharsis" items presented at the conclusion of each part for his consideration:

What of the common criterion that counselors in schools must first demonstrate teaching competence? Does this have any merit?

Are counselors members of a unique profession, are they specialists
within psychology or some other occupation, or are they educators with a
highly specialized role?

How about the question of the many non-professional assignments
which are so often handed to counselors?

Various extra-professional pressures may influence counselor role as
much as anything pertinent. What can counselors do about this? Should we
undertake to exert professional power? *Can* we exert professional power?

Does the question of *seriousness of the problem* have any relationship
to whether the counselor (as opposed to some other professional person)
should be involved?

What defenses have we against the administrator who misuses
counselors? Are "Shape up or ship out" our only alternatives?

What tools do (or should) counselors actually have with which to be of
help to people?

If we agree that the counselor should not be authoritarian, do we also buy the notion that he should not be an authority? If he *is* an authority, is it appropriate for him to make his authoritative competence available to others—or is this confusable with advice-giving?

How do we feel about all of the amateurs who provide "counseling" assistance to people? Is it desirable to try preserving our occupational identity better than we do? Would professional controls over certification lend themselves to improved role definition?

What about the counselor-teacher, counselor-administrator assignment? Do these represent appropriate professional function?

What *is* the counselor's professional role? What is *not*?

1

The Role of the School Counselor

Gail F. Farwell, Ed. D.*

Counseling is the primary function of the school counselor. In this function of counseling, the school counselor works individually with each pupil trying to help the counselee gain a meaningful perspective of his strengths and weaknesses, a clear vision of his opportunity, and a knowledge of the existing or possible interferences in his maturing and adjusting throughout life. It is not the function of the counselor to "tell" the pupil. There are enough "significant others" in each person's life committed to telling. Kahlil Gibran [1, p. 62] in *The Prophet* eloquently develops a philosophy for this counseling function:

> No man can reveal to you aught but that which already lies half asleep in the dawning of your knowledge.
> The *counselor* [mine] who walks in the shadow of the temple, among his followers, gives not of his wisdom but rather of his faith and his loving-ness.
> If he is indeed wise he does not bid you enter the house of his wisdom, but rather leads you to the threshold of your own mind.

The school counselor committed to assisting each pupil in the struggle for self understanding has his role defined for him. This counselor must recognize his prime commitment, the attendant functions associated with this commitment, and lastly, must have the courage to stand up and be counted in support of this commitment. Too many so-called school counselors do not have professional preparation for the task and consequently do not recognize the uniqueness of professional counseling. Rather, these school counselors (?) reflect much more vividly their experiential background as former instructor, and end up doing many things akin to this activity.

The role of the school counselor can be identified as: (1) He is a school staff member committed to education and the educational process; (2) It is his function to study human lives and the contingent environment in which they live; (3) The school counselor should devote a two-thirds majority of his time to counseling with individuals; (4) He is a consultant to teachers, administrators, and parents.

*Dr. Farwell is Professor of Education at the University of Wisconsin, Madison. His article appeared originally in *Counselor Education and Supervision*, 1:1:40 (Fall 1961), and is reprinted with permission of the author and of the journal. Dr. Farwell is President (1968–1969) of the American Personnel and Guidance Association.

Many implications attend this role for the school counselor. School administrators should demand professionally prepared counselors. They should not select chemistry teachers for counselors but chemistry teachers to instruct in chemistry. It has always been a wonderment why counselors aren't hired in terms of their knowledge about counseling and their commitment to counseling rather than those reasons which have persisted during the past decades. In 1961, antiquated notions about the proficiency of personnel prepared as experts in instruction for implementing counseling procedures should be dissipated. I will support wholeheartedly the necessary commitment of the school counselor to education and the purposes of the school. I will continually support the desirability of a minimal amount of teaching experience or associated experience to familiarize the school counselor with classroom realities, problems and setting. This enables the school counselor to be more accepted as a school staff member. However, those persons who demand year upon year of classroom experience are closing their eyes to the tunnel vision created. The person intensely committed to school counseling will learn more about the total curriculum, the total school situation, and a broader segment of the pupil enrollment from his vantage point of counselor than in the restricted environment of one subject matter area, in one classroom, for years ad infinitum.

With what instruments can the school counselor work? The first instrument at the disposal of the school counselor is his personality. In the instructional program at the University of Wisconsin a requirement of the course *Counseling: Theory and Issues* centers on a paper "My Counselor Person" which is an attempt to have potential counselors turn inward for self reflection and assessment. If you will, self-knowledge on the part of the school counselor is as important as the counselee's self-knowledge which the counselor attempts to promote. This paper is followed by interviews devoted to clarification, further expansion and self-growth—counseling if you will. Developmental counseling is a growth process—growth in self-understanding and enhancement of adjusting as a necessary construct of life. Counseling as growth is one segment of the helping relationship continuum. One end of this continuum involving a telling (advisor or instructional function) with progression to counseling (self-growth) to psychotherapy (cure and treatment). The basic instrument for implementation of the school counselor role is one's own person.

Second, many instruments developed on the measurement and human development scenes are necessary for implementation of counseling. Such items as statistical concepts, standardized tests, rating scales, anecdotes, autobiographies and others too numerous to mention in this discourse are essential for functioning in a school setting. Conceptual knowledge in career development, personality development, curriculum implementation, administrative protocol and the evolving societal scene are essential if self-growth in the school setting is to be enhanced and the base for effective adult adjusting is to be established. Research tools are an essential ingredient for the school counselor. The professional role of the school counselor demands that he be a good consumer of research studies in many fields of endeavor and that he too, research his own activity. The best way to improvement and development of quality in school counseling is to expand the research horizons.

Where will the school counselor function? Naturally in the school and at all school levels. We have minimized the work of the school counselor, through default, in the elementary school. The trait-factor theorists in counseling took us off on a measurement binge; the Rogerians made us face up to the real importance of relationship in counseling, not that people of other points of view didn't ultimately contend with relationships. With developmental counseling focused on growth and implemented in the school setting, the importance of each pupil developing a counseling relationship and being helped to know and understand the contribution a counselor can make should receive emphasis in the elementary school. If we would do this, junior and senior high school students wouldn't approach the counselor's office with trepidation and wonder "what have I done wrong now." The pupil would have an expectancy for the contribution the counselor can make. The school counselor that will give of himself to his relationships with each counselee is in a position to help each pupil understand more meaningfully the meaning of child study (pupil appraisal) and to promote optimal performance on the assessment and evaluative instruments employed. Maturity plays an important role in all of counseling but young counselees are as open to psychological love, acceptance and understanding as the octogenarian, maybe more so. Counseling and the attendant pupil appraisal activity is important when internal placement and interferences to learning are the focus of attention. The school counselor works here to assist in greater performance in subject matter learning. At the elementary level curricular choices for pupils are few and far between. They may have a role in planning implementation but society determines much of the experiential base to be provided. The school counselor at this level will spend considerable time in direct consultation with teachers and parents to assist them in decision making on behalf of the pupil.

As the pupil matures and moves into the junior and senior high school much more emphasis is placed on self-determination, decision and choice making, and self-understanding. Effective relationships established at the elementary level promote developmental counseling at this level in contrast to much of what goes on today—"closing the barn door after the horse has escaped."

The area of social adjustment has not received much mention. Surely we're concerned with this, so are most of society's institutions. We must remember that much of social adjustment in the school still centers in settings where subject matter of the curriculum takes front seat. I want the counselor to be sensitive to total development but the school counselor continues to exist as a professional worker in this institution if his services and skills contribute to the unique characteristics of that institution.

In summary, the role of the school counselor is envisaged as a catalyst of human growth and self-understanding. He should spend a 2/3 majority of his time in one to one counseling or consulting relationships. He is expert in his knowledge of counseling theory and procedures, career development, measure and the role of the school in developmental behavior of young people. He is an educator; he is also an applied psychologist. He is a counselor because he has preparation for the role and selects this role rather than being promoted to it as a reward for good instruction. Let us recognize the unique role of the counselor in the educational setting. Let us accept, select and prepare those who want to be counselors. Let us strengthen our profession by defining the school counselor's role so that confusion ceases to exist.

BIBLIOGRAPHY

1. Gibran, Kahlil. *The Prophet*. New York: Alfred A. Knopf, 1953.

2

The School Counselor and His Publics:
A Problem in Role Definition

Bruce Shertzer, Ed. D.
Shelley C. Stone, Ph. D.*

Recently it has become commonplace in psychology to speak of personal or individual identity. To borrow from contemporary sociological theory, we are speaking of an occupational identity which could be termed a role definition. In general, role theorists stress that individual behavior within a role is determined by the expectancies or demands of the role. By definition, at least in Parsonian theory, role is viewed as a set of complementary expectations which result in behavior [13]. The key word in this definition for the purpose of this paper is complementary. It is contended that much of the current difficulty and confusion surrounding the school counselor's role stems from the contradictory and conflicting expectancies of his various publics.

Why resurrect this old ghost and dress him in the latest continental garb, or for our female counterparts, the latest Cassini fashion? Precisely because lively ghosts such as this one, like unresolved, repressed material, do not stay buried for long. This resurrection has only one purpose: to increase our awareness of what we are as counselors or, in an ideal sense, of what we might become when and if the ghost truly is laid to rest.

One profitable means of seeing what we are, here and now, is to look at the counselor's role through the eyes of his various publics. Obviously, this produces a distorted image, or caricature. Caricatures are harsh but nonetheless revealing because they contain elements of truth which place in bold relief the most salient characteristics the individual conveys in his efforts to meet the demands of his role.

Who are the school counselor's publics? They are neither mysterious nor ethereal; rather, they are obvious and real. They are the groups who hold the conflicting expectancies . . . pupils, teachers, administrators, parents, and other segments of the public-at-large. In briefer terms, they are the groups the school counselor serves.

*Drs. Shertzer and Stone are Professors of Education, Purdue University, Lafayette, Indiana. Their article appeared originally in the *Personnel and Guidance Journal*, 41:8:687 (April 1963), and is reprinted with permission of the authors and of the journal.

PUPILS' OPINIONS OF COUNSELORS

What perceptions do pupils, the direct recipients of counselor services, hold of counselors? When questioned, most students indicate they believe a guidance program adds something of value to their school. Dr. Leona Tyler notes that a large number of inadequately controlled surveys reveal from 80 to 90 per cent satisfaction with counseling primarily because "there are certain social conventions that make for positive findings in studies planned this way" [16]. Consequently, such surveys can be deceptive since they tend to reveal only the positive and lead to heightened contentment with our lot. Dr. Robert Gibson's study of guidance services in 12 secondary schools within a three-state area is pertinent here. He found that more than one-fourth of the students indicated counselors had not assisted them personally in any way; that 56 per cent reported they were not sure what constituted the activities of their school guidance program; that one-third of them reported the program had not been described, explained, or outlined to them during their three or four years in high school; and that many felt shortchanged because test results were not interpreted to them [8]. Dr. Claude Grant studied the help given to students by counselors in educational planning, vocational planning, and personal-emotional problems. His analysis revealed that counselors were preferred as the students' first source of help in educational and vocational planning, but not with personal-emotional problems. Students at best perceived the counselor as playing a minor role in assisting them with problems of a personal-emotional nature [7].

Dr. Marilyn Heilfron, using an adaptation of Robinson's case descriptions, asked students to indicate the degree of counseling needed by students with various kinds of problems. Pupils felt that those who were bright and performing well in school did not need counseling; rather, it should be reserved for those who displayed marked character disorders [9]. Dr. Ralph E. Jenson's study of pupil reactions toward the guidance program in Phoenix, Arizona, high schools showed that while counselors generally were preferred over teachers, parents, and friends as sources of help, students preferred to discuss personal problems with parents and peers [11].

Studies such as these lead to the conclusion that students do not view the counselor as being an effective source of help except in the area of educational-vocational decision-making. However, it should be noted that students say others who are in critical situations should have the benefit of the counselor's skills, despite the fact that they themselves would not seek the assistance of a counselor.

One might easily pause here and ask: why is this service for *others* with problems? The readily available glib generalization that this tendency merely represents a student's reluctance to admit to his own problems is inadequate. While this kind of rationalization holds a measure of comfort, it suffers from the danger of leading to still more contentment. The painful but more profitable view might be that while students are willing to see *others* risk themselves to this service, they are reluctant to place themselves in such an obviously risky situation. Why should this be? There is no sure answer. A partial explanation might be found in counselors' inability or failure to convey to the group they serve directly the feeling of acceptance and understanding which most counselors claim to prize. Counselors who are heavily involved in a variety of tasks do not have time to exercise the basic function of counseling which is the indispensable means for communicating such attitudes. Obviously the full benefits of a school counseling program cannot be realized when such perceptions are held by those who are the primary recipients of the services.

TEACHERS' OPINIONS OF COUNSELORS

What caricature may be drawn from teachers' perceptions of the counselor? Dr. John G. Darley's forthright presentation of the attitudes of teachers provides a cutting fivefold description: (1) counselors are administrators and the nicest thing you can say about administrators is that they are a necessary evil which may be tolerated but better yet eradicated; (2) counselors provide ancillary services and are therefore expendable; (3) counselors coddle and pamper those who would, and perhaps should, flunk out; (4) the counselor's pseudo-Freudian, pseudo-psychometric jargon is the purest nonsense; and, (5) his pretense of confidentiality is merely a shield to hide behind when the welfare of the institution is involved or his activities challenged [5].

While it is tempting, for the purposes of this paper, *not* to soften the edges of Darley's conclusions, most school counselors come from the ranks of teachers and therefore carry with them some residual feelings from their own teaching days which make the above particularly harsh. A quote from Dr. George A. Pierson reveals one possible motive for such hostile opinions:

> . . . it is difficult for the classroom teacher to accept the need for specialists in human relations in the school. For to admit that specialists are necessary is to imply that teachers have certain limitations which they are reluctant to face [14].

However, the concern is with the seeds of truth within Darley's caricature not with Pierson's hypothetical explanation of the dynamics behind such attitudes for to slip at this point results only in contentment.

Possibly, teachers are largely correct in these negative assessments of the role of the counselor. If so, it then follows that: (1) to the degree that the counselor functions as an administrator he will be seen as an administrator; (2) to the degree that the counselor provides only an ancillary service, rather than an integrated, valuable service to students and teachers, he will be expendable; (3) to the degree that the counselor's acceptance and understanding of pupils is purposeless coddling and pampering of academic incompetents, teachers are justified in their misperceptions; (4) to the degree that counselors rely on jargon rather than clear, understandable communications to the staff, they risk the brand "charlatan" in its clearest sense—"one who pretends to knowledge"; (5) to the degree that confidentiality is used as a self-protective device rather than an indispensable part of ethical conduct, the counselor's activities are suspect. In all fairness, could any respectable teacher tolerate, let alone relate, to the individual occupying such a role?

ADMINISTRATORS' OPINIONS OF COUNSELORS

What impressions do administrators have of the school counselor? Grant reported that administrators believed that counselors were not particularly competent to handle students' personal-emotional problems [7]. In relation to this perception, a recent issue of *Look* quotes one anonymous principal as saying:

> I've honestly failed to see much good come out of the so-called counseling services, in schools or out, that these people (dropouts) are referred to. All too often, the counseling people are second-rate, both in their training and in their human makeup. They seldom get really close to the students. What they tell them has little to do with their problems; it's just jargon that bores them and makes them distrustful [4].

Another and better documented index to the amount of confidence placed in counselors exists in the assignments made by school administrators. A number of studies such as those by Kenneth Martyn [12], Florence Purcell [15], Theodore Vassello and Leslie Kindred [17], report counselors frequently functioning as clerks or quasi-administrators. Many administrators expect the counselor to be active in certain administrative and instructional areas such as curriculum planning, pupil attendance, schedule making, discipline, substitute teaching, and the like.

The caricature within the quote from *Look* is patently clear. Counselors are ineffective, if not incompetent, at any level one chooses to examine. It is implied that they do not earn their keep by producing the requisite number of "cures." The consensus of the other studies cited above is that the administrator views the counselor as a "jack-of-all-trades." While seemingly unrelated, these views are intimately intertwined. To view the counselor's job in terms of a favorite administrative criterion, that of "efficiency," seems particularly inappropriate in the light of the disparate and mutually incompatible expectations of administrators. To relegate an employee to the position of jack-of-all trades and then condemn him for his failure to perform the unique service for which he was originally employed is grossly unfair and possibly represents deceitful hiring practice. Clearly, if one hires an individual to do one thing, loads him down with a second and a third and a fourth set of tasks, he is unable to perform his *presumed* original assignment very competently.

The fundamental issue is why the counselor permits this sequence of events to occur. An even more disturbing thought of concern to counselors is that perhaps in a subtle and shrewd way they avoid facing the issue of a real test of their skills and services by tacit acceptance of inappropriate assignments or passive tolerance of such assignments.

PARENTS' OPINIONS OF COUNSELORS

What perceptual sets do parents have toward the role of the school counselor? Dr. William Evraiff reports that parents ranked counselor duties in the following order: programming, handling school problems, counseling pupils on future careers, and counseling pupils on personal problems [6]. Dr. Harry Bergstein and Grant completed a study of parents' expectations of school counselors based on interviewing 187 mothers and 179 fathers of students in Grades 6–12. The school was located in a small compact community with an established guidance program that had maintained good public relations. They found, at a statistically significant level, that counselors were rated as more helpful in the areas of educational-vocational-personal problems than were the family's best friend or the school principal. In the areas ranked, parents thought counselors were least helpful with personal-emotional-social problems [3].

Two issues are suggested by the rather skimpy material cited. Evraiff's study indicates that parents seem to view counseling in an outdated way since they rate program planning as the first duty of the counselor. The contention here is *not* that program planning is unworthy of the counselor's time but that it is no longer considered *the* major task of the counselor. Priority certainly should be given other duties. It is not the intention to detract from the research efforts of Bergstein and Grant but for the purposes of this paper it seems only slightly encouraging and more than a little saddening that counselors, who ostensibly devote the major portion of their energy to the so-called "helping relationship," are rated only a little more helpful than the family's best friend. In passing it is hoped that the "best friend" does not refer to "man's best friend" old dog Tray, even though pets may possess a certain therapeutic value!

Although it is difficult to find published statements related to parents' expectancies for counselors, there is no dearth of opinion among professional workers regarding what parents often do expect. There is little to be gained by belaboring the point that parents often wish the counselor to perform a persuasive function in the areas of educational and occupational choice or to somehow set right child-rearing errors which often have accumulated for years. Needless to say, the serving up of "instant aspiration" and the facile repair of long standing parent-child conflicts are unrealistic expectations. The question becomes: should counselors permit themselves to be used to persuade adolescents to make "right" choices and decisions especially when "right" is often synonymous with agreement or submission to parental demands?

CURRENT, EMERGING OPINIONS AFFECTING THE GENERAL PUBLIC'S VIEW OF COUNSELORS

What does the public-at-large expect of the counselor and why? Since the Russians launched Sputnik in October, 1957, counselors have been inundated with constant pleas to direct, pressure, channel, place, and put youngsters into careers demanded by America's manpower shortages. Counselors are seen as responsible for providing the appropriate number of workers to fill the jobs society needs. They are expected to coerce and seduce students into taking mathematics, science, and foreign languages. Especially pervasive has been the view that counselors are to identify, cultivate, and place students with exceptional talent in critically needed professions.

Thus, the mental health and welfare of the individual are relegated to a lesser position than manpower needs. Such expectations apparently minimize the well-documented relationship of personal adjustment and mental health to job satisfaction and productivity. Efficient manpower utilization is as dependent upon the former as the latter.

Appropriate counseling, from the economist's point of view, stems from the pressures of society and the shape of the nation's economy. The National Manpower Commission has stated:

> School officials use their guidance and counseling staffs primarily for vocational guidance purposes and, when expanded resources of staff and funds permit, also for counseling students with personal adjustment problems [2].

This statement implies that only when sufficient funds are available can schools legitimately be concerned with a full-fledged guidance program. Not only is this implication present but a rather clear indictment is made that this *is* what school officials do in actual practice.

Dr. Henry Weitz, in responding to some of the manpower pressures, has pointed out:

> The youth who is channeled into science or language study or engineering because he is "best suited" to this has been robbed of a chance to learn how this major life decision was made. He may be successful, he may be

well adjusted, he may be happy, but he has not learned the sense of responsibility which comes from making decisions and *accepting the consequences* of that choice [18].

Is there not danger in the imposition of the counselor's conception of social
needs upon the planning of an individual client's career? Manpower
trends are pertinent information for both counselor and client. The objection is to the effect of such suggestions by manpower experts on public
opinion. Will their statements eventually result in the ultimate public
impression that counselors are "hidden persuaders" or "flesh peddlers"
whose primary aim is to fill empty cells in the Bureau of Labor Statistics'
manpower matrix?

NECESSARY STEPS

It seems abundantly clear that counselors will continue to be the
target of criticism and will in fact deserve the contradictory blur of perceptions held of them until they themselves do something about it. A basic responsibility of any professional is to redirect people's attitudes toward his
role and to cultivate public understanding and support. Counselors cannot close their eyes to the harsh reality that constant interpretation of their
work to their publics is necessary. What steps must now be taken to provide
a set of complementary role expectations for the school counselor?

First, *it is of major importance that counselors articulate their own
identity.* Dr. William L. Hitchcock's comparison of the duties counselors
performed with what they believed they should *not* do revealed a striking
study of contrasts:

Of 1,154 counselors who now assist pupils with course planning, 40 per
cent do not feel it is their job.
Of 1,152 counselors who now assist pupils with occupational plans, 40 per
cent do not feel it is their job.
Of 1,101 counselors who now assist teachers with pupil's problems, 37 per
cent do not feel it is their job.
Of 893 counselors who now interpret test results to teachers, 33 per cent
do not feel it is their job.
Of 875 counselors now counseling with parents of failing pupils, 34 per
cent do not feel it is their job [10].

From these data it is apparent that school counselors as a group disagree
greatly with meeting legitimate demands which are basic to their reasons
for existence as a professional group.

As school counselors become identified with inappropriate activities
such as those described earlier in this paper, stereotyping sets in which
hampers and distorts their professional role. This is apparent when one
discusses school counselors' work with them. In some schools and communities counselors see their job as merely that of checking college re-

quirements for students. They hold the view that school exists only to prepare pupils for college. The purpose of counseling, therefore, is to set up
procedures for movement to college. In doing this counseling becomes
easy and automatic, providing a measure of stability for the counselor. In
other schools and communities, counseling is seen as a matter of test administration. The view held is that test results present students as they
really are and that the counselor can automatically predict students' fu-
tures from the results. Many counselors are long on test administration.
Cabinet drawers bulge with test results. However, few of these measuring
enthusiasts effectively implement test results. In other schools and communities counselors seem to view counseling as a matter of keeping records.
Their view is that past academic success or failure is the best predictor of
future success or failure. Hence, records are the prime focus of their existence. In still other places, counselors place all their energies in the technology of groups. The value of group experiences cannot be denied, but all
too often the emphasis is upon group technology and techniques rather than
upon the individual's experience in human relations provided by the group
setting.

All of this points to the fact that the counselor is a thoroughly confused
fellow. One reason for the confusion is that too often counselors serve dual
roles—that of teacher and counselor. Dr. Dugald S. Arbuckle reasons:

> It is interesting to note that of these groups [teachers, administrators, and
> specialized service personnel] it is only the school counselor who is willing
> to accept the part-time, dual-role status. Other professional workers may
> spend only part of their time in the service of the school, but they are not
> part-time doctors, or part-time nurses, or part-time psychologists, or psy-
> chiatrists. Like pregnancy, "they are or they ain't," and there is no in-
> between status. We have no doctor-teacher, or nurse-principal, or psy-
> chologist-janitor, but we have thousands of teacher-counselors, or even
> more absurd, principal-counselors, and even, horror added upon horror,
> superintendent-counselors. Even worse, this schizophrenic fellow doesn't
> seem to mind this dual or triple status, and goes blithely walking off in
> several directions at the same time, quite unaware that one set of feet is
> falling over the other [1].

Another reason for such confusion is that giving tests and being an administrator's handyman is the easiest, most secure role for the counselor.
Can counselors afford to waste their training and skills in this fashion?
The stereotypes of others are out of focus with the nature and purposes of
the counseling profession. Continued attempts to satisfy distorted images
can hardly promise much except further frustration and confusion.

*The second step is that counselors must communicate their role to their
publics.* Communication with teachers and administrators is especially
needed because students' and parents' perceptions of the school counselor
are reflections of how the counselor is viewed by teachers and administra-

tors. Their view, in turn, is dependent upon how counselors view themselves. How the counselor views himself will determine not only what he will do in the school and community but the effectiveness with which he does it.

Communication of role demands enlightened leadership. A talk at a single parent-teachers' meeting will not serve the purpose. It requires career-long contacts in which the counselor lucidly and frequently explains the purposes and methods of his work, *i.e.*, his reason for being. Such contacts must be frequent as well as lucid because the counselor's work is not static. Indeed, if he can adequately communicate the role expectancies he legitimately can and will meet as a professional, his activities and duties will grow and expand in a complementary fashion.

To some it may seem that this has been a harsh and unyielding condemnation of the counselor's failure to define his own occupational role clearly and unequivocally. This is intentional in order to stress professional responsibility as an indispensable part of an occupational role and to underscore the importance of the individual's own identity and personal integrity within that role.

The personal gain which can accrue to the individual counselor who actively enters the fight against misunderstanding, misperception, and distortion of his role is unlimited. However, the counselor cannot adequately handle this conflict until he is reasonably certain that he knows what he is, who he is, and where he hopes to go. In other words, he must seek his own unique identity within the cultural context of his professional setting.

Reliance on the traditional role of the counselor will not suffice, since the traditional role rapidly grows outmoded and ineffectual. An "other-directed," multiple identity based on an interpretation of opinions from segments of the school counselor's various publics leads into a blind maze of confusion. Therefore, in this context, occupational identity, like individual identity, is the responsibility of each counselor. As Allen Wheelis points out:

> "Modern man cannot recapture an identity out of the past; for his old identity was not lost, but outgrown. Identity is not, therefore, to be found; it is to be created and achieved" [19].

REFERENCES

1. Arbuckle, Dugald S. "The Conflicting Functions of the School Counselor," *Counselor Educ. Supv.* (1961), 1, 56.

2. Bray, Douglas W. "Vocational Guidance in National Manpower Policy," *Personnel Guid. J.* (1955), 34, 197.

3. Bergstein, Harry B., & Grant, Claude W. "How Parents Perceive the Counselor's Role," *Personnel Guid J.* (1961), 39, 698–703.

4. Brossard, Chandler. "Teenager Without a Job," *Look*, 26 (February 27, 1962), 33.

5. Darley, John G. "The Faculty Is Human, Too." *Personnel Guid. J.* (1956), 35, 228.

6. Evraiff, William. "Perceptions of the Counselor," *Sch. Couns.* (1961), 8, 78–82.

7. Grant, Claude W. "The Counselor's Role," *Personnel Guid. J.* (1954), 33, 74–77.

8. Gibson, Robert E. "Pupil Opinions of High School Guidance Programs," *Personnel Guid. J.* (1962), 40, 453–457.

9. Heilfron, Marilyn. "The Function of Counseling as Perceived By High School Students," *Personnel Guid. J.* (1960), 39, 133–136.

10. Hitchcock, William L. "Counselors Feel They Should," *Personnel Guid. J.* (1953), 32, 72–73.

11. Jenson, Ralph E. "Student Feeling About Counseling Help," *Personnel Guid. J.* (1955), 33, 498–503.

12. Martyn, Kenneth A. "We Are Wasting the Counselor's Time," *California J. of Second. Educ.* (1957), 32, 439–441.

13. Parsons, Talcott, & Shills, Edward, (Eds.). *Toward a General Theory of Action.* Cambridge: Harvard University Press, 1954.

14. Pierson, George A. "Aesop and the School Counselor," *Personnel Guid. J.* (1954), 32, 326–329.

15. Purcell, Florence. "Counselor Duties—a Survey," *Sch. Couns.* (1957), 4, 35–38.

16. Tyler, Leona F. *The Work of the Counselor.* New York: Appleton-Century-Crofts, 1953, p. 272.

17. Vassello, Theodore, & Kindred, Leslie. "How Counseling Can Be Improved," *Nations Schs.* (1957), 59, 58–60.

18. Weitz, Henry. "Creating a Climate for Accepting Guidance Services," *Personnel Guid. J.* (1959), 38, 190–194.

19. Wheelis, Allen. *The Quest for Identity.* New York: W. W. Norton, 1958, p. 205.

3

Professional Educators, Parents, and Students Assess the Counselor's Role

Richard S. Dunlop, Ed. D.*

Differences of opinion appear to exist between groups of persons interested in secondary schools as to the duties of the counselor as a professional person. Casual observation and more precise investigations suggest that tasks for which modern school counselors are trained are not necessarily the same tasks which they are actually expected by their various publics to perform on the job.

The counselor's role in the high school setting is a function not only of his own training and best judgment, but also of various professional and community pressures and expectancies. The counselor is not alone in his efforts to determine his role, nor are the influences of his various professional organizations alone in shaping the operational environment within which he will function. While the counselor's particular training and experience perhaps best qualify him to determine the appropriateness of numerous activities available to him, the boundaries within which he will be able to perform his services are affected by many forces not under his control, and perhaps not sympathetic or even in contradiction to the expectancies the counselor holds for himself.

Particularly influential forces might include those exhibited by school administrators, the teaching faculty, counselor educators, fellow pupil personnel workers, and the counselor's student clients and their parents.

Previous investigations have been addressed to the problem at hand. Dr. Claude W. Grant [6] found New York counselors to be insecure in appraising their own effectiveness in dealing with problems of a personal-emotional character, and more secure in the vocational areas of guidance. The role of the counselor as seen by administrators was investigated by Dr. L. D. Schmidt [11] and Grant [5]. Dr. James A. Stewart [12] surveyed teacher attitudes toward guidance practices, finding that women teachers tended to be more accepting of such services than men. Parent perceptions of the counselor's role were assessed by Dr. Harry W. Bergstein [1], who asked that they nominate persons who might be helpful to students under

°Dr. Dunlop is an Associate Professor of Education at the University of Missouri at Kansas City. His article appeared originally in the *Personnel and Guidance Journal*, 43:10:1024 (June 1965), and is reprinted with permission of the author and of the journal.

various circumstances; and in a study of student attitudes toward counselors, Grant [5] found that students perceived the counselor as giving acceptable assistance in the categories of vocational and educational planning, but as being less helpful in the personal-social area. Dr. Robert Gibson [4], in another assessment of student attitudes toward guidance, found that pupils regarded counselors as being persons who performed various interesting duties, few of which appeared related to counseling. Dr. H. W. Houghton [8] found that various groups of respondents to his questionnaire evidenced differing attitudes toward the school counselor's role, and differences between student and adult respondents were apparent. Dr. Herman Roemmich and Dr. John L. Schmidt [10] found that San Diego counselors seemed to be of limited assistance to students in college planning.

METHOD

The study was undertaken to test the hypothesis that no significant differences exist among various groupings of professional edu***** and lay persons in their opinions as to what tasks and f*****nes of similar tasks constitute appropriate parts of the school c*****selor's role.

Literature relating to cou***** and guidance was reviewed, and from the review a list was developed of 106 specific tasks that high school counselors might reasonably be expected to perform. The tasks were presented in a rating form to doctoral students in counseling and guidance at Arizona State University, who assigned each of the tasks to one of the following seven counselor responsibility areas: Vocational, Educational, or Personal Counseling; Testing and Diagnosis; Administrative-Clerical; Teacher-Role Expectancy; and Counseling Profession (tasks related to ethical and professional conduct of counselors behaving as members of an organized profession). After two rating form administrations, 81 items remained that had been consistently assigned by respondents to appropriate responsibility areas (task groups). Between 10 and 12 tasks were listed in each of the seven task groups.

Following a sub-study during the summer of 1963 in which the reliability of tasks was assessed as reported elsewhere [2], 42 tasks remained, including six in each of the seven task-groups, which were acceptable as to consistency.

The tasks were placed at random in an opinionnaire which was administered in the winter of 1963. Included in the randomly selected samples were 25 California counselor educators, 24 high school administrators, 25 high school counselors, and 35 male and 35 female teachers associated with a large Southern California high school district; 25 college-preparatory and 25 job-bound seniors, and the mothers of 25 college-preparatory and 25 job-bound seniors in the same school district.

All administrators, counselors, and teachers possessed appropriate California credentials. All but three of responding counselor educators held doctoral degrees in guidance and counseling. In large measure, the territory of the high school district from which the students and mothers were secured is a bedroom community for San Diego, and homes in the area range in price from among the most expensive to tract developments with prices spanning a wide range although a rural area is included.

Respondents to the opinionnaire were asked to read each task, and to indicate if in their judgment counselors (1) should, (2) probably should, (3) maybe should, (4) probably should not, or (5) should not perform the task. In addition, respondents were encouraged to add written remarks in response to broad, neutral questions relating to the school counselor's job.

Eighty per cent of persons contacted completed and returned their opinionnaires. Groups were then compared by assessing the significance of difference in the proportions of positive responses given by them (1) to each of the opinionnaire's seven task groups and (2) to each of its 42 discrete items, according to the procedures described by Gray [7], and tabled Omega values prepared by Lawshe and Baker [9]. "Should" and "Probably Should" responses were regarded as positive, whereas negative attitudes were assumed from "Probably Should Not" and "Should Not" responses.

It was assumed that differences at the .05 level were indicative of significant differences among respondent groups' perceptions of the appropriateness of counselor involvement in task groups, and that differences at the .01 level were indicative of significant differences among groups' perceptions of the appropriateness of counselor involvement in the performance of specific tasks.

FINDINGS

All responding groups were in agreement that it is appropriate for school counselors to engage in educational counseling. Similarly, all groups reacted favorably to counselor performance of tasks related to vocational counseling and to testing and diagnosis, except that job-bound seniors and the mothers of job-bound seniors were significantly less enthusiastic than other groups over tasks relating to the interpretation and explanation of test scores.

Sharp differences were observed among groups in their reactions to the appropriateness of counselors performing tasks related to personal counseling. While total reaction to the task group was favorable, students exhibited a level of agreement that was significantly less than that demonstrated by other groups. College-preparatory seniors, in particular, were conspicuous in their rejection of three tasks generally supported by other groups: they rejected the ideas that the counselor should learn as much as possible about the student's family in order to help the student better, help students work out problems they are having with their parents, and help parents and members of the school staff with personal problems. Written remarks prepared by college-preparatory students appeared to support the idea that the school counselor was a good choice for personal counseling only when no one else was available.

Differences were also observed among groups in their reactions to counselor performance of teacher-like tasks. Parents of college-bound students tended to consider such tasks as representing appropriate counselor behaviors, whereas they were rejected by counselors and counselor educators. Teachers considered it appropriate for counselors to teach at least two classes a day or spend a semester or two teaching, every few years (counselors and, interestingly enough, students, rejected this expectation). Parents and students reacted positively to the notion that counselors should be stern task masters with failing students, but counselors and counselor educators rejected this task. Parents of college-preparatory seniors gave greater proportional support than other groups to the notion that counselors should teach students the difference between right and wrong. Parents and students felt it appropriate that counselors "give lots of good advice to students," a task which received support from only one counselor educator (six counselors reacted favorably to the item, seven rejected it, and 10 weren't sure).

Parents and students supported counselor performance of administrative-clerical tasks. Counselor educators, counselors, administrators, and teachers rejected this task group. Only the parents of job-bound students regarded checking up on truant and tardy students as being part of the counselor's job. Administrators, parents, counselors, and students felt that counselors should see to it that lazy students get to work, but the task was rejected by counselor educators. Parents and students felt it was appropriate for counselors to set up class schedules for students, period by period, making sure they do not have two classes at the same time or other schedule conflicts, but counselors and counselor educators rejected the task.

Groups were generally in agreement as to the appropriateness of counselors doing those things defined as being professional in character. The single exception was the task which called on counselors to allow students to say what they want in the counseling interview, without fear of correction or punishment. Counselors and counselor educators felt this behavior on the counselor's part was appropriate; however, it was rejected by teachers, parents, and college-preparatory students.

In written responses, administrators did not appear willing to distinguish between teachers and counselors as professional specialists ("My teachers are my best counselors"), and related the desirability of counseling to the effect it might have on students' academic achievement. Female teachers tended more than their male colleagues to recognize professional differences between teachers and counselors, but both argued strongly in favor of increased attention to vocational counseling. Time limitations appeared to be a matter of concern to students, parents, and counselors.

DISCUSSION

It seems clear that efforts made by counselors to perform educational guidance services are welcomed and approved of by the counselor's colleagues and by lay persons with whom he comes in professional contact. This support suggests the presence of a special attitude toward the counselor as being a helpful person whose function is largely one of providing assistance to students in their efforts to achieve academic success in school.

All groups demonstrated a high level of support for the idea that it is appropriate for counselors to be concerned with vocational guidance, and it is interesting to note that the parents of college-preparatory seniors gave significantly greater support to vocational counseling than did the parents of job-bound students. Perhaps the feeling exists that college-preparatory students give more thought to getting into college than to what they are going to do afterward.

Groups were in agreement that counselors should be capable in the area of testing and diagnosis. Less support, however, was given tasks in this area by job-bound students and the parents of job-bound students than by other groups. This finding could be interpreted in a variety or interesting ways, but probably for present purposes it would be well to simply suggest that counselors might consider treading cautiously in test interpretation activities with such individuals, to whom tests may be threatening.

Professional educators rejected the appropriateness of the performance by counselors of administrative-clerical tasks, but lay groups supported the appropriateness of such involvement on the counselor's part. It might be suggested that if counselors are seriously interested in being something other than administrators or clerks that they not engage in clerical or administrative functions. Avoidance by counselors of routine clerical work would obviously free them for other sorts of activity perhaps more appropriate to the kinds of talents they presumably offer the school. Hopefully, such additional time might be spent by counselors in counseling.

Counselor educators and counselors appeared better able than members of other groups to distinguish professional differences between counselors and teachers. It seems clear that members of several groups that took part in the study were not aware of the distinct operational and philosophical differences that must be present in effectively functioning counselors as opposed to effectively functioning teachers. It is recommended that every effort be made to educate members of school staffs and public to the role of the counselor as it is distinct from that of the teacher. Such educational efforts should prove helpful in demonstrating why the counselor is not serving effectively when he teaches classes, behaves as a "stern task master," or sets out to provide "lots of good advice" to students.

Attitudes toward the appropriateness of counselor involvement with personal counseling activities varied widely. To the extent that counselors, who saw themselves as being usefully engaged when employed in such activities, feel comfortable with and adequately trained in counseling for personal-social adjustment, it could be recommended that efforts be made to communicate to others in the professional and lay community the necessity for such counseling opportunities in the school setting, and the competence of appropriately trained persons to perform services of this kind. If counselors do not feel comfortable or adequate in personal counseling, evaluation by counselor training institutions of their programs of preparation would seem called for, and in-service experiences for such counselors would seem to be highly desirable.

The expectation by students and parents that counselors should serve as advice-givers leads to speculation that their experiences with counselors have led to this kind of expectation. If counselors are willing to recognize that their clients' worlds are filled with advice-givers, that the earning of a counseling credential does not make one an especially well-qualified seer, and that counseling is something quite different from advising, then it could be recommended that counselors stop giving advice so that the expectation would in time disappear.

It would appear that there is no universally acceptable role definition for the high school counselor. However, if counselors are to do the work for which they are presumably best trained, i.e., counseling as opposed to clerking, administering, or teaching, and if in their work they are to meet with acceptance from their peers in education, from students, and from patrons of the school in the community, efforts must be made to promote the counselor's image along lines viewed as being appropriate by the counseling profession.

REFERENCES

1. Bergstein, H. B. "A Study of Parents' Perceptions of the Role of School Counselors in a Selected Community." Unpublished doctoral dissertation, New York Univ., 1960.

2. Dunlop, R. S. "An Analysis of the Expectations Held for School Counselors by Members of Several Professional and Lay Groups." Unpublished doctoral dissertation, Arizona State Univ., 1964.

3. Dunlop, R. S. "Mom Looks at the Counselor," *Journal of Secondary Education* (1965), 40 (2), 69–73.

4. Gibson, R. "Pupil Opinions of High School Guidance Programs," *Personnel Guid. J.* (1962), 40, 453–457.

5. Grant, C. W. "How Students Perceive the Counselor's Role," *Personnel Guid. J.* (1954), 32, 386–388. (a)

6. Grant, C. W. "The Counselor's Role," *Personnel Guid. J.* (1954), 33, 74–77. (b)

7. Gray, R. T. "Establishing the Significance of the Difference Between Two Uncorrelated Proportions Under Various Conditions." San Diego, Calif.: School of Education, San Diego State College, 1963. (Mimeographed.)

8. Houghton, H. W. "The Role of the Counselor as Perceived by Seniors, Administrators, Teachers and Counselors in Selected New York State Public High Schools." Unpublished doctoral dissertation, Syracuse Univ., 1956.

9. Lawshe, C. H., & Baker, P. C. "Three Aids in the Evaluation of the Significance of the Difference Between Percentages. *Educ. Psychol. Measmt.* (Summer 1950) 263–270.

10. Roemmich, H., & Schmidt, John L. "Student Perceptions of Assistance Provided by Counselors in College Planning," *Personnel Guid. J.* (1962), 41, 157–158.

11. Schmidt, L. D. "Concepts of the Role of Secondary School Counselors," *Personnel Guid. J.* (1962), 40, 600–605.

12. Stewart, J. A. "Factors Influencing Teacher Attitudes Toward and Participaton in Guidance Services," *Personnel Guid. J.* (1961), 39, 729–734.

4

Issues in School Guidance: Varying Perceptions of Administrators, Counselors, and Counselor Educators

Buford Stefflre, Ed. D.*

The typescript of this tape-recorded address to the 1964 Indiana State University Guidance Administrators' Workshop was edited by Dr. Lawrence Beymer of the I.S.U. Department of Education and Psychology. This text was submitted to and approved by Dr. Stefflre.

There are, I believe, some important issues needing discussion regarding the perceptions of administrators, counselors, and counselor educators of the job of school counseling. Problems, like elephants, can be perceived in different ways, and I'd like to look at this elephant as he is seen by the counselor, his teacher, and at the same elephant as he is seen by the administrator.

First let us consider issues regarding what kind of people should be doing school counseling, then how many of these counselors there should be, what they should be doing, and finally, why counselors and administrators sometimes disagree on these and other matters.

WHAT KIND OF PEOPLE SHOULD BE DOING COUNSELING IN THE SCHOOLS?

One of the issues that gets talked about and worried about is whether or not teaching experience is an essential prerequisite for counselors. It is my belief that administrators feel, "Yes, of course, you couldn't possibly do a good school counseling job if you haven't faced 35 students in a classroom." In general, counselor educators are not so sure this is true; they sometimes have the feeling that when they get around to educating a counselor they first have to undo what those years in the classroom have done. Counselors' views are more difficult to determine but since they have all been teachers it would seem likely that they would tend to agree with administrators on this issue.

*Dr. Stefflre is a Professor of Education at Michigan State University, East Lansing, and is editor of the *Personnel and Guidance Journal*. His article appeared originally in the *Teachers College Journal* (Indiana State University), 36:195 (March 1965), and is reprinted with permission of the author and of the journal.

In any event, this is an issue which I think will become more important in years to come. A number of counseling organizations have gone on record as saying that teaching experiences are not an absolute essential for counselors. I have managed to perch precariously on a fence in regard to this issue because I don't feel strongly about it. I do think the controversy parallels our experience in Michigan with school psychologists. In our state you don't have to be a teacher first to be a school psychologist. So sometimes when you talk with teachers about school psychologists they say, "Well, what does this fellow know about education? You know, he has never taught school." So you take away that psychologist and you bring in another one who has taught school. Then the teachers say, "Oh, yeah, I know why he is in school psychology; he taught school and couldn't stand the classroom so he got out!"

There seems to be no sure-fire method of winning this argument. If you require all your counselors to have been teachers first you are apt to end up with a lot of refugees from classrooms. But if you permit people to counsel without first having taught, you end up with a certain amount of staff skepticism because the counselor is then not really a part of the "in" group.

Now what about counselor training? There is a movement, the wave of the future in counselor education, that is calling for two years of graduate education. In Indiana you now require two years for directors of guidance, but I refer to the movement towards two years for all school counselors. I do not know how enthusiastic school administrators are about this change. I am not even sure how enthusiastic school counselors are about this. Counselor educators think it's great! So here we have another kind of issue which can produce division.

Two years or one, what do you do during that time to the counselor-in-training? In general, counselor educators (and perhaps counselors) think that a good deal of this training should be psychological. Maybe a third to a half of it should be. I'm not so sure school administrators agree; I'm not sure they want all of that psychology muddying up the halls of the school. This is a matter that needs to be thrashed out among administrators, counselors and counselor educators.

Of course, only a few years ago the big problem was whether you needed any kind of special training or not. Certification seems to be a pretty dead issue now. By that I mean there is a little tampering with it here and there, but by and large nearly every state requires certification for counselors. A few don't—Mississippi, Michigan, and a handful of others. (In Michigan we create counselors by the laying on of administrative hands!)

To summarize this matter of what kind of a person should be a school counselor, I think we need the phenomenon of professionalization. Nobody is really opposed to professionalization, nor motherhood, nor the flag. But there is some question as to what professionalization really means.

It appears to me that often the school counselor and his administrator think of professionalization in terms of a united profession—we are all in NEA together. Our profession is education. This isn't what a counselor educator means when he talks about professionalization. To him it means that counselors should join the American Personnel and Guidance Association and the American School Counselor Association. Our profession is counseling.

But in fact, not many school counselors belong to APGA—less than a third of them do at the present. They report that they read the *NEA Journal*, not the *Personnel and Guidance Journal*, and I can't imagine why! So here is another division in perception. We are all for professionalization, but what does that mean? Does it mean that the counselor is primarily an educator so he joins the NEA and the Indiana State Teachers' Association? Or does it mean that he is primarily a counselor, and attends APGA conventions and meetings and reads in that area? What kind of creature do we want as a counselor?

HOW MANY COUNSELORS SHOULD THERE BE?

Assuming that some kind of person is going to do this job, how many of them do we want and need? In 1958, when the National Defense Education Act was passed, we had 1 counselor for every 1000 students. We now have—after the great leap forward—about one counselor for every 500 students. Thus we are getting, if not better and better, at least more and more numerous. Where do we go from here?

The North Central Association says we ought to have 1 counselor for every 300 students. The American School Counselors Association, not to be caught napping, says we ought to have 1 for every 250.°

The range of regional variation in counselor ratios is surprising. In California there is 1 for every 350. In the Northwest the ratio is 1:450, in the Northeast and Middle Atlantic 1:400, in the South 1:850, and in the North Central region, 1:650. So this area is worse off in regard to counseling ratios than any other place in the country except the South.

Of course there are two ways to interpret these figures—perhaps we are a little backward, or perhaps our students need less counseling. I am a little suspicious of such figures, however, because it is difficult to tell just who is a counselor. When you take somebody out of a Latin class and shove him into a counseling office, does he become a counselor? Or is he only a counselor after he meets state certification requirements? And if so, if he crosses into a state with different certifications requirements, does he lose his counseling tag because he hasn't had some specific course which is felt to be vital by that state?

°North Central's thinking is now that a ratio of 1:500 is appropriate for accreditation of the employing school. The counseling specialty is not represented on North Central's governing board. [Text Editor]

In any event, despite the figures which are a little suspect, it appears that we have about half as many school counselors as we need to attain a 1 to 300 ratio. Since 1959 we have just kept even with population growth, and maintained a deficit of about 20,000 secondary school counselors each year. Extending counseling down into the elementary schools at the ratio of one counselor for each 600 pupils will call for about 40,000 more counselors. The big issue here is, do we as a nation want to quadruple the effort we have been putting into guidance for the past six years? Do we want to ear-mark enough money for guidance to close the present gap of 60,000 counselors.

Here we get quite a little difference in opinion among administrators and counselors and counselor educators. When I listen to administrators I hear them being very critical of ear-marked funds. They seem to feel that the school district ought to use funds as its sees fit. Some counselors and counselor educators, however, feel that it would be much better if funds went to districts to be used only for guidance.

I find strange things happening in Michigan because we have ear-marked funds for Special Education. Suddenly in most every district in the state, the top educational priority has become Special Education. No district seems to need improved libraries or band uniforms or other real educational essentials. What they need is Special Education because that's what the state is paying for this season. If we have more ear-marked guidance funds, obviously what we're going to get is more ear-marked counselors! If we are going to funnel money into guidance, I would hope that administrators will be able to assess the situation clearly enough to determine if that is in fact our top priority. Is guidance the one thing that every school district needs more of now?

WHAT SHOULD THE SCHOOL COUNSELOR DO?

Endless lists of counselor duties and functions could be related here. I'll try to stay with a rather simple one.

There seems to be pretty good agreement that counselors ought to do something called counseling. I'm not really convinced that counselors are doing lots of this, but there is a lot of encouragement for them to. Most people in the field of counselor education say that a counselor should spend at least half of his time counseling.

They ought to be doing pupil appraisal. This is assessing students to find out what they are like so that teachers might deal with them more effectively. This function implies consulting with teachers and others to help them use the data derived from pupil appraisal.

Program development and management—setting up a guidance program and keeping it going.

Educational and occupational planning—telling students that plumbers make $2.35 an hour—is part of the counseling role expectation as is referral work, which often means passing the buck to somebody else.

Placement which involves both educational placement (should we put him in Miss Brown's room or not?) and sometimes job placement. Working with parents is included in typical lists of functions.

Counselors should do research. (No educator ever gives a list of expected functions without including research, otherwise he gets drummed out of the party for being insufficiently respectful of science.)

Finally, public relations, which means not blowing it when a board member comes in to visit. And other more solemn matters.

This list of duties can be argued about, but in general it represents what counselor educators and counselors think that counselors ought to be doing. Now, what are some of the issues dividing administrators, counselors, and counselor educators?

For one, we often train counselors in counseling with an emphasis upon personal counseling, dealing with social and emotional problems. Counselor educators don't do this intentionally, but any reasonably bright student working on a degree in guidance soon catches on that when something nice and emotional and affective occurs during an interview, his supervisor is a lot happier than if the counselor and the student had grubbed around in occupational information and data for the whole hour. So the student perceives that we grant special prestige to personal counseling during his training. And I'm not too sure that administrators are simply mad about counselors doing all this personal counseling. When counselors do personal counseling it is possible that they will be helpful, but it is probable that they will threaten the whole school structure whether or not they are helpful. Unfortunately, we have some counselors who rather relish other people's problems, and think they have really drawn blood if they can get the student to complain about his siblings or wallow around in other family problems. So here is another issue: how much personal counseling do administrators want school counselors to do? And if counselors aren't supposed to do it, does this mean that the school has no responsibility for personal counseling, or we hire someone else with another kind of training to do it?

Then testing. Since the NDEA became law, we have doubled the number of tests which are given to school pupils. In 1963 the total reached 20 million. I don't really know if we ought to quadruple that figure, or triple it, or halve it, but it sounds like a lot of tests just off hand. I vision car loads of tests rolling out of Chicago, and other car loads of pins to jab into them. The only really worthwhile suggestion about testing that I have come across was one made by Ed Roeber of the University of Michigan. It was his suggestion that we ought to handle the disbursement of money for testing the same as the USDA handles money for agriculture problems: we should give each school so much money for each test they don't give. (Twenty cents for each interest inventory not given; thirty cents for ungiven personality tests, etc.). This I think is a reasonable solution, because our schools seem to be filled with tests that are taken, scored, filed, and forgotten.

Why is testing an issue? I think it is because one thing a counselor learns in his program that other specialists may not learn about is testing. The students and their parents don't know much about tests, and often the administrator is not very sophisticated in this area either, so if the counselor rides the white horse of testing nobody can catch him. The insecure counselor may be tempted to say, "I know all about tests and you don't, so let's give lots of them, shall we, and then let me tell you about yourself." This is only one of many ways in which tests and testing can become problems.

Another issue, the extent to which counselors ought to be involved in attendance and discipline problems, is getting its second wind. It used to be that this issue was disposed of in the first guidance course. After 16 weeks when you were asked to sum up what you had learned, you could always say, "The counselor shouldn't be a disciplinarian!" But just about the time we sold administrators on this idea, we began to have second thoughts on the matter. Now we're not nearly as firm and fervent about keeping the counselor clean of all contact with discipline as we were ten years ago. Why? Because in practice, all of the students who need help desperately, all the hoods, pre-dropouts, the trouble-makers, now talk to the administrator, who is trained in administration. The students with the delicate problems, like "Should I take French this semester or next semester?" get to talk with a counselor, who has had a year's training in getting ready to help them with such earth-shaking decisions. So perhaps we are not making the best use of counselors if we insist that they have nothing to do with discipline and attendance. I have a hunch, however, that most counselors like the present situation just as it is.

Let us look now at the consulting function. The supposition that anyone in the school really wants the counselor to talk to administrators and teachers about human relations and human development may very well be a myth. In the teaching profession we have the idea that only the weak need to be helped. After student teaching, you have arrived and they give you a class of your own. You close the door, draw the shades, and nobody else is present—just you and the students. Only the weak teacher has anybody else in there helping him. Social work is different in its ethos. In social work the strong take help. The social worker seeks consulting, talks his problem over with others, says, "How does this case look to you?" As a matter of fact, social workers like this business of being helped so much that if you suddenly take a consultant away from a social worker he gets the bends, so you must do it gradually, if at all. Therefore if we're going to train counselors to do consulting (and I don't think anybody really knows how to do this), then maybe we ought to think a little about whether administrators really want to hire counselors to do consulting. If we don't do this, we run the risk of producing a lot of highly polished, wound-up counselors eager to be consulted, but with nobody willing to consult them. This situation would be very frustrating to all concerned.

Now, elementary school counseling—here is another interesting problem area. All of us are discussing elementary school counseling, administrators are trying to find elementary school counselors and hire them, and school boards are asking why their schools don't already have elementary school counselors. I think we are on the threshold of a big expansion in elementary school guidance and counseling, aided by the new NDEA funds which are being made available for training elementary school counselors.

But as far as I can tell, nobody has figured out very clearly just what it is that these people are to do. We seem to be saying: "Counseling is good in secondary schools, therefore, we need more of it, and sooner," Perhaps this is reasonable. But again I doubt that America is teeming with elementary school teachers who every night pray, "Please send us a counselor." And yet, we are preparing to send them, and I wonder what kind of a welcome they are going to get and what they think they are going to do when they get there, and what the administrators who hire them think they are going to do.

Four general patterns seem to be developing. One model is that of the secondary school counselor, a person who talks to kids one at a time about their concerns. ("Just take a secondary school counselor, teach him to lisp, and he's in.") A second model resembles the psychologist. This kind of elementary school counselor is seen as primarily interested in testing and appraisal. He is a psychologist at least in self-concept if not in training. He would handle the group tests, and give individual tests. The third model is the consultant—a person who works with teachers to try to aid them in understanding their students, or if he really wants to live dangerously, to understand themselves. This person would be educated in child development, mental health, and interpersonal dynamics. The fourth model I've been able to identify is the social work model. Here you would have the counselor work with those children who are exhibiting obvious social and emotional problems. He might work with them individually as well as visit their homes, to elicit the cooperation and understanding of their parents. There may be other models but these four seem most prominent now.

I see no consensus among either counselor trainers or school administrators as to what an elementary school guidance specialist should do. And yet I'm convinced that we are going to train them and hire them, because this is the way America handles problems. The first thing we do after we get around to recognizing that a problem exists is to pass a law about it. If that doesn't work, we take courses about it. (For example, if you are having troubles with your wife, or somebody else's wife, you go to school and take a course in marriage and family relations and live happily ever after.) If these two approaches fail, we hire a counselor. So we see lots of problems—dropouts, low motivation, deliquency—and we are reacting instinctively by advocating hiring more and more counselors to magically solve these many problems.

To conclude this section on counselor functions let us look at the revolution ahead. Already in California machines are taking over most of the routine clerical jobs of guidance—machines which can figure out a master schedule for the school, assign students to classes, score, analyze, and record test results, prepare class lists, and so on. And machines can do these tasks faster, more accurately, and take into account more factors than can any counselor.

The trouble comes from the fact that when machines liberate counselors from the paper work they tend to complain so much about, there will be time to do other things. And many counselors have hidden behind this paper curtain for years, all the time because of all of the paper work. When the machine appears on the scene, they panic. The experience has been in California that counselors are so upset by this that they sabotage the program by figuring out ways to make sure that the machine can't do the job—perhaps by the punching of extra holes in IBM cards. Therefore when the machine arrives counselors must be trained—or retrained—to counsel.

The administrator may ask himself, "Well, now, I've used this fellow for scheduling for ten years, but since I can get a better, faster, and more efficient scheduling job from a machine, do I really need him anymore? Do I really want him anymore? Or should I send him back to the classroom?" Perhaps we are nearing that point where administrators will be forced to think about what they want counselors to do when they no longer need them for the routine functions which can be automated.

(Sometimes I think that a counselor is someone who is doing scheduling, thinks he should be doing therapy, but who would really like to be doing administration!)

WHY ARE THESE SITUATIONS SEEN DIFFERENTLY?

It seems apparent that some basic differences do exist between counselors and administrators. As evidence I would refer to four little pieces of research which neither alone nor together form any sort of breakthrough, but are, it seems to me, worth our attention.

Dr. Grant Kemp of Ohio State studied a large group of Ohio counselors and administrators. He found that principals were more concerned with achievement, order, aggression, and were more evaluative than counselors. On the other hand, counselors were more concerned with affiliation (being nice to people), intraception (stewing about their problems), and understanding other people.

In a Kentucky study both counselors and principals agreed that principals were more competitive and aggressive than were counselors. And they both agreed that counselors were more kind, understanding, and reassuring. So both groups see counselors as more considerate and encouraging and principals as more autocratic. The important finding however, was that both the counselors and the principals said that they would like the other fellow to be more managerial and autocratic. Each wanted the other to run a little tighter ship. Moreover, the principals said in this study that they would like their counselors to be a little less indulgent, a little more firm, and more businesslike. In other words, to "get with it."

The third study was conducted in Nebraska by Dr. Robert W. Filbeck. He constructed some hypothetical critical incidents which occur in the work of counselors, and sent them out to both principals and counselors to see how they thought the counselor should react in each situation. Both groups agreed, at least on paper, that the counselor should not spend so much time on such things as scheduling, and that he should be more "other-people" oriented and not be so concerned with keeping himself clear of others problems. The big difference was that the principals were more concerned with group welfare, and the counselors more concerned with individual welfare. The principals were concerned with policy, norms of behavior, and making sure that the school norms were not challenged. Counselors were more concerned with individual kids, and didn't care too much about the policies of the school, rules, and the rest of it.

Finally, I did a study in Michigan which shows that counselors are more concerned with altruism and self-realization than principals, who are more concerned with money and with control.

It seems to me that the common denominator of these studies is the fact that principals have a job of running a total institution, and counselors don't always appreciate the difficulties of such responsibilities. So some conflict ensues. The principal, on the other hand, would like to have a counselor who is warm and outgoing and student-centered and concerned about individuals and their problems, but every time the counselor gets warm and outgoing and student-centered and concerned with individual problems he scares the principal because this behavior makes waves—makes problems for the principal and threatens the status quo. The counselor wants some protection from his own impulses, and likes to have an administrator who knows how to use power, who controls things, who is business-like.

Oh, he may complain about his administrator, but this is analogous to the adolescent who says, "You are a mean father because you won't let me do so." Actually, both are privately pleased that somebody else is holding the reins.

At least part of the difficulty, then, seems to come from the ways in which power is used. Nobody likes to talk about power much—it's sort of unclean. But administrators have power in the schools, and they have to use it in the interest of society. They are forced to balance what the counselor wants with what other things must be done to run the school properly. Counselors may say, "Oh, I shy away from power. I don't have any, you know," but at the same time they want to make real sure that the power that is in their school is used in a way that their job can be the job they want it to be.

I have been talking about the varying perceptions we have about our problems in guidance, and where these variations come from. I recognize that I haven't given you many if any clear answers to these problems, but I'm not holding out on you. If I knew the clear answers to these problems you could have had them for the same fee that you are paying just for the questions.

Even without definite answers, however, it may be helpful to remember that administrators, counselors, and counselor educators see the same issues from different occupational perspectives. They disagree, when they do, not out of perversity but because of the private vision they have of education, the schools, and guidance. By mutual professional respect they may learn more from the others' views and succeed better in communicating their own.

BIBLIOGRAPHY

1. Kemp, C. Gratton. "A Comparative Study of the Need Structures of Administrators, Teachers, and Counselors," *Journal of Educational Research*, 57: 8, pp. 425–427.

2. Chenault, Jo Ann, and Seegars, James E. "The Interpersonal Diagnosis of Principals and Counselors." *Personnel and Guidance Journal* (1962), 41: 118–122.

3. In print, *Personnel and Guidance Journal*.

4. Stefflre, Buford, and Leafgren, Fred. "Value Differences between Counselors and Administrators," *Vocational Guidance Quarterly* (1962), 10: 4: 226-228.

5

The Elementary School Counselor's Unique Position

Edna Harrison, M. A.*

The idea that teachers are the key persons in guidance has led many to presume a natural ability to counsel. To draw a dividing line between the work of the teacher and that of the counselor in guidance has thus become next to impossible.

But there is a clear distinction. The teacher as a guidance person can, as Dr. Dugald S. Arbuckle [1] says, function as follows:

1. Provide in the classroom a climate and atmosphere such that learning can take place

2. Provide a psychological atmosphere conducive to mental health

3. Help the child adjust to his environment

4. Provide the child an example of healthy, ethical and moral behavior

5. Provide the child an accurate, objective and truthful picture of the knowledge and the understanding of mankind, and help the child to use this knowledge for his own good and for the betterment of mankind.

COUNSELING

These precepts of guidance could and should be practiced in every schoolroom, but they are not to be confused with the professional service called *counseling*. Along with the professional training and practice mentioned above, the following differences are to be found:

1. The counselor functions as a professional in the interview, as opposed to the lay person who, in conference, uses advisement, persuasion and even, at times, threats and cajolery.

2. The counselor engages in a professional diagnosis, as opposed to the lay person's mere recognition that a problem exists.

3. The counselor functions in professional treatment using sound psychological methods, as opposed to the hit-or-miss efforts of the lay person.

4. The counselor functions as an expert in prognosis, as opposed to the lay person, who makes unstudied predictions.

°Mrs. Harrison is a psychologist with the Diagnostic and Resource Center, Wichita, Kansas. Her article appeared originally in *The School Counselor*, 11:2:107 (December 1963), and is reprinted with permission of the author and of the journal.

5. The counselor functions as the professional leader of small-informal child-entered groups, as opposed to the lay leader, whose classroom group situations are larger, more formal and leader-centered.

Counseling in the elementary school is in danger of being watered down to the level of everybody's business. Dr. Ruth Strang has written a comprehensive definition of counseling.

> Counseling and psychotherapy have much in common. All forms feature a face-to-face relationship in which growth takes place—a relationship in which the client develops understanding of himself and others and ability to cope with his personal problems and other life situations. All forms aim to help personalities attain a higher level of personal and social development. [4]

Unless the counselor can be freed from the "visiting teacher" conception, unless the concept of counseling can be restricted to that of the counselor at work carrying out the above functions and their related responsibilities, unless educators are helped to make a clear distinction between the work of the teacher and that of the counselor in guidance, then the terms "counselor" and "counseling" may as well be done away with.

Where and in what classroom does a teacher have the time, the training and the skill to adequately counsel his students? Confer with, yes, but counsel, no. Time is something the teacher does not have for the one-to-one relationship even if he had the training.

It is not likely that a person qualified to provide professional counseling services would be found among the teachers in the elementary school. And skill cannot be had without practice.

FUNCTIONS

To clarify further the responsibilities of the elementary school counselor as opposed to the duties of the elementary school teacher, one might describe those functions the counselor performs as director of guidance services as follows:

1. *The counselor acts as consultant to the principal.*

Robert McIsaac [3] suggests that the counselor study factors that might lead to teacher and curriculum improvement, that he provide administrators with information that will help them identify students' needs which may not be served by the present program, and handle many of the opportunities for promoting public relations, among other things. He may also recommend and participate in the placement of children and assist in their orientation into new situations. He may counsel with the principal on personal matters when invited to do so.

Dr. Kenneth Hoyt voices the need for professional autonomy in performing a unique service in a professional manner:

"The true professional has to have elbow room. . . . He needs and can countenance no supervision in the exercise of his own professional actions and judgments" [2].

He has the responsibility to safeguard the interests of the public he serves. There is no place in his counseling situation (the interview) for a third person. The principal is his supervisor in an administrative capacity only. Together the principal and counselor set the *direction* of the guidance program.

In an administrative sense the counselor is a member of the principal's staff, but as a specialist the counselor determines the specific *means* by which desired objectives are met. This is another clear distinction between the position of the teacher and that of the counselor in their relationships to the principal of the school.

2. *The counselor acts as consultant to the teachers.*

He assists the teachers in their interpretations of pupil data. Providing the environment that would be of benefit to elementary school pupils in their study of occupations, the counselor may suggest talks by certain parents who take pride in their jobs and can thereby remove the stigma that may surround the "blue-collar" jobs in the community. He encourages teachers to work individually with children in classroom guidance activities, holds in-service training periods for teachers with specified objectives in view, and counsels with them personally when invited to do so.

In return the counselor receives help from teachers in the knowledge of pupils through observation and conversation within the classroom. He works with the teacher in group situations based upon the developmental needs of the children, using the small informal child-centered group for the purpose of furthering children's growth in human relations. He plans frequent conferences with teachers in small groups and singly in order to carry out objectives and evaluate results.

3. *The counselor acts as consultant to parents.*

He may counsel them concerning family relationships that have a bearing upon the behavior of the child or upon certain stages in his development. Or, if the seriousness of the situation so indicates, he may refer them to agencies outside the school for family consultations. He brings influence to bear upon the attitudes and feelings of parents toward the school and its staff to effect cooperation in the interest of the child.

OTHER DUTIES

As a consultant to other members of the school staff, the counselor often calls together a team for purposes of holding a case conference concerning a child with whom each member of the team has worked. The team may be composed of principal, teachers, school nurse, speech specialist and parents, with the counselor as chairman. The counselor may sometimes work with a committee to plan certain aspects of the guidance program that involve various members of the staff.

The five aspects of the counseling function are the professional earmarks of the counselor and are used in the various guidance services as necessary. Sometimes the elementary school counselor must also be psychometrist and social worker, depending upon the circumstances in which he finds himself. Some counselors feel that the individual testing situation gives them a better insight into a child's essential character than a series of interviews, but most prefer to leave social work to the professional in that field.

In short, being a counselor in the elementary school is not a job for any other member of the staff, no matter how guidance-minded that member may be. Nor is it an easy one.

Dr. C. Gilbert Wrenn makes a most pertinent observation: "No counselor need be a superman but he must be a person who is able to live with the awareness that he can never quite live up to his job. All who want a placid self-contained life should apply elsewhere" [5].

REFERENCES

1. Arbuckle, Dugald S. *Guidance and Counseling in the Classroom.* Boston: Allyn & Bacon, 1957.

2. Hoyt, Kenneth B. "Guidance; A Constellation of Services," *Personnel and Guidance Journal,* 40: 690–697.

3. McIsaac, Robert H. "Guidance Services (Wichita)." In Lester C. Crow and Alice Crow, (Eds.) *Readings in Guidance.* New York: David McKay, 1962.

4. Strang, Ruth. "Criteria of Progress in Counseling and Psychotherapy," *Journal of Clinical Psychology,* 3: 180–183.

5. Wrenn, C. Gilbert. *The Counselor in a Changing World.* A Preliminary Report of the Project on Guidance in American Schools. Washington, D. C.: American Personnel and Guidance Association, 1961.

6

The School Counselor: His Unique Mental Health Function

I. N. Berlin, M.D.*

It may be somewhat presumptuous of a psychiatrist to try to help clarify and define the particular function of colleagues in an allied professional group. However, it has become clear to me from my almost 12 years of work as a psychiatric consultant to several school systems that among the most troubled, overburdened, and perhaps most unappreciated group of people in a school are its counselors. One of the plaints I've heard repeatedly is that as a group, counselors are expected to be all things to all people within the school, and of all the professional people in the school system their jobs are the most poorly defined and most subject to constant change in emphasis, depending upon the pressures then current in a particular school system.

I have thus encountered such wide and varied ideas and concepts of the counselors' job as on the one hand being held strictly responsible for the disciplinary control of the antisocial, delinquent youngsters assigned to them, and on the other extreme the surveying of large groups of youngsters, spending only a few moments with each, diagnostically, in order to "spot" potential problems, so that the administrator could say he had his counselors in touch with every child in his school. In addition to these duties, counselors are expected to possess a particular brand of magic so that after one interview with an antisocial, hostile youngster, or a frightened, withdrawn one these students should return to the classroom completely changed in attitude and behavior.

It should be evident that I am talking about the "personal problems" counselor, and his "primary" job of helping disturbed youngsters, not the counselor whose job is essentially one of program evaluation and planning with students. I am aware that the personal problems counselor is expected and is often trained to do vocational counseling, aptitude testing, etc., and often has administrative duties as well.

The counselor's job is usually so ill defined and at the mercy of the fates because of the demands placed on schools by the increased number of problems due to ever larger numbers of disturbed students. These conditions

°Dr. Berlin is a Professor of Psychiatry and Pediatrics, School of Medicine, University of Washington, Seattle. His article appeared originally in the *Personnel and Guidance Journal*, 41:5:409 (January 1963), and is reprinted with permission of the author and of the journal.

have followed the Second World War with the resulting population shifts and increases. The schools, in an effort to deal with the, in many instances, overwhelming number of difficult youngsters, usually have appointed as counselors teachers with sensitivity and greater than usual concern about children. Sometimes these are designated as full-time jobs, more frequently as part-time functions, and in some instances as a duty in addition to their regular teaching assignments.

Despite the increasing number of specialized curricula in counseling and guidance, and the increased number of trained personnel, most counselors have not had much specific training for their jobs. Most counselors have conscientiously taken courses in psychology and in counseling and guidance. Rarely have they had an opportunity once they begin to function as counselors to learn about counseling through a formal course of didactic lectures and seminars and supervised field work experience. I have been repeatedly amazed at the outstanding work that counselors do as a group, despite all the above problems and pressures.

THE OUTSIDE VANTAGE POINT

I would like to discuss several aspects of the counselor's job from the vantage point of an outsider, one who, while concerned with the ways in which people, and especially children, can be helped with their problems, is not subject to the pressures which beset the counselor who may try to define his job. I have a hope that any discussion which helps make the counselor's job progressively clearer to him and encourages him to define it more and more precisely for himself may help him to help others in the school setting and in the community to recognize his unique function.

Thus I'd like to try to describe my impressions of the kinds of work the counselors I've known have been involved in, the kinds of expectations the school administrators and community have of school counselors, and the realistic functions school counselors can have in which they might function with maximal effectiveness for the benefit of the school. I'd like to attempt one other kind of clarification from my particular vantage point, that is, to describe what I have felt to be the unique function of the school counselor. Over and over I have heard counselors ask with some discomfort, "How is what I do different from the social worker or psychologist in the school department or community agency?" It seems to the counselor that the expectations are often the same. The confusion may be greater when such expectations of the counselor carry no added training or remuneration as part of the job. Inherent in this question also is how counseling differs from casework and psychotherapy as practiced by others. It has been my increasing feeling and belief that the school counselor's job is a unique one. It is a unique function requiring clearly describable techniques which borrow from dynamic psychology and psychotherapy, but which is distinct from it in practice. As I think of the task I have just outlined for myself, I have some qualms about how clearly and succinctly I can complete it. I'm aware that what I will say is not especially new, but I hope it will put various familiar elements into a different context which might stimulate critical evaluation and assessment of what I am trying to say.

The counselor's job as I now know it seems to center primarily around trying to help those youngsters who are disturbing to their teachers or to the school. Thus, most youngsters come for counseling, usually after prolonged difficulties with various classroom teachers, or repeated truancy and hostile, defiant behavior which disturbs the administration. The counselor is thus often faced with an enraged, distraught teacher or administrator on the one hand and a disturbed, angry, hostile, defensive student on the other. Under these "auspicious" circumstances, he is frequently asked to do several things: first to try to understand the child's problems and explain them to others, second to secure the cooperation of the parents, and third and above all to use a few talks with the youngster to help him become a good citizen of the school. In other instances the counselor is asked to deal with the learning problems of a youngster who is failing in his academic work and is beyond whatever remedial help the classroom teacher can offer. In this case also he is expected to diagnose and "cure" a problem of many years' duration with a few interviews. More rarely the withdrawn, socially isolated, schizoid youngster is referred for counseling. Usually the expectations are not so great with those youngsters because this type of student is not as troublesome to the teacher as is the hostile, defiant, or sullen, nonlearning student.

THE UNWARRANTED DEMANDS

In addition to the expectations of teachers and administrators that such problem children will be quickly "cured," there are other expectations which make the already difficult job even more difficult. These expectations are in part at least the result of an ever growing demand from communities that schools assume more and more parental functions in addition to or often instead of their prime function of educating children. To the extent that administrators go along with these demands and expectations, they then expect the counselor to be parent to the disturbed child, *i.e.*, to discipline him. The counselor is sometimes required to accept responsibility for the student's behavior, and above all he must keep him out of the administrator's hair. In a few schools the counselor has actually had to face the wrath of administrators for "allowing" a youngster to continue to get into trouble. Perhaps the most difficult expectation the counselor has to deal with from fellow teachers, administrators, and community is that of the magic effect. When a parent, teacher, administrator, or other adult human being has failed to help solve the disturbance of a youngster with whom he is related as a parent, teacher, etc., and when he finally turns to someone else for help, there are rather ambivalent feelings involved. On the one hand he hopes the other fellow has some magic that he does not have since there really should be some easy answer to the problem with the child. On the other hand, if someone else does succeed where parent or teacher has failed, it means that he is not very effective and there is a half hope that the other fellow will not be successful. Thus the emphasis on the magic change that should occur carries with it a great deal of feeling. Sometimes the counselor accepts such assigned expectations. He hopes that he can affect a magical cure or change to prove his worth and his abilities. Such unrealistic self-expectations make things even more difficult for the counselor and counselee. When the hoped-for magic does not occur, the teacher, parent, administrator, etc., is angry overtly or covertly with the counselor since the problems are still theirs to cope with and they often do not know where else to turn for help. Also the youngster may have been led to expect an easy solution to his problem and when this does not occur he feels again let down and even more angry with the unhelpful adults.

Where does the counselor fit into the mental health team? What is unique about his function? What special methods can he use and how may his particular competence be best used by the school?

The counselor, by virtue of his being a teacher, brings to his work not only his understanding of children and techniques of education, but also an experience that no other mental health worker can have. In his work as a teacher usually he has come to recognize the important integrative and even healing function that learning can, and often does, have for many children. He has often observed that for many children from deprived and/ or conflict-ridden homes, school may be a haven, and that learning, *i.e.*, the mastery of the techniques for acquiring knowledge, may be an important help to the child in making him feel better able to cope with the world. When he can at least adequately cope with and master the skills necessary for learning and achieving in school he feels less at the mercy of forces he cannot master in his environment.

Thus learning and mastery of academic material may give some youngsters a sense of self-worth, a glimpse of their own abilities, and a feeling that they need not be stuck in the same circular impasses in which they see their parents and other adults mired.

Out of just such experiences, the counselor may get a feeling of how important learning and mastery of skills are to a youngster and may begin to recognize that often the hostile, antisocial, truant youngster is one who has never learned. Such a youngster feels incompetent as a student among his peers and angry at the insistence of teachers that he perform school work that his parents have never felt was important. In fact, the child has experienced that he was not important enough to be helped with school work and encouraged to learn. Each succeeding year of failure in academic mastery increases the frustrated, hopeless, angry feeling with the sense that the future holds little for him. He can only see for himself a future full of the problems and miseries with which he sees his parents vainly trying to cope. He thus turns his anger against the adult world and tries to get his satisfactions (kicks) from any short-term respite from tension through alcohol, drugs, stealing, sex, etc.

Thus the counselor has a particular point of view, the educator's, about why and how the school setting may help or increase the child's difficulties, and he may often have a sense of at least a partial solution to the youngster's aggressive, defiant behavior via learning.

It may not be surprising to many of you here to know that in psychoses of childhood one of the more recent important therapeutic tools has been the use of educative techniques. The mastery first of skills of self-care and then of academic skills is important in the total effort toward the recovery from this most serious mental illness [1, 3].

Similarly, recent experiences in an anti-delinquency project revealed that helping delinquent adolescents to begin to learn was vital to their improvement and their relinquishing their delinquent ways [4]. How then can the counselor use his unique vantage point to help his counselee? It seems to me that the use of insights from recent developments in ego psychology and with certain psychotherapeutic techniques the counselor can be of some help to the disturbed student.

A DEPENDABLE REALIST

First the counselor tries to develop a relationship of some trust and dependability with the troubled student. Since most students are angry, hostile, defiant, and unable to trust any adult, much less rely upon him, the job of showing some interest in the student without over-identification with him and thus being regarded as a sucker is important. Perhaps the most important aspect of developing such a relationship is regular interviews and careful follow-up of the student's behavior and activities in school. I can recall those instances when hostile, defiant students have accused counselors of being stool pigeons or spying on them and have felt relieved when the counselor has been able to say, nondefensively, "Look, my job is to help you. I know you're going to try to con me and avoid telling me the truth if you can, so I'm getting all the facts I need to help me help you with or without your help." Also helpful is the effort to define for the youngster the clear alternatives for continuous destructive, antisocial behavior without its being either a punitive "behave or we'll kick you out," or a seductive "We wouldn't want this to happen to you, so please be a good boy," but a realistic "I want you to know where we stand and what may happen if we aren't able to work together successfully."

It also becomes important that the counselor use his task-oriented attitudes to help cement his relationship with the student. That is, if he can spend the required time with the student, first assessing his learning problems realistically, spelling out what his current academic status is, and helping him make plans for the next steps he must take to begin to achieve and feel better about himself, then learning can begin. It's also important to be quite truthful and yet to extend one's help in overcoming the difficulties. If in the face of the student's feeling of overwhelming hopelessness and dread of beginning the monumental task the counselor can help him take but one tiny step, much has been accomplished. No false hopes, unrealistic formulas, or dreams of glory without the inevitable attendant drudgery must be subscribed to by the counselor. Often after prolonged backing and filling, equivocating and avoidance, when the youngster really knows the counselor will hold firm a beginning is made, and the student grudgingly and warily will make the attempt to begin to work. The counselor helps by being clear within himself and with the counselee that it won't be a straight path and that there will be many false starts. With each small step forward, such a youngster will often try to quit and try to avoid the next step up and will have to be encouraged with more frequent interviews for a short time. At such times the student can use the personal relationship and beginning trust in the counselor as an aid in reducing the anxiety attendant on beginning to learn.

In this work, the counselor's enlistment of the student's teacher is vital. As teachers begin to understand the problems and the difficulties of the undertaking, the teacher's help with the learning by special attention and encouragement may spell the difference between success and failure. Here the counselor uses his insights about the particular teacher-pupil relationship. He can help the teacher by being available to him at moments of discouragement and anger about the impossible task. He also needs to keep reminding the teacher to send him regular reports of the student's work in the classroom, so that the counselor is always informed about the counselee's current status. When the counselor clarifies for the classroom teachers the therapeutic value of learning for the youngster, he makes of them important allies in a mutual undertaking. It is helpful to clarify with each teacher how long, slow, gradual and frustrating the process will be, but also how important it is.

Another aspect of this task-oriented psychotherapeutic work is that the counselor's work with the parents also has as its focus the academic achievement of the youngster rather than control of antisocial behavior, which implies blame of the parent for his failure as a parent. It is thus sometimes easier for the parents to help encourage their child to be interested in his school work when this is made part of their task than to exercise control which they have long ago relinquished. Interestingly enough, such an emphasis has in many instances brought child and parents together for the first time.

Obviously what I've tried to describe for the hostile, antisocial youngster applies equally to the sullen, indifferent nonlearner. The help of the counselor to teachers in assessing the child's academic status accurately and then the firm and steady help in beginning the learning of fundamentals is here also essential and often very effective.

In addition to the core therapeutic task of the counselor, he also needs to follow his usual practice of assessing the teacher's role in the particular child's problems and planning how these may be worked out. Further, it is informative to try to understand the particular disturbing behavior of a counselee as a request for some counter action of an integrative kind from some adult. Thus the insolent but not destructive youngster is often asking for the adult to look beneath his insolent words and attend to his actions so that he may experience someone who is concerned with him, the youngster, rather than with one's own hurt, pride, and self-esteem. Much hostile, insolent, aggressive behavior is aimed at unmasking the phony attitudes of adults who say they care about youngsters. These young people seem to be looking for honesty, firmness, and security in the adult with which to identify and emulate since such patterns were absent in the adults at home.

Often the counselor's contacts with the child's family will give him clues to the student's behavior as he assesses the emotional deficiencies in the family situation.

An important therapeutic agent is the student's beginning relationship with his counselor whom he begins to see as an honest adult who believes in the student's human potential for growth, who does not deceive himself about the gravity and difficulty of the situation, and who is willing to expend the time and energy to help the student toward self-realization. It is especially important that the counselor do his task because it is his job which he wants to do well and not out of any unclear altruistic love of the student. Such love the student knows from bitter experience could not withstand the frustrations and disappointments which the work brings. The firm expectations of teachers and counselor that a student can learn, and their willingness to stand by until he does may be the necessary reliving of an important part of the parent-infant relationship which these youngsters have not yet experienced, and may provide an important model for the youngster, a model he has never encountered.

The counselor continues his help when he responds to the inevitable cries with spot appointments and clear, consistent presentation of the two roads open to the youngster. The student can persist at his learning tasks or he can give up and revert to his usual pattern of running away from work. Slowly as the alternatives are presented, his usual pattern of behavior becomes clear to the youngster and he is encouraged to try a different solution this time.

As elsewhere described, there is no more rewarding experience than having lived through such difficult times with a youngster [4]. It is especially gratifying to recognize how much differently the student sees himself and the world around him and how differently he functions.

I can hear as I have described the counselor's therapeutic task the cry of counselors everywhere. It sounds interesting and even promising, but where can we find the time to do such a job? It is impossible. It is for this reason that a beginning at definition of the professional job to be done is so vital, because then and only then can one begin to clarify the task, plan for, and get others to help in getting recognition of the job to be done, and finally discovering the means to do it.

Thus, I've tried to emphasize that the school counselor's job is a unique one. His experience as a teacher permits him to focus on the mental health aspects of learning in helping his counselees. He uses techniques from ego psychology which focus on the here and the now, that is, the task to be mastered in the present rather than focusing on past experiences. Such therapeutic activities borrow from psychotherapeutic techniques common to social work, psychological counseling, and psychiatry in its use of the developing relationship between counselor and counselee and the conscious use of the process of identification (providing a model) to help the counselee to accomplish his task—beginning to learn. In this light no one outside of a school setting is in the position to help the counselee as fully from his knowledge of the teachers, the school, and learning theory as the school counselor. Personal problems counseling is thus a mental health profession, distinct and unique with much promise if time to practice it and time to acquire training in it are provided.

REFERENCES

1. Berlin, I. N., Henry, A., *et al.* "Improving Learning Conditions for Delinquent and Predelinquent Adolescents," *Calif. J. Second. Educ.* (1960) 35: 175–202.

2. Boatman, Maleta J., & Szurek, S. A. "A Clinical Study of Childhood Schizophrenia." In *The Etiology of Schizophrenia*, edited by Don D. Jackson. New York: Basic Books, 1960.

3. Szurek, S. A. "Childhood Schizophrenia: Psychotic Episodes and Psychotic Maldevelopment," *Am. J. Orthopsychiat.* (1956) 26: 519–543.

4. Szurek, S. A., & Berlin, I. N. "Elements of Psychotherapeutics with the Schizophrenic Child and His Parents," *Psychiatry* (1956) 19: 1–9.

7

Administrator, Advocate, or Therapist?

Dan C. Lortie, Ph.D.*

These are days of high excitement for those engaged in school coun-seling.[1] A new recognition of the import of counseling services prevails: extensive assistance to guidance is a significant feature of the National De-fense Education Act, strong endorsement for increased counseling service occurs in that potent source of legitimation, the Conant Reports, and pro-grams directed toward assisting the urban disadvantaged—programs of in-creasing moment—place heavy emphasis on augmented guidance activi-ties. Small wonder that members of the counseling field show heightened self-awareness and concern for their occupation and its future. Small wonder that counseling leadership seeks to seize the moment to attain pro-fessional status for their timely work.

The sociologist who is invited to comment on these trends is likely to find himself, like the late arrival at a lively party, in a somewhat ambiguous situation. He can, of course, jump in and join the festivities, but this line of action contributes no special benefit. Yet should he stand aside, calm and detached, his sobriety may simply inhibit the vitality of others. Permit me to make one point early in the hope that subsequent observations will not ap-pear to be anti-convivial. The continued development of counseling serv-ices is, in my opinion, crucial in the construction of a more specialized, rational order in the public schools—a kind of order which will be more and more necessary in the years ahead. The issues involved in refining coun-seling activities are too critical to set aside; of the questions pressing for scrutiny, few are more urgent than the professionalization of school coun-seling.

To professionalize an occupation is to crystallize it in specific, formal and even rigid ways. Careless decisions can "freeze" inappropriate solu-tions to problems in organizing a complex field of work. Serious risks are involved—an inadequate structure can result in the unwitting sabotage of earnestly sought goals. Counselors could, in short, organize their work in such a way that future years will see them doing things they never intended in ways they never planned.

°Dr. Lortie is an Associate Professor of Education with the Midwest Administration Center, at the University of Chicago. His article appeared originally in the *Harvard Educa-tion Review*, 35:3 (Winter 1965), and is reprinted with permission of the author and of the journal.
[1] In this article no distinction is made between counseling and guidance [Editor].

Indications are that guidance does face serious problems in professionalization. Dr. C. Harold McCully, in a review of major writers in the
field, could find no consensus on what are the essential and primary services
offered by counselors.[2] In the pages that follow I shall argue that without
such a consensus—without a clear image of core services and skills—effective professionalization of guidance will not occur. I shall attempt to demonstrate that the current position of the counselor contains diverse, contradictory functions and that members of the occupation will be forced to
resolve thorny issues in moving toward the professional model of work
organization. The analysis, however, is not exhaustive; logical rather than
empirical, it seeks to isolate issues which require attention from the professional group. It should become clear, however, that resolution of these
issues will require extensive and thorough research into the current work
reality of counselors and others working in schools. I hope that the ideas
put forth here will prove to be hypotheses capable of empirical confirma-
tion, rejection or amplification.

I

To make a profession of an occupation requires monumental effort of
those so committed.[3] It calls for the development and diffusion of collective
beliefs, it involves patterning relationships the practitioners will have with
persons inside and outside the profession, and it permeates the personalities
of members of the colleague group. It is, in fact, the construction of a sub-
society within the larger community, for it features a unique culture, peculiar modes of interaction and an apparatus for the socialization of would-be
members. Some of this effort is informal and emerges spontaneously in the
course of day-to-day activities, but an enterprise of such scope also requires
formal political work—a working constitution must be hammered out.
Constitution-making is a sequential process in which alternatives which are
selected early constrain later decisions; the cumulative effect is not only
something new and unique but a structure in which many logical alternatives have been ruled out. In a sense, we can describe professionalization as
a "narrowing" process—a narrowing process, however, which rests on
basic agreements hacked out over the years.

[2]Harold C. McCully, "The School Counselor: Strategy for Professionalization,"
Personnel and Guidance Journal (April 1962).

[3]Although there is no one definition of profession which is commonly accepted, certain
elements found in established professions can be used effectively in analysis of the process of
professionalization. Good illustrations can be found in Myron Lieberman, *Education as a
Profession* (Englewood Cliffs, New Jersey: Prentice-Hall, Inc., 1956), and Howard S.
Becker, "The Nature of a Profession," *Education for the Professions*, Chapter II, *The Sixty-
first Yearbook of the National Society for the Study of Education.* Edited by Nelson B. Henry.
University of Chicago Press, 1962.

Although we cannot engage in a complete analysis of professionalization processes here, we can illustrate some of the typical mechanisms by a brief review of three problems which face every profession. (1) Who will be admitted for training? (2) How will candidates be prepared for practice? and (3) How can members of the profession be induced to comply with its standards of conduct? The answers selected to these questions become the structure within which individuals are shaped to the professional ideal. Conversely, perhaps without awareness, the answers chosen reflect the group's conception of what its members seek to become.

Modern professions must come to terms with the university system, and the latter has much to do with the answers given to the admission question. The casual entry of an earlier era gives way to a controlled, single route of specific educational requirements which frequently imply allied characteristics. The age of entrants, for example, usually goes down, for university regulations and/or facilities frequently proscribe participation in later periods of the life cycle. Beginners are truly beginners who come to the field without previous experience and specific commitments to given ways of doing things. The newly formalized requirements are usually longer, and these greater time demands increase the direct costs of education and such indirect costs as income foregone; the social class background of students, often linked to financial resources, may change as a result. The sex balance of the occupation may shift as rigidly specified training makes it more difficult for women to combine the career with family responsibilities. Thus does insistence on new academic qualifications introduce social homogeneity that was absent before the new requirements; unintended but significant consequences can flow from any one of these alternations in the social composition of entrants to the field.

Occupational leaders find that as they construct a system of professional preparation, many difficult issues require resolution. What should the balance be, for example, between scientific and intuitive components in the curriculum? In fact, what sciences are relevant to their profession? In assessing a given candidate, how should they weigh his demonstration of practical skills versus his performance in academic work? How do they test those elusive personality characteristics they feel are so important in practice? Those preparing professionals seem almost compelled to find standard answers to such questions and to apply them to institution after institution; perhaps this drive for standardization stems from the professional's insistence that his special preparation is so significant—it is chiefly the training, after all, which separates the legitimate practitioner from the quack. Established professions have, however, managed to develop complex curricula featuring a surprising amount of internal consistency, of unity in socialization experiences. But such standardization is possible, after all, where there is consensus on what the practitioner should do and how he should do it. Where the image of the practitioner's future work is diffuse or ambiguous or controversial, educators and senior practitioners have no criteria to assist them in arbitrating the many decisions they must make in building a system of professional preparation. Not knowing what kind of man they wish to produce, they cannot design a program with repetitive, consistent experiences intended to personify the professional ideal; lacking just such a unifying theme, the impact of their program is never quite strong enough.

Inducements for compliance in the established professions are many and subtle, and they range from internalization of ethical principles ("professional conscience") to controls built right into the career system and the distribution of rewards. Law and medicine, for example, test the young practitioner's technical competence and moral qualities at crucial points in the career—professional success is gained or lost largely in the context of colleague judgments.[4] A long period of socialization follows the university period—young physicians and lawyers learn much, technically and otherwise, from the senior colleagues who oversee their early years in practice. This system of instruction, however, rests upon the consensus felt by those who rule the profession and influence the fates of young aspirants to high position. It also requires a highly effective system of communication to implement the values which underlie the judgments and influence the allocation of money, prestige and power rewards. The system defines who is in and who is outside the professional group; one knows, in short, who one's colleagues are.

This brief discussion may suggest some of the complexity connected with answering the questions cited earlier—the questions of entry, preparation and control which face every group seeking professional status. Many specific questions and issues must be resolved and similar answers adopted by members of the professional group; adoption implies a willingness to accept rules of the game which affect one's career and life fate. The group must agree on what is important to do and how it should be done in specific terms.

Where does school counseling stand in regard to these problems of professionalization? The current role of the counselor combines several different functions which are difficult to project into a unitary professional model. We shall examine the counselor's role in terms of three clusters of tasks which focus on different functions within the school's social organization. Scrutinizing each in turn (we shall begin with administrative functions in the counselor's role), we shall find that selection of any one of the

---

[4]For medicine, see Oswald Hall. "The Stages of a Medical Career," *American Journal of Sociology*, LIII (March 1948), pp. 327–336. For law, see Dan C. Lortie, "Laymen to Lawmen: Law School, Careers and Professional Socialization," *Harvard Educational Review*, 29 (Fall 1959), No. 4.

three components as the core would lead in a different direction and would result in a distinctive type of professionalization.°

II

The duties of guidance counselors generally include some activities which are administrative in function. Among these are situations where counselors route students to speicfic teachers or specific departments of the school. In so doing, they are performing an important executive function— using Talcott Parsons' phrase, they are allocating primary materials.[5] Few matters influence a teacher's work or a department's status more deeply than the operation of the assignment system. Such decisions, by exerting an important influence on the technical level of work, are clearly managerial in nature, and since they require choices among members of that level, they must be made by persons either above it or apart from it. The counselor's decisions, unlike those made by most administrators, may be accompanied by esoteric techniques and special psychological knowledge, but the *functions* of such decisions, from the organizational point of view, are essentially administrative in nature.

Counselors may also engage in another administrative activity of some consequence—the maintenance of the school's system of order and discipline. The counselor who works with "behavior problems" referred by teachers and principal deals with an individual at any given moment; in acting with a succession of deviations from the school's normative order, however, counselors give that cultural system significant support. The techniques used do not matter very much; strong sanctions or subtle suasion, the ends served are the same. To uphold the school's norms is more than a simple police function. Problem behavior and its control invariably raise judicial issues and judicial decision-making requires the counselor to diagnose the likely effects of alternative decisions not only on the child but on the school as an organization.

Schools and counselors differ in the importance they attach to these and other administrative aspects of the counselor's role. Some school districts, for example, consider the counselor's position the first rung on the administrative ladder; in these schools, the counselor is an administrator-in-training. (We find the same thing in some colleges and universities where the dean of students position is clearly linked with an administrative career.) Although many counselors may scorn the "administrative trivia" of their jobs, some spokesmen for guidance assign great weight to the administrative function.

°For further discussions of several points raised above by Dr. Lortie, see the several papers in Parts I and II [Text Editor].

[5]Talcott Parsons, "Some Ingredients of a Theory of Formal Organization," *Administrative Theory in Education,* Edited by Andrew W. Halpin. Chicago: Midwest Administration Center, University of Chicago, 1958.

Dr. Edward J. Shoben, for example, advocates a position for the counselor akin to that of the pathologist checking the surgeon's work, for the implementation of his suggestions would require the counselor to report, and therefore appraise, the effect of teachers and others on the climate of the school.[6] The Meyerson and Michael viewpoint is more dramatically administrative, for their depiction of the counselor as a master pedagogical engineer leaves administrators little by way of educational leadership in the school.[7] Administrative functions are more than accidental elements in the counselor's role if school systems and professional spokesmen are prepared to give administration the central place in guidance work.

It seems reasonable, in light of what we know about men and their work, to expect that a man's outlook will be heavily influenced by the repetitive problems and interactions he encounters on a day-to-day basis.[8] Much time spent in allocating students, for example, could lead to preoccupation with balancing the often conflicting values of fairness-justice and individual appropriateness. The assignment of students to a vocational program versus a college preparatory course, for example, is not a private affair—it involves the vital interests of students, their families, local employers, colleges, etc. The public nature of these decisions increases the decision-maker's concern with their legitimation and the result is that he places greater reliance on "objective" indicators of capability, interest and the like. Since such modes of thought require categories (bright versus dull, high versus low motivation, etc.), the counselor, no matter how profound his dedication to individuals, must constantly classify individual students into relevant groups. Such categorical considerations, although intended to clarify single decisions, introduce their own constraints. Once used and announced, any objective basis for allocation may be cited by others as justifying a similar decision. Willy-nilly, the counselor finds himself enmeshed in a round of precedents and judicial decisions; his actions, far from being free in each new instance, are constrained by an ever more complex set of policies and rules.

The counselor can become a man deeply committed to solving a recurrent series of complicated interpersonal as well as individual problems. As is true of the general school administrator, the counselor finds that he must become skilled in suggesting as well as implementing policy, and that he acts for the organization as it classifies and routes students into potentially

    [6]Edward Joseph Shoben, Jr., "Guidance: Remedial Function or Social Reconstruction?" *Harvard Educational Review*, 32 (Fall 1962), No. 4.
    [7]L. Meyerson and J. Michael, "A Behavioral Approach to Counseling and Guidance," *Harvard Educational Review*, 32 (Fall 1962), No. 4.
    [8]This assertion has, of course, become a central thesis of the sociology of work. Perhaps the most significant article in granting it formal attention was that written some years ago by Hughes. Everett C. Hughes. "Institutional Office and the Person," *The American Journal of Sociology*, XLIII (November 1937), 404–413.

different life careers. In all these matters, he must heed his official position, the wishes of legal superiors and the consequences decisions may have for the organization's ability to help future students. He is not only, as an employee, committed to working toward the goals of the organization, but his tasks make it difficult for him to deviate from the organization's means for meeting those goals. The counselor who allocates students has a relationship to the individual student which is not a pure dyadic transaction free of other entanglements. It must be filtered through a complex set of policies, relationships to various publics and organizational loyalties.

Protracted engagement in the work of order maintenance is also likely to lead to preoccupation with administrative issues. In this instance, the goals and means of the organization are especially important—the counselor is acting to protect them, in fact, against the incursions of deviating students. It need not be true that the organization's interests and those of the student be always in conflict for this to be problematic; it is enough that where such a conflict arises, the counselor cannot disregard established school ways. The latter alternative is frequently ruled out by considerations of justice or expediency stemming from the visibility of disciplinary decisions. Furthermore, those responsible for upholding any established order sense the need for some minimum predictability in its rules if those rules are to have validity. School counselors know full well that continued "bending" of established school rules will, after a period of time, undermine the very relevance of the rule system. The law may need changing, but until changed, it is the law.

How would counseling be affected were it to professionalize around such administrative functions? This definition of the role would, of course, fix it clearly as an official position—it would place counselors as specialized administrators, sub-officials within the school hierarchy. Their special expertise might include such unique knowledge as recent advances in psychology, measurement, and peculiar skills (diagnosis, test administration and interpretation, the psychology of persuasion, etc.). The work, however, would not feature unique ends, for the counselor's proximate goals would not differ in any appreciable way from those of other functionaries in the school system. As with other administrators, one would expect him to demonstrate his loyalty to the organization by showing enthusiasm for its goals and respect for its ways. He would act inappropriately were he to put a personal conception of counseling (or one asserted primarily by the professional colleague group outside the organization) ahead of established school policy. He would, of course, work for changes he considered desirable, but at any given moment, his decisions would necessarily flow from pre-existing policy.

Research might reveal that counselors engaged in administrative functions vary in their relationships with general administrators and teachers, but I believe that assigning priority to this function necessarily involves distance in the counselor's interactions with students. The student, at least the perceptive student, will recognize the role the counselor plays and his possession of power to affect him, the student; rational behavior on his part, therefore, would dictate caution in relating to the counselor. (Where a student has a clear and specific purpose, in fact, rationality would include efforts to manipulate the counselor to assist in realization of that purpose.) The shrewd student would, at the very least, seek to make a "good impression" on the counselor, and such an orientation would generally discourage revelatory outbursts which might put him in an unfavorable light and tarnish the image he is attempting to project. The counselor, for his part, could not adopt the non-judgmental stance recommended for therapists. As a school official charged with implementing specific policies, he could only pretend to no prior commitments were he willing to engage in hypocrisy. Holding power and authority, he would find it impossible to be "buddy" and "boss" simultaneously. Counselors playing administrative roles no doubt differ in some of the ways in which they interact with students, but like all who possess power, they sooner or later know the toughness of the boundary which separates those on different sides of an authority relationship.

Some may question the usefulness of counseling if it is primarily administrative in nature—why differentiate it at all under these circumstances? There is at least one answer to this query, although that answer does not dictate, in any way, the choice counselors should make in the years ahead. There seems little doubt that the advance of school administration will require some effective link to the world of applied psychology and will need persons skilled in the use of such knowledge in those areas where it is most relevant. Someone, no doubt, will play this role if school counselors do not; schools will not be able to ignore a large and important area of substantive knowledge in making rational provision for allocation, order maintenance, and allied matters. Leaders in the field of guidance may or may not choose to organize the field around administrative core tasks. Whatever their decision, there is a positive contribution of specialized knowledge and ability that rests in the application of modern psychology to the governance of public schools.

III

Dr. C. Gilbert Wrenn and others have remarked that counselors currently perform many administrative and clerical duties.[9] Yet we know better than to leap from this fact to the conclusion that the counselor's role is identical to that of the principal or any school official. Among the special

[9]McCully, *op. cit*

attributes of the counselor's role is the private nature of his relationship with students and the dyadic setting within which it takes place; although the outcomes can be highly visible, the processes usually take place under conditions of greater privacy than found in principal or teacher dealings with students. Teachers may employ the rhetoric of individual instruction, but the ecology of their work offers them small opportunity for private interaction with students.° Principals may see students privately, but the context is usually special and often involves "trouble." The counselor, however, routinely spends many hours in face-to-face conversation with students. The regularity of these private encounters has important repercussions for his role and could lead to a definition quite distinct from that we have been examining.

No social system works perfectly—all, to at least some extent, sacrifice individual interests in the operation of the whole. Schools are no exception, and as quasi-bureaucracies, they promulgate and enforce rules which do not always fit the individual's needs. The privacy and access which the counselor has in relating to students make it likely that he will become aware of such disjunctions more frequently than will other professionals in the school. In fact, the counselor's job title encourages students to define him as the logical person to hear their dissatisfactions. Undistracted by thirty other students needing attention, the counselor can more readily react by empathizing with the student before him; furthermore, counseling, as a position, probably attracts more persons who wish to "help" individuals, than do teaching or administration. This combination of factors—privacy, dyadic relationships, students frustrated by the organization, and counselors oriented to helping youngsters—can readily lead to counselor identification with beleagured students. Such identification, were it to occur on a large scale, could bring about another logically possible formulation of the counselor role. Lacking a prior term, I shall call this function "advocacy."

The counselor who acts as advocate (specifically, as defendant's attorney) treats a given substantive complaint presented by a student as a serious matter. Where convinced that the complaint is valid, his inclination is to act, to press for a change in the situation which is problematic for the student. His eye is on reality problems, not on the emotional turbulence and distorted perceptions of the psychologically troubled student. Where this type of counselor finds a problem needing action, he is willing to go to bat for the student even where such attention might cause embarrassment to other professionals in the school. Although

---

°This is less true in schools which have adopted flexible-modular instructional designs. Such designs permit much more personal contact between teacher and student than has been possible before [Text Editor].

he needs and uses diagnostic skills in descerning valid from invalid complaints (in terms of *his* criteria), his is not the therapist's stance. His interest is in helping individual students cope effectively with the sometimes impersonal juggernaut of the school.

Significant changes in the organization of our schools would be necessary before the advocate function could become the central activity of school counselors. Though current role arrangements may permit the counselor to battle for some individual students, there is little evidence that regular conflict of this kind has become institutionalized in our school structure. If counselors are to engage in strenuous, prolonged advocacy in the interests of individual students, they will need protection to do so and a clear set of rules guiding their behavior and the behavior of those with whom they debate. Fighting the cause of the individual student could easily put the counselor in direct conflict with administrators and teachers. He would need a special license to perform this function, a license which defined his actions as professional, not personal, and which made it clear that he was not attacking the solidarity of the professional group. Mechanisms would have to be developed which placed the counselor as a loyal member of the group justifiably engaged in opposition.[10]

Counseling organized around advocacy would not resemble the administrative formulation or, as indicated, the therapist conception. Persons engaged in this kind of role would, we imagine, begin to look like lawyers and stress the skills of pleading and analysis; we might even see the emergence of a kind of administrative law system in schools with formal arrangements for dispensing justice and arbitrating issues. Advocate counselors would probably emphasize such values as humanism, individualism, and concern themselves deeply with "the good of the child." One suspects they would leave to others such matters as the integrity of the organization and the logics of cost and efficiency. This kind of specialization, in other words, would include moral as well as technical specialization. The drive underlying the role would be the *relevant* treatment of the individual child, and the school would be held accountable for the human implications of its general procedures, rules, and policies. Nor is the stance that of the therapist who, in helping the student work through his problems, locates the problem as something within the student. To the advocate counselor, reality *is* a problem and students have the right to skilled in-

---

[10]There are promising opportunities here for research on the current situation. On what occasions do counselors stand ready to go out on a limb for a student? Do some counselors occupy a position which permits them to play the advocacy role regularly? If yes, what are the bases on which this position has been built? Are counselors who incline to this formulation different in personality terms? For example, are they more generally rebellious than those who have little interest in advocacy function? These and many other questions need answering before we can assess the force behind this particular formulation of the guidance role.

tervention and support in getting the treatment most appropriate for them. The curriculum or the schedule—even an individual teacher—can be wrong.

We can speculate that were counseling to move in this direction, different skills and values would emerge to dominate the profession. Forensic abilities, the preparation of a "brief," skill in discriminating between neurotic and realistic complaints—these would probably emerge as valued abilities among such counselors. One would also expect counselors to develop an ideology consistent with their function—a set of beliefs stressing, in this instance, the importance of offsetting bureaucratic and standardizing forces in our schools. Research might center on such issues as how situational factors inhibit or encourage learning and personal growth, and on how individual variations affect response to different educational structures. The core ethic of this type of counselor would be one which placed clear priority on the responsibility of the counselor for the individual child.

Answers would have to be found for many complicated questions were counselors to move toward this conceptualization of their mission. What norms, for example, should govern the relationship between the counselor and the student he decides to assist? What powers, if any, should counselors be given to right wrongs they uncover? Should counselors intervene in family matters? If so, in what ways do their responsibilities differ from school social workers? To simply list these questions dramatizes the complexity involved in moving to this definition of the counselor's role. Yet one can question very seriously whether American schools can make good on their affirmations of individualism in the years ahead unless specific arrangements are made to defend the individual student against powerful bureaucratizing forces. Will counselors be the ones to seize this responsibility as their core task?

IV

Those expert in the art and science of psychotherapy agree on the importance of the therapist-client relationship in influencing the outcome of the therapeutic transaction. Such authorities maintain that the client must be able to extend full and unquestioning trust in the integrity and ultimate sympathy of the counselor, and that the establishment of this trust is a primary task confronting the therapist. Yet few authors raise questions about the sociological context necessary for achieving this kind of relationship, for most discussions focus on the counselor's obligations to win trust without serious analysis of the constraints which can act on him from his broader role commitments. Imagine, however, the likelihood that a student called by the counselor for disciplining will perceive the complete absence of "explicit or implicit disapproval" stressed by Dr. Adrian van

Kaam.[11] What chance does the counselor have to convey the "warm and acceptant" feelings emphasized by Rogers where he is tightly bound by pre-existing policies which he must implement?[12] We know intuitively the impossibility of these juxtapositions yet we often ignore the situational and role prerequisites to effective psychotherapy.

It is clear that the trust relationship rests upon the client's feeling that his interests will come first, and that he is free, as client, to explore a variety of alternative actions, emotions, etc. without excessive moral constraint emanating from the therapist. (Some moral constraints will, of course, always exist.) Specifically, the client must never feel that the solutions he considers and assesses in association with the therapist will be screened in terms of unique organizational requirements. The therapist must be able to convince the client, legitimately, that he is assisting him and placing his interests before that of an employer, a school official, or a court.[13]

The therapist must also be free to follow the client's total interests and be in a position to explore many facets of his total life situation. Schools, for example, generally treat youngsters in their charge in terms of a specific status—that of "student." The existence of the latter status, paired as it is with several counter-statuses, limits the nature, extent and expression of interest school personnel show the individual youngster. But no troubled young person is ever, in his eyes, solely a student in School X—he possesses other statuses, crucial affiliations and concerns which transcend one particular organization. The person who would, through therapy, seek to help him explore and understand his world must be willing to accompany him down many paths which lead away from his school experience. An externally imposed definition of psychological problems into "educational" or "noneducational" is hardly likely to coincide with the actuality of the youngster's inner experience—the therapist, in sum, must interact with the student as a total person.

This double imperative of therapy—the necessity to give priority to client interests and the need to relate to him in a total way—makes it extremely difficult to incorporate the therapeutic relationship into a pre-existing hierarchy of authority and formal status. Inasmuch as the therapist

[11]Adrian van Kaam, "Counseling from the Viewpoint of Existential Psychology," *Harvard Educational Review*, 32 (Fall 1962), No. 4.

[12]Carl R. Rogers, "The Interpersonal Relationship: The Core of Guidance," *Harvard Educational Review*, 32 (Fall 1962), No. 4.

[13]When the counselor "counsels" a student he may be doing, as I see it, one of three things. He may be giving him information about the school and its operations—this is essentially an instructional function, and does not differentiate the counselor from the teacher. He may be, as discussed in our review of the administrative function, be directing the student in ways congruent with the organizational plan—this is clearly administrative. Therapy would presumably include all situations where the counselor seeks to improve the student's capacity to deal with problems which occur in his life space—the end goal is, in this instance, increased psychological capacity on the part of the student.

must enforce even limited aspects of the organization's special expectations, he cannot be certain to place the interests of the client first. Inasmuch as the therapist must limit his relationship to predesignated spheres of life, be they work, study or citizenship, he cannot engage himself with the object of his help as a whole person; yet to show interest in all relevant spheres of the client's life is to create suspicion that the organization is overreaching its boundaries. Almost all therapeutic relationships outside of mental institutions are *separated* from other critical facets of the person's round. Individual psychotherapy is, as well, frequently mediated by a fee-for-service arrangement which dramatizes the professional-client relationship, but even where the service is provided in a publicly-supported clinic, the actual therapy is conducted in a physically isolated setting and with no regular communication channels to other persons who figure prominently in the client's life. These structural arrangements are, it seems, not accidental—they relate closely to the double imperative we have examined.

What would be involved in establishing counseling in schools as essentially psychotherapeutic in nature? The counselor would have to be relieved of all administrative and semi-administrative responsibilities, and special mechanisms would be necessary to clarify his lack of organizational authority; he could not, as we noted earlier, expect full trust and revelatory behavior from students who perceived him as a person with influence over their daily school life. The counselor would have to show an interest in many sides of the student's life which are not currently part of the school's mandate. Nor would student expectations which are consistent with the therapist's stance accord with those sought by the advocate counselor. One wonders, in fact, just how he could be placed in the school's regular social structure since the usual ties and obligations of a school professional have disruptive potential for his therapeutic work. The problematic nature of his role would place him under a particular strain to justify his location in the school—he would be asked what he does in school that he could not do as well outside it.

To institutionalize therapy as the core function of the school counselor would require differentiation of his role from that of others engaged in psychotherapeutic activities. Organizationally, one would expect school boards and top administrators to resist the therapeutic emphasis if it involves what they perceive as a major change in the overall function of the school. Creating a new profession of school counseling based on therapy would also be difficult if close examination revealed that school counselors feature the same skills, knowledge and social relationships needed in already established psychotherapeutic fields. Can school counselors develop a new and special conception of therapy which is clearly suited to the school situation and requires the location of the therapist on site?

Our era is one marked by a new realization of the significance of mental health among children as well as among adults. It is ironic that of the three functions we have examined, the psychotherapeutic formulation of the counselor's role would require the most extensive redefinition of that role and, indeed, of the mandate and organization of our public schools.

V

Selection of any one of the three functions we have reviewed as the core activity of school counselors would result in a different profession. Entry arrangements, professional training and career system would differ for administrative, advocate and therapist types of counseling. Guidance based on the administrative function, for example, would probably feature relatively late entry (our tests for leadership potential are not yet good enough to stand in for demonstrated capacity), a curriculum largely similar to that used in preparing school administrators and a career line which could logically terminate in the superintendency.

The preparation of advocates and therapists, however, would call for different persons to start with and different curricula in their training. Recruiting advocates would be challenging, as it would require persons with unusual intellectual abilities, commitment to individualistic values and the personality which would lead to effective work under conflict situations. Furthermore, a new career line would have to be developed to reward the core values of this new profession. But the recruitment, training and career routing of therapists, unless a new and profound differentiation of school therapy emerges, would be based on patterns already worked out in clinical psychology, psychiatry, and social work. Three different central functions would require three different sets of answers to questions facing all new professions.

If one major value of the author underlies this discussion, that value is the belief that counselors should select the function, or functions, they wish to serve and build a structure appropriate to it or to them. There is a genuine risk that if they fail to do so, structural decisions (e.g., admission requirements, educational programs, job organization, etc.) will coerce functional outcomes. Counselors might, for example, recruit new members primarily from those established as teachers only to find that prior socialization makes it impossible to move toward an advocate or therapeutic definition of the role. On the other hand, university curricula might produce graduates imbued with an advocacy mission but no school in which to express it. In social affairs, function *can* follow structure.

The decisions facing counselors are difficult, manifold and time-consuming. As leaders toward a more refined and rich division-of-labor in schools, it is my hope that they will persist in efforts to find the set of duties which makes the maximum contribution of which they are capable. This will, I believe, require extended study and analysis not only of counseling but of other functions and groups within schools; counselors are not the only persons in schools who, concerned with their status, are considering important changes. We need thoughtful estimates of what services will be critical in the future and close analysis of the interlocking relationships of counselors and teachers and social workers and assistant principals. We will need much careful work, protracted discussion and, I suspect, considerable good will on the part of all if a more effective organization of our schools is to emerge.

Counselors must ask themselves what services they can best perform over the years ahead. Thorough and sensitive research, coupled with frank, widespread discussion is the only strategy that I can visualize which will lead to a reasonably harmonious and rational division-of-labor in our public schools. If school counselors wish to play a vital part in that emerging order, they had best heed Robert Park's advice to another occupation and find their craft before they build their profession.

8

Counselor—or What?

C. C. Dunsmoor, Ed. D.*

"What you will *be*, you are now becoming." So said the speaker at an Iowa high school commencement some 30 or more years ago, and it is the one point which I still remember from his remarks. And so, it seems to me that what the Counselor of Tomorrow is going to be, he is now in the process of becoming.

Millions upon millions of words have been written upon the "counselor" and "counseling" these past few years, and with acceleration to the point where it seems that nearly everybody wants to get in on the act. Even many psychiatrists, clinical psychologists, and psychotherapists who have their own domains of therapy rather neatly staked out for many years are now talking about the "counseling" they are doing; and, as if threatened or even a bit insecure themselves, are, at least by implication, indicating that many of the thousands of well-prepared and qualified "counselors" in America are at best only "amateurs" and that the only real "counseling" after all, is being done by themselves.

Counseling, if it is to become a *real profession*, must have the dedicated informed, and constant allegiance of a core of counselor educators and real counselors in the field who aren't the least bit ashamed to be known as counselors. We must quit bowing so deferentially to the psychotherapy oriented, who for some reason or another are willing to claim much of the glory, but who at the same time seem to be unwilling to do very much to help the counselor prepare for the types of tasks which he realistically faces on the firing line in the school, in the college, or in the agency.

Counselors everywhere are striving for maturity in their profession and they are beginning to snip a few apron strings and to ask a lot of questions of the "father-figures" about the facts of life in our evolving profession. And, I shudder a bit when I hear of the answers which some of our learned "leaders," who seemingly are a bit reluctant to shed their mystic robes and to mingle meaningfully with those of us who must practice some of the doctrines which *they* preach.

*Dr. Dunsmoor is retired Director of the Board, Cooperative Educational Services, Bedford Hills, New York, and is a former president of the American Personnel and Guidance Association. He now makes his home in Seminole, Florida. Dr. Dunsmoor's article appeared originally in the *Personnel and Guidance Journal* (October 1964), and is reprinted with permission of the author and of the journal.

The counselor has a sort of *mobile*, or perhaps I should say *ever-dynamic*, set of factors with which to deal.

1. He is working with individuals who are constantly changing, even from week to week.

2. Both he and his counselees or clients are living in a changing world—we have this from no less an authority than our good friend Dr. C. Gilbert Wrenn—and at least in *our society* and in *our time*, it is a world in which the tempo and pressures have become so great that the social and economic aspects of our lives may be said to be *changing almost from day to day.* Just imagine what a modern Rip Van Winkle, awakening today, would discover he had been missing during the past twenty years.

3. The character of our occupational and educational structures is undergoing revolutionary changes. The pace of automation, for example, is putting to shame the industrial revolution of the 18th and 19th centuries. Along with this we find a worldwide social revolution going full blast, with new nations being born every year and with overthrows of government coming at the rate of "a dime a dozen."

Meanwhile, education is experiencing an *extensive* and *vigorous* overhaul and retooling—in fact, education is having a renaissance of its own. The American dream of "education for all" is getting a great deal of play these days as Federal impetus is being given to vocational education, special education, the reduction of school dropouts, and upgrading the performance of the unemployed and the disadvantaged. And, under President Lyndon B. Johnson's leadership, we are taking the first major steps in launching an all-out war on poverty in this country. In all these, it is inevitable that education, accompanied by adequate counseling, must play a leading part.

In such a changing environmental situation, in which about the only thing that is certain is change, the moral to our story is that the counselor himself must change, and he must be constantly on the alert and ready to *adapt* to change. It is thus somewhat inconceivable that some counselors strongly oppose increased standards of counselor preparation which will help them adapt to these changes. The world—be it physical, economic, or social—moves on, and to merely maintain the *status quo*, is but to fall behind.

We've heard a great deal in recent years about the urgency of more and more rigorous academic standards for students at all levels. But we should at the same time remember that the tougher the schools become, the greater the obligation of the school to be concerned with the fitness of the individual pupil to meet the demands of the "toughness." We have reintroduced the "sweatshop" into millions of homes in America by demanding extensive homework assignments of our pupils, even down in the elementary grades, and we are often demanding a working day for our children that is far in excess of what Dad or Mother put in on their respective jobs. Is it any wonder, then, that we have had steadily mounting numbers of individuals with emotional problems, both among children and adults? Many students today are working under pressures and tensions that *just should not exist.*

Dr. Clovis Hirning, a member of the counselor education staff at Teachers College and a part-time psychiatric consultant on our staff in Northern Westchester, who has had some 25 years of experience as a psychiatrist, said awhile back, "I feel after so many years of pulling people out of the river, that I'd like to meander upstream and find out who's throwing them in." It is high time, he feels, that we introduce more preventive or anticipatory problem-solving programs of pupil study and counseling in our schools, which are really the only "common denominator" of children and youth from age 5 through 16 at least. Obviously, this means the introduction of extensive programs of elementary and junior high school guidance in which counselors and school psychologists would play leading parts, with the able assistance of school social workers, psychiatric consultants, and health service workers on the pupil personnel services team. Dr. Hirning conceives of the school counselor as the watchdog of mental health in the schools and as the guardian of individualization in education.

Limitations of time prevent more than this passing mention of the preventive or development approach here, but I personally feel that in it lies the best prognosis for greatly improved school and college counseling programs in the years ahead. Without effective programs of this type, we inevitably have a great, and largely needless, waste of "pupilpower" and manpower. The most fruitful strategy is to anticipate problems and head them off, or to deal with them in their early incidence, when the prospects of success are most favorable.

If we accept the basic premise that counseling and guidance services are for *all* students in the school, and not just for the 15 or 20 per cent who have special problems, then our work is indeed cut out for us in the years ahead, for the "hurricane" represented by the widely discussed population explosion is rapidly bearing down upon us. There is no hope of meeting adequately the counseling needs of school pupils and college students, or of out-of-school youth unless we are to have a great increase in the number of qualified counselors, or unless we are able to discover and provide new approaches whereby we can materially extend the influence of those counselors that we now have, or can prepare in the next few years.

Necessity has always been the mother of invention and she is certainly knocking loudly at our door right now and demanding to know how we are going to provide the amount and quality of counseling which somehow needs to be done for our boys and girls, young men and young women—the most valuable assets of our respective communities—each worth, on the average, a cool $200,000. Early guidance was largely based upon individual counseling. Then came rather extensive group guidance activities, followed by a return to the idea that essentially all counseling had to be done in a one-to-one relationship.

Today, however, it appears that we may be approaching a "reincarnation" of group processing for doing a part of the counseling job, and probably upon a higher professional level today, because it would be more likely to be handled by qualified counselors. It appeared for a time that the term "multiple counseling" would be used to describe this newer type of counselor activity, but now the term "group counseling" is coming rapidly into common use. Just what is meant by group counseling doesn't seem to be uniformly understood—at least there seems to be no consensus as to just what is meant by it. Those who first did group counseling have been wont to think of it as dealing with problem youngsters only, and in small groups of six or eight, meeting over a relatively longer period of time. But is there any reason why group counseling has to be confined to so-called problem children only? And does it always have to be long term? If it's good for problem groups, why isn't it even better for other groups? If research demonstrates that satisfactory results can be shown with these latter groups as well, then perhaps here is an approach that has much promise as one means of helping out the over-burdened counselor.

Let us quit our bickering about whose job it is to do counseling and "who is the greatest." Stake out our areas of responsibility and influence if we must, but let's be on with the job—because figuratively, "Rome is burning" while we are "fiddling around" and sometimes with discordant tunes, while millions of children, youth, and adults are clamoring for counseling on their choices and their problems.

There is plenty of work for *all* to do and more than we collectively, as counselors, can possibly do both now and for the future. Thus, it is high time that we desist from such immature approaches as trying to make inadequate psychotherapists and/or clinical psychologists out of "counselors"; and to make disdainful "counselors" out of psychiatrists and clinical psychologists. Perhaps we should also include in our "desists," that of trying to make "counselors" out of every teacher who comes along and says that he or she wants to *become* a "counselor." And, in the same vein, shouldn't we get away from the idea of having every teacher masquerade as a counselor, when most of them have had no basic preparation for it and seemingly are not interested in attaining it?

Until we establish a hard core of well-qualified counselors, both in terms of preparation and personal qualifications, we cannot hope to advance rapidly as a profession. The ASCA *Study on Counselor Role and*

Function, under the leadership of Dr. Paul Fitzgerald and Dr. John Loughary, has constituted a major step in the advancement of counseling toward recognized professional status.

Thus, as we continue to grow in stature as an evolving profession—and the growth in the next decade and the ensuing ones will be tremendous— we must find a better answer to the question, "Counselor-or what?" We must come to realize what we *can* and what we *cannot* do, as we carve out our niche in the vital area of human endeavor in which we are striving to serve. This idea is most aptly expressed in this little anonymous verse:

> I am *only one,*
> But I *am* one,
> I can't do everything,
> But I *can do* something,
> And, what I *can* do,
> By the grace of God,
> I *will* do.

As we stride down the roadways of counseling history—and I mean "stride," because ours is becoming and *rightfully*, a proud profession— we, with our vision keenly alert to the constant changes of a dynamic world, must keep in primary focus the humanistic concepts and values in counseling.

9

A Survey of Effects Arising from Differential Practices in Employment of School Counselors

William D. Dannenmaier, Ed.D.*

Directors of guidance have, for some time, shown concern with the effect that the employment of counselors in full-time, as opposed to part-time, capacities has on teacher morale and counselor effectiveness. Although no longer a major topic in professional journals, this concern continues to be demonstrated in varied employment practices. It is also a frequent topic in private conversations among guidance directors. In practice, some directors employ counselors on a full-time basis, meaning that all of their duties are within the personnel services. Others prefer to employ counselors as part-time teachers, dividing their responsibilities between the counseling of students and the teaching of academic subjects. Reasons for the regular utilization of such differential employment procedures are generally centered about the questions of teacher acceptance of the counselor and counselor effectiveness with the student.

The approach taken in textbooks on administration concerning this problem varies widely. Some authors tend to ignore the question completely. A few make statements from which inferences as to their position can be drawn [2, 4, 6, 8, 9]. Others will state the reported advantages and or disadvantages [1, 3]. References to empirical studies in the area apparently are nonexistent.

THE PROBLEM

Many counselors appear to accept the premise that counselors who teach will find greater acceptance by other teachers in the school. They feel this will be reflected in more referrals and in the creation of an atmosphere in the school which will be friendlier and more acceptant of counseling. A second point is frequently made concerning counselor availability and counselor growth. The argument concerning these is that persons whose duties are concerned solely with counseling will be better able to remain

*Dr. Dannenmaier is Assistant Registrar, University of Calgary, Calgary, Alberta, Canada. His article appeared originally in *The School Counselor*, 13:1:107 (December 1963), and is reprinted with permission of the author and of the journal.

abreast of current developments and that they will have greater availability to the students. A counterpoint sometimes made is that eight half-time counselors will have more exposure to the students than will four full-time counselors. The above arguments suggested the following hypotheses:

1. Part-time counselors will find greater acceptance by teachers than will full-time counselors.

2. Full-time counselors will be more effective in working with students than will part-time counselors.

THE METHOD

THE INSTRUMENTS

Questionnaires were devised to measure each of the variables. The Teacher-Counselor Relationship Questionnaire was intended to elicit teacher opinions on the use of counselors in the school as well as to permit statements concerning the use made of the counseling services by the responding teacher. The assumption was made that schools in which teachers reported referring students to the counselors and favoring the advancement of counseling could be considered as having favorable teacher-counselor relationships. Conversely, if teachers did not make such referrals or indicate approval it was assumed that teacher-counselor relationships were poor. The questionnaire for students was of a more factual nature. Among other items, students were asked their counselor's name, the location of the counseling office and resource material. A basic postulate of the questionnaire was that if the student did not know his counselor's name, the location of the counseling office, and did not report talking with the counselor or referring friends or parents to the counselor, the counselor could not be considered effective.

THE SAMPLE

Two schools were selected for study on a basis of apparent similarities in all respects except that of the proportion of school time assigned for counseling to the counselors. Both schools served suburban communities which were primarily residential. School A, while of approximately the same size as school B, was somewhat newer, not having an established residential area which had been in existence longer than 15 years as did school B. Both were senior high schools, school A having, at the time of the study, a student population of 1,141 while school B had a population of approximately 1,500. In school A about 50 per cent of the graduating seniors enrolled in a college, while in school B about 40 per cent did so.

The pupil-counselor ratio in school A approximated 285:1, in school B the ratio was approximately 375:1. In neither school was there a basic salary difference between counselors and teachers, although in school A opportunities were provided for counselors to work an extra week in the summer for additional pay. The counselors in both schools were certified by the State of Missouri. School A employed two professional counselors, one teacher-counselor, and one temporary counselor. These categories represent differential levels of training as specified by the State Department of Education. School B employed four professional counselors, two teacher-counselors, and one temporary counselor.

In school A, counselor duties included counseling, course selection, and, to a limited extent, scheduling. In school B, counselor duties included teaching one-half time, counseling, and course choice. The single exception to this in school B was the director, who was on a full-time basis. In neither school was the counselor expected to assume other duties.

THE ADMINISTRATION

Both questionnaires were administered in both of the schools concerned in the final month of the academic year. The Teacher-Counselor questionnaire was administered, in both schools, during teachers' meetings and at a time when the counselors were not present. The teachers were informed, in each case, that neither the counselors nor the school administrators would be informed of the answers given by any individual.

In school A the student questionnaire was administered during class time and in different classrooms to the different students. In school B the questionnaire was administered during a general meeting of the seniors. Beyond this difference, the situations were highly similar in both schools. Only senior students were tested, students were guaranteed the confidentiality of their responses, and no counselors were present in the rooms at the time of, or immediately prior to, testing.

STATISTICAL TREATMENT

Two-by-two contingency tables were utilized to examine the results for the existence of any regular differences between the schools. Those in which the probability was less than 10 chances in 100 that such a difference had occurred by chance were deemed significant enough to be considered as trends.[1]

RESULTS

On the survey of teacher-counselor relationships, few differences ap-

[1]Yates correction factor was applied when the lowest expected frequency in any of the contingency tables fell below 5.

Table 1

Results of the Teacher-Counselor Questionnaire According to School

Items	School	Yes	No	X^2	P
1. I frequently refer students to the counselor	A	21	28	.09	.80
	B	23	27		
2. I have discussed with a counselor the role of counseling in the schools	A	26	23	1.22	.30
	B	32	18		
3. The counselor has a greater need for a private office than does the classroom teacher	A	43	6	.29	.70
	B	42	8		
4. The counselors should have a somewhat higher pay scale than the classroom teachers	A	4	45	.0006	.99
	B	3	47		
5. I have occasionally discussed a problem concerning myself with the counselor	A	13	35	.01	.95
	B	14	36		
6. A counselor needs to spend his free time in advancing his skills and knowledge in counseling and guidance	A	43	6	.33	.70
	B	41	8		
7. Counselors should have the responsibility of teaching courses in psychology and sociology in high school	A	9	40	28.71	.001
	B	36	14		
8. I feel that the counselor has helped me to understand certain students	A	37	12	.06	.85
	B	38	11		
9. Counselors need continuing teaching experience	A	37	11	3.25	.10
	B	46	4		
10. All counseling should be the responsibility of the teacher	A	2	47	.16	.70
	B	4	45		
11. I usually refer parents to the counselor with questions involving their children which are not specifically appropriate to my subject	A	34	14	.26	.70
	B	31	16		
12. A counselor should be proficient in some academic field appropriate to high school teaching	A	44	5	.001	.98
	B	46	4		
13. I sometimes refer to the counselor students whom I feel I could help to some extent but who would receive more assistance from the counselor	A	40	9	.08	.80
	B	38	12		
14. Counselor and teacher training are about the same and consequently there is no real need for the employment of counselors as such	A	2	46	.001	.98
	B	4	45		

peared between schools. In fact, the only two items on which the teachers in the two schools could be said to have differed appeared to reflect the difference in the employment of counselors. In school A, where counselors did not teach, teachers saw no need for counselors to teach the courses in psychology, and fewer teachers felt that counselors needed to teach any course. In school B, where counselors were also half-time teachers, the teachers felt that the counselors should teach the psychology courses and more teachers felt that counselors should teach.

In the Knowledge-of-Counselor questionnaire, senior students were asked to record such items as the name of their counselor, the location of educational and vocational materials, and what they considered to be the counselor's duties. Certain of the questions could be answered with a yes or no. Of 17 possible differences, seven were significant. In school A, where

Table 2

Reports Concerning Counselors by Senior
Students in Each of Two High Schools

The Student	School	Yes	No	% Yes	x^2	P
1. Felt the counselors had been helpful	A	94	6	92	1.67	.20
	B	79	10			
2. Had referred a friend to the counselor	A	72	28	74	.48	.50
	B	68	21			
3. Knew the name of his counselor	A	100	—	97	3.78	.10
	B	84	5			
4. Reported he had visited his counselor on his own	A	98	2	95	3.29	.10
	B	81	8			
5. Felt his counselor was interested in him	A	91	9	90	.27	.70
	B	79	10			
6. Had discussed personal problems with his counselors	A	30	70	29	.083	.80
	B	25	64			
7. Knew where job information was kept	A	65	35	63	.19	.70
	B	55	34			
8. Had read literature about occupations	A	82	18	65	26.75	.001
	B	41	48			
9. Had received new ideas from these	A	54	46	45	6.99	.01
	B	31	58			
10. Knew where educational information was kept	A	69	31	77	7.09	.01
	B	76	13			
11. Had read educational information	A	70	30	76	3.696	.10
	B	73	16			
12. Had received new ideas from these readings	A	31	69	30	.071	.80
	B	26	63			
13. Had had his parents talk with his counselor	A	19	81	23	2.18	.20
	B	25	64			
14. Felt these discussions had helped him	A	24	76	26	.41	.70
	B	25	64			
15. Felt the counselor duties were those of general aid to the students, including help with personal problems	A	49	51	44	1.78	.20
	B	35	54			
16 Felt the counselor duties were to include helping the student make long range plans	A	59	41	59	.063	.90
	B	52	37			
17. Felt the counselor duties were to include things of a technical nature, i.e., scheduling, record keeping, and testing	A	39	61	46	3.621	.10
	B	47	42			

counselors devoted full time to counseling, more students knew the name of their counselor, and more students reported that they had visited their counselor voluntarily and read occupational literature. In school B, where counselors taught half time, more students considered scheduling as a counselor duty, more knew where educational information was kept, and more reported having read educational literature. (There was no difference between the schools in the gaining of ideas from education literature.)

SUMMARY AND CONCLUSIONS

Counselors do not appear to be differentially accepted by teachers on a basis of whether or not their workday consists solely of counseling duties or includes teaching assignments. The teachers in both of the schools studied appeared to have essentially the same feelings toward the counselors. Those differences which existed conformed with the official school policy.

When the effectiveness of the counselors was implied from the student knowledge of details concerning counseling and from student reports as to their percepts of counselors, there were, however, several differences to be noted. In that situation in which counselors devoted full time to counseling duties, more students knew the name of their counselor, and more students reported that they had visited their counselor voluntarily, read occupational literature, and received new ideas from reading occupational literature. In the school in which counselors taught as well as counseled, more students considered scheduling and record keeping as a counselor duty, more knew where educational information was kept, and more reported reading it.

The differences between the schools in counselor effectiveness might be partially explained through the more favorable student-counselor ratio in school B. Against this explanation, however, is the general argument that two counselors, with partial teaching duties, will have greater contact with students and, consequently, greater effectiveness than would one counselor with full-time counseling duties. Also of interest is the more academic direction which counseling appears to have when counselors are teaching as well as counseling. Again, this might be explained by the fact that more graduates of the school in which this was true attended college than did graduates of the school in which counselors were solely responsible for counseling duties. This difference would not, however, explain the lack of differences between the schools in the reported gaining of new ideas.

The results of this study would tend to refute the hypothesis that counselors whose duties include the teaching of academic subjects have better professional relationships than do counselors who do not have academic responsibilities. The hypothesis that full-time counselors are more effective in counseling than are half-time counselors is supported by the study.

REFERENCES

1. Crow, Lester D., & Crow, Alice. *An Introduction To Guidance: Principles and Practices.* New York: American Book Co.

2. Hamrin, Shirley A. *Initiating and Administering Guidance Services.* Bloomington, Ill.: McKnight and McKnight, 1953.

3. Hatch, Raymond N., & Stefflre, Buford. *Administration of Guidance Services.* Englewood Cliffs, N.J.: Prentice-Hall, 1958.

4. Hutson, P. W. *The Guidance Function in Education.* New York: Appleton-Century-Crofts, 1958.

5. Jones, Arthur J. *Principles of Guidance.* New York: McGraw-Hill, 1945.

6. Mathewson, Robert H. *Guidance Policy and Practice.* New York: Harper, 1955.

7. Stoops, Emery. *Guidance Services: Organization and Administration.* New York: McGraw-Hill. 1959.

8. Strang, Ruth. *Pupil Personnel and Guidance.* New York: Macmillan, 1940.

9. Warters, Jane. *High School Personnel Work Today.* New York: McGraw-Hill, 1946.

10

Time, the Counselor's Dilemma

W. Wesley Tennyson, Ed. D.*

Dr. Arthur H. Brayfield [1] has taken a critical view of studies of counselor functions which give no quantitative statements regarding the proportion of time devoted to various activities. The importance of his criticism is readily apparent to counselor educators who have daily contact with public school guidance personnel. A familiar refrain is voiced in such counselor comments as "I would like to, but first things first," "Followup is important, but there just isn't time," and "Time doesn't permit carrying students on a continuing counseling basis." The plight of time appears to respect few guidance workers, regardless of the worker's level of training. One may well wonder what it is that counselors believe they should be doing and if there is not some explanation for their "lack of time" for important guidance services. The present paper, based upon one aspect of a larger study made by the writer [5], endeavors to show how counselors in Missouri perceive their job functions and why it is that some of these persons face the time dilemma.

PROCEDURE

A proper assumption is that the well-trained counselor has obtained some degree of sophistication as to how his time should be allocated among various job functions. It would seem logical, then, to explore the problem at hand by analyzing discrepancies between time spent by counselors on various functions and these person's perceptions of how their time should be spent. Operating on this premise, the investigator attempted to find answers to the two specific questions: First, how do counselors apportion their time among several guidance functions? Second, what do counselors believe to be a proper allocation of time with respect to these functions? Data are presented dealing with these questions. They were obtained in March, 1956, from 152 certified guidance workers in Missouri. The data represented 95 per cent of all persons in Missouri who met the criteria (1) of holding some one of three titles,[1] (2) of devoting at least one class period

°Dr. Tennyson is an Associate Professor of Educational Psychology at the University of Minnesota, Minneapolis. His article appeared originally in the *Personnel and Guidance Journal,* 37:129 (October 1958) and is reprinted with permission of the author and of the journal.
[1]Director of Guidance, Counselor, and Teacher-Counselor.

per day to guidance work, and (3) of being employed in public secondary schools of the four-year, six-year, or three-year type. The interview was used to collect additional data from 29 of the counselors. In selecting persons to be interviewed, a sampling plan was adopted in which the group was stratified according to several variables and then randomly selected by making use of a table of random numbers.

The null hypothesis was set forth in testing the differences between the percentage of time spent by counselors and the percentage of time they felt they should spend on guidance services and functions. To test this hypothesis, F's [4] and t's were computed. Nomographs developed by Zubin [6] for determining the significance of the difference between the frequencies of events in two groups were used in finding the t values. For the most part, the investigator was concerned with how these persons as a group spent their time and how, as a second group, they believed their time should be spent, *i.e.*, whether a difference existed between the means of the two groups. Actually, a large number of F values were found to be significant at the 0.02 and 0.10 levels of confidence. In these cases a method proposed by Cochran and Cox [3] was used to test the hypothesis that the population means were equal without any hypothesis concerning the variances.

FINDINGS

Functions performed by the counselors were classified under four major services: (1) assistance to students; (2) assistance to teachers; (3) assistance to administration and general school program; and (4) research assistance to the school. Table 1 shows the mean percentage of time which the re-

Table 1

Comparison of Percentage of Time Spent and Percentage of Time Counselors Believed
They Should Spend on Four Guidance Areas [†]

Guidance Service	Mean %	S.D. %	df	F Value	P	t Value	P
Assistance to students							
Time now spends	60.65	19.87	142	1.80	< 0.02	2.25*	—
Time should spend	65.49	14.83	118				
Assistance to teachers							
Time now spends	13.68	8.34	142	1.18	> 0.10	1.93	—
Time should spend	15.59	7.69	118				
Assistance to administration							
Time now spends	21.67	17.08	142	5.41	< 0.02	5.38*	0.01
Time should spend	12.18	7.34	118				
Research assistance							
Time now spends	4.00	2.67	142	4.48	< 0.02	4.97*	0.01
Time should spend	6.80	5.65	118				

*Cochran and Cox Test of Significance between means when the variances are unequal [3, p. 297].
†Percentages are based on the total amount of time counselors devoted or felt they should devote to the guidance program.

spondents spent during the school year on each of these major guidance services and the mean percentage of time they believed should be spent.

It is evident that the counselors' job was one in which primary assistance was given to students, although there were wide differences in the amount of time given to this service. Both teachers and the administration drew on the counselors' services, but it appears that the administration with its varied responsibilities for the total school program was making somewhat greater use of this person and the assistance he had to offer. Wide variability in the amount of time which was given to assisting the administration suggests, too, that practices differed greatly in this respect from school to school. The fourth type of assistance, planning and assisting with the school's research, occupied a minor part of the counselors' time in comparison with their other services.

As shown in Table 1, this distribution of time was not entirely satisfactory to these guidance workers. The counselors seemed to feel that they were spending too much time assisting the administration and general school program. There are indications that these guidance workers felt that a portion of their time spent in helping the administration should be re-allocated so that more time could be given to assisting students and teachers, although the amount so distributed was not great enough to be significant in either case with respect to the mean percentages. Because of wide variability within the groups, it is probable that at least some of the counselors believed they should give substantially more time to assisting students. A significant finding is that counselors believed they should be giving more of their time to assisting with the school's research.

With these general differences existing between the time spent on various guidance services and counselors' perceptions of how that time should be spent, it was appropriate to consider in greater detail any such time differences relative to specific functions within the four major guidance services. Significant differences between certain specific functions performed and counselor perceptions of specific functions were found in the areas of (1) assistance to students and (2) assistance to teachers. Further analysis of these two areas is herewith presented.

ASSISTANCE TO STUDENTS

It was shown that the major portion, 60.65 per cent, of the counselors' time was spent providing counseling and its supportive activities in order to assist students in making adjustments and formulating and carrying out plans. The counselors were asked to estimate what per cent of this total time devoted to assisting students was spent on each of the specific functions performed in this area. These functions are shown in Table 2. This table reveals that almost half of the time spent by counselors in assisting students was devoted to individual counseling, a function generally recog-

Table 2

Comparison of Percentage of Time Spent and Percentage of Time Counselors Believed
They Should Spend on Major Functions in the Area of Assistance to Students[†]

Major Function	Mean %	S.D. %	df	F Value	P	t Value	P
Orientation and articulation							
Time now spends	7.71	7.10	137	1.74	< 0.02	0.57*	–
Time should spend	8.16	5.38	110				
Individual appraisal							
Time now spends	15.43	12.61	137	2.43	< 0.02	2.34*	–
Time should spend	12.34	8.09	110				
Welfare							
Time now spends	5.80	6.45	137	1.40	< 0.10	1.01*	–
Time should spend	5.04	5.46	110				
Counseling							
Time now spends	47.00	18.45	137	1.12	> 0.10	2.10	–
Time should spend	51.78	17.47	110				
Occupational and educational information							
Time now spends	17.42	12.49	137	1.85	< 0.02	3.18*	0.01
Time should spend	13.05	9.19	110				
Placement							
Time now spends	3.91	4.92	137	1.13	> 0.10	1.66	–
Time should spend	4.92	4.62	110				
Follow-up							
Time now spends	2.40	2.78	137	1.96	< 0.02	5.45*	0.01
Time should spend	4.79	3.89	110				

*Cochran and Cox Test of Significance.
[†]Percentages were based on the total amount of time counselors devoted or felt they should devote to the one service of Assistance to Students.

nized as the heart of the guidance program. A slightly greater emphasis was being given by the counselors to collecting occupational and educational information than was being given to the functions involved in appraising the individual. Placement and follow-up activities were allocated a minimum amount of the counselors' time. In terms of amount of time spent in the various activities, orientation and articulation appeared to be more a part of the counselors' job than did placement and follow-up.

An activity to which these persons thought they should be giving more time was follow-up, as shown by the significant difference between what the counselors were doing and what they believed they should be doing. Since significance was established between the time spent and the time counselors felt they should spend on the occupational and educational information function, it would seem that if time were to be taken away from any activity these persons would prefer it to be in this area.

Because of the importance attached to counseling in any guidance program, this function was analyzed in further detail. The counselors were asked to estimate what percentage of their total time devoted to the counseling function was spent on various kinds of problems. The results shown in Table 3 points up the prevalence of problems relating to school, future education, and vocation. Over a third of the time devoted by these persons to counseling was spent in academic advising. This means that a

Table 3

Comparison of Percentage of Counseling Time Spent and Percentage of Time
Counselors Believed They Should Spend on Various Problems †

Problem	Mean %	S.D. %	df	F Value	P	t Value	P
Academic planning							
Time now spends	38.46	17.57	144	1.66	< 0.02	0.89*	—
Time should spend	36.60	13.62	108				
Educational and vocational							
Time now spends	35.15	15.95	144	1.73	< 0.02	0.77*	—
Time should spend	33.79	12.11	108				
Other problems							
Time now spends	26.40	19.79	144	1.57	< 0.10	1.43*	—
Time should spend	29.61	15.81	108				

*Cochran and Cox Test of Significance.
†Percentages are based on the total amount of time counselors devoted or felt they should devote to the one major function of counseling.

large portion of the counselors' interviewing time was spent helping students determine their educational needs in high school and plan courses of study in line with these needs, and periodically checking with these students to see if they were receiving maximum benefit from the planning. Table 3 shows that this was an area in which these persons felt that a large portion of their time should be spent, although wide variability among the counselors probably indicates that at least some would spend less time with this type of problem.

Not apparent in this table was the impossibility of the counselors' position with respect to academic advising. The guidance workers who were interviewed were asked to give their opinions concerning the role they felt the counselor should assume in this program-making. The impression drawn from these discussions was that academic advising posed a serious problem for the guidance person, a problem which was professionally self-defeating for at least some of these workers. Here was a program in which the counselors were extensively involved, a program which was almost monumental in its demands on the counselors' time. Here, then, was an explanation for part of the counselors' "lack of time" for important guidance services. The conflict which these counselors experienced lay deeply embedded in their professional concern and conscientiousness for the well-being of the individual student. Over and over again they remarked, "I feel a responsibility which I cannot ignore." One counselor said, "Who in the school but the counselor would have the intimate knowledge of both the student and the world of work so necessary in order to do a good job of advising?" Another said, "I feel responsible for helping them plan courses in line with their abilities and interests." From another the comment ran, "It's part of my job." Still another remarked, "Being guidance oriented, the counselor probably has a better understanding of student needs." For these counselors, as well as for the majority of those responding to the information form, academic advising was an important and logical part of their job. The conflict, and it may not have been recognized as such by the counselors, was not whether to do academic advising, but whether or not to attempt to provide the other various and important guidance services.

ASSISTANCE TO TEACHERS

A mean of 13.68 per cent of the counselors' time was shown to have been spent in assisting teachers, considerably less than the 20 per cent recommended by Dr. Willis E. Dugan [2] for this area of relationship. The major functions performed by counselors in giving this assistance to teachers were classified as follows: (1) helps teacher to develop guidance skills; (2) assists teacher with children who have problems; and (3) helps teacher to adapt class instruction. The counselors were asked to estimate what per cent of their total time given to teachers was spent on each of these major functions.

The largest percentage of their time was spent helping teachers with youngsters who have problems, as shown in Table 4. Although there was great variability among the counselors in the amount of time devoted to this function, it would appear that these guidance workers were student oriented, even in their relations with teachers. In their perceptions of the job, however, the counselors would have redistributed their time so that less emphasis would be given to this type of teacher help. Although the respondents still felt that they should spend a considerable percentage of their time helping the teacher with children who have problems, they believed they should give significantly more time than was their practice to assisting teachers in developing skills for handling these problems better. Those counselors who were interviewed envisioned an evolving program of guidance services in which the teacher plays a more prominent role as a member of the guidance team.

Table 4

Comparison of **Percentage** of Time Spent and Percentage of Time Counselors Believed They Should Spend on Major Functions in the Area of Assistance to Teachers[†]

Major Function	Mean %	S.D. %	df	F Value	P	t Value	P
Develops guidance skills							
Time now spends	17.25	17.37	131	1.03	> 0.10	3.39	0.01
Time should spend	25.94	17.63	107				
Children with problems							
Time now spends	71.96	21.40	131	1.04	> 0.10	4.40	0.01
Time should spend	59.60	21.86	107				
Adapts class instruction							
Time now spends	10.87	11.87	131	1.16	> 0.10	2.43	—
Time should spend	14.46	11.04	107				

[†] Percentages were based on the total amount of time counselors devoted or felt they should devote to the one service of Assistance to Teachers.

ASSISTANCE TO ADMINISTRATION

Although these guidance workers would prefer to devote less time to serving the administration and general school program, a further analysis of specific functions performed in this area (data not presented in this paper) revealed that such functions were not affecting the counselors' time significantly. Thus, functions such as attendance and discipline were not being performed by a large number of the counselors, nor did these counselors believe they should be performing such functions.

SUMMARY

This study reveals that great variability existed in the time spent by Missouri counselors on guidance activities and their perceptions concerning how their time should be spent. In general, there was somewhat closer agreement concerning how time should be spent than how the counselors did spend it, thus giving some validity to the expectation that well-trained counselors have obtained a degree of sophistication as to how their time should be allocated among various job functions.

The counselors' job was one in which a major portion of their time was spent assisting students, a proper allocation of time in the opinion of these persons. Although teachers were using his services, the faculty received less time from the counselor than has generally been advocated by authorities in the field. The respondents felt that a greater proportion of the time given to the faculty should be used to upgrade teachers' abilities to deal with problems of students. It appears that the administration may have been making greater use of this professional person and the assistance he had to offer than were the teachers, but the counselors would prefer to reduce the amount of time given to the administration. Further analysis of specific functions performed in the administrative area, however, revealed that those functions performed were considered appropriate by the counselors. Research assistance to the school occupied a minor part of the counselors' time in comparison with the other services, and it was generally felt by these persons that not enough time was given to assisting with this program.

In giving assistance to students, most of the counselors' time was devoted to counseling individuals with problems. Over a third of the counseling time was spent in academic advising and such advising was considered by the counselors an important and logical part of their jobs. The counselors believed that more time should be given to follow-up activities and that if time were to be taken away from any activity it probably would be the occupational and educational information function.

DISCUSSION

It appears that these counselors are faced with the continuing problem of defining their roles and job functions. Undoubtedly, there are factors operating within the schools or communities in which these persons are employed which affect this problem, but the evidence presented here seems to suggest that there also are factors within the counselor himself which may affect the way he defines his job. The fact that a disproportionate amount of the counselors' time was spent in collecting and filing occupational and educational information, a function which normally would be affected only in a small way by conditions in the working situation, suggests that the counselor must yet learn how to delegate responsibilities by enlisting the aid of others.

A more complicating factor for the counselor who is striving to define his proper role in the school grows out of his professional conscientiousness. In his concern for the individual student, the guidance worker will, in the course of his day, see many ways to be of service. Because of special qualifications and his unique relationship with students, many demands will be made of him. Academic advising is a case in point. To be successful in helping students select courses wisely requires several kinds of knowledge. In the first place, a faculty member who does advising must understand the student—his abilities, interests, aspirations, and family pressures coming to bear upon him. This is not enough, however, for good advising also requires knowledge of the occupational and training opportunities available to the student. Who in the school is most logically suited to perform this function? The counselor, by virtue of his training, commands the understanding so necessary to successful advising. Yet, the task is an impossible one unless the counselor is content to define his role narrowly as that of an academic advisor. The question is one of values. If the counselor is to function in the broader aspects of the job as it is coming to be viewed by authorities—*i.e.*, assisting students in their understanding of self, consulting with teachers and coordinating their efforts to help students receive optimum benefits from learning, providing leadership in the organization and administration of guidance services, and acting as a liaison between the school and community in the use of resources for guidance—then he never can realize fully a role as *the* academic adviser in the school.

A solution to this problem is available. The school staff must first recognize that all teachers have a responsibility in the academic program. The guidance worker, too, has a responsibility, as has been recognized by counselors in Missouri, but this responsibility must be defined as a coordinative one. Viewed in this light, the counselor's role becomes one of organizer and developer of teacher efforts and skills in academic advising.

This is not to imply that the counselor will be divorced completely from the direct responsibility of assisting students in selecting courses. He still works with the whole individual, and in his day-to-day counseling contacts with students course selection frequently will be included in the joint planning of the counselor and student. The counselor also will serve as a resource person to whom the teacher may refer students whose planning problems require information or counseling skill which the teacher does not possess. In this coordinative role the counselor functions in the program of academic advising, but his talents are used in a manner which permits a more appropriate allocation of his time.

This study and the major one of which it is a part point up the continuing need for clarification of job functions of professionally prepared guidance workers in Missouri. One may speculate that the school counselor will continue to have considerable freedom of action in defining and acting out the component parts of his job. It behooves the counselor to focus attention on how his time is divided and used and the effects of such time distribution on the school's guidance program.

REFERENCES

1. Brayfield, Arthur H. "Functions of the Counselor in Secondary Schools," *Calif. J. Second. Educ.* (1948), 23: 468–471.

2. Dugan, Willis E. "Counselor and His Relationships," *Bull. Nat. Ass. Second. Sch. Prins.* (1951), 35: 55–56.

3. Edwards, Allen L. *Statistical Analysis.* New York: Rinehart & Co., 1946.

4. McNemar, Quinn. *Psychological Statistics.* New York: John Wiley & Sons, 1955.

5. Tennyson, Willard W. "An Analysis of the Professional Guidance Position of Certified Secondary School Counselors in Missouri." Unpublished doctoral dissertation, University of Missouri, 1956.

6. Zubin, Joseph. "Nomographs for Determining the Significance of the Differences Between the Frequencies of Events in Two Contrasted Series or Groups," *J. Amer. Statist. Ass.* (1939), 34: 539–544.

Catharsis

1A. Dr. Farwell suggests that "Counseling is the primary function of the school counselor." Yet the counselor is also chief *guidance* officer of the school. *Guidance* is a good deal broader than *counseling*, which is only *one* of *several* ways in which guidance is carried on. *Can* counseling be the *primary* function of the school counselor? *Should* it be?

1B. According to Dr. Farwell, there are enough "significant others" in each person's life to tell him what he needs to know. But do all of these people have access to the same quantity and quality of information as the counselor? While the counselor is not a giver of advice, are there not times when it's desirable for him to be a provider of *professional recommendations*? Is this not an important part of his guidance responsibility and of his role as an educator? *Or is the counselor an educator?*

1C. Dr. Farwell supports "a minimal amount of teaching experience or associated experience to familiarize the school counselor with classroom realities, problems, and setting." He feels this experience lends itself to heightened acceptance of counselors as members of the school staff. Does this suggest that the longer the classroom experience the greater the acceptance, and the greater the acceptance the better the counseling? Is this demonstrably correct? Is there any evidence that teaching experience makes a difference in counselor performance? If school nurses had teacher training and teaching experience would they perform their specialized functions better because of improved acceptance? Or are nurses unlike counselors in that nurses are not educators? Are counselors educators?

1D. The suggestion is made by Dr. Farwell that a better basic training in the problems of education might be gained in the counselor's office than in the classroom. Instead of spending two or three years (or sixteen!) in the classroom how might it work out if counselors in training worked as interns in the guidance suite—as Counseling Associates, clerks, aides, or what have you? Might not a year or two of this experience be preferable? What problems might be involved?

1E. Dr. Farwell says that the counselor should spend some two-thirds of his time in "one-to-one counseling or consulting relationships." Does "consulting" imply provision of specialized information to people, or the making in some cases of professional recommendations? What portion of the two-thirds of total time might be included in "consultancy"? What does this do to the notion that "Counseling is the primary function of the school counselor"?

1F. It's a very useful project for members of an advanced class in counseling to try drawing up a precise list of tasks which counselors *should* do, and a similar list of tasks which they *should not* do. This is a good exercise for the individual, too.

2A. Drs. Shertzer and Stone tell us that "to the degree that counselors rely on jargon rather than clear, understandable communications to the staff, they risk the brand 'charlatan' in its clearest sense—'one who pretends to knowledge'." What is there in our professional language (jargon) which is offensive? Should we avoid specialized language simply because not everyone understands it? Can we not, as educators who have specialized in counseling, assume that our colleagues who have specialized in teaching know the language of their profession? Must we communicate through grunts and chest thumpings?

2B. Counselors' "passive tolerance" of non-professional assignments is referred to by Drs. Shertzer and Stone. *Why are counselors passive in the face of such assignments? Have we not the courage to insist upon certain prerogatives of our specialty?*

2C. The quotation from Dr. Arbuckle's paper, "The Conflicting Functions of the School Counselor" (*Counselor Education and Supervision,* 1: 56, 1956) seems especially pertinent in the Shertzer-Stone reading. Can we assume that we are teachers who dabble in counseling? Or counselors who dabble in teaching? Can we not be educators who have specialized? And can we not insist that those who would share our specialty show evidence of adequate preparation, and that they devote their full time and attention to it? Must we tolerate the teacher in our midst for whom insufficient Latin classes were created, and who has been placed in the counselors' office to keep his load balanced? Must teachers tolerate *us,* practicing *their* specialty on a part-time basis? Have not students the right to competent persons in the various specialties?

2D. Is the counselor a counselor by profession or an educator who has specialized? Or is he some kind of psychologist? Social worker? Assuming that the reader is a counselor or a counselor trainee, how does he identify his occupational role? Where is his allegiance? (If the response comes easily, it has probably been given inadequate attention.)

3A. What earthly difference does it make *what* a flock of other people think counselors ought to be doing? Why can't we just practice our profession and let others take advantage of our services or leave us alone?

3B. How does the reader account for the finding that many people seem to feel comfortable with the image of the counselor as a person who provides occupational assistance and renders educational aid, but become upset when it is suggested that counselors might be able to help people who are having personal-social difficulties?

3C. When administrators or teachers suggest that counselors should teach regularly "so they won't get out of touch with the kids," are we prepared to suggest to the principal that he get back into the classroom too, for the same reason? Or that teachers should serve as principals every few semesters to broaden their viewpoints? What's *wrong* with teachers, as a group of professional specialists, if they're willing to let *anyone* practice in the classroom? Do counselors make good teachers? Could it be true, as some of the crustier types maintain, that the best counselors were also the best teachers? Is it remotely possible that someone who was a weak teacher— or someone who made waves—might make an excellent counselor? In how many specialties should we insist that educators show continuing competence?

3D. Why might it be that counselor educators and practicing counselors are at odds with other groups of people as to what the counselor's role is? Is there anything we counselors can *do* to communicate the character of our specialty more effectively? Or is the projection of professional image beneath our dignity?

4A. Considering Dr. Stefflre's paper, is the counselor an educator who has specialized, or is he a member of a unique profession (counseling) who *happens* to function in the school setting? This question is fraught with many far-reaching implications, from which a number of our most basic assumptions about ourselves must come. The question can't be taken—or answered—lightly.

4B. Dr. Stefflre mentions that "In Michigan we create counselors by the laying on of administrative hands." But isn't this true even in states with certification laws and standards? *Counselors* don't select counselors— *administrators* do. And administrators are chosen by administrators. Thus, it may seem that school administrators, as specialists, come closer to meeting one of the basic criteria of professionalism than the rest of us, through maintaining controls over admission to practice. Why do we as counselors permit persons to be admitted to our specialty by administrative fiat? Or is this not the concern of practitioners? Should we rely on school superintendents to fight this battle for us? Do we leave it to counselor educators? To the State Department of Education? Are criteria for the selection of counselors the proper province of laymen on state commissions? *In the reader's state, how many professional educators sit on the credentials committee in the capital? How many barbers sit on the committee which licenses barbers?*

4C. Dr. Stefflre mentions that some counselors shy away from power or its exercise. Is it undesirable for counselors to develop and use power within the practice of their own specialty? What kinds of power might counselors harness? In what effective ways might it be used? Is there a moral question here? An ethical one? Is there something wrong with looking after Number One, as a means to an end (the end being better service to clientele)?

5A. Mrs. Harrison makes several distinctions between counselors and the "lay person." Teachers appear to be included among the ranks of laymen. Again this raises the question: Are we professional educators committed to specialized practices (teaching, counseling, administering, etc.) or are school people actually representatives of various professions who happen to work together in one building? If the latter is the case, and if counseling is a unique profession, then do we also admit the existence of a profession of school administration? Do we admit that teaching, *per se*, is a profession? If teaching is a profession, do we regard ourselves as laymen *vis-a-vis* the teacher and his classroom practice? And if we are laymen, what right have we to evaluate the character of the professional teacher's work, suggest different approaches to him, function as his first line of defense against a sometimes hostile citizenry, or presume (as Mrs. Harrison recommends) to consult with the principal as to means of improving teachers? One would think that if we are unique professionals *teachers* would be primarily concerned with improving their colleagues' performance.

5B. How do you feel about Mrs. Harrison's suggestion that the school counselor might function as a counselor to members of the school staff? Is the distinction clear between the counseling and consulting functions? Are both appropriate?

5C. Mrs. Harrison suggests that the counselor should be involved in a consultant relationship to parents, except that when "the seriousness of the situation so indicates, he may refer them to agencies outside the school for family consultation." Does this indicate that the counselor is not prepared to deal with problems which are "serious"? At what points should referrals be made? Under what circumstances should the counselor be prepared to assume full responsibility for this clientele? Is the counselor never to deal with serious problems? Is it appropriate to refer "serious problems" to a school psychologist whose competence in counseling may be inferior to the counselor's? Perhaps ours is a profession (or a specialty) which concerns itself with simple things. Is this the image we have of ourselves? Is this the image we project? Is image important?

6A. The views of laymen concerning educators, and especially concerning counselors, are almost always interesting to behold. Dr. Berlin, a psychiatrist, tells us that "The counselor's job . . . seems to center primarily around trying to help those youngsters who are disturbing to their teachers or to the school." Is this *really* the focus of our work—even in the Real World? What of the broad helping relationship, the educational guidance, the occupational exploration, and the therapeutic role?

6B. Dr. Berlin indicates that in a few schools the counselor has actually had to face the wrath of administrators for "allowing" a youngster to continue to get into trouble. Granted that the behavior of some administrators is a continuing embarrassment to all, is this kind of thing common enough to merit attention? Are not the overwhelming bulk of school administrators thoroughly professional in commitment and behavior? Have we no defenses against the few who prompt ideas such as the one proposed by Dr. Berlin?

6C. An interesting point is made in Dr. Berlin's paper about the "magic effect" which many people expect the counselor to have in solving complex problems affecting individual students' school performance. While the magic effect is surely present, have we not the tools to be helpful with many people? Are we consigned to perpetual hand-wringing because we're fresh out of magic? Can the reader list a number of specific ways in which the school counselor is uniquely qualified to provide assistance to people?

6D. How does the reader react to Dr. Berlin's notion that the counselor is a teacher? Is it possible that many people, especially laymen but often professional educators, don't grasp the differences between counselor and teacher? Could it be that some *counselors* don't see these differences? *Can one be an educator without being a teacher?*

6E. Dr. Berlin says, ". . . students . . . have felt relieved when the counselor has been able to say . . . , 'Look, my job is to help you. I know you're going to try to con me and avoid telling me the truth if you can, so I'm getting all the facts I need to help me help you with or without your help'." Now this kind of verbal behavior in a counselor would surely cause a great deal of discomfort among adherents of the "non-directive" school; but is it completely out of place in the school setting? Are there some students with whom it might be effective? Dr. Berlin appears to think so. If he is correct (and many counselors would agree that he is), then must we throw out client-centered techniques and approaches? Or are we in the position of having to constantly make judgments as to what technique in our repertoire is more apt to be effective with this particular client at this particular time under these particular circumstances? If this is our position, then is it meaningful for a counselor to describe himself as "Rogerian," or "directive," or "reinforcement-oriented," when in actuality he is a professional who chooses his tools as they seem appropriate for the varying tasks at hand?

6F. Non-educators frequently seem unfamiliar with the broad range of techniques available to the counselor. Dr. Berlin indicates that the counselor's attitude is "task-oriented" and that his principal function is one of diagnosing problems and working out solutions. How might the reader react to this description of prime function? Is the medical "complaint-diagnosis-treatment" approach the only valid one?

6G. Dr. Berlin (and many administrators and guidance directors) would have the counselor remind teachers to send him "regular reports of the student's work in the classroom." Is the counselor a checker-upper? If progress reports sent to the home with carbons to the counselor at nine-week intervals are not adequate or regular enough, then is it realistic to ask for individual reports several times a year in addition to those sent regularly? If the counselor has 400 clients, and if by "regular reports" Dr. Berlin implies as many as four a year, from each of six teachers which any student sees daily, is it fair to ask *when the counselor is to perform his professional services* if, in addition, he is asked to review 9600 teacher write-ups and 1600 report cards every year? At the rate of ten minutes per report, the time demand on the counselor would work out to about ten hours a day. Teacher time needs to be considered here, too. The importance of anecdotal reporting cannot be overstressed, but aren't we able to define means of encouraging such reports without the sorts of demands implicit in this recommendation?

7A. Dr. Lortie suggests a dichotomy between "educators and senior practitioners" who are involved in "building a system of professional preparation." What might the differences be between "educators and senior practitioners"? Are "educators" people who work in colleges and "senior practitioners" people who don't? What of the *junior* practitioners? Are not practitioners properly identified as "educators"? Can't we identify ourselves as educators who have specialized in counseling, some at the practitioner and some at the training levels?

7B. According to Dr. Lortie, many school hierarchies regard the new counselor as being on the first rung of the administrative ladder. What are some of the implications here?

7C. Classification of students into relevant groups is seen by Dr. Lortie as presenting continuing problems to the counselor, who "finds himself enmeshed in a round of precedents and judicial decisions . . . constrained by an ever more complex set of policies and rules." Is the problem really this bad? Is the counselor prevented from exercising professional judgment in individual cases? Cannot professional judgment be exercised free from reference to irrelevancies? Must the administrator be called to bail the counselor out when his recommendations run counter to the demands of parents?

7D. Dr. Lortie refers to "the toughness of the boundary which separates those on different sides of an authority relationship." Is the reader able to distinguish between counselor-as-authority and counselor-as-authoritarian figure? If the counselor behaves as an authority in making a professional recommendation, does this necessarily make him authoritarian? Has the client a right to anticipate, that when he consults a school counselor he is consulting an expert on education and on means of resolving problems students and parents encounter in dealing with the school? Or does the reader feel that the counselor (unlike the dean, principal, or teacher) has no business, under any circumstances, making professional recommendations?

7E. Dr. Lortie suggests that "counseling . . . probably attracts more persons who wish to 'help' individuals than do teaching or administration." If *all* educators are not engaged in a helping relationship (that is, if education is not a helping profession), then in what kind of relationship *are* we engaged?

7F. What does Dr. Lortie's paper suggest in reference to the most desirable physical location for guidance offices in a school setting? What implications might this have in the reader's school?

7G. With reference to Dr. Lortie's suggestions, can the reader develop a notion of or rationale for a clearly defined form of *"school therapy"*?

8A. Referring to Dr. Dunsmoor's paper, how does the reader feel about the amateur counseling being done by psychiatrists, physicians, and others? Some of these people seem concerned that we are invading their domain. Are we concerned that they are invading ours? What is the difference between "counseling" and "therapy"? If "counseling" can be broadly defined, then can't "therapy," too?

9A. What implications does the reader identify from Dr. Dannenmaier's study?

9B. How does the reader react to the proposition that administrators should teach occasionally? Should teachers occupy themselves in the mechanical details of school administration from time to time? Why is it that virtually every specialist in education imagines himself to be an accomplished teacher? Should administrators and counselors be inflicted upon students in the classroom?

10A. In one section of his paper, Dr. Tennyson says that "good advising . . . requires knowledge of the occupational and training opportunities available to the student." Are "advising" and "counseling" synonymous? Can the reader distinguish among "advising," "counseling," and the "making of professional recommendations"? Are these, in fact, discrete terms? Jargon?

10B. With reference to Dr. Tennyson's concern with the counselor's dilemma in use of time, what effect might the counselor exert in this connection through the expedient of careful establishment of a daily calendar, and assigning time to himself largely as he sees fit? Could he not then say to the administrator, "I'm booked up for three weeks with counseling appointments, but if this filing can wait until two weeks from next Thursday, I'll have twenty minutes free at about one o'clock. Why don't you ask a clerk to do the job today?" Or is the reader opposed to the use of a daily appointment schedule? Is the reader fearful of offending the principal (Daddy might spank)?

part II

The Training of Counselors and Their Admission to Practice

PRESENTING PROBLEM

Let's face it. There is a gap—perhaps an abyss—between much of counselor education and much of school counseling practice. To be sure, the vast portion of what counselors get in training should be put to use in schools, and much of what counselors are expected to do on the job is absurd. However, the Real World of Counseling in the schools is not the same as the Real World of Counseling in private agencies and college centers. Responsibilities overlap, but there is a uniqueness in each which many school counselors feel is not dealt with at appropriate depth in many schools of education—thus, the remark of the experienced school counselor to the neophyte: "Forget what they taught you, and start from scratch." If such comments were heard but infrequently, they would represent an indictment deserving of our most serious attention within the profession; the fact that they are heard commonly suggests that in training we have problems of greater enormity than many of us have perhaps been willing to accept.

The professional specialty of counseling in the schools is unique enough that review of the problem is called for. It is to this problem that this part of the book (and some of Part III) addresses itself.

The readings which follow have to do with the training of counselors and their admission to practice. Standards for the preparation of counselors as formulated by the American Personnel and Guidance Association are included. Also included are articles regarding the education of the school counselor by Dr. Dugald S. Arbuckle; on inadequacies in counselor education as perceived by Dr. Ralph A. Meyering, of Illinois State University; on the question of national certification of counselors by the University of New Mexico's Dr. George L. Keppers; and on their selection, by Dr. George E. Hill. The question of the varied sorts of characters who perhaps too frequently inhabit the guidance suite is treated by Dr. Stanley W. Niehaus; Dr. Beverly Swan, of the Florida State Department of Education, comments upon the common practice of requiring years of teaching experience as a prerequisite to certification.

For whatever assistance they might give the reader as he studies the papers included, the major points which follow seem to be among those which deserve special attention. They might be kept in mind as reading progresses.

If the training of counselors is inadequate, how might it be improved?

If a two-year post-graduate program of preparation is advocated, how can this be justified in the face of the mediocre salaries which the typical graduate will find offered him?

How can candidates be found, of the quality needed, if to become a counselor one must undergo four years of undergraduate preparation, a year of teacher training, two or more years of teaching experience, two years of counselor preparation, and, in some states, a year or more of experience in non-school employment? Does a ten-year training program seem excessive?

What influence should the organized profession have upon training practices, *vis-a-vis* lay boards, administrators, teacher organizations, curriculum committees in colleges of education?

What influence should practitioners exert on training practices?

How might the quality of training be evaluated, and by whom?

Which is better: guidance services offered by poorly trained and possibly incompetent counselors, or no formal guidance other than that made available by relatively untrained teachers and administrators? (The North Central Association, as one example, presently requires that counselors in approved secondary schools show evidence of only 15 semester hours of graduate preparation in their professional specialty. Is *this* representative of the kind of quality control which is necessary? North Central also holds that a 1:500 counselor-student ratio is satisfactory for accreditation, which is a horror of another color.)

Who should be responsible for certifying counselors? Who should govern the admission of counselors to practice?

11

Standards for the Preparation of Secondary School Counselors—1967*

INTRODUCTION

The 1967 revision of Standards for the Preparation of Secondary School Counselors represents another step toward establishing the quality of programs for preparing secondary school counselors. In 1964 the Association for Counselor Education and Supervision, a division of the American Personnel and Guidance Association, issued the first edition of these Standards. Five years of study went into that 1964 edition, study that involved hundreds of counselor educators, state supervisors, city supervisors and school counselors. This five-year program was chaired first by Dr. Willis E. Dugan and later by Dr. Robert O. Stripling.

The 1967 edition of Standards for the Preparation of Secondary School Counselors constitutes a revision of the 1964 edition based upon use of the standards in more than one hundred institutions and reactions from more than one thousand members of the Association. The 1967 edition of the Standards was endorsed almost unanimously by respondents to a mail poll of all ACES members.

These Standards are intended to be used in such ways as the following:

1. For institutional self-study by counselor education staffs and their school colleagues.

2. For the evaluation of counselor education programs by state departments of education which determine what programs will be recognized as adequate to prepare candidates for certification.

3. For the evaluation of professional counselor education by appropriate accrediting bodies.

4. For use by agencies and persons conducting research in the field of counselor education.

A manual to aid in the use of these Standards, entitled *Manual for Self-Study by a Counselor Education Staff*, has been prepared by the Committee and it is available from the American Personnel and Guidance

---

*This statement of standards is reproduced with consent of the Association for Counselor Education and Supervision, an affiliate of the American Personnel and Guidance Association, and is an updated revision of the statement on standards published in 1964. The 1967 statement occurs also in the September 1967 edition of the *Personnel and Guidance Journal*, p. 96 ff. It should be noted that a committee chaired by Dr. Merle Ohlsen is currently preparing a statement on "Standards for the Preparation of Elementary School Counselors."

Association (Price: $1.50). The *Manual* provides useful suggestions for institutional self-evaluation and several guides for simplifying the use of the Standards.

It is the expectation of the Committee, as it was of its predecessor committee, that further efforts will be made in the years ahead to continue the refinement and improvement of these Standards.

> Association for Counselor Education and Supervision-
> Committee on Professional Preparation of Secondary
> School Counselors

George E. Hill, *Chairman*
Emeliza Swain, *Coordinator, Southern Region*
Benjamin Cohn, *Coordinator, North Atlantic Region*
Paul F. Munger, *Coordinator, North Central Region*
Phelon J. Malouf, *Coordinator, Rocky Mountain Region*
James A. Saum, *Coordinator, Western Region*

STANDARDS FOR THE PREPARATION OF SECONDARY SCHOOL COUNSELORS-1967

SECTION 1: PHILOSOPHY AND OBJECTIVES

1. The institution has a stated philosophy of education and has developed a set of objectives for counselor education with that philosophy.
   a. Such statements have been prepared cooperatively by the staff members in counselor education.
   b. Such statements are in harmony with the institution's philosophy and objectives, have been accepted by the administration, and are supported at the policy making level.
   c. State and local guidance personnel have been consulted in reviewing the institution's objectives for counselor education.
   d. The statements of philosophy and objectives are reflected in pamphlets, brochures and other publications.
   e. Philosophy and Objectives are reflected in the attitudes and behavior of students in the program.
2. The objectives of the counselor education program were developed by a staff who are aware of the total secondary school program, aims, needs, and trends.
   a. The objectives reflect the staff's awareness of the structure and setting of public and non-public school education in the country.
   b. Due consideration is given to developments and trends in school organization, curriculum and program provisions.
   c. The objectives include a recognition of the role of guidance services in encouraging and facilitating desirable change in education.

3. The institution's philosophy and the objectives of the counselor education program are accepted and implemented by staff members.

    a. The counselor education program is developed, extended, and improved on the basis of the stated philosophy and objectives.

    b. Philosophy and objectives are implemented on a planned basis in all areas of the program including student selection, curriculum, instructional methods and facilities, research and administrative provisions and procedures.

    c. The objectives are applied in the use of staff members representing other disciplines and in the use of outside personnel and resources.

4. The staff continues to review the objectives of the program.

    a. The objectives are reviewed in the light of the needs of youth in a changing society.

    b. The objectives are reviewed in the light of local, state, and national studies of guidance program status and needs.

    c. The objectives are reviewed in the light of studies and recommendations of local, state, regional, and national groups concerning educational needs.

    d. The objectives are reviewed in the light of significant research findings related to guidance, education, and the behavioral sciences.

5. There is a continuous study of the extent to which the stated philosophy is transmitted and the objectives are accomplished.

    a. There is a planned program for assessing changes in attitudes and behavior of students as they move through the counselor education program.

    b. Flexibility of assignments and experiences is provided for students with differing backgrounds of preparation and experience.

    c. Personnel in cooperating schools and agencies participate in the evaluation process.

    d. Evaluation of the effectiveness of preparation is accomplished through evidence obtained from former students, the schools in which they work, and the state departments of education. This evaluation is based upon the stated objectives of the program of counselor education.

SECTION 11: CURRICULUM:
PROGRAM OF STUDIES AND SUPERVISED EXPERIENCES

A. General Program Characteristics.

1. The institution provides a program in counselor education, based primarily on the program of studies and supervised practice outlined in B and C below. The institution provides a minimum of one year of graduate

counselor education. In order to fulfill the requirements of the studies and supervised practice detailed in B and C below, the institution provides at least one additional year of graduate study in counselor education either through its own staff and facilities or through cooperative working relationships with other institutions which do have at least a two-year program of counselor education.

    a. The opportunity for full-time study in counselor education is provided throughout the academic year.

    b. Flexibility is provided within the curriculum to allow for individual differences in competencies and understandings developed prior to entering the institution's counselor education program.

    c. The organized curriculum for the program is published and is available for distribution to prospective students. This description includes information relating to the institution's requirements for full-time study.

2. There is evidence of quality instruction in all aspects of the counselor education program.

    a. Syllabi or other evidences of organized and coordinated instructional units of the curriculum are available.

    b. Appropriate resource materials are provided.

    c. Responsibilities are assigned to or assumed by staff members only in those areas for which they are professionally qualified by preparation and experience.

    d. Provisions are made for periodic evaluation by students, staff, former students, and employers of all aspects of the counselor education program, such as course content, methods of instruction, and supervised experiences both on and off campus.

    e. Evaluation is followed by appropriate revisions and improvements, if indicated.

3. Planned sequences of educational experiences are provided.

    a. A sequence of basic and advanced graduate courses and other associated learning experiences is defined and provided.

    b. The program provides for the integration of didactic instruction, seminars, and supervised experiences in counseling and other related guidance services throughout the sequence.

    c. Prerequisites are identified.

4. Cooperation exists among staff members directly responsible for the professional education of counselors and representatives of departments or schools offering courses in related fields.

    a. Cooperative working arrangements are in existence.

    b. Staff members from related areas meet with the counselor education staff for planning, implementing and evaluating the counselor education program.

    c. Course work in other areas is identified for the counselor candidate with respect to its appropriateness for graduate credit or for background work.

    d. There is evidence of interdisciplinary planning with respect to both student and staff participation in designing, conducting, and evaluating research.

5. Within the framework of the total counselor education program, there are available curriculum resources as well as prodecures that make it possible for the counselor candidate to develop understandings and skills beyond the minimum requirements of the program.

    a. Elective courses are available.

    b. Staff time is provided for the supervision of individual study in the areas of counselor education.

    c. Advisers make counselor candidates aware of such opportunities.

6. The counselor education staff encourages the spirit of inquiry and the production and use of research data.

    a. The statement of objectives of the program reflects an awareness of the role of research in the work of the counselor and the competencies to be developed.

    b. Instructional procedures make frequent use of, and reference to, research findings. Areas in which research is needed are identified.

7. Opportunities for self-evaluation and the further development of self-understanding are provided for the counselor candidate.

    a. Opportunities are provided through such activities as laboratory experiences, supervised counseling, and self-analysis through tape recordings and/or video tapes.

    b. Opportunities for improvement of interpersonal relationships are provided through small group activities.

    c. Counseling services provided by persons other than the counselor education staff are available to students in counselor education.

B. Program of Studies.

1. Opportunities are provided for the development of understanding and competencies in the following:

    a. The foundations and dynamics of human behavior and of the individual in his culture.

    b. The educational enterprise and processes of education.

    c. Professional studies in school counseling and related guidance activities:

        (1) Philosophy and principles underlying guidance and other pupil personnel services.

        (2) The nature and range of human characteristics and methods of measuring them in individual appraisal.

    (3) Vocational development theory.

    (4) Educational and occupational information, its nature and uses.

    (5) Counseling theory and practice.

    (6) Statistics and research methodology, independent research, and familiarization with data processing and programming techniques.

    (7) Group procedures in counseling and guidance.

    (8) Professional relationships and ethics in keeping with the APGA Ethical Standards.

    (9) Administration and coordination of guidance and pupil personnel services.

  (10) Supervised experience (See C below).

C. Supervised Experiences.

    1. Supervised experiences in counseling and other guidance activities are provided as an integral part of the total counselor education program.

    a. Settings in which such experiences are provided are appropriate for the preparation of secondary school counselors.

    b. These supervised experiences, including both observation of and work directly with secondary age youth, frequently are provided in the actual school situation.

    c. Opportunities are provided for working under supervision with parents and with a variety of school and community agency personnel.

    d. All such experiences are conducted under established ethical policies.

    e. Primary responsibility for all supervised experiences is assigned to counselor education staff members, qualified as stated in C-3-a below; secondary school counselors and advanced graduate students may be assigned subsidiary responsibilities.

    2. Three aspects of supervised experience are recognized in the counselor education program-laboratory experiences, practicum experiences, and internship.

    a. Laboratory experiences are provided in the first and/or second years.

    (1) Opportunities are provided for both observation and participation in activities related to the total guidance program, e.g., role-playing, listening to tapes, testing, organizing and using pupil personnel records, working with professional personnel, preparing and examining case studies, and using educational and occupational information materials.

    (2) Laboratory experience appropriate to the counselor candidate's needs are a continuing part of the counselor education program.

      (3) Plans and procedures adopted by the staff clearly describe the integration of such experiences.

  b. Practicum experiences are provided in the first and/or second years.

      (1) Practicum consists of counseling and small group work, both under supervision.

      (2) Practicum is conducted in settings which are appropriate for the preparation of secondary school counselors and which include young people with a variety of educational and vocational potential.

      (3) Practicum includes opportunity for continuing experiences in a series of counseling relationships with each of several secondary age youth.

      (4) A stated number of hours is spent by each counselor candidate in actual counseling relationships. This does not include time required for preparation and for supervisory consultations.

        (a) Counselor education students completing the two-year program spend 60 hours as a minimum.

        (b) Counselor education students completing a one-year program spend 30 hours as a minimum.

      (5) Opportunity is provided within the total work load for staff to supervise practicum experiences.

      (6) Media such as tape recorders, television, and one-way vision screens are utilized in the supervision of the practicum activities.

      (7) Practicum provides for a growth experience which is spread over a period of time.

      (8) Supervised experiences are provided as an integral part of courses throughout the counselor education program of the student.

  c. Internship may be provided. This is optional, though recommended.

      (1) Internship is an advanced level of on-the-job supervised experience offered in a school setting.

      (2) It is under the systematic supervision of qualified members of both the school staff and the institution's counselor education staff.

      (3) It is normally a paid experience.

      (4) Opportunities are provided for the counselor candidate to share responsibilities in all phases of the school guidance program.

  3. A well-qualified staff with adequate time allocated to supervision is provided.

    a. Members of the on-campus staff responsible for supervision

      (1) Have earned advanced degrees (preferably the doctorate) from accredited institutions.

      (2) Have had experience in counseling and related guidance activities with secondary age youth.

    b. Secondary school staff members who supervise counselor candidates concurrently with the institution's staff should have at least two years of graduate work in counselor education or have equivalent preparation developed through long-term service and professional activity.

    c. Doctoral students who supervise practicum as a part of their preparation are under the supervision of staff members with appropriate advanced degrees and experience.

    d. The counseling practicum is virtually a tutorial form of instruction; therefore, the supervision of five students is equivalent to the teaching of one three-semester-hour course. Such a ratio is considered maximum.

    e. Supervision of internship is provided regularly by the cooperating secondary school staff and adequate staff time is allocated both for day-to day supervision and for weekly supervisory conferences.

    f. Supervisors from the institution's staff have internship consultations and supervision assigned as part of their total work load.

    g. Time is allocated by the school system for secondary school staff members to assist in supervision of laboratory, practicum, and internship experiences.

    4. Appropriate facilities, equipment, and materials are provided for supervised experiences in both on-and off-campus settings. (See Section IV.)

D. The institution assists cooperating school systems, state departments of education, and individual school counselors with activities which contribute to in-service growth and to the improvement of the schools' guidance programs.

    1. There is a planned means of communication to encourage school and pupil personnel administrators to seek the institution's assistance in planning and conducting in-service education and program improvement activities.

    2. The institution's staff is provided load recognition for their part in in-service and program development activities in the schools.

    3. The institution's staff in counselor education involves its graduate students in its in-service and program development activities in the schools as a means of enriching their experiences.

SECTION III: SELECTION, RETENTION, ENDORSEMENT, AND PLACEMENT

1. The institution has a procedure for identifying and selecting candidates for counselor education.

    a. The counselor education staff has cooperatively developed criteria and procedures relating to selection, retention, endorsement, and placement.

    b. The criteria used for selection are consistent with the philosophy and objectives of the institution's counselor education program.

    c. Information about the counselor education program and about certification in the several states is available to the candidates.

    d. Qualified candidates may be drawn from various undergraduate fields and from various occupations.

        (1) Candidates who have been teachers have demonstrated superior competence as teachers.

        (2) Candidates from fields other than teaching demonstrate their understanding of the secondary school and their competence to perform guidance and counseling functions in secondary schools by completing courses and supervised experiences planned for this purpose.

    e. Members of the counselor education staff are available to confer with prospective candidates.

2. The institution follows a defined procedure for the selective admission of candidates to the program of counselor education.

    a. The candidate is assessed with respect to:

        (1) Capacity to do graduate work.

        (2) Familarity with the objectives of the program.

        (3) Potential for developing effective relationships with youth, teachers, administrators, and parents.

        (4) Potential for engaging in research.

    b. The counselor education staff admits to the program only those candidates who meet the requirements established for admission to study in counselor education. These requirement may be in addition to those established by the institution for admission to graduate study.

    c. Decisions with respect to admission to the counselor education program are made by the staff (or by a committee) and not by any one staff member.

3. The institution administers a planned program of selective retention, designating points within the program for evaluation of progress, and informing of procedures for selective retention.

    a. The counselor education staff has the responsibility of denying continuation in the program to any candidate whose level of

    academic performance and/or personal characteristics do not
adequately meet institutional or professional standards.

   b. Each counselor candidate is encouraged to enter into a program
of self-evaluation related to his retention in the program. To
assist him in his growth in self-understanding, a counseling
service separate from the counselor education program is
available to him.

   c. When appropriate, cooperating school counselors and state
supervisors and administrators are consulted concerning decisions about retention of candidates.

   d. Decisions with respect to retention or dismissal of a candidate
are made by the staff (or by a committee) and not by any one
staff member.

  4. The institution endorses successful candidates for certification and
employment.

   a. A statement of policy relating to the institution's procedure for
formal endorsement has been adopted by the staff and approved
by the proper administrative authority.

   b. Each candidate is informed of procedures for endorsement for
certification and employment.

   c. The counselor education staff participates in this endorsement
procedure.

   d. Endorsement is given only on the basis of evidence of proficiency. This implies that the candidate has completed a substantial part of his graduate work in counselor education, including supervised counseling experience, at the endorsing institution,
and that his personal growth is considered to have been satisfactory.

  5. The institution provides a placement service.

   a. Placement service organization and procedures are consistent
with established principles of student personnel work.

   b. Provision is made for the participation of personnel from the
state department of education and cooperating schools in the
placement of candidates and their induction into the profession.

   c. Students are assisted as needed in the preparation of placement
papers.

   d. Staff members utilize individual professional relationships to
assist in the placement of their graduates.

   e. Assistance is provided in the evaluation of job opportunities and
in the selection of positions appropriate to the individual's qualifications.

   f. The placement service provides continuing assistance to the
candidate throughout his professional career.

6. The institution maintains a program of research designed to evaluate its selection, retention, endorsement and placement procedures.
   a. School counselors, administrators, and state department of education personnel, when appropriate, participate in the planning and execution of the follow-up program and other evaluative procedures.
   b. The program of evaluation and follow-up includes early leavers as well as those who complete the program.
   c. Evaluation is followed by appropriate revisions and improvements.

SECTION IV: SUPPORT FOR THE COUNSELOR EDUCATION PROGRAM, ADMINISTRATIVE RELATIONS AND INSTITUTIONAL RESOURCES

1. Administrative organization and procedures provide recognition of and designated responsibilities for a counselor education program.
   a. The program is a clearly identified part of an institutional graduate program.
      (1) There is only one unit responsible for the preparation of school counselors.
      (2) The program is oriented toward and administered through the unit responsible for graduate work in education.
   b. Cooperative relationships exist between the counselor education program and other units of the institution related to the program.
      (1) Contributions of other units to the program are defined.
      (2) Channels of communication with staff members in other units are identified and maintained.
   c. Use is made of a wide range of professional and community resources.
      (1) Sound working relations exist with state department of education, public and private schools, community agencies, and professional organizations.
      (2) Effective use is made of a wide variety of resource material and personnel.
2. The institution provides for the professional development of the staff as well as students in the counselor education program.
   a. Staff members are active in professional leadership and research on a local, state, regional, and national level.
   b. Staff members are participating in voluntary professional service capacities.
   c. Staff members engage in programs of research and contribute to the literature of the field.
   d. The institution provides encouragement and financial support for the staff to participate in such professional activities.

  e. The program exemplifies high professional standards in all relationships to students.

  f. Students learn about and participate in the activities of professional organizations.

3. The institution provides adequate faculty and staff for all aspects of the counselor education program.

  a. An individual is designated as the responsible professional leader of the counselor education program.

   (1) This individual is an experienced counselor and possesses an earned doctorate from an accredited institution in counselor education, or a closely related area.

   (2) This individual has a primary and preferably a full-time assignment to the counselor education program.

   (3) This individual's other responsibilities are consistent with and supportive of his primary obligations to the program of counselor education.

   (4) This individual is recognized for his leadership and service activities in the profession.

   (5) This individual is qualified by preparation and experience to conduct or to supervise research activities.

  b. A minimum basic staff includes the equivalent of at least three full-time qualified persons whose primary assignment is in counselor education, to insure staff depth to carry out curricular responsibilities of the professional studies and of the supervised practice and to provide program advisory service and supervision of research.

   (1) In addition to the designated leader of the staff this includes at least the equivalent of two full-time faculty members with qualifications comparable to those of the chairman, or director, of the counselor education program.

   (2) Additional basic staff members are provided in a ratio of approximately the equivalent of one full-time staff member for every eight full-time graduate students or their equivalent in part-time graduate students.

   (3) The full-time teaching load of these staff members is consistent with that of other graduate departments in the institution.

   (4) This individual is recognized for his leadership and service activities in the profession.

   (5) This individual is qualified by preparation and experience to conduct or to supervise research activities.

   (6) The total work load of staff members includes a recognition of time needed for professional research.

   c. Faculty in related disciplines are qualified in their respective areas and also are informed about the objectives of counselor education.
   d. Off-campus school personnel who supervise counselor candidates are qualified through academic preparation and professional experience.
      (1) A basic policy provides for the identification and recognition of these staff members as an integral part of the counselor education staff.
      (2) Such staff members have two or more years of appropriate professional experience.
      (3) These staff members have at least two years of graduate work in counselor education or have equivalent preparation developed through long-term service and professional activity.
   e. Graduate assistantships are provided to reduce routine demands on staff and to provide additional experiences to students in the program.
      (1) Regular procedures are established for the identification and assignment of qualified students to these assistantships.
      (2) These assignments are made in such a way as to enrich the professional learning experiences of the graduate assistants.
   f. Adequate secretarial and clerical staff is provided in the counselor education program.
      (1) Clerical responsibilities are defined and responsibility for supervision of clerical staff is clearly identified.
      (2) A minimum of one full-time secretary is provided for the clerical work of the counselor education program.
      (3) Additional clerical service is provided on a ratio of approximately one full-time clerical assistant for every three faculty members.
   4. For the counselor education program the institution provides facilities and a budget which are sufficient to insure continuous operation of all aspects of the program.
   a. The institution provides a designated headquarters for the counselor education program.
      (1) This headquarters is located near the classroom and laboratory facilities used in the counselor education program.
      (2) The headquarters area includes well-equipped private offices for all professional staff members.
      (3) The headquarters area includes office space for clerical staff and graduate assistants.
   b. Practicum facilities are provided on and/or off campus in cooperating schools or other agencies.

    (1) These facilities include an adequate number of counseling offices.

    (2) Facilities are equipped with recording and listening devices for observation and supervision.

    (3) One-way vision screens are located in such a way as to provide for observation by an individual or by a whole class.

    (4) If the institution has closed-circuit television facilities, these are available to the program of counselor education.

    (5) Conference rooms are provided for tape analysis and small group conferences.

    (6) Portable recorders are available in sufficient numbers.

    (7) Seminar rooms are provided.

    (8) Ample and appropriate audio-visual and demonstration materials are available for staff and student use.

    (9) A variety of resource material is available for the demonstration and use of current information services in guidance. Included are files of educational and occupational information materials.

c. Library facilities provide a rich supply of resource material for both research and study in counselor education.

    (1) These include basic resource, both books and periodicals, in guidance, counseling, personality appraisal, psychology, sociology, economics, and other related disciplines.

    (2) Both current and historical materials are available.

    (3) Library resources are available during both evening and weekend hours.

    (4) Inter-library loans, microfilm, and photocopy services are available.

    (5) Multiple copies of frequently used publications are available.

d. Guidance and counseling center facilities are utilized on and/or off campus for the supervised experiences.

    (1) Opportunities are provided for both observation and participation.

    (2) These facilities provide for a broad variety of types and levels of experience and thus provide an understanding of a wide range of professional guidance and counseling activities both in and out of the school setting.

e. Testing laboratory facilities are available.

    (1) Files of tests and test interpretation data are available.

    (2) Space for both group and individual testing is provided.

    (3) Students have access to test scoring equipment.

f. Research facilities are available to both staff and students in counselor education.

(1) Facilities include offices and laboratories equipped to provide opportunities for collection, analysis, and summary of data.

(2) Calculators are provided in these offices for research work.

(3) Consultants' services are available from research specialists on the institution's staff.

(4) Access is provided to campus computer centers and other data-processing laboratories.

(5) Settings are provided in which research can be conducted, including campus laboratories and secondary schools which provide enabling relationships to student and staff in counselor education.

5. The institution recognizes the individual needs of graduate students and provides services for personal as well as professional development.

   a. Since full-time academic-year attendance is possible for most graduate students only if some form of financial assistance is available, every effort is made to develop appropriate assistantships and fellowships in counselor education.

      (1) The counselor education program is assigned a proportionate share of the total number of graduate assistantships and fellowships provided.

      (2) Part-time work opportunities appropriate for students in the program are identified and efforts are made to secure assignments for those desiring such assistance.

      (3) Loan resources are made available to students in counselor education.

      (4) Prospective students are provided information about possible sources of financial assistance.

   b. Personal counseling services are available to all counselor candidates.

      (1) Available counselors are identified.

      (2) This service is available from staff members other than the members of the counselor education staff.

      (3) Patterns for referral are known to all staff members.

12

The Education of the School Counselor

Dugald S. Arbuckle, Ph.D.*

When one attempts to examine recent research on the education of the school counselor, the first difficulty faced is the attempt to answer the question: What is a counselor? Is it true, as Dr. George F. Lehner [12] says, that a counselor works with an undefined technique which is applied to unspecified problems with nonpredictable outcomes? If anything, it would seem that this difficulty has been accentuated in the past few years rather than decreased. In speaking at a workshop for rehabilitation counselors and social workers in June of last year, the author was somewhat surprised to find that to a man, or a woman, the social workers felt that their primary, indeed their only function, was counseling. Similarly, discussion with school psychologists reveal that many of them feel that most of what they do might be described as counseling. Clergymen feel that a very major part of their task is counseling, and physicians are beginning to believe that they are counselors.

There are, of course, some specifically designed counseling programs. At the doctorate level, the counseling psychologist is probably the best known, while the program for the rehabilitation counselor, at the "two years beyond the bachelor's" level, is also quite specific. On the whole, however, the evidence would tend to indicate that a number of different professional workers feel that their primary function is counseling, and yet for this function they vary widely in their background and professional education. And of all these the school counselors appear to be the group which has the most varied background of education and expectation. This is understandable, since a person who has a "school social worker" degree will usually go out as a school social worker, while one who has a "school psychologist" degree will usually perform the duties of a school psychologist. The person who receives a degree in guidance and counseling, however, may be going into any one of a variety of occupations. Programs at the master's level show some similarity, of course, partly due to the state certification regulations. Thus most school counselor preparation programs at the master's level have one or more courses in counseling, one or two in occupations, some psychological measurement, and a course in adminis-

*Dr. Arbuckle is a Professor of Education at Boston University. His article appeared originally in the *Journal of Counseling Psychology*, 5:58 (1958), and is reprinted with permission of the author and of the journal.

tration. Once beyond the master's level, however, there is a good deal of flexibility. Not all of this is bad since a great and wondrous variety of people do post-master's work in guidance and counseling. Thus the Boston University Guidance and Counseling Department has present and future clergymen, nurses, teachers, deans of men and of women, heads of residence halls, directors of admission, directors of guidance, school and college counselors, and so on.

State certification is, of course, a major factor affecting the education of counselors, but it is unlikely that certification will go beyond the master's level in the foreseeable future, although there may be a move in the direction of an attempt to develop levels of counseling proficiency, which might be given in programs which would represent the master's degree as the first level, the advanced certificate as the second level, and the doctorate as the top level.

A report by Royce E. Brewster [5] indicates that by this year all but nine states will have certification regulations for school counselors, or plans for establishing such regulations. It must be admitted, however, that nine hours of course work as a "professional" preparation does look, at best, rather feeble! A significant development has been the adoption, in California, effective this year, of regulations which provide for a common core in the preparation of counselors, social workers, child welfare and attendance workers, psychologists, and psychometrists employed in the public schools of the state. Connecticut has recently appointed a Director of Pupil Personnel Services, and Dr. Robert H. Mathewson, in his report on the training of counselors in New York State [16] emphasized the need for inter-relationships of *functions* among those who perform the counseling *function*. Florida is another state moving in the direction of a total personnel services concept.

Thinking specifically of the education of the counselor, it would seem that we might look first at some of the programs of education, then at some of the techniques used in these programs, and finally at the counselor as a person.

PROGRAMS OF PROFESSIONAL EDUCATION

Although in the past few years there has been some progress toward agreement regarding the general areas which should be included in counselor training, as indicated in reports by Dr. Dorothy Clendenen [6] and Dr. C. Gilbert Wrenn [29, p. 338], there is still much diversity in content, techniques, and organization of programs for the professional preparation of counselors. The arduous task that is being been done by Dr. Frank Sievers and his associates at the United States Office of Education, in attempting to compile, in much detail, all of the programs that are offered throughout the country, will do much to publicize the differences and similarities in training programs. The task of improving the content and the techniques of counselor preparation, however, is vastly complicated by the multiplicity of the tasks of the counselor, by our lack of understanding of the counseling process, by confused inter-professional relationships, and by problems of semantics.

Mathewson [14] has recommended that the professional training of the general guidance counselor should be preceded by 24 hours of undergraduate work in psychology and sociology, that the candidate should have had teaching experience, and should meet high standards of intelligence and personality. On the other hand, a committee of APGA, in 1955, reported that there were at least 205 colleges and universities which had programs for the preparation of school counselors. A multiplicity of courses were offered, and the "education" in the "program" ranges from the offering of one course, taught by one who has taken one course, to a program of several years of intensive study, culminating in a doctorate degree. Dr. F. W. Miller's survey [18] in 1953 revealed significant differences in facilities and requirements among 157 colleges and universities.

Dr. G. A. Pierson's report [19] indicated that many counselors and guidance directors felt the need for a better planned preparation in terms of coordination of courses, the relative emphasis on many aspects of their work, and the practical application of theory. Dr. Claude W. Grant [9] points out that the tendency of some students to look to others rather than counselors for counseling assistance raises some questions as to the direction and emphases in counselor education.

Mathewson [15] proposed a two-year sequence for the preparation of the general counselor, the content of which he related closely to an analysis of appropriate functions. Dr. Harold F. Cottingham [7] has suggested a series of positions and broad training levels for college personnel workers, and has related these levels to functions. As Wrenn [29] has indicated, the recommendations of the Division of Counseling Psychology of the APA should provide a basic structure for the evaluation of doctoral programs. Some of the suggestions made by the Committee on Sub-Doctoral Education of the APA 7] might well be used in the formulation of sub-doctoral programs, which will likely continue to represent the education of the great majority of school counselors for some time to come.

TECHNIQUES AND METHODS USED

In a study of 102 colleges and universities made by a committe of NAGSCT [20] it was found that provision for supervised experience was reported by only 68 institutions. Only a few institutions could probably report that supervised experience was given for all master's candidates. The part-time candidate poses a problem on this question, since for such a student very often neither the supervision nor the experiences which might be available would be desirable. The practical application of skills and understandings is a highly desirable experience in the education of the counselor, but a carefully supervised educative experience for every counselor who must be graduated to fill the now available positions poses an impressive problem of staff and facilities.

Mathewson and Dr. Isaiah Rochlin [17] have described techniques for the close structured analysis of recorded initial interviews to increase counselor-self-awareness and sensitivity to silent self-perception. The question of the effect of an observer during an interview was studied by Alfred Kadushin [11], who also described means by which the presence of the observer could be minimized. Ruth P. Anderson and O. H. Brown [3] described their use of tape recordings in three stages of supervision, emphasizing that the supervisor is concerned less with specific counselor responses than with the meaning and understanding communicated in the totality of his responses.

Counselor trainees are generally encouraged to experience personal therapy, but the author knows of no evidence to indicate that a group of "normally abnormal" counselors were any better or any worse, as counselors, after experiencing psychotherapy. A blanket requirement for personal psychotherapy might be questioned, although there is little danger of this ever happening as far as the education of the average school counselor is concerned. Dr. Leona Tyler [26] has pointed out that psychotherapy is not the only method to help counselors to develop an awareness of their own biases and sensitive areas. Dr. Ronald Shor [23] described a "recorder self-therapy" technique for use in counselor training to help students understand themselves. Dr. Milton Schwebel [21] has suggested that the counselor might be helped to learn about his own motivation through small classes specifically designed for that purpose. Dr. M. Slomowitz [24] compared personality changes and content achievement gains in two parallel classes, one conducted in a student-centered setting whereas the other was conducted in a problem-oriented setting. Dr. William E. Hopke [10] and R. H. Van Zelst [27] have reported on the development and use of instruments to measure attitudes and empathy. Dr. E. A. Wicas [28] developed an instrument with which trainees could compare their responses to client talk with those of expert counselors.

THE COUNSELOR

There is an increasing accumulation of evidence, such as that found in reports by Dr. Edward Shoben [22] and other *Annual Review* writers, which indicates the influence of counselor personality and attitudes on the counseling process. Dr. Calvin Daane [8] found differing patterns of scores on the MMPI for counselors with high and low empathy scores. Dr. Walter M. Lifton [13] had a report of significance to counselors on the relationship between empathy and aesthetic sensitivity. Clendenen [6] found that "good" trainees usually have an A or B rating on three groups for the Strong for Men, most frequently on the Scientific, Social Welfare and Literary. Arbuckle [4], in a study of trainees who had either been chosen or rejected by their fellows as potential counselors, found significant differences on scores on the MMPI, the Heston and the Kuder. Those who were accepted, when compared with those who were not accepted, tended to show more "normal" scores on several scales of the MMPI, a higher degree of confidence on the Heston, and a higher degree of interest in such areas as social service, persuasive, literary, and scientific, as measured by the Kuder. Dr. William Snyder [25], in a study of the personality of clinical students, found that "good" students were more aggressive, independent, unconventional, intellectual, and social, and were less religious. "Poor" students tended to have feelings of inadequacy and neurotic concerns. While these "good" students were not necessarily good counselors, this and other studies tend to indicate that the counselor trainers should tread carefully when we come forth with the usual unverified comments about good and poor counselor personality traits.

SUMMARY

All this, then, would seem to point out that:

1. We need more research to determine whether or not there are specific counselor traits that definitely contribute in either a positive or a negative way to the total effect of the counseling process.

2. We must become more concerned with the problem of the extent to which a counselor preparation program should be therapeutic or educative—does a graduate program in this field have counselees or students, or both?

3. The two national associations which are apparently most concerned with this problem are the American School Counselors Association and the National Association of Guidance Supervisors and Counselor Trainers° since these represent the individuals who do the counseling and those who certify and prepare them.

4. We must work to develop two or more realistic levels of counseling, with the functions of the counselor being related to his preparation. The "master's level" counselors would likely be generalists, with specialization coming at the post-master's level.

5. The American Personnel and Guidance Association should take the lead in attempting to see that there is a movement toward more unity between several disciplines so that there is at least a common core of preparation in the education of those individuals who are going to be counselors,

°Now the Association for Counselor Education and Supervision [Text Editor].

whether they be called counselors, social workers, psychologists, or any other name.

6. Personnel workers, counselors, and psychologists should exert themselves to see if they cannot reduce the traditional lag between research and service. How can we put into effect what we already *know*, so that *all* students who are clients rather than just a few in a research situation, may undergo a more effective counseling experience?

BIBLIOGRAPHY

1. American Personnel and Guidance Association, Committee on Professional Training, Licensing and Certification, APGA committee reports on professional training, licensing, and certification. *Personnel & Guid. J.*, 33, 356–357.

2. American Psychological Association, Education and Training Board, Committee on Subdoctoral Education. The training of technical workers in psychology at subdoctoral levels. *Amer. Psychologist, 10*, 541–545.

3. Anderson, R. P., & Brown, O. H. "Tape Recordings and Counselor-Trainee Understandings," *J. Counsel. Psychol.*, 2, 189–194.

4. Arbuckle, D. S. "Client Perception of Counselor Personality," *J. Counsel. Psychol.*, 3, 93–96.

5. Brewster, R. E. *Guidance Workers Certification Requirements.* Guide Lines. Office of Education, U.S. Department of Health, Education and Welfare. Washington, D. C.: The Office, February 1956, p. 44.

6. Clendenen, Dorothy M. "Selection and Training of Counselors," *New Perspectives in Counseling.* Minnesota Studies in Student Personnel Work, No. 7. Minneapolis, Minn.: Univer. of Minnesota Press, 1955, pp. 49–58.

7. Cottingham, H. F. "Roles, Functions, and Training Levels for College Personnel Workers," *Personnel & Guid. J.*, 33, 534–538.

8. Daane, C. J. *A Study of Empathic Ability and Related Variables Among Trained and Practicing Counselors.* Doctor's Thesis. Bloomington, Ind. Univer., 1955, p. 168. Abstract: *Dissertation Abstracts* 15, 2096; No. 11, 1955.

9. Grant, C. W. "The Counselor's Role," *Personnel & Guid. J.*, 33, 74–77.

10. Hopke, W. E. "The Measurement of Counselor Attitudes," *J. Counsel. Psychol.*, 2, 212–216.

11. Kadushin, A. "Observing the Interview in Counselor Training and Supervision," *Personnel & Guid. J.*, 34, 405–408.

12. Lehner, G. F. J. Comments. *Amer. Psychologist, 7*, 547.

13. Lifton, W. M. *A pilot study of the relationship of empathy to aesthetic sensitivity.* Urbana, Ill.: Univer. of Illinois, Bureau of Educational Research, 1956. 49 p. (mimeo.)

14. Mathewson, R. H. "The General Guidance Counselor," *Personnel & Guid. J.*, 32, 544–547.

15. Mathewson, R. H. *Guidance Policy and Practice.* Rev. Edition. New York: Harpers, 1956. 424 p

16. Mathewson, R. H., Chairman. *The Training of Counselors in New York State.* Report of the Committee on Counselor Training. New York: Division of Teacher Education, 500 Park Avenue, 1954. 37 p. (mimeo.)

17. Mathewson, R. H., and Rochlin, I. "Analysis of Unstructed Self-Appraisal: A Technique in Counselor Education," *J. Counsel. Psychol.*, 3, 32–36.

18. Miller, F. W. "Counselor Training Programs in Colleges and Universities," *Personnel & Guid. J.*, *32*, 132–134.

19. Pierson, G. A. "Aesop and the School Counselor," *Personnel & Guid. J*, *32*, 326–329.

20. Polmantier, P. C., Chairman, *Report of the committee on supervised practice in counselor preparation.* Preconvention Workshop, National Association of Guidance Supervisors and Counselor Trainers. Chicago: the Committee (Chairman Paul C. Polmantier, Univer. of Missouri at Columbia), April 1955, p. 12 (mimeo.).

21. Schwebel, M. "Why Unethical Practice?" *J. Counsel. Psychol.*, *2*, 122–128.

22. Shoben, E. J., Jr. "Counseling," *Annu. Rev. Psychol. Vol. 7*, Stanford, Calif.: Annual Reviews, 1956, pp. 147–172.

23. Shor, R. E. "Recorder Self-Therapy: A Technique," *J. Counsel. Psychol.*, *2*, 150–151.

24. Slomowitz, M. *A Comparison of Personality Changes and Content Achievement Gains Occurring in Two Modes of Instruction.* Doctor's Thesis. New York: New York Univer., 1955. Abstract: *Dissertation Abstracts* 15, 1790, No. 10, 1955.

25. Snyder, W. U. "The Personality of Clinical Students," *J. Counsel. Psychol.*, *2*, 47–52.

26. Tyler, Leona. *The Work of the Counselor.* New York: Appleton-Century-Crofts, 1953.

27. Van Zelst, R. H. "Validation Evidence on the Empathy Test," *Educ. Psychol. Measmt.*, *13*, 474–477.

28. Wicas, E. A. *The Development and Evaluation of a Free Response Instrument Measuring Counseling Perception for Use in Counselor Training.* Unpublished docotral dissertation, Boston University, 1956.

29. Wrenn, C. G. "Counseling Methods," *Annu. Rev. Psychol. Vol. 5.* Stanford, Calif.: Annual Reviews, 1954, pp. 337–356.

13 | The Wonderland of Counselor Education

Ralph E. Myering, Ph.D.*

> All in the golden afternoon
>   Full leisurely we glide;
> For both our oars, with little skill
>   By little arms are plied,
> While little hands made vain pretence
>   Our wanderings to guide

(From *Alice's Adventures in Wonderland* by Lewis Carroll, Introduction)

Counselor educators are basically an uncreative lot. For the most part, we are intellectually lazy, inefficient, egocentric, and have a real commitment to maintenance of the status quo.

It is the purpose of this paper to indicate the current status of our profession, to offer suppositions as to how this came about, and to submit suggestions for possible solutions to our predicament. The references to Alice's Wonderland are made to illustrate the point that one never-never land is like another and that the wonderland of counselor education may not really be unique.

Guidance as we know it developed out of the educational pragmatism of the early twentieth century. The concern at that time was with helping youth in decision making which would have an immediate effect upon their lives. Problems of educational and occupational choice naturally received a great deal of attention. Counselors were technicians; and since that time counselor educators, for the most part, have trained technicians.

School counselors of today are still most concerned with problems of choice which have an immediate impact upon the life of the counselee. Counselor educators still spend a large percentage of their time dealing with the technical aspects of the counseling process. Counselor educators examining the job analyses of counselors find that ninety per cent of counseling time is spent in educational and vocational counseling. Therefore, they set up programs which emphasize the techniques of educational and vocational counseling so that counselors will feel comfortable in spending ninety per cent of their time in these functions. The approach is backward

°Dr. Meyering is Professor of Education and Psychology, Illinois State University, Normal. His article appeared originally in *Counselor Education and Supervision*, 4:1:37 (Fall 1964), and is reprinted with permission of the author and of the journal.

and cannot alone answer the question of what should be included in an adequate counselor-education program.

Counselors are pragmatists and are interested in aiding students answer immediate questions. "For which occupation should I prepare?" however, is only one of the problems which trouble our youth. "How can I develop mature social relationships with fellow students?" "How can I achieve emotional independence within my family?" "How should I go about choosing a marriage partner?" "How can I reconcile the social standards of my peer group with adult expectations?" "How can I maintain socially acceptable behavior in these two societies?" "I need to develop a set of values upon which to base my behavior; where do I start?" These are some of the problems of the adolescent with which the school counselor ought to be concerned. We do not need more techniques so much as a deeper understanding of the students we wish to serve. We do not need new skills so much as a deeper commitment to the broader goals of guidance.

> "Would you tell me, please, which way I ought to go from here?"
> "That depends a good deal on where you want to get to," said the Cat.
> "I don't much care where . . . " said Alice.
> "Then it doesn't matter which way you go," said the Cat.
> ". . . so long as I get *somewhere*," Alice added as an explanation.
> "Oh, you're sure to do that, said the Cat, "if you only walk long enough."
> (From *Alice's Adventure in Wonderland*, Chapter 6)

Too often we as counselors are content to allow students to drift. Many problems take care of themselves in time. Value systems and codes of conduct will develop whether or not counseling takes place. The question is whether or not we can afford to let them develop without helping the adolescent carefully assess himself and his environment. We may not be able to persuade students through counseling to revise their basic values, but we do have a responsibility to encourage them to examine themselves as worthwhile entities existing in an objective world.

How can the school counselor aid students in the solution of developmental problems? The basic counseling process is the same whether the youth is attempting to choose a life partner or a life occupation. The key to developmental counseling lies in helping the student evolve an adequate self-concept and then helping him implement this self-concept in the decisions which he must make. In this process the counselee is the investigator, always striving toward a greater understanding of himself.

This emphasis on self-understanding, self-direction, and self-development encourages creative individuality. With this knowledge of self, the counselee is in a position to make responsible application of current knowledge in the solution of particular problems. Counselors must be prepared to help students in this process. Counselor-education programs must be geared to train the counselors not as technicians, but rather as perceptive and understanding catalytic agents in the process of student development.

"The first thing I've got to do," said Alice to herself, as she wandered about on the wood, "is to grow to my right size again; and the second thing is to find my way into that lovely garden. I think that will be the best plan."
It sounded an excellent plan, no doubt, and very neatly and simply arranged: the only difficulty was, that she had not the smallest idea how to set about it.
(From *Alice's Adventures in Wonderland*, Chapter 4)

When one looks back on the progress of counselor education during the past twenty-five years, one realizes what a short way we have come. When one looks at the totality of clear-cut and conclusive research evidence dealing with counseling, one realizes how much more we have to learn. Research acitivity in guidance and counseling has been undesirably random in nature. We have become bogged down with extremely complex research designs in our attempts to demonstrate the obvious or the inconsequential. At times it appears that we have not the smallest idea of how to set about achieving our goals.

We need not, of course, go back to the beginnings in our research. We have learned some things in our desultory attempts to understand the dynamics of human personality, and thus the dynamics of counseling. What we need to do is fill in the gaps and synthesize what we have learned. We must develop a body of knowledge which each counselor can draw upon in dealing with a particular student.

More specifically, we need to identify the developmental problems of youth. This should involve less concern with symptoms and complaints and a more intensive investigation of the psychological needs of adolescents. We need more research dealing with the importance of realistic self-concepts on the decision making process. How does the individual's ability to relate himself to his environment affect his ability to solve developmental problems?

We must develop theories which can serve as adequate models for the short-term, ego-oriented counseling carried on in our schools. The theories should provide a frame of reference which the school counselor can apply to "normal youth with normal problems." Along with new theories of counseling, new techniques also need to be developed. Although techniques may facilitate the counseling process, care must be taken to prevent school counseling from becoming technique dominated. The sensitivity of the counselor, his commitment to an approach, his understanding of personality dynamics, and his ability to establish an effective relationship will all be more important than his knowledge of specific techniques.

Finally, ego-oriented school counseling should be evaluated in terms of the broad objectives of guidance in our schools. We have enough research which has used intermediate criteria. What we want to know is whether our counseling is helping students satisfy their developmental needs. We must be thinking not in terms of what is now taking place in our schools, but rather in terms of what help school counselors could be providing our youth.

> She generally gave herself very good advice (though she very seldom followed it), and sometimes she scolded herself so severely as to bring tears into her eyes; and once she remembered trying to box her own ears for having cheated herself in a game of croquet she was playing against herself, for this curious child was very fond of pretending to be two people. "But it's no use now," thought poor Alice, "to pretend to be two people! Why, there's hardly enough of me left to make *one* respectable person!" (From *Alice's Adventures in Wonderland*, Chapter 1)

It is easy to scold ourselves severely for there is truth in the assertion that we are uncreative; one merely has to look at how little has been created in our field. We are intellectually lazy. The thinking of many counselor educators is only the thinking of their major advisor warmed over. The disciples repeat the words of their masters with little attempt to evaluate critically the quality of the thought. We are inefficient. Old research is constantly being redone. The perspicuous and the inappreciable are not only included in our courses, but they are duplicated in others so that students will not miss their full impact. We are egocentric and overly concerned with the level of our prestige. We write to be published whether or not we are contributing to the field. We jealously guard our professional status against invasion by all outsiders no matter what they might have to offer. Like Alice, we pretend to be two people but owing major allegiance either to education or psychology when there is hardly enough of us to make one respectable person.

Finally, we are firmly committed to maintenance of the status quo. Innovations in our profession are rare, and are frowned upon by the group as a whole. At the present time our national organizations are concerned with the establishment of standards for counselor-education programs. For the most part, their recommendations only rigidify our present procedures. We become overly concerned with whether we should require a one or two-year master's degree program, but allow our recommendations for the content of either to be guided by what we now include. In short, the attitudes of many counselor educators are geared to resist change and to continue the curriculum which they knew in their own training.

Counselor-education programs must begin to reflect the broader objectives of guidance. Now is the time for creative thinking. If we look first to the children we would like to help, determine how we can best prepare them to face the problems which they must face, and develop counselor-education programs which prepare counselors to carry out these functions, we will have made great strides.

The wonderland of counselor education is a delightful place, no doubt; but sooner or later, like Alice, we must return to reality. We shall never be able to completely escape. There will always be the frightened mice of our profession, the Queen ordering someone's execution, the shrieking Gryphons, and the sobbing Mock Turtles, but these will be merely vestiges of a bygone day, charming reminders of where we have been. Counselor education will have progressed into a profession of status, with a contribution to offer to our society.

14

National Certification of Counselors

George L. Keppers, Ed.D.*

Why national certification of counselors? Is it necessary? Is it possible? These questions and others are being asked regarding certification of and preparation programs for counselors. We are not preparing counselors just for New Mexico or New York or Washington. Our population is becoming more mobile all the time. Thus there is a need for standard preparation for counselors not only from the standpoint of the counselors moving from one college to another or one job to another but also in helping them in their work with people who will be living in various parts of the world. Much has been done and continues to be done to improve the situation such as requirements established by the North Central Association and other accrediting agencies for public schools. The institutes under NDEA have done much to provide stability to preparation programs. All too often the specifications deal only with hours of course work and not specific preparation. In many instances as above the impetus to improve the situation has come from more or less outside agencies rather than counselor educators. Similarly suggested programs for the preparation of counselors have come from such groups as a) the American Psychological Association Committee on Subdoctoral Education of the Education and Training Board, b) The National Vocational Guidance Association, Counselor Preparation, c) the Ann Arbor Conference, sponsored by Division 17 of the A.P.A. and the University of Michigan and more recently, d) Standards for Counselor Education in the Preparation of Secondary School Counselor [3]. The latter represents the most significant contribution by counselor educators through the American Personnel and Guidance Association.°

Counselor educators must and will be held responsible for not only the quantity but the quality of the counselor preparation programs and as a consequence certification of counselors. We must not allow this important responsibility to be taken over by default by the North Central Association, the National Council for the Accreditation of Teacher Education, or other similar groups. In a survey of counselor educators in 1962 regarding such

°Dr. Keppers is a Professor of Education at the University of New Mexico, Albuquerque. His article appeared originally in *Counselor Education and Supervision*, 4:4:202 (Summer 1965), and is reprinted with permission of the author and of the journal.

°For APGA's most recent statement on preparation, see the lead article in Part II [Text Editor].

topics as counselor education, certification, and reciprocal agreements on these topics some very specific suggestions were made. The remainder of this paper will be devoted to a presentation and discussion of these statements.

A statement or idea that was very frequently mentioned was that reciprocal or national accreditation and certification is needed. This seems to be a reasonable expectation. The National Association of State Directors of Teacher Education and Certification has for the past several years considered problems in establishing standards for national reciprocity in all areas. This group has been concerned with the character, adequacy and quality of collegiate programs of preparation. If we are to profit from these studies we should proceed along these same lines, that is, look to the counselor preparation programs in our colleges and universities and certify counselors on the basis of this preparation.

A second frequently mentioned approach to the problem was to the effect that counselor preparation programs should be approved by some agency outside the college or university. It was suggested that this could take several forms: a) a committee from the American Personnel and Guidance Association to visit, evaluate and approve or not approve the program or b) work with existing accrediting agencies such as the National Council for Accreditation of Teacher Education (NCATE). In either case this indicates a need for evaluative criteria for counselor education programs. How can we evaluate if we don't know what to look for? All too often in the past NCATE has approved or disapproved a program without the assistance of qualified personnel or a set of criteria by which to rate the institution.

Following this line of reasoning we come to a third factor, namely, what sort of preparation do counselors need to carry out their work effectively? It was suggested by many respondents that we contact the American School Counselors Association to see how they view the preparation counselors are currently receiving, or have received, and how appropriate it is to their job.

The fourth point which received considerable emphasis was: Determine the role of the counselor and develop a statement of functions of the counselor. This again seems a very logical approach to the entire problem of national accreditation. If we can't agree on what counselors should be doing, how can we prepare them adequately and how can we certify them? This should be based on what we think counselors should be doing, as well as on what they are doing.

To put all this in its proper perspective, let's reverse the order of these suggestions and we have a rather logical approach to the problem as follows: a) prepare a statement pertaining to duties of the school counselor, b) establish preparation programs to prepare counselors to carry out these duties, c) Evaluate counselor preparation programs to see that they are equipped to carry out such a program, and d) recommend and carry out accreditation and certification on a national basis. To make this complete there should be a fifth point and it should be basic to this entire discussion, i.e., the needs of the individual student to make a satisfactory adjustment in our society. This should be the starting point for any discussion of accreditation and certification at the local, state, regional, or national level. Therefore, let us begin with this in mind and see if we can develop a reasonable approach to standards across the nation.

Much has been written and rewritten about the areas in which individuals need assistance, but they can be reduced to such areas as vocational and educational planning and personal and social adjustment and development. There seems to be general agreement that counselors should work in the areas of vocational and educational planning, but there is considerably less agreement that counselors should do personal counseling. This is unfortunate since it is almost impossible to work with a student with a vocational or educational problem (expressed problem) without getting involved in the personality of the individual. Just ask any counselor who is counseling or do some counseling yourself, and the facts speak for themselves. Whether counselors should do intensive psychotherapy is one issue, but to say they should not work with students with emotional problems is another. Truancy, discipline, and under-achieving are all complex problems and are certainly packed with emotional tension. There is no point in going into great detail about the duties of a counselor because they are discussed at length in the literature. If we accept the statement above, and we must, then it is quite obvious what types of counselor preparation programs we should have in our colleges and universities. It is sufficient to say that in keeping with what the counselors' duties should be and suggestions included in the questionnaire returns, these programs must include work in such areas as sociology, psychology, curriculum and the usual courses in guidance. One of the best guides to a good program of counselor preparation is the pamphlet *Counselor Preparation* [1], published and distributed by the National Vocational Guidance Association. I know some of you are saying "Oh, that was 1949." There still isn't a better set of criteria and suggestions available under one cover.

It is one thing to set up a program on paper, but most difficult to carry it out. The situation at the level of preparation is similar to the problem counselors face—that is, this is what we want to do but how can we carry it out with limited staff, facilities, funds, and most of all support and understanding from the administration. We need to do a much better job of selling the administration on what needs to be done. Sometimes national accrediting groups can bring pressure to bear on institutions of higher learning to improve their programs. It seems we listen to the expert from without before we listen to ones from within. This leads us to the point dealing with evaluating counselor preparation programs. Several suggestions were made regarding procedures to follow in carrying out this evaluation: a) set up our own evaluation committee similar to the American Psychological Association, b) work with such accrediting groups as the North Central Association and the National Council of Accreditation of Teacher Education, or c) have the programs certified by state departments of education. May I be so bold as to suggest that we work with existing groups, especially NCATE? This should be done by providing this group with recommendations for adequate counselor preparation programs and insist that one member of the visiting team be competent in the area of counselor education. It is not enough to provide an evaluation team with a checklist of evaluative criteria; someone on the team must be capable of making value judgments as to how effectively the materials, staff, and facilities are being utilized.

Now we come to the main point of this presentation, namely, national accreditation. If we accept the suggestions made so far, national or reciprocal accreditation will be a relatively simple task. Certification should be based on what counselors should be doing as well as what they are doing. This in turn should determine preparation programs and, if these programs are approved, certification is accomplished. This does not imply lockstep programs, but there is sufficient similarity among people throughout the nation that we can prepare counselors to deal with them wherever they may be.

In spite of such a simple approach (to some, simplicity is an indication of mediocrity or complexity is synonymous with excellence) we have differences of opinion as to minimum standards. In the above survey, articles in journals, reports and general discussions, several points need to be made regarding changes in counselor certification. One has to do with work experience—this requirement has already been excluded from many credentials (required in only fifteen states) and could very easily be eliminated as a specific item from the others. This is a reflection of the days when vocational guidance was the primary role of the counselor. Another is the requirement pertaining to teaching experience (all states with certification require teaching experience). The fact that 20 per cent of the respondents to the questionnaire said teaching experience is not a necessary prerequisite to counseling indicates this requirement is not universally accepted. There is no evidence that teaching experience is a necessary and sufficient prerequisite for good counseling. Only one comment is necessary, "Eliminate teaching experience as a requirement for counselor certification." Why have only one path leading to certification? If school administrators wish to include this requirement, fine. In fact they may impose other standards as well.

If we eliminate these two controversial requirements, we have only the preparatory programs to consider. Here we have so much general agreement, at least regarding areas of preparation, that one might ask, "Why haven't we established national or reciprocal certification before?" Perhaps the reason is that we haven't given it much "serious" thought. There are some other considerations such as two levels of certification, practicum or supervised experience, psychological background and the behavioral sciences in general, and minimum number of hours of course work. At present two levels of preparation seem appropriate but so organized that the counselor will eventually be fully certified or be eliminated from the profession. Currently, the North Central Association recommends 15 semester hours of graduate credit for certification. It has been suggested by many and with the NDEA institute program moving in the direction of full year institutes, (except for refresher courses or upgrading) it would be reasonable to require a minimum of 24 semester hours of graduate work for the "provisional" certificate. The "professional" certificate should specify at least a minimum of 45 semester hours of graduate work and as much as two years beyond the Bachelor's degree. There doesn't seem to be any vigorous opposition to increasing the course requirements for certification. In a recent survey of counselors in New Mexico the majority expressed no opposition to such an increase and consequently the change has been made. There is also general approval of an expanded and improved program for practicum or internship so this should be no problem. If we are concerned in guidance with all aspects of an individual's development, that is a "commitment to individuals," we need to include work in the behavioral sciences. Therefore, it can be concluded that reciprocal and/or national certification is merely waiting to be put into effect.

The following recommendations are proposed to facilitate reciprocal or national certification:

1. Acceptance and implementation of the standards for the preparation of school counselors, as approved at the APGA National Convention in 1964.°

2. Establish a working relationship with the National Council for Accreditation of Teacher Education. Through this group reciprocal teacher accreditation has been agreed upon by 27 states. We need to provide this group with a set of standards for evaluating counselor education programs and certification requirements with which they can work.

3. Further work on the Counselor Education Standards and reciprocal certification should involve increasing participation by members of the American School Counselor Association. This should be a continuous process. After all, since guidance is a dynamic process, why not preparation and certification?

°Presumably the author would now be willing to substitute the 1967 statement [Text Editor].

4. We need action, not more words. Therefore, it is suggested that we move as rapidly as possible to achieve our goals of accreditation of counselor education programs and certification of counselors on a national basis.

REFERENCES

1. *Counselor Preparation.* National Vocational Guidance Association, 1949.
2. *Guidance Workers Certification Requirements.* U. S. Department of Health Education, and Welfare, Office of Education, Washington, Revised 1963.
3. *Standards for Counselor Education in the Preparation of Secondary School Counselors, A Report.* American Personnel and Guidance Association, 1964.

15

The Selection of School Counselors

George E. Hill, Ph.D.*

The selection of persons to engage in an occupation ought to fit into a sensible pattern involving the following steps.

1. Job analysis to provide guides for selection, training, placement, and evaluation. This entails establishment of a fundamental point of view regarding the nature of the work to be done.
2. Identification of persons who might do the job well and their selection preliminary to training.
3. Screening during the preparation program.
4. Training realistically related to the occupation. In a profession this involves a considerable period of pre-employment preparation plus continued growth on the job.
5. Placement of the worker in a position most nearly fitting his peculiar attributes.
6. Follow-up and evaluation to determine needed adjustments in the selection, training, and placement program.

Have school counselors been selected along lines such as these? An analysis of the literature on their selection and preparation covering the past two decades warrants the following answers.

First, the literature on the selection and preparation of school counselors is meager as compared with the general guidance literature. Only 14 of the 411 articles in the *Personnel and Guidance Journal* classified by Ruth Barry and Beverly Wolf [12] dealt with "counselor training."

Second, as a professional group, counselors and counselor educators have apparently done only a limited amount of research on the problems suggested by the six points listed above. Of the 136 articles based on research which Barry and Wolf [12] classified, two were on counselor training. A recent search for research reports [26] revealed a disappointingly small number, in fact no major longitudinal study of selection, training, placement, and evaluation.

Third, the guidance profession has arrived at a point where concerted attention to these problems is imperative.

*Dr. Hill is Distinguished Professor of Education, Ohio University, Athens. His article appeared originally in the *Personnel and Guidance Journal*, 39:355 (January 1961), and is reprinted with permission of the author and of the journal.

THE NEED FOR SELECTION

Most writers on counselor education have expressed concern about selection [3, 6, 52, 54]. It has also been generally agreed that selection is a continuing process, not a single event [7, 20, 37]. Selection should begin prior to preparation, continue through the preparation program, and be involved in the placement and evaluation of the school counselor. The actual effects of inadequate selection have received little attention. One writer [18] has suggested that the general public puts counseling in the same category as kissing insofar as there is any need for selection and training prior to practicing the art!

There is widespread concern for selection both among counselors and among counselor educators. This has been shown by several surveys of selection practices [33, 36, 41] and by the pronouncements of counselor groups [3, 6]. Little attention has been given, however, to the problems of selection involved in the widespread practice of school administrators identifying and encouraging members of their teaching staffs to train for counseling work. It has been shown [23, 27, 31, 43] that school counselors come chiefly from the teaching ranks and largely from the staffs of the schools in which they become counselors.

COMPLEXITY OF THE SCHOOL COUNSELOR'S WORK

The problem of selecting persons to prepare for and engage in the work of the school counselor is greatly complicated by the following conditions.

1. There is a variety of roles and relationships involved in the work of any given counselor [3, 6, 29]. His position is complicated and demanding.

2. There is a diversity of skills, understandings, interests, and attitudes expected in the counselor's position from one school to another [10, 29, 34, 45]. One disturbing aspect of this variability is the evidence that many counselors are expected to perform duties that have little, if any, relation to what the profession has agreed they should be doing [40, 50].

3. There is a variety of personalities involved in the work of the counselor. Counselors themselves differ one from another. Studies of the characteristics of counselors in service have not produced anything resembling a standard personality pattern [38, 47].

4. There is a hierarchy of guidance positions, if we may take seriously the many pronouncements regarding the specialties in guidance and personnel work [4, 9, 17, 19]. One of the more troublesome distinctions is that which seeks to differentiate between the general school counselor and the counseling psychologist. The latter is emerging more and more as a person prepared beyond the master's degree level. This distinction, however, may not last since many school counselors are achieving advanced levels of training.

These four variables have been delineated briefly in order to underline a few facts of life about the selection of counselors.

1. Selection and training programs must be geared to some clear conception of the nature of the educational personnel work for which the trainee is headed [16].

2. Selection and training programs will become more realistic as the guidance profession evolves greater clarification of its own goals and responsibilities.

3. Selection and training programs that assume counseling to be the sole, or even major, activity of all school counselors are currently not realistically geared to the demands of school situations.

4. Selection and training programs must prepare workers of tremendous breadth. Currently the school counselor must fit a professional demand of almost impossible complexity.

5. Significant research assessing the effectiveness of selection procedures must cope with the evaluation of the counselor's effectiveness. This poses problems of considerable complexity.

QUALIFICATIONS NEEDED BY COUNSELORS

The literature includes many pronouncements [2, 35, 49, 52] regarding the personal characteristics and the competencies needed by guidance and personnel workers. While relatively little of this literature may be said to be based upon research, the change in emphasis over the past two decades has been notable. This has constituted a shift from the search for a fixed list of desirable traits to general acceptance of the concept of the total personality pattern and its impact [27, 28, 46, 54]. There has also been a strong resurgence of emphasis upon the role of the counselor as an educator, a member of a team striving to achieve defined educational goals [46, 54].

Several good studies have been made of the tested characteristics and the reported status of counselors-in-training and of guidance workers in service [1, 14, 22, 29, 38, 42, 55]. These have not revealed that either group may be characterized in any standarized way. These studies of the known qualifications of counselors have not provided us with sure guides for the selection of school counselors except for certain characteristics known to be required to achieve the required graduate preparation—scholastic aptitude for graduate education, desire to secure such an education, personal qualities adequate to satisfy counselor educators and employers.

What has just been said is not intended to minimize the significance of the qualifications problem nor to discount the importance of counselor educators, counselors, and school officials seeking to clarify their concepts and their techniques of selection. Those concerned are going to continue to select persons for counselor training and for school counselor positions. The fact that there seems little promise of achieving blueprints of counselor qualifications only makes the selection problems more challenging; it does not erase the problems.

Perhaps one of the more hopeful research channels through which clearer selection procedures may emerge is that having to do with the evaluation of the work of the counselor. Such research, so far, has centered almost entirely upon the counseling process as such [1, 2, 11, 29, 32, 39]. This research has been scattered and diverse. There has been enough done, however, to provide much sharper tools for use in counselor education, especially in the practicum, for evaluating the effectiveness of trainees. The studies of counseling evaluation have depended heavily upon client reactions to counseling and upon expert ratings of counselors-in-action.

Another type of research that has been done in scattered sections and which gives promise of considerable help in the selection and training of school counselors has been the studies of what counselors do on the job [40, 45, 48, 49, 51]. These studies, among other things, raise serious questions regarding the definition of the counselor's proper role in the school. They reveal serious gaps between what is being done in counselor education and what is expected of counselors in the schools. That counselor education should merely reflect what school administrators expect of school counselors is hardly to be desired. Yet some reasonable harmonizing of job requirements and the selection-preparation processes is imperative.

CURRENT SELECTION PRACTICES

Those who become school counselors have been chiefly persons chosen from the teaching staff of the school in which they assume guidance responsibilities. To a considerable degree, school counselors are persons whom administrative officers identify as potentially good guidance workers [23, 27, 31, 43]. Little research has been done to determine the criteria used at this point in the selection process. There is little evidence that the universities recruit counselor-trainees or that the guidance workers themselves, individually or in groups, enter into the selection process.

Educational institutions report that their pre-training selection processes center about the question of eligibility and potential competence for graduate training [33]. Selection while in training centers is chiefly in the practicum aspect of preparation [5, 24, 25, 33, 53]. When the counselor-trainees get into supervised practice the counselor-educators give serious attention to the trainees' effectiveness and potential. Numbers of institutions administer various tests and inventories to trainees; but there is little evidence that actual selection transpires as a result of these having been administered.

In short, in practice, the selection of counselors transpires typically in about these steps:

First, a teacher becomes interested in guidance work, takes some training and is assigned guidance duties, or an administrator identifies a teacher on his staff whom he regards as potentially a good guidance worker and encourages him (or her) to seek training.

Second, the university screens applicants for counselor education as to their potential for pursuing graduate work. This screening varies from merely the requirement that the applicant hold a bachelor's degree to rigorous aptitude testing and the requirement of a high undergraduate point average.

Third, in the preparation program the trainee is assessed as to potential, usually in the practicum. In some institutions this involves careful and rigorous evaluation accompained by a strong emphasis upon self-evaluation and planning. In many institutions this in-training evaluation is loose and unplanned.

There have recently been a few attempts at the development of instruments giving some promise of usefulness in counselor selection. These have centered upon the measurement or attitudes toward and interest in educational and psychological training [13, 22, 30, 38, 44]. No one seems, as yet, to have attempted to develop a counseling aptitude test. One of the more interesting and promising selection techniques in counselor education programs has been the group process evaluation procedure. Counselor trainees have been subjected to various group experiences, under observation in most instances [21, 25, 53]. Ratings of their reactions in group discussion and group activities have been made by expert observers. These ratings have been shown to bear a surprisingly close relationship to their effectiveness in counseling as rated by other experts. Self-evaluations by counselor trainees have also been shown to bear a relationship to their counseling effectiveness [8, 21]. While such studies do not provide easy, pat selection procedures, they do indicate that attention to selection in the training processes can enrich the preparation program and provide information of considerable usefulness to the trainee. The selection processes that are emerging as most promising are those, then, that most nearly conform to accepted counseling theory. They are the processes that recognize the counselor trainee as a person whose dignity and worth will be enhanced by his being treated with the respect and care we insist we should accord our counseling clients.

SELECTION THROUGH CERTIFICATION

There has been some hope expressed that the processes of certification would ultimately become selective. While state after state has been added to the list now providing certification for school counselors, there is no real evidence that this has enhanced the selection process. The latest report [15] indicates that 37 states have certification for school counselors that has been classified as "mandatory." Four states have optional certification. The requirements vary from the very loosest minimum course requirements to the master's degree with specification as to preparation for the beginning counselor certificate. As a selection device certification depends primarily upon the practices of the training institutions.

SELECTION THROUGH SUPPLY AND DEMAND

It is clear that there is currently a serious shortage of school guidance workers [31, 33]. There are some signs that the shortage situation has, if anything, had the effect of relaxing selection and preparation criteria. For example, one state that had been moving toward required certification for guidance workers found it necessary, with the demand created by NDEA provisions, to lower its minimum training requirement when part-time guidance workers were involved. It is clear that the school counselor profession faces a serious problem in seeking to keep up with the demand for guidance workers while, at the same time, trying to maintain reasonably high training requirements. The anomalous situation in which part-time counselors are assumed to need less preparation than full-time counselors puts the profession in an indefensible and uncomfortable position.

SELECTION THROUGH PROFESSIONAL ACTION

All of the professional organizations have some sort of committee or commission concerned with selection and preparation. Most of the work of these groups, so far, has been in the pooling of opinions and the preparation of pronouncements. The more vigorous and extended of these have come from the counseling psychology groups. Without doubt, there is serious need for these professional groups to pool their efforts and to give concerted attention to such questions as the following:

1. How can the profession do a better job of encouraging research that will contribute to better selection and preparation of school counselors?

2. What can be done to make better use of the research already done on the selection and preparation of school counselors? What can be done to get more of the unpublished dissertation and thesis research into print and available to the profession?

3. What can be done to get the school counselors and the counselor educators into closer working relationship? Is it possible for these two groups to effect better working relationships with school administrators to the end that the selection processes be better conceived and better coordinated?

4. Would it be possible for these groups to secure adequate financial aid for some fundamental, longitudinal studies of counselor selection,

preparation, and evaluation? Could financial aid be secured for a truly definitive study of the proper role of the school counselor? Without more such studies, selection and preparation programs are bound to continue to be lacking in basic unity of meaning and approach.

The profession of the school counselor is in danger of losing the status and acceptance it has so recently achieved. Only the most earnest attention to such questions as those listed above will make it possible for the school counseling profession to achieve those goals we all recognize as essential to the proper maintenance of our educational system. "Selection" is an integral and important aspect of the larger, more comprehensive campaign to make of this profession a truly effective instrument of educational progress.

REFERENCES

1. Abeles, Norman. "A Study of the Characteristics of Counselor Trainees." Unpublished doctoral dissertation, University of Texas, 1958.

2. American College Personnel Association, Professional Standards and Training Committee. Personal Characteristics and Job Success, *Personnel Guid. J.* (1957), 35, 463–468.

3. American Personnel and Guidance Association, Committee on Professional Training, Licensing and Certification. "Professional Training, Licensing, and Certification," *Personnel Guid. J.* (1958), 37, 162–166.

4. "American Personnel and Guidance Association Committee Reports on Training, Licensing, and Certification," *Personnel Guid. J.* (1955), 33, 356–357.

5. American Psychological Association, Division of Counseling Psychology, Subcommittee on Counselor Selection, Counselor Training. *J. Counsel. Psychol.* (1954), 1, 174–179.

6. American Psychological Association, Education and Training Board. "Criteria for Evaluating Training Programs in Clinical and Counseling Psychology," *Amer. Psychologist* (1958), 13, 59–60.

7. American Psychological Association, Division of Counseling Psychology, Committee on Counselor Training. *Amer. Psychologist* (1952), 7, 175–181.

8. Arbuckle, Dugald S. "Client Perception of Counselor Personality," *J. Counsel. Psychol.* (1956), 3, 93–96.

9. Arbuckle, Dugald S. "The Education of the School Counselor," *J. Counsel. Psychol.* (1958), 5, 58–62.

10. Arnold, Dwight L. "Time Spent by Counselors and Deans on Various Activities," *Occupations* (1949), 27, 391–393.

11. Bandura, Albert. "Psychotherapists' Anxiety Level, Self-insight, and Psychotherapeutic Competence," *J. Abnorm. Soc. Psychol.* (1956), 52, 333–337.

12. Barry, Ruth, & Wolf, Beverly. "Five Years of the Personnel and Guidance Journal," *Personnel Guid. J.* (1958), 36, 549–556.

13. Bendig, A. W. "Development of the Psychological Activities Interest Record," *Educ. Psychol. Measmt.* (1958), 18, 159–166.

14. Brams, Jerome M. "The Relationship Between Personal Characteristics of Counseling Trainees and Effective Communication in Counseling." Unpublished doctoral dissertation, University of Missouri, 1957.

15. Brewster, Royce E. *Guidance Workers Certification Requirements.* Washington, D.C.: U.S. Office of Education, Bull. 1960, No. 14.

16. California State Department of Education. *The Preparation of Pupil Personnel Workers.* Bull., Vol. 21, No. 5, April, 1952.

17. Council of Guidance and Personnel Associations. Interim Report by the Study Commission. *Job Analysis of Educational Personnal Workers,* Part II, October, 1951.

18. Dressel, Paul L. "Evaluation and Counseling," *Concepts and Programs in Counseling.* Minnesota Studies in Student Personnel Work, No. 1, 1951, 70–81.

19. Fletcher, Frank M. "Occupations in Counseling," *Educ. Res. Bull.* (1949), 28, 93–98 & 127–137.

20. Fletcher, Frank M. "Problems Relating to Counseling Personnel, *Concepts and Programs in Counseling.* Minnesota Studies in Student Personnel Work, No. 1, 1951, pp. 27–41.

21. Fougner, Herbert M. "A Self-Concept Course for the Preparation of Guidance Personnel." Unpublished doctoral dissertation, University of California at Los Angeles, 1955.

22. Gibby, Mabel K. "The Use of the Minnesota Teacher Attitude Inventory in Appraising Counselor Attitudes." Unpublished doctoral dissertation, University of Missouri, 1952.

23. Goedke, M. T. "What's Going on in Guidance?" *Sch. Exec.* (1959), 78, 68–71.

24. Hackney, Ida May. "Client and Counselor Variables Related to Outcomes of Counseling." Unpublished doctoral dissertation, University of Michigan, 1958.

25. Heist, Paulus A. "An Experiment Utilizing Group Psychotherapy—a Self-analytical Procedure for Counselors' Training." Unpublished doctoral dissertation, University of Minnesota, 1956.

26. Hill, George E., & Green, Donald A. "The Selection, Preparation, and Professionalization of Guidance and Personnel Workers," *Rev. Educ. Res.* (April, 1960), 30, Ch. 3.

27. Hitchcock, Arthur A. "By What Means Can the Quality and Quantity of Guidance Services in the High Schools Be Increased?" *Curr. Issues Higher Educ.* National Education Association, 1958, 116–121.

28. Hobbs, Nicholas. "The Compleat Counselor," *Personnel Guid. J.* (1958), 36, 594–602.

29. Hoffman, A. Edward. "An Analysis of Counselor Sub-roles," *J. Counsel. Psychol.* (1959), 6, 61–67.

30. Hopke, Wm. E. "An Investigation of a Test of Several Basic Counselor Attitudes." Unpublished type C project report, Teachers College, Columbia University, 1950.

31. Hulslander, Stewart C., and Scholl, C. E. "U. S. School Principals Report Their Counselor Needs," *Voc. Guid. Quart.* (1957), 6, 3–7.

32. Jenson, Ralph E. "Student Feeling About Counseling Help, *Personnel Guid. J.* (1955), 33, 498–503.

33. MacMinn, Paul, & Ross, Roland G. *Status of Preparation Programs for Guidance and Student Personnel Workers.* Washington, D. C.: Office of Education, Bull. 1959, No. 7.

34. Martinson, Ruth A. "Duties of Elementary School Counselors," *Occupations* (1951), 30, 167–170.

35. McCreary, W. H. "Who Should Be a Guidance Specialist?" *Calif. J. Second. Educ.* (1957), 32, 426–432.

36. Miller, Frank W. *Current Trends in Counselor Selection and Training Among Schools Located in the North Central Region of N.A.G.S.C.T.,* Northwestern University, 1959.

37. National Vocational Guidance Association. *Counselor Preparation.* Washington, D. C.: NVGA, 1949.

38. Nelson, James H. "A Study of Personnel and Guidance Workers: Some of Their Characteristics, Interests and Attitudes." Unpublished doctoral dissertation, Denver University, 1952.

39. Porter, E. H., Jr. "The Development and Evaluation of a Measure of Counseling Interview Procedure," *Educ. Psychol. Measmt.* (1943), 3, 105–126 & 215–238.

40. Purcell, Florence E. "Counseling Assignments and Efficiency," *Voc. Guid. Quart.* (1957), 5, 111–113.

41. Santavicca, G. Gene. *A Summary of a Study Concerning Supervised Experience and Selection of Counselor Trainees.* Miami University, Ohio, 1958.

42. Snyder, W. U. "The Personality of Clinical Students," *J. Counsel. Psychol.* (1955), 2, 47–52.

43. Stevens, Nancy D., & Hoppock, Robert. "Employment Prospects for Guidance and Personnel Workers," *Voc. Guid. Quart.* (1956), 5, 9–12.

44. Symonds, P. M. "An Educational Interest Inventory," *Educ. Psychol. Measmt.* (1958), 18, 377–385.

45. Tennyson, Willard W. "Time: the Counselor's Dilemma!" *Personnel Guid. J.* (1958), 37, 129–135.

46. Tooker, Ellis D. "Counselor Role: Counselor Training," *Personnel Guid. J.* (1957), 36, 263–267.

47. Tuma, Abdul H., & Gustad, J. W. "The Effects of Client and Counselor Personality Characteristics on Client Learning in Counseling," *J. Counsel. Psychol.* (1957), 4, 136–141.

48. Vassallo, Theodore P. "The Status of Guidance Counselors and the Services rendered in Public Secondary Schools Located in the Middle Atlantic States." Unpublished doctoral dissertation, Temple University, 1956.

49. Warnath, Charles F. "Ethics, Training, Research: Some Problems for the Counseling Psychologist in an Institutional Setting," *J. Counsel. Psychol.* (1956), 3, 280–285.

50. Wellman, Frank E. "A Challenge and Some Problems," *Proceedings of the First Annual Invitational Conference for School Counselors,* Ohio State University, 1957.

51. Wendorf, Robert A. "Qualifications and Duties of Guidance Counselors in Ohio High Schools." Unpublished doctoral dissertation, Western Reserve University, 1955.

52. Williamson, Edmund G. "Value Orientation in Counseling," *Personnel Guid. J.* (1958), 36, 520–528.

53. Wilson, Phyllis G., & Robbins, Irving. "An Evolving Technique for Appraising Interpersonal Effectiveness," *J. Teach. Educ.* (1955), 6, 233–238.

54. Wrenn, C. Gilbert. "Status and Role of the School Counselor," *Personnel Guid. J.* (1957), 36, 175–183.

55. Wrenn, C. Gilbert. "The Selection and Education of Student Personnel Workers," *Personnel Guid. J.* (1952), 31, 9–14.

16

The Counselor Menagerie, or What to Avoid in Counselors

Stanley W. Niehaus, Ed.D.*

Ever since someone pushed the panic button when the Russians shot off Sputnik back in 1957, counselors have been popping out of training centers faster than a hatchery programmed for a 28-hour day. Everyone, it seems, has been climbing onto the counseling bandwagon in order to get into the act. So much myopic attention has been centered on what training counselors should have and from whence they should get it, that there is an increasing concern that not nearly enough attention has been given to what counselors should *not* be. Unfortunately, this inappropriately aimed preoccupation has contributed to the unleashing of a hoard of shaggy rabbits who aspire and claim to be counselors. It is now high time that a long, hard look be taken in the direction of what should *not* be included in the background and personality characteristics of counselors. As in other fast-emerging professions, too many alleged counselors have emerged ahead of their accomplishments and capabilities.

As a consequence of the recent and rapidly expanding demand for counselors, a veritable Noah's Ark has come sloshing over the horizon. After 40 days and 40 nights of rain and scarcity of counselors, the Ark has now touched land. At the lowering of the gangplank, off march an assortment of counseling varieties and types the likes of which civilization has not hitherto beheld. With bright and beady eyes, this miasmic procession moves forth onto the dry and productive land of a currently expanding counseling-awareness to seek its habitat and fortune. From high up on a limb above the water line, one can look down and behold the species which have debarked. In one way or another they seem to have come off in the following order, not that the order was due to any planning; it was just a matter of who got there first. These, then, are the species which have come to ply their trade in the counseling kingdom:

1. The "Furtive Animal"—hides in his office most of the time—no one knows quite what he is doing. When startled, he has to be coaxed down out of a tree with a saucer of milk.

*Dr. Niehaus is Dean of Student Personnel Services, Illinois Central College. His article appeared originally in *The School Counselor*, 13:1:42 (October 1965), and is reprinted with permission of the author and of the journal.

2. The "Predator"—everyone needs counseling—sort of an over-achiever who is just oozing out all over—has a compulsion for entering into a counseling relationship.

3. The "Kickster"—a type of spasmodic eclectic who varies from week to week in his approaches to counseling.

4. The "Nosey Nelly"—to him, counseling is fascinating because he learns so much about what is none of his business—sort of a "buttinski" where angels fear to tread.

5. The "Gossip"—"I really had a tough case today. Did you know that etc., etc., etc.—but don't tell anyone that I told you, it would not be ethical, you know."

6. The "Problem Personality"—a high-grade neurotic imbued with terrifying dedication—feels that he is exceptionally well qualified because he too has problems. If he runs out of problems he sets about making some.

7. The "Bandwagon Rider"—an opportunist who keeps close watch on the emerging and receding educational trends. At one time it was the Smith-Hughes program, before that the NYA and before that the CCC. He has also been involved in distributive education, driver training and the physical fitness program. Now the tide seems to be flowing in the direction of counseling. When the trend moves toward bigger and better school bus drivers, he will stop counseling and start driving a bus.

8. The "Hobbyist"—one who has always loved to help boys and girls and who doesn't like to play bridge, enter sack races or feed pigeons.

9. The "Jammer"—also referred to as "The Huckster"—he is so busy telling who he is, what he is doing, and what his opinion is, that no one ever hears from the counselee.

10. The "Self-Justifying Professional"—exceedingly careful of his new-found professional dignity—has to remind himself and others constantly of how very, very professional he is. If he had his way, counselors would not counsel, they would just do research on counseling.

11. The "Unprofessional"—most willing to give advice, makes him feel like a big shot. Unwilling to assume responsibility for his counseling activities. "Sorry kid, but that is the way the cookie crumbles," or "The administration did it."

12. The "Attorney for the Prosecution"—one who snitches on counselees "for their own good." "Tell me about your problems." "By the way, you are suspended for three days."

13. The "Attorney for the Defense"—"There is no such thing as an uncooperative student, just uncooperative teachers from whom I must protect these innocent lambs." This one seems to look with suspicion on anyone who is over 12 years of age.

14. The "Fixer"—no such thing as channels or appropriate procedures. If the student wants to be transferred to that other class just put him there and let the IBM machine find out for itself.

15. The "Pal Counselor"—a type of lowest-common-denominator counselor who seeks to establish rapport by being less mature than the counselees.

16. The "Pygmalion"—"I counseled this sixth-grade boy. He was 22 years of age, with an IQ of 85. I have now arranged for him to enter college and study engineering."

17. The "Busy, Busy Bee"—he doesn't get much work done, but man, is he busy!

18. The "Logician"—all information worth knowing comes from a test profile. "According to your test scores, Mr. Jones, you are somewhat shy and retiring." Jones is cowering under his chair, but the counselor has not bothered to look at him yet.

19. The "Bucketeer"—has a bucket full of credits in everything from animal husbandry to structural dynamics. He insists that all of these courses be counted toward his specialist certificate in counseling.

20. The "Credit Picker"—through workshops and institutes there is no place like a sponsored summer vacation program.

21. The "Training Avoider"—he would rather fight than take even one course which he needs desperately. He has fallen asleep too close to the place where he entered.

22. The "Politician"—a promoter-type professional organization man with an ax to grind. So busy attending conventions and getting himself elected that he never helps anybody but himself.

23. The "Committeeman"—a type who feels insecure unless he is surrounded by a committee as fuzzy as he. He has a particular urge to participate in "grope" sessions.

24. The "Contract Jumper"—A "job hopper"—leaves his counseling job two days after school begins in order to work in a neighboring state at a higher salary. One jumper is reputed to have left because he did not like his room. Has had nine jobs in five years.

25. The "Good Sam"—naive to the point of stupidity. Could not find a gorilla in a zoo.

26. The "Recognition Seeker"—spends most of his time posing for pictures in the new guidance wing.

27. The "Moral Paradox"—a Jekyll-Hyde type who counsels by day and prowls by night.

28. The "Chameleon"—in order to establish rapport, gets lost in any group. In fact, he can get lost in a group of two people. "Call me Bob, I'm your buddy."

29. The "Particularistic Counselor"—a nitpicker—a voice crying in the wilderness, "Who am I? Who am I? Who am I?"

30. The "Gadgeteer"—always armed with some kind of counseling tool. He is intrigued with gimmicks, trickles and trifles.
31. The "Role Definer"—so busy defining his role as a counselor that he never accomplishes anything.
32. The "Bundle of Insecurity"—"Yap, yap, yap, I am very much concerned." So concerned that he never has an original thought or a productive idea.
33. The "Bleaker"—a bleak personality—a prophet of doom and gloom.
34. The "Pollyanna"—"Ha, ha, ha, so many people have so many problems. I just love to counsel them. I'm enjoying every minute of it."
35. The "Backlooker"—"Yes, I now have all of my academic trappings. It was rough, rough, rough. I have really accomplished something." This is the kind of Jasper who looks at the graduate candidate as if he is contemplating jumping off the Empire State Building when the candidate has the temerity to suggest that he too would like to attempt that rough program.
36. The "Tedious Timothy"—or "Fussbudget"—leaps about his office like a cat with the hives. Puts the client in such tension that he wants to counsel the counselor.
37. The "Quick Study"—at first he resembles a "nervous" intelligent hamster who is eager for knowledge. After a quickie eight-week course in counseling he becomes a veritable Oracle of Delphi. "By George, as I see it, etc., etc., etc."
38. The "Late Bloomer"—after coaching cross-country, track, and supervising study halls for 30 years, he decides he wants to become a counselor. He once took a course under Frank Parsons.
39. The "Good Old Uncle Ned"—grandfathered his way into counseling through courses he took in 1920. Students and faculty look upon him as sort of a mascot.
40. The "Helper"—"I want to help boys and girls." "I want to help people." This is the same character who misses his appointments and, if inconvenient, will not lift a finger to help anyone who really needs help.
41. The "Bird Dog"—one who measures his effectiveness by the number of scholarships he can extract and promote for his counselees. Seems to have his sense of values mixed up somewhere. Fails to recognize that to work or even to borrow for an education is not a fate worse than death.
42. The "Cream Skimmer"—is enthralled by the intellectually brilliant. Seems to be attempting vicariously to bolster his own insecure intellectual ego. The very thought of anyone with an IQ of less than 120 makes him ill.

43. The "Leveler"—considers anyone with an IQ of over 120 a personal threat and a menace to society.
44. The "Johnny One-Note"—a former chemist, or whatever, turned counselor, who allows as how anyone not aspiring to become a chemist, or whatever, is just not worth the bother.
45. The "Old Fraidycat"—a "gutless wonder" who won't stand up to anybody for anyone for anything. Rumor has it that he once had some convictions. He is now able to keep them well under control.

As one observes the inhabitants of this menagerie, the thought occurs that these are exaggerations and caricatures which might also apply to other educators. It is not the purpose of this commentary to be unkind or humorous; rather it is an attempt to focus attention on a situation which is tremendously important. In counseling as in the other educational and healing arts, the capacity for hurting always exceeds the ability to heal. It is indeed fortunate that counselors who are afflicted with the menagerie characteristics described are not prevalent. Nevertheless, even a few are too many.

It serves little constructive purpose to lay the blame exclusively at any particular doorstep. Everyone—counselors, supervisors, trainers and administrators alike—has contributed to and shares a responsibility in this matter. These problems have been perpetuated through loopholes and deficiencies. More care must be exercised by counselor trainers in the selection of candidates for counselor training. Academics per se are not enough. Someway, somehow, counselor educators must determine what kind of persons knock at the portals of this profession. Administrators have the responsibility to select their counselors intelligently. Practicing counselors must see to it that the ethics of their profession are upheld and promoted. Too often there has been a misplacing of emphasis on what is not practical or worthwhile. The ranks of counselors must be comprised of people who are emotionally stable, are imbued with a blessed sanity, are sincere, and are possessed with an articulate sense of dedication. They must be knowledgeable, with a broad frame of reference combined with specialized skill. They must not be so broad in outlook that they are hazy and indefinitive. Neither must they be so specialized that they are esoteric and impractical. Their value concepts must be realistic and in appropriate perspective. Insofar as possible, counselors should be:

Sophisticated but not slick
Objective but not disinterested
Articulate but not glib
Dignified but not sonorous
Sympathetic but not maudlin
Young in heart but not immature
Emphatic but not intrusive

Needs yet to be met include:

1. More specific definition of what is expected by school or agency consumers of counselors' services.
2. More standardization of training course descriptions and terminology.
3. More experience and training for counselors in the humanities and the social sciences.
4. More experience in the practical, workaday world.
5. Better understanding and knowledge of the local community.
6. A sharpened sense of professional responsibility on the part of those now working in any area of the counseling profession.

This is indeed a big order. Yet any profession, if it has a right to exist and a hope for survival, has no choice but to face up to its responsibilities. If the counseling profession fails to assume these necessary tasks, it could very well become impaled on a picket of its own devising. The required investment for achieving appropriate goals should yield dividends which could accrue to the benefit of both the individual and society.

17

The Back Door Approach to Becoming a Counselor

Beverly B. Swan, Ph.D.*

The guidance movement came into being as a direct result of one man's impatience with a system which provided no help to students with their choices of occupational goals. Self-knowledge and long-range planning were stressed by the pioneers in guidance. As the movement gained impetus, it captured the imaginations of educators and was found to fill a real gap in the process of preparing youth to take suitable places in the adult world. Slowly, the concept has widened. Some original goals seem to have been abandoned. Other ideas about services to be provided have been advanced. Occasionally, feelings of disloyalty to the founding fathers have drawn members of the guidance profession back to a restatement of the original purposes of the Vocation Guidance Bureau. Whenever the stresses are placed on the need for more scientists or the desirability of providing vocational education for potential dropouts, the pendulum swings back to Parsons.

It seems strange that high school counselors are not encouraged to give educational and vocational facts about their own profession to students. It seems equally strange that counselor educators and supervisors appear determined to make entry into the counseling profession as difficult and as devious as possible for those who show a budding interest in it. In order to become a high school counselor, the aspirant must first be educated for some other job in education. He must prepare to teach English, mathematics, or history. Then he must actually enter into his second-choice profession and achieve experience in it. After that, he may pursue a graduate course which will lead him to certification as a counselor.

The skills demanded of teachers are not necessarily those demanded of counselors, and the achieving of competence in the teaching of subject matter has little bearing upon the achieving of competence in the skill and techniques of counseling. It is even possible that acquiring the necessarily authoritarian techniques of classroom teaching inhibits the development of the required "accepting" techniques of the counselor.

*Dr. Swan is Consultant in Guidance and School Psychology, Florida State Department of Education, Tallahassee. Her article appeared in *Clearing House*, 40:70 (October 1965), and is reprinted with permission of the author and the journal.

Most of the state certification standards for guidance personnel require that a prospective counselor prepare to teach and enter into a teaching job for at least a year. Many require more than a year's teaching experience. After that probationary period as a teacher, the candidate may return to graduate school and prepare for the quite different specialization as counselor. A question may be raised here as to the motivation to teach if such a job is viewed primarily as a stepping stone to another career and not as a career in itself. It may be that the counselor-candidate's lack of real interest in classroom teaching will prevent his doing an acceptable job with the students who study with him during his "qualification" period.

Returning to graduate school may work unusual hardship on the counselor-candidate. If he elects to attend a series of summer sessions, he prolongs the preparation period and confronts the added disadvantage of being unable to avail himself of a unified program. There is learning loss to be compensated for from summer to summer, and the ever-present possibility that it will not be possible to return to the university every summer for a period of several years. If he chooses to leave his job and return to graduate school to obtain a unified and cohesive counselor-preparation program, he may face personal and economic inconvenience and the disruption of a smooth family life. It is possible that many potential counselors are "lost in the leap." The chasm is too wide; their jump-power is inadequate.

If such circuitous educational routes were the practice in other professional fields, counselors who must work with students in vocational choice and preparation might find justifiable reason to criticize. If, for instance, the prospective physician were required to prepare for a medically-related profession such as physical therapy and to enter into the practice of that profession before he were considered an acceptable candidate for the graduate preparation of medical school, much time and many prospective physicians would be lost. Other professional-school educators work under the assumption that one does not have to practice in a related area in order to understand its dynamics. Not only do medical students receive instruction in related areas, but they also serve an internship period in which they may profit from close observation of the functions of medically-related specialties. This time-tested practice seems to have served adequately the need for understanding the role of other specialists within the field of a responsible profession.

Careful thought should be given to the reasons which support the preparation detour which is required of aspiring counselors. There may be a tendency on the part of those who have entered the counseling profession to believe that the route which they took is not only the best preparation for the job but the *only acceptable preparation. The psychological need to believe in one's own competency and therefore in the method by which the*

competency was attained should be apparent to the average college sopho-
more.

Postponing the time when study toward guidance certification is encouraged serves an additional purpose which is usually considered to be
"good." The stereotype of the usual counselor is of a person who has passed
the first blush of youth. "Maturity" is thought to be desirable for those
who enter into the counseling profession. There are, however, some unresolved issues surrounding the concept of "maturity." It is possible that one
does not achieve maturity by the simple accumulation of years. There is no
research which establishes the fact that a 35-year-old counselor is, ipso
facto, a "better" counselor than one who is ten years or more younger. No
one has yet determined who the "better" counselors are, much less defined
the many variables which contribute to the state of being "better." If the
job of the counselor were to dispense advice, it might be true that a seasoned
and mature person with many years of experience in a variety of life's situations could tell very young students which of several courses of action would
constitute the wisest choice. Since, however, advice-giving is not the function of the counselor, age and experience should have little bearing on the
kinds of counseling techniques which generally are considered within the
profession to be desirable ones.

It may be that the guidance profession has arrived at its standards for
counselor certification as a result of expediency. When the demand for
counselors far exceeded the supply in the years immediately following
World War II, the prospect of educating persons in both an undergraduate
and a graduate program seemed too time-consuming. It seemed at the time
far better to seek candidates for counseling jobs who had at least completed
the undergraduate program and urge them to qualify for counseling jobs
by undertaking graduate courses. Since some undergraduate prerequisites
in education were deemed necessary for the building of an acceptable counselor education program, it seemed natural that teachers be encouraged to undertake such graduate preparation. Now that the demand for
counselors has been at least partially satisfied, expediency need not necessarily determine the selection of candidates. We may have reached the time
when the goals of counseling should determine the methods used to prepare persons for the job to be done.

Perhaps because of expediency, when teachers who were considered
personally qualified for the job were sought out by their principals or supervisors and encouraged to seek the education which would prepare them to
be counselors, an element of false humility was introduced into counselor
selection and preparation. It has come to be considered more seemly for
someone else to urge the startled and wide-eyed teacher to enter into a
counselor preparation program than for the aspiring counselor to be self-
nominated. Anyone who chose for himself the job of counselor may be

regarded with some distrust by established members of the profession. However, no one seems surprised when men offer themselves as candidates for public office, declaring that they consider themselves competent to assume a responsible position. Since one of the cornerstones of the counseling philosophy is that help in achieving self-understanding is forthcoming from the guidance program, it seems a little incongruous to declare that a student should not decide that his strengths and competencies may lie in the counseling field. If a person declares himself competent to assume leadership functions on the basis of certain self-understandings, why may not similar self-understandings help another to determine his capacity for a counseling function?

The time may have come for counselors to start practicing what they preach. Perhaps counselors should help young people select and prepare for entrance into the counseling profession. Now that guidance services are well established in most secondary schools, high school students have had adequate opportunity to observe the work of the counselor. They may be able to decide, on the basis of this observation, that the job of the counselor is attractive to them, and want information about how to enter into this employment. Since goal-directed young people would seem to make better candidates than those who just drift into the profession from other jobs, we need to seek ways in which plans for counselor preparation may be made by the high school student.

A five-year planned program leading from high school graduation to the business side of the counselor's desk is a reasonable and realistic goal. The undergraduate "enabling" courses might include such studies as child development, adolescent psychology, the history and philosophy of education, sociology, psychology, economics, marriage and the family, and human biology. Such a spectrum of courses might serve as excellent background for the specialized guidance courses which would be undertaken immediately after the baccalaureate degree was attained. Such course content might also cut down on the time needed for graduate preparation, since much of the time in graduate school is devoted to "shoring up" the deficiencies of an undergraduate program. An internship served in a school setting is designed to provide the necessary insights into the practices and policies of other educational specialists as well as to gain deeper understandings of the functions involved in the counseling job itself.

It may be that those in leadership positions in the counseling and guidance movement should begin to reassess the mazes through which aspiring counselors are being led. With greater and greater pressures from both laymen and other educators for effective counselors, and with the ideal ratio of students to counselors shrinking before our eyes, counselor preparation programs should be strengthened and opportunities to enter into them should be broadened. It is inconsistent for persons who are interested in becoming counselors to have to be educated in another area and then spend precious graduate time in learning concepts which could have been learned earlier in the educational career. By requiring such divaricate preparation, the counseling leadership is placing a low value on the educational specialty which is guidance. If the profession is worth practicing, it is worthy of having a preparation program all of its own.

Catharsis

11A. Some educators tend to complain at length about the quality of their training. Others get into the act as well, including all kinds of professors, housewives, and even sailors. The reader, using the APGA guidelines, a local university's catalog, and his own experience and creativity should be able to design a curriculum for training counselors, including course titles, credits earnable, and brief course descriptions, which would be good enough to stifle complaints from all quarters.

11B. What realistic steps can the reader suggest that might be practical for practitioners to employ in causing a new counselor education curriculum to be developed and adopted?

12A. With reference to Dr. Arbuckle's paper, school counselors are trained, to be sure—but to do *what*? If social workers, psychologists, clergymen, and physicians all imagine themselves to be counselors, then what is the *counselor's* role? Don't we need to know this before we undertake to determine how he should be trained?

12B. People from various professions and occupations receive portions of their training in departments of guidance, associated with schools of education. Should counselor education programs be the same for all, or do future school workers have unique requirements? Specifically, what might the differences be? *Or is a counselor a counselor a counselor?*

12C. Dr. Arbuckle suggests that the master's degree, advanced certification, and the doctorate might represent three levels of counselor training. Can the reader foresee a time when all school counselors might hold the doctorate as prerequisite to admission to practice? There is at least some thought that dissertations, foreign language competence, and advanced familiarity with statistics represent irrelevancies in the training of school people, and thus have no place in Ed. D. programs designed for the practitioner. Can the reader suggest meaningful alternatives in doctoral-level preparation?°

12D. Dr. Arbuckle refers to the statement of the American Psychological Association on the training of counselors. Is it really appropriate that APA, even through its Division of Counseling Psychology, undertake to concern itself with the training of school counselors? What effect do APGA,

°For another discussion of this question, see R. S. Dunlop, "Not Enough Doctors in the Schoolhouse," *Journal of Secondary Education*, February 1968.

ASCA, NEA or AFT have upon the training of psychologists? Or are school counselors really just junior-grade psychologists, properly under the jurisdiction of senior psychologists?

12E. Dr. Arbuckle refers to a 1955 study in which it was found that somewhat over half of the colleges offering counselor training included supervised practicum as a part of the program, and suggests that "only a few institutions could probably report that supervised experience was given for all master's candidates." Conditions have changed since 1955; however, a basic question remains: why do we permit marginally trained people to practice? What pressure do *practitioners* bring to bear upon colleges which offer short-cut programs? Must we tolerate inadequate preparation because the demand is great? Is incompetent service better than no service? To what extent do we concern ourselves with public needs, those of the clientele with whom our poorly prepared brethren will deal?

12F. How might the American School Counselors Association (ASCA) play a more effective role in the area of counselor training, certification, and admission to practice? *Should* ASCA play such a role?

13A. Dr. Meyering indicates that 90 per cent of the counselor's time is spent in educational and vocational counseling, and that 90 per cent of the training effort is related to educational and vocational counseling applications. Is this statement consistent with the reader's experience? In either case, is the main thrust of the training experience appropriate in terms of demands of the job? Or are "demands of the job," probably defined by administrators, sensible criteria for what should be included in training?

13B. Readers who reacted to item 11A, devised a curriculum for the training of counselors. In what ways might Dr. Meyering's paper affect that proposed curriculum? What changes might be proposed now, by the reader? If Dr. Meyering's proposals suggest no changes in the reader's curriculum, how does the reader react to the proposition that counselor educators are uncreative, tradition-bound, etc.?

14A. Dr. Keppers feels that "Counselor educators must and will be held responsible for not only the quantity but the quality of the counselor preparation programs and as a consequence certification of counselors." How does the reader feel about the involvement of practicing counselors in this connection? Honestly, how does the reader regard counselor educators as a group? Are they colleagues who work in a different setting, or are they college professors primarily, with allegiances and problems other than those seen as important by school practitioners?

14B. Dr. Keppers appears to prefer working with established groups (such as NCATE) to the notion of groups of counselors undertaking to evaluate their own training programs and presenting suggestions as to the later training of others. Which approach seems to the reader to offer greater opportunity for professional growth? How about cross-fertilization—counselor graduates of College A evaluate the training program at College B?

14C. What possible justification is there for the requirement in several states that potential counselors have work experience in settings other than the school? Why do practitioners permit such requirements to exist?

14D. What point is there in having multiple levels of counselor certification—or even two such levels? Is it not true that one is either qualified to practice or he is not? If he is not qualified to practice, what business has he offering services in a school under a lower-level certificate?

14E. If multiple-level counselor certification is defended, is it then assumed that counselors will deal with different sorts of client problems, diverse in terms of complexity? Will there be salary differentials? Will marginally qualified persons be permitted to assume supervisory positions? If multiple-level certification is opposed, then what might the reader suggest as means of meeting demands in schools for counselors?

15A. Dr. Hill quotes another writer who has likened counseling to kissing, in the sense that neither require selection and training prior to practice. What are some ways in which counselors might communicate their unique preparation and skills to the lay public?

15B. Attention is drawn by Dr. Hill to the problem which Dr. Buford Stefflre has called the creation of counselors "by the laying on of administrative hands." What can individual counselors do about this grotesque practice, with their own colleagues, in their own buildings, and in cooperation with counselor educators?

15C. Dr. Hill points out that various schools expect various things of their counselors, and intimates that in many cases the occupational responsibilities of counselors have little reference to the professional training which these persons have undergone. What can practitioners do about this? What are some realistic means of seeking relief? Can the reader come up with some methods which are *not* necessarily "realistic" but which are far out, idealistic, theoretical, wild-eyed?

15D. According to Dr. Hill, the assessment of a trainee's potential is, in some colleges, "loose and unplanned." Is rigor desirable in the training of counselors? If so, how might practitioners arrange for the introduction of rigor in counselor education programs, if little exists? What responsibilities must be assumed by practitioners, in the reader's judgment, for the conduct of training programs and admission to practice?

15E. Dr. Hill says, "It is clear that the school counselor profession faces a serious problem in seeking to keep up with the demand for guidance workers while, at the same time, trying to maintain reasonably high train-ing requirements." React to the following proposition:

> "Dr. Hill's statement is irrelevant. Highly qualified applicants will be available for all schools where compensation, autonomy, and working con-ditions are commensurate with training brought by the professional school counselor to his position. Schools willing to attract qualified people will get them. The profession can't be cheapened, nor can it allow me-diocre practice in its name, because of local mediocrity in salary and other considerations."

16A. Dr. Niehaus has given us an impressive list of undesirable coun-selor "types." If counselors were selected by counselors, rather than by administrators, might these "types" be so prevalent? If counselors were dominated numerically by Bundles of Insecurity (Type 32), might they not tend to approve only other Bundles of Insecurity for employment?

17A. Dr. Swan tells us that "counselor educators and supervisors appear determined to make entry into the counseling profession as difficult and as devious as possible." Is it possible that Dr. Swan is blaming counselor edu-cators and supervisors for matters outside of their control? Might the blame better be placed at the doorstep of lay boards of education and lay creden-tials committees which, incredibly enough, set standards for admission of counselors to practice? What might counselor educators and supervisors do to create better circumstances? What might *practitioners* do?

17B. Setting aside the argument over whether or not teaching experi-ence is desirable for school counselors, can the reader suggest some *other* ways in which the trainee might get the broad experiential background in education which most would regard as desirable?

17C. What might happen to counseling as a school profession if teachers decided not to allow persons to engage in classroom practice if their career goals lay in areas other than teaching?

Professionalism, Autonomy, and Competence in School Counseling

PRESENTING PROBLEM

The assumption is made at the outset of Part III that professionalism is preceded by broad areas of autonomy for the practitioner, and that before such autonomy may be assumed by him, the occupational group of which he is a part must demonstrate that it is competent in the performance of whatever tasks it assumes responsibility for and that it has developed means of promoting competent performance and of protecting the public from the incompetent practitioner.

Any close examination of school counseling shows all too clearly that we lack many of the criteria commonly accepted as evidence of professional standing and that we are far from enjoying the recognition afforded by the public to occupational groups composed of such workers as attorneys, accountants, barbers, beauticians, and others who train and license each other and monitor occupational practices so that the grossly inadequate are not inflicted upon the public. Given competence, considerable autonomy is often granted the vocation by a public which is willing to say that the practitioner knows more of the specialty than the layman, and reliance is placed in the specialized worker's judgment and ability. From these bases, professional standing may follow, depending upon various other criteria.

The value judgment is made here that school counselors are interested in professionalizing, that many of us are willing and anxious to work toward that evidence of occupational maturity so commonly associated with the helping vocations, and that we recognize that becoming a profession will take a great deal more than simply hanging a label on ourselves and making assumptions which are not necessarily shared by others.

The papers in Part III have been selected with a view toward presenting a spectrum of opinion relating to the question of professionalism of the school counselor, the autonomy which should be his, and the question of competence in professional school counseling practice. The papers should all stimulate counselors to discussion, should provoke varying amounts of controversy among readers, and may in some cases antagonize even the most open and progressively-oriented practitioners.

In the first paper, Dr. Mona B. Shevlin defines professionalism with special reference to its legal implications and particularly to privileged Communication. She analyzes counseling in the light of these criteria. Next, some blunt views of the banal way in which the term "professional" has been misused in education are discussed by Dan Fulks, an elementary school principal, who challenges his readers in several ways.

A variety of problems inherent in professionalism is discussed by Dr. Buford Stefflre, of Michigan State University, in the third paper of this collection. This overview is followed by an article devoted to the question of what professionalism is and what counselors might do to achieve professional status. Dr. C. C. Dunsmoor, one of whose papers appears in an earlier section, is present again—this time with a lively call for counselors to exercise vigor in establishing themselves professionally.

Problems encountered by the new counselor, just beginning his office practice, are dealt with by Dr. Bernard A. Kaplan, Jr., who is associated with the New Jersey State Department of Education.

Two contributions bear directly upon the question of the professional person's need for autonomy in determining how he will function in his unique occupational role. Dr. James R. Barclay, of California State College at Hayward, discusses in detail the matter of attacks leveled by vigorous but often unenlightened persons against testing and counseling in the public schools; and the whole range of the rights of educators to be free from irrelevant interferences of various sorts in their professional practices and personal lives is stated with emphatic clarity in the "Bill of Rights for Teachers," a publication of the American Federation of Teachers.

Part III's final paper relates to the matter of counselor autonomy and competence, and details a variety of ways in which each might be monitored and governed by appropriate professional people without interference either from laymen or other school personnel who are perhaps ill-equipped to make such judgments.

The following questions are central to many points raised in this section of the book, and attention to them at this stage would seem desirable if they will help the reader to maintain focus as he proceeds through the materials presented.

How responsible should the counselor be? As responsible as a *professional person*?

If professional training in education is less than desirable, what can be done about it?

Where stand the teacher and the counselor in the "Education Establishment"?

What about "professional identification" and the counselor?

What professional model does the counselor emulate?

How much autonomy should the counselor insist upon?

How might autonomy best be achieved?

What are the relationships among autonomy, professionalism, and competent service?

To what extent should professional judgments be subject to lay control? How may the public best be assured that professional judgments (such as those made by the counselor, teacher, or administrator) are sounder than their own?

To what extent should classroom teachers be autonomous, and what role must counselors play in defending that autonomy?

What relationship is there between the *rights* of educators and their *responsibilities*?

Who should evaluate the counselor's competence? How?

18

The "Professionalization" of Guidance Counselors

Mona B. Shevlin, Ph.D.*

The author's attempt to reconcile various definitions of the concept of a profession has led to a rather frustrating conclusion, to wit: published definitions and the supporting statements of elements which constitute a profession are dependent upon the particular occupation seeking public recognition as a "profession." For instance, it has been stated that:

> By definition, a profession is a service. A professional worker is required to have certain knowledge, and he is expected to possess certain knowledge, and he is expected to have certain skills, but very important also is the fact that he is designated by society as the person responsible for performing certain serviceable acts.[1]

Profession has also been defined as a calling or vocation, especially one that requires a good education.[2] It has also been asserted that professional status has been ascribed chiefly on the basis of earning power.[3] Perhaps an accurate, although uncomplicated definition is contained in *The Practical Standard Dictionary*:

> An occupation that properly involves a liberal education or its equivalent and mental rather than manual labor . . . Hence, any calling or occupation other than commercial, manual, etc., involving special attainments or discipline, as editing, music teaching, etc. . . .[4]

*Dr. Shevlin is Assistant Dean for Admissions and Counseling, The Catholic University of America, Washington, D.C. Her article appeared originally in the May 1967 issue of *Catholic Education Review*, and is republished with consent of the author and of the journal. Dr. Shevlin wishes to call attention to two companion articles, published in the February and March 1967 issues of *Catholic Education Review*.

[1] George Pierson and Claude W. Grant, "The Role Ahead for the School Counselor," *Personnel and Guidance Journal*, XXXVIII (November 1959), 207. Although this definition would apply to bootblacks, golf caddies, baby sitters, steeplejacks, garage mechanics and perhaps even sanitary engineers (formerly known as garbagemen).

[2] *Webster's New School and Office Dictionary* (Greenwich, Conn.: Fawcett Publications Inc., 1963), p. 578.

[3] Herman J. Peters, Colins W. Burnett, and Gail Farwell, *Introduction to Teaching* (New York: The MacMillan Company, 1963), p. 173. Earning power is seen as one of many variables which serve to identify a profession.

[4] Funk and Wagnall's, p. 1045.

Certain definitions of a profession recognized by the law are contained in Black's *Law Dictionary*:

> A vocation, calling, occupation or employment involving labor, skill, education, special knowledge, and compensation or profit, but the labor and skill involved is predominantly mental or intellectual, rather than physical or manual. (citation omitted) The method or means pursued by persons of technical or scientific training. (citation omitted)
>
> The term originally contemplated only theology, law, and medicine, but as application of science and learning are extended to other departments of affairs, other vocations also receive the name, which implies professed attainments in special knowledge as distinguished from mere skill. (citation omitted)[5]

There is little doubt that the practice of teaching, including the specialized function of guidance, falls within the classifications involving social service practice. In the field of education, it would appear that discussions relating to professionalization are more concerned with the increased prestige or status of particular components of the field than with the general recognition accorded to educators. Relatively minor emphasis has been directed toward the legal effect of recognition of educational specialists as separate professions.

It has been noted that the degree of public recognition of an occupation has significant weight in determining the legal standard of care to which an individual practitioner may be accountable for actions directly or indirectly causing injury to others,[6] the criteria for requiring licenses or permitting certificates of qualification for the practice of certain occupations,[7] and the degree to which an individual practitioner may be accorded that status of an expert witness and thereby entitled to offer opinion testimony.[8] So far as the guidance counselor is concerned, the discussions relating to his qualification as a professional are perhaps more material in the area of privileged communications than in the other legal topics.

A review of the extent to which the legal privilege to refrain from testifying as to communications given in professional confidence suggests three basic qualifications which are essential to judicial or legislative sanction of such immunities for particular professional groups:

(1) The community recognizes and accepts the merits of a distinct occupation in holding itself out as a "profession";

(2) secrecy of the professional-client relationship is essential to the established discipline and practices of such professionals;

---

[5] Black, *Law Dictionary*, 1375 (4th ed., 1051).
[6] See: Mona B. Shevlin, "Guidance Counselor and the Law," *Catholic Educational Review*, LXV (February 1967), pp. 78–80.
[7] Ibid., pp. 74–76.
[8] Ibid., pp. 88–91.

(3) the community recognizes and accepts the necessity of nondisclosure of professional secrets even in cases where an individual member of society may be denied his usual legal right to compel relevant testimony from any person.

Initially these qualifications would not appear to differ materially from the four fundamental conditions set forth by Dean Wigmore. It has been asserted that Wigmore's standards are ambiguous.[9] In any event, the author submits that the concept that only such occupations as are recognized and accepted by the public as "professions" are granted privilege is a fundamental element which is lacking in the Wigmore test. As a practical matter, the extent to which an occupational group, by utilizing modern methods of public relations in the creation of a favorable "image" and the exertion of pressure on legislative bodies, has obtained public and legal approbation of its professional status, as distinguished from a purely theoretical appraisal of the merits of the occupation, is essential to an evaluation of the reasons certain groups have been granted or denied the privilege. The Wigmore test does not contain these considerations.[10] There is no doubt that the historical "learned" professions of law, medicine, and theology are generally recognized as being entitled to the privilege by the law as well as the general public. However, Wigmore himself states that the medical profession does not meet his tests although there has been no effort to abolish the medical privilege.[11] Some of the newer professions, which would appear to meet all of Wigmore's conditions, have had great difficulty in securing the privilege while other professions, which obviously fail to meet such standards in one or more aspects, have had considerable success in being accorded the privilege.[12]

Educational literature contains many attempts to define the dividing line which separates the professions from other occupations. However, these attempts have resulted only in the establishment of a complex of characteristics by which it is intended to distinguish between professions and occupations on the one hand and the relative status among professions on the other hand. These writings reflect a yearning on the part of occupational groups to become professionalized and the ambition of professionalization set forth in these writings are essentially self-serving, that is, a method of allowing one to hoist himself by lifting his own bootstraps. It is nevertheless incumbent upon an occupational group seeking recogni-

[9]Note 71, *Yale Law Journal*, 1226, 1230 (1962).

[10]It has been suggested that the reference by Wigmore to a community's evaluation of a relationship might more accurately have been phrased in terms of society as the community of lawyers sees it. Id. at 1234.

[11]8 Wigmore, *Evidence*, Sec. 2285, *McNaughton Rev.* (1961).

[12]Psychiatrists and psychologists are examples of the former, while journalists, accountants and public officials are examples of the latter.

tion to proceed in a manner by which both he and the community are convinced of the arguments in favor of professionalization.[13]

The eleven criteria listed by Dr. C. Harold McCully reflect a clear
consensus of the elements of a profession from the viewpoint of the guidance
counselor and it is proposed by the author, as a practical method of organization to present the arguments for and against professionalization of
guidance counselors within such a framework.

McCully defined a profession as an occupation in which:

1. the members perform a unique and definite social service;
2. performance of the specified social service rests primarily upon intellectual techniques;
3. society has delegated to qualified members of the occupational group
   exclusive authority to provide the specified social service;
4. the members possess a common body of knowledge which can be identified and can be communicated through intellectual processes of
   higher education;
5. entry into qualified membership requires an extensive period of
   specialized training;
6. the members as a corporate group assure minimum competence for
   entry into the occupation by setting and enforcing standards for selection, training and licensure or certification;
7. the members possess a broad range of autonomy in performing the
   specified social service;
8. the members accept broad personal responsibility for judgments
   made and acts performed in providing the specified social service;
9. emphasis is placed upon service to society rather than upon economic
   gain in the behavior of the corporate groups as well as in the performance of the specified social service by individual members;
10. standards of professional conduct for members are made explicit by a
    functional code of ethics; and
11. throughout his career the member constantly takes positive steps to
    up-date his competency by keeping abreast of relevant technical lit-
    terature, research, and participation in meetings of the corporate
    group members.[14]

The cause for professionalization of the guidance counselor will be analyzed
with respect to each of these characteristics.

1. The members perform a unique and definite social service.

It may be conceded that guidance counselors perform a social service.

[13]See C. Harold McCully, "The School Counselor, Strategy for Professionalization,"
Personnel and Guidance Journal, XL (April 1962), 681–689; C. Harold McCully, "The Counselor as an Instrument of Change," address delivered before the Secondary School Section of
the New York State Association of Deans and Guidance Personnel, Concord Hotel, Kiamesha
Lake, New York, November 3, 1963; C. Harold McCully, "Memoranda to an Emerging Profession," address delivered before the American School Counselors Association 1963, APGA
Convention, Boston, Massachusetts, April 9, 1963; C. H. McCully, "Conceptions of Man and
the Helping Professions," *Personnel and Guidance Journal,* XLIV (May 1966) 911–918.
[14]Ibid., p. 682.

However, whether such service is unique or definite has been the subject of substantial discussion and it must be admitted that no general agreement has been reached in this area. A study by Dr. W. L. Hitchcock attempting to reveal the responsibilities of a guidance counselor resulted in a negative conclusion to the effect that certain areas were generally considered as being outside the scope of the practice of guidance, but there was no concurrence as to what lies within the scope.[15] Nor can it be established that the guidance counselors' services are unique since psychologists and social workers, among others, perform substantially identical services.[16] The failure of the guidance counselor to meet the standards of McCully's first characteristic, unfortunately, is rather obvious.

2. Performance of the specialized social service rests primarily upon intellectual techniques.

Intellectual techniques are commonly defined to mean the utilization of the powers of perception and thought as distinguished from the senses or memory. The practice of guidance involves services ranging from the purely intellectual to the quasi-mechanical.

The five major services of guidance, individual inventory, counseling, information, placement, and follow-up, employ various techniques.

The individual inventory service concerns the acquisition of information regarding the individual student, his home and community, scholastic achievement, and social background. Although the technique of obtaining this information is quite mechanical in form, the material acquired is utilized and analyzed in a manner which must be considered intellectual.

The counseling service requires the establishment of a relationship with the student whereby the counselor attempts to help the student better understand himself with respect to his present and future problems.[17] The process demands a complete analyzation by the counselor and student together of the student's problems, and a joint determination as the possible solution thereof. Whether the counselor is directive, eclectic or nondirective, it is evident that the service is wholly intellectual.[18]

The information service is intended to provide information concerning educational, vocational, and social opportunities to students. The dis-

[15]W. L. Hitchcock, "Counselors Feel They Should," *Personnel and Guidance Journal,* XXXII (October 1953), 72–74.

[16]Compare the descriptions of the respective roles of the administrator teacher, school psychologist, school social worker and school counselor as contained in Walter Johnson, Buford Stefflre, and Roy Edefelt, *Pupil Personnel and Guidance Services* (New York; McGraw Hill Book Co., 1961), pp. 93–216, and Dugald S. Arbuckle, "Counselor, Social Worker, Psychologist; Let's Ecumenicalize," *Personnel and Guidance Journal,* XXV (February 1967), 532–538.

[17]James F. Adams, *Problems in Counseling: A Case Study Approach* (New York: McMillan Company, 1962), p. 1.

[18]Ibid., p. 2; Clifford P. Froehlich, *Guidance Services in Schools* (New York: McGraw-Hill Book Company, 1958), p. 207.

criminate usage of available literature by the sophisticated counselor involves some degree of intellectual technique. This is evidenced in the criteria established by the Guidance Information Review Service Committee of the National Vocational Guidance Association.[19]

The placement service is responsible for assisting the individual in determining the "next step" towards his educational or vocational goals and for affording the means of adjusting to post-school experience.[20] Unfortunately, this service is conducted, all too often, as a liaison or clearing-house function whereby job or education descriptions are matched against job or educational qualifications in a mechanical fashion. Needless to say, the efficient performance of this service necessitates a comprehensive utilization of mental skills.

The follow-up service involves mechanical techniques in the form of informational surveys concerning the educational and vocational experiences of former students. However, decisions with respect to the form in which such information is gathered and the effective utilization of the information received (decisions on curriculum revision, evaluation of the total guidance services, and the like) are undoubtedly intellectual.

Mechanical functions are a necessary and time-consuming activity of the guidance service as in any professional endeavor. However, the employment of intellectual techniques in effectuating the guidance services is the only rationale upon which a service separate from school administration and instruction can be justified. It must be concluded that this specified social service rests on intellectual techniques.

3. Society has delegated to qualified members of the occupational group exclusive authority to provide the specified social service.

Were it not for the word exclusive, the guidance worker would probably qualify under this characteristic. However, the classroom teacher, who is less specialized and trained in guidance matters, and the school psychologists and social workers are among others who are specially trained in limited aspects of guidance service. Cooperation among all of these individuals is essential. While the guidance counselor is the main force in this area, he is not exclusively responsible for total performance.

4. The members possess a common body of knowledge which can be identified and can be communicated through intellectual processes of higher education.

This characteristic is somewhat vague. The training of the guidance counselor must necessarily be accomplished through the facilities of institutions of higher education and he must be versed in a variety of sub-

---

[19] Willa Norris, Franklin Zeran and Raymond N. Hatch, *The Information Service in Guidance* (Chicago: Rand McNally and Company, 1960), p. 21.
[20] Ibid., p. 17.

ject areas including economics, statistics, sociology, international relations, personnel management, psychology, as well as the philosophy and methods of education. If "a common body of knowledge" is to be interpreted as a subject area exclusive to guidance, this characteristic is not fulfilled. If it is to be interpreted as a corps of subject areas in which guidance workers generally must be proficient, this characteristic is fulfilled.

5. Entry into qualified membership requires an extensive period of specialized training.

Ideally, guidance counselors should fulfill this requirement. This is evidenced in a report of the Committee on Professional Training, Licensing, and Certification of the American Personnel and Guidance Association which recommends that minimum counselor preparation include the acquisition of a master's degree predicated on study in the areas of personality organization and development, environmental factors in adjustment, individual appraisal, statistics and research methodology, philosophical and professional orientation, counseling, group guidance, and supervised practicum.[21] At present such a standard is far from uniform. Some states have no specified requirements, others require token formal training, and some have adhered to standards consistent with the American Personnel and Guidance Association recommendations.[22]

6. The members as a corporate group assure minimum competence for entry into the occupation by setting and enforcing standards for selection, training, and licensing or certification.

Except in those states which require licensing or certification of individuals included within the specific category of psychologists, this characteristic is not fulfilled. However, the requirement is definitely capable of fulfillment and efforts have been undertaken to establish standards of minimum competency for entrance into the work of school counseling. The prestige and authority of a national organization is a necessary prerequisite in this matter. The accomplishment of this characteristic will depend upon the full support of counselor educators, supervisors, administrators, and school boards as well as the school counselors themselves.

7. The members possess a broad range of autonomy in performing the specified social service.

"Autonomy" is defined as the power, right or condition of self-government and practical independence with normal subordination.[23] The school counselor is not, at present, at liberty to exercise such independent

---

[21]"Professional Training, Licensing and Certification," *Personnel and Guidance Journal*, XXXVII (October 1958), 162–166.

[22]Dolph Camp, *Guidance Workers Certification Requirements*, U.S. Department of Health, Education, and Welfare, Bulletin 1960, No. 14 rev. OE 25005A (Washington: U.S. Government Printing Office, 1960), pp. 1–107.

[23]Funk and Wagnall, p. 98.

judgment nor has he the degree of latitude and personal responsibility which could be considered as autonomous. This characteristic is also capable of fulfillment but not until such time as the counselor has demonstrated a proficiency to the degree that school authorities may deem to free him from direct and continuous supervision.

8. The members accept broad personal responsibility for judgments made and acts performed in providing the specified social service.

The counselor, of course, must accept personal responsibility for his decisions and actions within the scope of his specific duties. Primary responsibility, however, remains with the school administration. It may be assumed that increased responsibility will be delegated to counselors in direct proportion to the showing of their capability to assume such responsibility. Again, this characteristic is capable of fulfillment but the counsleor has shown no particular proclivity in this direction. The public stand of the American Personnel and Guidance Association in connection with the brief submitted as amicus curiae in the Bogust v. Iversin case, wherein the Association was apparently reluctant to admit that an individual counselor should be charged with a legal standard of care higher than that expected of the ordinary prudent man, did not enhance the cause for professionalization in the context of this characteristic.[24]

9. Emphasis is placed upon service to society rather than upon economic gain in the behavior of the corporate group as well as in the performance of the specified social service by individual members.

This characteristic may be more significant to a profession in which services are compensated directly by the client. However, a professional in the employ of a private or public institution should not be of less regard. The author submits that the very nature of the guidance counselor's duties, as generally regarded, are inconsistent and incompatible with personal economic enrichment. In most cases the qualifications of counselors would permit their acceptance into more lucrative occupations. The very choice of his employment within the education setting is a strong indication of his motivation for social service.

10. Standards of professional conduct for members are made explicit by a functional code of ethics.

The American Personnel and Guidance Association has published a code of ethical standards for persons functioning in the field of personnel and guidance.[25] Whether or not this code is "explicit" is questionable. However, it is clear that the code is not "functional" since membership in the Association is a matter of individual choice and there is no provision

[24]Shevlin, 80–83.
[25]American Personnel and Guidance Association, "Ethical Standards," *Personnel and Guidance Journal*, XL (October 1961), 206–209.

within the code relating to the enforcement of its contents. Furthermore, it is doubtful to what degree members or non-members are knowledgeable of the code or make positive effort to adhere to its provisions. Regardless of the shortcomings thereof, publication of this code is a laudable effort toward professionalization.[26]

11. Throughout his career the member constantly takes positive steps to up-date his competency by keeping abreast of relevant technical literature, research, and participation in meetings of the corporate group of members.

It is estimated that of approximately 50,000 full-time counselors, some 24,895 are members of the American Personnel and Guidance Association.[27] It may be assumed that the technical literature and research of the American Personnel and Guidance Association and its eight divisions is utilized by non-members as well as the active participants. Again, the realization for fulfillment of this characteristic is possible within the framework of the national organization; however, to date, the percentage of active participation is not sufficient to meet such standards.

A tally of the eleven characteristics with respect to the current activities of guidance counselors shows that only three can be answered in the affirmative. The majority can be fulfilled within the foreseeable future, if the members of this occupational field strive diligently toward this goal and are able to enlist the sympathetic support of members of related disciplines. The two characteristics which indicate the least possibility of fulfillment (that is, that members perform a unique and definite social service, and that society has delegated to qualified members of the occupational group exclusive authority to provide the specified social service) are fundamental to the quest for professionalization of the guidance counselor and deserve utmost concentration if the individuals operating in this field are sincere concerning their desire for personal and professional status. No one can achieve the dignity of a professional by his own reiteration in calling himself or his work "professional." Positive and dedicated efforts are necessary to effect such a goal.

[26]McCully, "Strategy for Professionalization," p. 687.

[27]Personal communication to the author from the Information Department of the American Personnel and Guidance Association, Washington, D. C., (March 1967). It may not be valid to assume that all of the 17,000 members are within the category of full-time counselors.

19

Professionalism: A Misunderstood and Maligned Word

Dan Fulks, M.A.*

The most misunderstood and maligned word in the public education vocabulary is the word "professional." Essentially the best definition is simply the opposite of "amateur." A person, regardless of what he engages in, is either an amateur, a novice, inept, or he is a professional. All other considerations are incidental.

But in the public schools of the United States, where amateurs abound, both the leaders and the led have inflated the meaning of professionalism until the word has become banal and literally without import. An intellectual excursion into professionalism as defined in educationese will explain why.

NEBULOUS TERMS

The code of the education establishment consists of a myriad of nebulous terms and phrases intentionally designed to enable the hierarchy to define professionalism at its own convenience and its own terms. A random sampling of these terms and phrases reveals the following abstractions: dedication, minimum of a bachelor's degree, professional workshops and conferences, unified opinion in problems, active support of professional associations, setting examples through acceptable behavior patterns, and non-affiliation with pressure groups. An examination in depth of these misty epitomes yields a number of significant revelations.

In an article in *Time* (May 6, 1966), Dr. Anthony Athos, Associate Professor of Business Administration at the University of Southern California, was quoted as saying that "You've got to be concerned—not dedicated, which sounds as if you're doing something you ought to do." Although careful reading of the *Time* article reveals that Dr. Athos is indeed a professional, the establishment continues relentlessly with its narrow profundities, dedication and professionalism are synonymous.

*Mr. Fulks is principal of Obetz Elementary School, Columbus, Ohio, and is completing his Doctor of Education degree in school administration at the University of Tennessee. Mr. Fulks' article appeared originally in the December 1966 issue of *Ohio Schools*, and is used with permission of the author and of the journal.

Because of such vagaries, the term dedication can become a convenient tool in the hands of local administrators for squelching rebellion in the ranks. After all, dedicated workers are doing something because they ought to do it, and therefore, should be content regardless of the trivia attached to their primary task. Moonlighting in service stations to support families, spending one-fourth of the working day counting lunch and picture money, filling out needless forms in triplicate, or making textbook inventories are not sufficient causes for grievances to the dedicated teacher. And often, if a recalcitrant teacher does have the audacity to complain, the administration will become apprehensive about the teacher's dedication and/or professionalism. This can happen only in public education.

Does the physician spend his valuable time checking whether there are enough clean sheets in the hospital? Does the aircraft commander pump gas into his plane before takeoff? Does the lawyer type his own legal briefs? The answer is no. These fields are inhabited by professionals—not amateurs.

The establishment defines competency for its adherents through the minimum of a bachelor's degree augmented periodically by professional workshops and conferences. Yet this degree may, and often does, consist primarily of nondescript courses in kindergarten theory, story telling, plays and games, and other hackneyed nonentities. Evidence of scholarship in significant academic disciplines is seldom suggested as a means toward professionalism.

MALIGNANT ORIENTATION

Since disciplinary excellence is apparently not a prerequisite to professionalism, the small malignant orientation continues during actual practice. Local boards of education will often provide released time and expenses for certificated personnel to attend workshops on inter-action analysis or mental health problems, but are very loath to provide the same benefits should a teacher wish to study the works of Thomas Carlyle. And often, a teacher who returns to summer school at his own expense to study American foreign policy or the life and times of Dylan Thomas is actually suspected of being avante-garde and something other than professional.

Moreover, the professional associations exhibit the very same provincialism by confining their workshops and conventions to textbook publishing company representatives and unknown speakers who rehash the same trite educationese. Seldom, if ever, are the arts and sciences, labor, history, or political science scholars invited to speak or participate in seminars where teachers are in attendance. Apparently professionalism can only be enhanced by keeping the education people engaged in their own native expertise.

THE PROBLEM OF UNITY

An amateur would probably find no objections to the statement that the professional teacher recognizes the necessity for unified opinion in problems affecting the future of public education. Professionals, however, will not accept this statement without reservations. When no sophisticated definition of just what the unified opinion should consist of exists, local groups of teachers can readily be asked to acquiesce to whatever consensus is developed in any given community. And if a member of the organization fails to accept the prevailing orientation, he may find his career at stake as the brand of "unprofessionalism" is applied smartly to his personal file. Thus any unruly member who prefers to think for himself is immediately threatened by the withdrawal of the sweet security of collectivism.

HIDDEN FALLACIES

In a further attempt to gratify all given forces, the professional teacher is asked to set a proper example through acceptable behavior patterns in his work and community life. Proper examination of this philosophy immediately reveals the hidden fallacies. While it sounds impeccable and impossible to criticize, it very carefully and deliberately fails to define proper behavior. Therefore, each local power structure has the liberty to evaluate morality based on its own peculiar emotions and experiences.

The existence and deployment of the rationale of "proper behavior" can cause teachers to be denied basic rights and privileges under the semblance of "unprofessionalism." Therefore, if a given community finds a teacher's behavior improper when he engages in partisan politics, expresses controversial views, supports racial integration of schools, or perhaps even supports the United Nations or the Supreme Court, then the local hierarchy can cast doubts upon the teacher's character with the full support of professional ethics.

The prevailing view of the education establishment equates identification with so-called pressure groups with unprofessionalism. And the meager salaries teachers universally receive are directly related to this non-pressure theory. While the group mouthpiece traditionally proclaims that teachers should earn perhaps $13,000 per annum, it produces little success in turning this dream into reality. While going up one side of the street proclaiming that professionals do not resort to pressure tactics, it goes down the other side beseeching local taxpayers to bail the teachers out of their sorry financial situation.

An average salary schedule in the public schools suggests that a 25-year-old married male, after spending some $65,000 on a college program that led to a master's degree (includes $10,000 per year he could have earned driving a truck instead of going to college), starts his career at something above $5,000. Should he survive the vicissitudes of the public schools, 15 years and 4 children later, he can earn the princely sum of $8,000.

And so the proud platitudes of the administration continue to calm the nerve cells. "The teacher is the key person in any school system. He is the priceless entity," proclaims the daily memoranda and the flyers sent home by the innocent children. Yet the salary scale peaks the teacher below $9,000 as the superintendent's salaries reach $20,000 and up.

But the question remains—who is the professional? In the public schools he is easily identified by his courage, conviction, and intelligence.

A REALISTIC APPROACH

Public education must begin now to take a realistic approach in its quest for professionalism. Representative leaders from all areas in the field should be drafting codes that reflect today's knowledge and understanding. Instead of emphasis on a provincial dedication, individual concern for a global humanity should be the consideration; instead of a bachelor's degree minimum, evidence of significant scholarship should be required. Professional workshops and conferences should provide the teacher with opportunities to participate in seminars that are broad in scope and significance. A unified opinion approach should be expanded to include and encourage the creative individual; the artist with character and guts who finds no comfort in phony artifacts such as 20-year pins and certificates of honor.

Acceptable behavior patterns should be defined in a broad statement which includes support for persons who affiliate with pressure groups. Indeed, this should be a significant part of any code of ethics. Malpractice in teaching, as it is in law and medicine, should be defined and arrangements made whereby offenders can be disciplined by their peers—and only by their peers through due process.

AT THE CROSSROADS

The field of public education is at the crossroads in its historic quest for professionalism. And education will be a profession when true professionalism is properly defined and demanded. These goals will not be achieved by waving magic wands or proclaiming that "all's right with the world."

20

What Price Professionalization?

Buford Stefflre, Ed.D.*

Several recent discussions have been concerned with the desirability of encouraging or requiring the school counselor to become more professional and the strategy to be used in achieving that goal [4, 5]. Systematic study of professionalization previously has been largely the interest of sociologists, and their conceptualizations may help us understand what we are now experiencing [1, 2]. This article is an attempt to look at the problem of professionalization in a sociological perspective which reveals some of the difficulties and sequences of behavior typically accompanying this process and to apply this knowledge to the situation presently faced by the school counselor.

IDENTIFICATION AS AN ASPECT OF PROFESSIONALIZATION

One mark of a profession is that its practitioners identify with the occupation—see themselves as wedded rather than temporarily related to the activities constituting the occupation. At the present time there is much evidence of a lack of identification of the school counselor with his profession. One indication of this lack is the nature of much recruitment into counseling which often results in a teacher becoming a counselor through a combination of largely accidental circumstances. A department declines in enrollment, a counselor is called away to another job, NDEA funds suddenly make possible the expansion of the counseling program—these and other, largely fortuitous, events determine that a teacher will be selected and placed in a counseling position. A second indication of lack of identification is the movement out of the occupation resulting from so called "waste" recruitment. Many counselors remain counselors only a few years while they gather their strength for the climb to the next plateau. Former counselors who are now administrators, supervisors, or college instructors are all evidences of "waste" recruitment in the sense that they did not have a lasting and firm identification with the occupation of the school counselor. It seems clear that at the present time most of the school

°Dr. Stefflre is a Professor of Education at Michigan State University, East Lansing, and editor of the *Personnel and Guidance Journal*. His article appeared originally in the *Personnel and Guidance Journal*, 42:7:654 (March 1964), and is reprinted with permission of the author and of the journal.

counselors in America do not identify with this occupation. Less than a third of them, for example, are members of the national organization devoted to their special interests—the American School Counselor Association. They think of themselves rather as teachers who are temporary refugees from the classroom or as potential administrators waiting in the wings for their cue.

One of the causes of this lack of identification is illuminated by the concept of the marginal man. In education, the most recognized, valued, and consensually accepted roles are those of the classroom teacher and the administrator. The counselor role is not as clear nor as well validated by educational history, and the other workers in schools may have some difficulty in classifying this marginal position. Is this marginal man—the school counselor—simply a teacher who has a new assignment; is he a psychologist who has strayed temporarily from his clinic; is he a sub-administrator who has not managed to place himself on the administrative salary schedule; or is he a kind of office worker who is giving prestige and dignity to what are essentially clerical tasks? Because his job may be seen as marginal, the counselor inevitably suffers from some isolation and segregation. He must continually tell himself that he is important to society, to the school, to the student. To dramatize his importance he may become somewhat obsessed with such matters as professionalization. His joining of organizations, his discussions of the proper balance between psychology and sociology in his training, his phobia regarding discipline and attendance enforcement all may be simply ritualistic externalizations of his feeling of isolation and segregation and his need to validate his role.

ELEMENTS IN IDENTIFICATION WITH A PROFESSION

The process of identifying with an occupation has been analyzed by Howard Becker and James Carper [1] into four elements. The first element concerns acceptance of the name of the occupation as a part of the self-concept of the worker. In our society, the individual changes as he matures from one who achieves his status through the name of his family to an individual who achieves his status through the name of his job. This shift implies a change of attitudes and an alienation from the past. With continuing career changes we have continuing alienations. As a counselor moves out of the classroom and into the private office some alienation from his former colleagues occurs. This process and concern is epitomized in the naming of the occupation for it has been said that the name of our occupation is our price tag and our calling card. Note that the term "guidance counselor" is now shunned by most all of us. The term "school counselor" is currently most commonly used but causes some twinges of embarrassment to the more psychologically oriented practitioner. The most promising label in terms of prestige seems to be "psychological counselor." (School counseling may soon be "out," psychological counseling "in"!) Labeling does not involve mere distinctions without differences for as soon as we think of ourselves as psychological counselors rather than school counselors we tend to be different and so to behave in different ways. To summarize, our identification with an occupation involves labeling which influences the self-concept which influences behavior through internalization of motives. From guidance worker, to guidance counselor, to school counselor, to psychological counselor, to psychologist is one possible path toward "professionalization."

The second element in this process of identification is the commitment to the task of the occupation. The attempt to clarify the nature of this commitment has resulted in sharp differences in viewpoints that are now testing the cohesiveness of our organization. Are we to be psychologists who would turn the schools into junior grade Menninger Clinics or are we to be consultants and resource people to teachers? Is it any wonder that we cannot agree on appropriate training programs when we have not yet agreed on the definition of our task? The counselor-in-training or the teacher accepting a counseling job cannot have an emotional and psychological commitment to the task of the counselor for it has not yet been clearly defined and accepted throughout the profession. What is done under the name of counseling is diverse and many splendored. Professionalization will require a degree of consensus regarding the appropriate functions of the school counselor.

The degree of commitment to the goals of the institution—in this case the school—which is the third element in identification would seem to vary a good deal from counselor to counselor. Some very "psychological" counselors may evidence little interest in curriculum, finance, and other "bread and butter" educational problems. They go to school as they would go slumming, with some curiosity but with little involvement. Other counselors may have a commitment to the goals of their institutions that does not make sufficient use of their uniqueness. Their attitudes and values may not be distinguishable from those of teachers or administrators and therefore may not add to education the flavor that should come from their specialty.

A recognition of the significance of the occupation to society is the fourth element in identification with an occupation. The nature of the significance may vary with the orientation of the counselor. It is the argument of those who insist on teacher training for school counselors that people who have this kind of experiential commitment to education see the significance of the school in a clearer light than do those who approach counseling from the field of psychology. Their opponents remain unconvinced and point to the importance to society of the process of counseling itself. The difference here would seem to be between those who emphasize the "school" in school counseling and those who emphasize the "counseling."

PROCESS OF PROFESSIONALIZATION

The sequence of professionalization involves predictable steps that have been identified by Herbert Biano [2]. The first step is the establishment of an occupational association and it must be remembered that the school counselor, as such, has had his own association for only a relatively few years. Second, there comes the process of name change which has already been discussed. The important point here is that the new name symbolizes the direction and process of change in the occupation. Third, a code of ethics is set up for internal control of the activities of the workers. School counselors have a code of ethics although it is of doubtful value considering the variety of tasks that the school counselor performs, the variety of settings in which he works, and the variety of sole expectations held for him by the community, the students, and other workers in education. The very existence of such a code, however, makes the counselor feel more "professional"—and probably even more "ethical"—such is the magic of incantations. Another step in the process of professionalization is control of the recruitment and screening of workers in the occupation. This control must be shared with the departments of education of the various states because the profession as presently organized cannot establish certification standards. Therefore the control in reality is divided among the universities doing the education and the states doing the certification. Obviously the power lies with the states but the influence of the universities is considerable.

CONSEQUENCES OF PROFESSIONALIZATION

As the education of the school counselors has become more specialized there are some who think that they have grown too far apart from the teacher; there are some who think that they are too much drawn toward psychologists; there are some who think the skills of the social worker are being duplicated. In any event, we need to conceptualize the relationship between changing the job of the school counselor and changing the other occupations in the school for it must be recognized that the school is a dynamic social system. In such a system the parts are interrelated so that changing one inevitably changes the others. Better-educated school counselors may threaten the teachers by seeming to belittle their level of training or may support the teachers by visibly demonstrating that these key education personnel know how to make use of auxiliary services. The psychologist may be unleashed to become more clinical or more research oriented. The administrator may need a higher level of executive skill to understand and manage a more complex educational system.

As an occupation becomes a profession its members select an appropriate "hidden audience" for which their role will be played. What is the hidden audience for school counselors? Some seem to be doing their job so as to merit the attention and the applause of psychologists. They identify with psychologists, they think of themselves as psychological counselors, they have little feeling for education, and may wince at being called educators (or worse—"educationists"). Other counselors may select as their hidden audience the school administrator and behave in a way to attract his admiration. Still others may select as their hidden audience teachers or students or the community. However, the number of school counselors who select other school counselors as their hidden audience would seem to be few. Our professional identification is so diffuse that we cannot select a model for ourselves from among ourselves but rather must look elsewhere for significant professional others.

CONFLICTS RESULTING FROM PROFESSIONALIZATION

As an occupation expands, and certainly ours is doing that, we are at first apt to get recruits from old occupations who are self-taught while only later will there be formal training and screening. We have seen this process in school counseling. Many of the "old-timers" were teachers who presumably taught themselves how to do the job of counseling. Some obviously did this very well and some obviously did it not at all. Most states now demand formal training and screening of new recruits. This change from self-selection and self-teaching to formal university screening and education leads to some conflicts. There may be a conflict, for example, within a professional association between its leaders who are very concerned about advancing professionalization and the rank and file members of the association who are less eager for changes [4]. It is possible for the association leaders to want and demand "advances" that its membership by and large resist. Do we have an example of that conflict in our own organization? Is the typical member quite well satisfied with a standard of certification met by a one-year training program and a generous grandfather clause? Is it largely the leaders of the association who ask for a more rigorous and extensive training program?

A second conflict that occurs is between the professional association and the association of other professions. We are now girding for conflict of this type. A guerrilla war against the American Psychological Association is already taking place and sadly straining the loyalties of many. Trouble brews with the National Council for the Accreditation of Teacher Education. School administrators in some states have effectively blocked or weakened regulations requiring certification of counselors. There may be still other associations whose interest will seem to conflict with ours.

A third conflict consists in the selection of one professional "fiction" from all of the possible "fictions" available. We have a conflict regarding the kind of fictionalized, glamorized image of the school counselor that we are going to accept and project. (This seems to be the basis of the disagreement between Dr. Kenneth Hoyt [3] and Dr. C. H. Patterson [6].) Is the idealized school counselor to be a psychologist working in the schools or is he to be an educator with a specialized guidance assignment? There may be other possible images that could be adapted for our purposes but until we agree to act as if one of them were real we are not going to become a profession because we are not going to have a clear image of what we think a counselor should be and do. It is obvious that this fictionalized image need not have much relationship to reality. Its only reality is that we agree to accept it as our idealized image. (The physician who works in the Veterans Administration Hospital, in the General Motors first-aid department, or in the Naval Recruiting Station may still maintain as his idealized fictional image of the medical doctor, the man in private practice going his appointed humanitarian nocturnal rounds.)

A final conflict is intrapersonal and results in growth or rigidity. During the period of change in an occupation some members will become more experimental and open-minded in regard to functions while others will become more worried and apprehensive. We might all examine our own reactions to the controversies regarding professionalization. Do we see this period of change as an opportunity to experiment with approaches that we previously could not try or do we see it as a threat to the familiar and comfortable? Certainly the currents that flow with professionalization have potentiality for good and for harm. Our definitions of progress as opposed to retrogression may be understood better through a personal examination than a professional one.

DANGERS OF PROFESSIONALIZATION

While, generally speaking, to be for professionalization is about as brave as being for motherhood or the flag, it is true that some dangers may result from the process. One possible danger is the assumption of an automatic and necessary harmony between occupational and societal interest. All of us are quick to scoff at the notion that what is good for General Motors is good for the country. Are we equally skeptical of this sometimes unstated relationship that what is good for APGA is good for the schools? While our demand for more education for the school counselor may reflect a concern for the student and society it may also reflect a concern for more prestige for the counselor or counselor educator and represent a justification for higher salaries, a kind of protection against job competition, or a method of legitimatizing aloofness and status. The notion that only altruistic motives lead us to demand more and more training for school counselors is naive. If we can spell out a tight, rigorous, and lengthy training program we can demand more money, more status, less competition. The movement is toward higher and higher certification standards and universities usually set their standards above the legal ones set by the state. Where is the proper balance between societal and professional needs? We could take the giant step and demand a doctor's degree plus appropriate post-doctoral experience for every school counselor. Or we could shrug off any need for additional training beyond a teaching certificate and piously repeat that after all "every teacher is a counselor." In striking the proper balance we not only need suspicion of the existing state of affairs but also considerable insight into our own motives. It is unlikely that we live in the best of all possible worlds but it is equally unlikely that our efforts to shape it nearer to our hearts' desire stem only from selfless concern for others. Perhaps we can see the problem better if we look across the fence at the social worker. Social workers insist on a two-year master's degree program and some of them believe that even more training is needed. In the meantime, many jobs that logically call for social work skills are being filled by completely untrained people because the supply will not fill the demand. Would it be better for society if we had somewhat less well-trained social workers filling a larger percentage of jobs that call for their skill or is it better that completely untrained people be placed in many jobs while well-trained people are placed in a few? Is it possible that sometimes what is good for us as counselors or as counselor educators and what is good for our organization is not necessarily good for teachers, for students, for education?

A second danger in professionalization comes from the fact that prestige is sometimes granted illogically. On occasions a kind of Gresham's law may operate so that the poor practice drives out the good. Prestige may come from putting on a cloak of wisdom so fine-spun that no one dares cry out "the emperor is naked." One result may be professional disassociation. As we become more identifiable do we tend to disassociate ourselves from teachers, from administrators, and from the total process of education? This may be a necessary consequence of the acceptance of our own identification or it may simply be a way of dramatizing our difference and our prestige.

Many groups as they rise in status are inclined to emulate the entrepreneurial professional rather than the employed professional. This may be happening even in school counseling. Perhaps we see the really good counselor as behaving more and more as though he were in private practice and less and less as though he were employed by a school system— becoming more and more rigorous and rigid about confidentiality and less and less concerned about school problems, more and more concerned about sibling rivalry and parent hostility and less and less concerned about curriculum and academic achievement. There may tend to be greater emphasis on the individual and the therapeutic functions rather than on the community and the preventative ones. As the counselor becomes better trained does he seek out personal-social as opposed to vocational-educational problems? Is he increasingly impatient (or defensive) in discussions concerning possible differences between counseling and psychotherapy? Does he see his work as remedial rather than developmental? Does he see the individual as more important than the group? Does he see the counseling office as the center of the school and the classroom as its periphery? Finally, does he depreciate the non-clinical procedures (that is, doing little things) and feel that he is only being fulfilled when he is doing "depth" counseling?

SUMMARY

In this discussion of professionalization we have said that there is at present good evidence that the school counselor still does not really identify with the profession of school counseling. He is often recruited accidentally and he waits sometimes impatiently to move on to other occupations. Part of his uneasiness as he works as a school counselor stems from the fact that he may be seen and may see himself as somewhat marginal to the central purposes of the school system. As he restructures his self-concept on his new job he must inevitably undergo some alienation from his teacher colleagues and some concern about which label he will wear and its influence on his self-concept and behavior. Will he think of himself as a guidance counselor, a school counselor, a psychological counselor, or simply a generic psychologist? What task will he feel committed to? Is he a guidance coordinator or a therapist? If the leaders in the profession cannot come to any agreement on this question, certainly it is not surprising that the counselor himself cannot. Will he have a commitment to institutional goals that reflects his unique training and function or will he feel alienated from the school? Conversely will he simply echo the values which could more appropriately originate from administrators and teachers?

Next, what significance does he see in his job? Is he somewhat embarrassed to be associated with schools and does he wish rather to be in a psychological service agency or is he proud to be a part of the task of education? As he goes about his work does he perform for a hidden audience of psychologists, of teachers, of students, of administrators? Is he aware that, because the occupation is changing, there will be inevitable conflict between his professional association itself and many of its members as well as between his professional association and other professional associations? What kind of a fictionalized image of an ideal or model school counselor will he support and emulate?

Some of the dangers of professionalization have been discussed. One danger lies in assuming that constant upgrading of the occupation is motivated only by the purest altruistic concerns. It is possible that in increasing the training necessary to qualify as a school counselor we may be simply engaging in a kind of academic featherbedding that permits us to ask for more money, prestige, and protection that we otherwise could have. And last, is it possible that as we become more professional we tend to think less about the purposes of the school and emulate more the private practitioner? Do we want to withdraw more and more with the individual student and deal with his personal problems rather than involve ourselves with the teacher, the school, and the goals of education? What price professionalization?

REFERENCES

1. Becker, Howard S., & Carper, James W. "Development of Identification with an Occupation," *Amer. J. Sociol.* (1956), 41, 289–298.

2. Biano, Herbert. "Professional Status and Professional Policies: A Heterodox Analysis," *Couns. News & Views* (1960), 12, 4–11.

3. Hoyt, Kenneth B. "Guidance: A Constellation of Services," *Personnel Guid. J.* (1962), *40*, 690–696.

4. Johnson, Walter F., Jr. "The Counselor and His Professional Education," *Personnel Guid. J.* (1959), 37, 694–695.

5. McCully, C. Harold. "The School Counselor: Strategy for Professionalization," *Personnel Guid. J.* (1962), 40, 681–689.

6. Patterson, C. H. "Which Way for the Guidance Worker," *Personnel Guid. J.* (1962), 41, 160–161.

21

Criteria and Goals en Route to Professional Status for School Counselors

Richard S. Dunlop, Ed.D.*

INTRODUCTION

In the preamble to its statement on ethical standards, the American Personnel and Guidance Association has asserted that there are ten "marks of a profession." These include such notions as the possession of specialized knowledge, preparation at the college level, the concept that the organization "constantly examines and improves the quality of its professional preparation and services to the individual and society," the statement that organizational membership and professional practice must be limited to those who meet established standards of preparation and competency, the concept of a life career, and the thought that the public recognizes and has confidence in members of the profession.

In his markedly significant text, *Education as a Profession,* Dr. Myron Lieberman [1] wrote on generally accepted characteristics of professions. He dealt, at least tangentially, with each of the premises of APGA's code but, in addition, suggested other characteristics which are not included directly in the APGA statement. Three of his important points are: (1) there is a broad range of autonomy for both the individual practitioner and for the occupational group as a whole, (2) there must be an acceptance by the practitioner of personal responsibilities for judgments made and acts performed by him, and (3) there should be an organization of practitioners governed by practitioners.

In addition to these characteristics, several other traits may be mentioned which appear to be common among the established professions. These include:

1. The notion that one who enters a profession subscribes to its ethics, holds himself responsible to them, and very probably takes some sort of oath to conduct himself accordingly.

2. The idea that the profession is self-disciplining and self-licensing.

3. Attitudes of courtesy exist within the profession which extend to protect and exalt the profession in members' interactions with one another and with the lay public.

*Dr. Dunlop is an Associate Professor of Education at the University of Missouri at Kansas Cuty.

4. Public understanding of the nature of the professional activity and the special competence of its practitioners is promoted through encouraging appropriate presentations of that activity through mass communications media and discouraging inappropriate, harmful, or misleading representations.

5. Practitioners actively advise the public in regard to their areas of special competence and warn the public concerning marginal, incompetent, or unqualified persons who offer services represented as being similar or equivalent to those offered by qualified members.

6. Training institutions are controlled, at least indirectly, by practitioners; and there is insistence that teachers in such institutions be, in the main, licensed to practice the profession and eligible for membership in associations which represent it.

7. Insistence that occupational titles associated with the profession be limited in use to qualified members of the profession is observed.

8. Prior to certification or licensure, a rigorous examination for competency must be passed at appropriate levels of performance by candidates.

9. Professional courtesies and interaction are limited in large measure to practitioners who are members in good standing of the appropriate society.

DISCUSSION

One criterion suggests that practice of a profession is limited to those who have met established standards of preparation and competency—to those who in fact possess and know how to employ certain specialized knowledge. But looking around, it is not difficult to see a plethora of "counselors." One sees used car counselors, negotiates with finance counselors, is advised by Mother's Day counselors, perhaps reviews dunning notices from his "friendly mortgage counselor." Even peddlers of real estate, when not busying themselves in the never-ending battle against adequate school levies, may call themselves "property acquisition counselors." ° If individual professional counselors avoid the active protection of their occupational identity from unqualified encroachments, they subvert their calling. Related to this is the matter of those hundreds of junior administrators, Super Clerks, and release-time teachers who have never undertaken to prepare themselves appropriately but who hold "counseling" positions in schools where standards for specialized competence may be lax or nonexistent. "Emergency," "postponement-of-requirements," and other forms of certification protection for the untrained practitioner, the corner-

---

° In a Missouri community's self-service laundry, a sign advises, "If the washing machine don't work, consult with the washing machine counselor."

cutting administrator, or the school board reluctant to establish attractive levels of compensation can be found without difficulty.

APGA's statement includes reference to the member's commitment to the profession as a life career, "as long as services meet professional standards." This criterion implies that professional people control for standards and discipline themselves. We should, then, face the question of what our reaction is—locally and at higher levels—when the practice of a colleague falls beneath acceptable standards, verges on the incompetent, or becomes unethical. Dismissal from the local Guidance Association seems an empty gesture, particularly if membership is open to "anyone who is interested in guidance." Rejection from the national association would appear to be equally futile, particularly since relatively few school counselors are members. And since we have evidenced a general reluctance to police ourselves, the disciplining of errant colleagues is left to administrators and to laymen on school boards. Our failure to meet another criterion of professionalism is profound.

Dr. Lieberman has suggested that among criteria of professionalism is the notion of

> A broad range of autonomy for both the individual practitioner and for the occupational group as a whole. . . . (There is) an acceptance by the practitioner of broad personal responsibilities for judgments made and acts performed within the scope of professional autonomy.

Yet in schools, the professional behavior of counselors is under surveillance and subject to the veto of administrators who may be totally without competence in the counselor's area of specialization. An administrator may insist upon reviewing student requests for counseling appointments, or he may want to initial routine class changes, or review correspondence mailed by the counselor, or invade the privacy of the counselor's files, or invent other means of interfering in the specialist's work. Professionally trained counselors may have spent years learning the skills of their specialty, but *how many are willing to insist upon autonomy to function within their areas of expertise, on their own responsibility, without interference from unqualified persons*? (The need for autonomous function within one's area of special competence is quite distinct from institutional requirements for competent administrative management; specialized function and management need not be locked in a death struggle nor should they be, but the responsibility and role of the practitioner should not be subordinated to the *vagaries of administrative structure*.)

Another generally accepted criterion of a profession is subscription to a code of ethics. But allegiance to APGA's statement on ethical standards is not required for state certification or for membership in the association. Graduates take no public oath (excepting possibly a negation of disloyalty) nor does anyone require even a private affirmation of the individual's intent to practice ethically or consistently with accepted procedures. Neither the profession nor the public have any kind of guarantee that practitioners will adhere to any standards whatever. We avoid a pertinent aspect of professionalism by default.

One looks in vain through APGA's statement on ethics for implication that counselors should be mindful of simple courtesy in dealing with one another and with followers of other educational specialties, especially in relationship with the lay public. Attorneys, by ethical commitment, must exercise "every honorable means to uphold the dignity and honor of (their) vocation, to exalt its standards and to extend its sphere of influence." No such commitment binds the counselor or any other educator. Thus, we have the spectacle of school people—counselors included—referring to each other disrespectfully in the presence of students and other laymen; of counselors and administrators pouncing into teachers' classrooms without invitation; of administrators and counselors permitting clerical and custodial personnel to speak disrespectfully of and to teachers; of educators of varying specialties arguing among themselves in public social gatherings over the extent of the superintendent's incompetence; of counselors and teachers regaling acquaintances with tales of students' inadequacies (one teacher made a fortune out of her wastebasket!), and so on. These kinds of behaviors demean rather than exalt our profession, and we invite condemnation by the sensible and avoidance among the sensitive.

Members of other professions make conscious efforts to keep the public aware of their expertise, and undertake actively to warn the public concerning tangential services offered by unqualified persons (physicians appear to have been so successful in this effort that their influence has extended to include virtually everything under the sun). But in spite of all the recent research on counselor role and the demonstrably confused attitudes among laymen as to what counselors are, efforts to educate the public in this sphere have been sadly neglected. They represent only a fraction of what must be done.

A profession typically controls its own training institutions. Teachers in such institutions are, themselves, qualified and licensed practitioners, for the most part; and, at least in medicine and barbering, some sort of practice is typically maintained. While counselor training institutions may be responsive to the demands of accrediting agencies, the effect of school counselors on their practices is limited at best.

In other professions we observe such phenomena as Bar and CPA examinations, medical boards, and tests to qualify applicants for registration as nurses, pharmacists, beauticians, and so on. Such examinations are supervised by attorneys, CPA's, physicians, nurses, pharmacists, hair stylists, and others with appropriate competencies. It may be true that the percentage of candidates who pass these examinations is enormous and that the relationship between test performance and skill is remote or at best unclear. Still, the administration of an examination for competence gives assurance to the public that persons without at least minimal skill will not be permitted *by their professions* to inflict services on an unsuspecting and trusting citizenry. No such examination is administered universally under the auspices of APGA, nor do state associations require profession-administered examinations prior to certification. Tests are sometimes devised and administered by local administrators or school boards, whose qualifications are uncertain, but he who fails the local test is able to seek employment in a neighboring district. Thus, neither the public nor the profession are protected against the profoundly incompetent, except through the offices of counselor educators and their various evaluational procedures. And in ludicrous fact, admission to practice is governed in nearly all states by laymen.

Finally, it is common knowledge that among established professions one does not gain acceptance to his professional society unless he has met all requirements to practice. Those practitioners who do not qualify for admission to the society are regarded as outlanders whose occupational existence is either ignored or terminated. Folkways in APGA are interesting to review, by way of comparison. One may become a member of APGA if he is "interested in and wishes to help promote the vocational aspects of guidance and personnel work." To be sure, such membership (through NVGA) does not include voting rights. To vote, the prospect must have a bachelor's degree and be regularly employed in guidance or personnel work. Non-voting memberships may also be obtained in APGA by anyone who is *interested* in college personnel work (ACPA), counselor education (ACES), teacher education (SPATE), or testing (AMEG).

Some years ago the Professional Training, Licensing, and Certification Committee of APGA formulated certain minimal standards for the training of school counselors—standards which have been and are still being expanded. Those early standards, with us now for over ten years, included possession of the master's degree, and course work in the following specific areas: personality, environmental factors in development, individual appraisal, statistics, research, philosophical and professional orientation, counseling theories, group guidance, and supervised practicum. One would imagine that compliance with these appropriate though minimal standards would be prerequisite to membership in the American School Counselors Association. But no. To become a member of ASCA one need only be doing something "directly related to guidance" for a third of his time; hold a bachelor's degree; and be the survivor of fifteen semester hours of graduate work, only eight of which must be in course work related to guidance. Surely membership in APGA, through whatever affiliate, should have some relationship to the criteria established by APGA as representing minimal competence. Surely membership should be consistent with criteria of professionalism as stated by APGA in its own statement of ethical standards.

GOALS

It is possible to suggest a number of steps which might be given our most serious attention for implementation if, as counselors with a firm sense of commitment we are seriously interested in attaining professional status and the public confidence and trust implicit in the according of that status, and if we are really prepared to accept the levels of responsibility associated with professionalism. Given an acceptance of these assumptions, it is possible to make the following suggestions.

1. We must be prepared to assure ourselves and the public that counselors are appropriately trained professional people.

a. The American Personnel and Guidance Association should create a printed "Certificate in Counseling," suitable for framing and display, to be awarded on request to any member who has completed minimal standards of preparation as specified by APGA, and a printed "Diploma in Professional Counseling," also suitable for display, to be awarded any member who in addition to minimal standards has completed postmaster's preparation of a defined quality.

b. Counselor organizations should make every effort to assure that at least two-thirds of the trainee's professional education is under professorial management of counselor educators who are certified to practice in the particular state, and who are holders of the Diploma in Professional Counseling.

c. Every local, state, and national effort should oppose the employment in school settings of persons who are not fully trained in accordance with minimal standards established by APGA, if the services to be offered by such persons, on a part-time or full-time basis, are implied by administration or by themselves to be of a counseling nature.

d. In order that there may be encouragement for counselors to be competently trained, APGA should publish annual books in which are listed, by state, community, and school, the names of counselors who hold Certificates in Counseling and Diplomas in Professional Counseling. Cooperation among counselors should be limited to persons listed in these books; and any school which allows unqualified persons to perform "counseling" duties should be listed and denied by qualified counselors any but the most essential courtesies.

e. State associations, working in cooperation with the national association and with close participation of counselor educators skilled in psychometrics, should cause to be created examinations covering all of the specifiable knowledges which should be held by and common to school counselors. These examinations should be completed acceptably by all persons engaged in school counseling or seeking such employment, and prior to application for either the Certificate in Counseling or the Diploma in Professional Counseling. Local schools should be advised by State associations when persons are employed by them as counselors who have not undertaken the examinations or who have completed them with unsatisfactory results.

2. Membership requirements of the American Personnel and Guidance Association should be modified so that voting privileges are enjoyed only by persons who meet minimal standards for counselor training as established by the American Personnel and Guidance Association.

3. We must work toward establishing responsible autonomy, discipline, and self-government in order that our services might be rendered with close regard to established professional expectations.

   a. Counselors in school districts should create Committees on Ethics and Standards, which would hear and review complaints and recommend for or against employment or dismissal of counselors, and monitor professional practices in the school district as they relate to the pupil personnel services.

   b. It should be a responsibility of such committees to encourage counselor membership in appropriate professional societies, and to evaluate carefully the qualifications of non-members to engage in the practice of the profession.

   c. We must make every effort to encourage the development of professional control of certification in the various states. Counselor certification might be the function of a sub-committee composed of certified counselors responsible to an educator-controlled board of education examiners.

4. We must give the most serious attention to developing an appropriate public professional image.

   a. It should be regarded as essential that counselor organizations undertake public information programs designed to communicate the counselor's role and specialized competence to the lay public.

   b. The public has a right to know the qualifications of those who serve it, and the practitioner has a responsibility to his profession to make his specialized competencies known. It should be expected that to serve these ends every counselor would display upon the walls of his office his diplomas and credentials; that counselors with masters' and doctors' degrees would place the initials of their degrees after their names in correspondence (as is the fashion of nurses, public accountants, certified life underwriters, motion picture editors, priests, and so on); that holders of the doctorate would use the title as an obligation to their profession; that counselor associations in local communities would arrange for plates to be affixed to the doors of counselors' offices specifying the counselor's full name and highest degree.

c. Every effort should be made by individual counselors and by their organized societies to discourage use of the title, "Counselor," by untrained persons, including untrained school persons employed as counselors, and to retain this title for the use of fully qualified practitioners.

5. Control of training institutions should be vested, in large measure, in practitioners through their chosen representatives.

a. Every department of guidance and counseling should create a committee of practicing school counselors which would advise training personnel regularly on changing needs in the field and offer constructive criticism of the counselor training program.

b. Active involvement of practicing school counselors in the training of candidates should be encouraged.

c. Counselor educators should be encouraged to engage in the practice of their profession. Their regular practice in the school setting should be regarded as a routine obligation.

Our dilemma, as counselors, is that if we expect to be regarded as professionals we must be prepared to start out on a lengthy and tortuous road leading toward that goal—and, on the way, become actively schizophrenic in a figurative sense: perhaps non-judgmental, non-threatening, and permissive with our clients as circumstances demand; but judgmental of ourselves and of those who would share our work, and responsibly tough in establishing and protecting our unique responsibilities and prerogatives as specialized practitioners. We can do no less. Our challenge, indeed, is to do a great deal more.

REFERENCE

1. Lieberman, Myron. *Education as a Profession* (Englewood Cliffs, N.J.: Prentice-Hall, 1956).

22

Yes, More Than Vigilantes

C. C. Dunsmoor, Ed.D.*

There comes a time in the life of a professional group, as in the lives of men, when we can no longer stand idly by and ignore or "forgive them for they know not what they do." And I, for one, believe that the time is here right now—not next week, not next month, not next year, but *NOW*.

In the past several years and with somewhat greater intensity within the past few months, it seems that there have been increasing numbers of "snipers" taking pot shots in the press, in the publications field, and on various homefronts, at such things as "testing," psychology and/or psychiatry as instruments of the Devil, guidance and personnel work as interfering with the rights of individuals (witness such books as *The Brain Watchers*, *The Tyranny of Testing*, and others with "innuendo-ish" titles).

Such books have just enough truth in them to confuse the lay reader or the slightly unsophisticated professional one. Mixed in with the elements of truth are many distortions of the truth, the taking of isolated items out of context, resorting to clever phraseology so often used by demagogic journalists to give false impressions, invoking sensationalism or argument, implying that a single misguided instance of questionable practice is the representative or typical practice of the profession, etc.

No one with a proper sense of professional values becomes unduly concerned about honest and justifiable criticism—in fact he welcomes it if it is made in a constructive way. But when accompanied by vilification often akin to slander and falsification, distortion or omission of related facts, this often damages materially the public image of what honest and dedicated professional workers are endeavoring to accomplish.

One might use the somewhat trite saying, "Don't throw out the baby with the bath water." Automobiles and airplanes kill people because of mistakes in judgment, equipment failure, and the like. But, with the millions of benefits we derive from them, we don't hear anyone clamoring for their elimination. Tests and counseling properly used by competent, informed, and ethical people provide benefits to millions of people, though

*Dr. Dunsmoor is retired Director of the Board, Cooperative Educational Services, Bedford Hills, New York, and is a former president of the American Personnel and Guidance Association. He now makes his home in Seminole, Florida. Dr. Dunsmoor's article appeared originally in the *Personnel and Guidance Journal*, 41:651 (March 1963), and is reprinted with permission of the author and of the journal.

there undoubtedly are isolated instances where their improper or indiscreet use may have harmed individuals or at least have done the clients little good.

It seems to me that there are several morals to this story, the first of which is to continue to expand our efforts everywhere toward the professionalization of "counseling." The Counselor Role and Function Study and the Counselor Preparation Studies, and others, are helping, to be sure, though this is a never-ending process.

A second implication is that we as a professional group and as individuals must launch both local and nationwide campaigns to put on the defensive, and wherever possible to remove the inept, the unethical and any misguided practitioners from our midst. We should not be merely in the position of "firemen" alert to "putting out the fires" of criticism and harassment which inevitably seem to break out in one community after another from time to time.

We must not be merely defensive and thereby "dignify" every little allegation leveled at us by endeavoring to counter it. But, let's take the offensive—now and everywhere—and start telling our story with a strong, vigorous, and continuous program of public information. Let's start a backfire, as it were, and stop our critics in their tracks or put them on the defensive instead.

We must assume the initiative and become aggressive in our efforts to serve and grow strong as a professional group. In this, YOU, TOO, have a vital stake—and, if you've read this far, you should be one of the "regulars" on our team.

23

The New Counselor and His Professional Problems

Bernard A. Kaplan, Ph.D.*

As a first year counselor, I had to seek help—the administrator was very weak in giving me needed information."

"If I had known guidance was anything like I find it to be here, I don't think I would enter it again. It might be this situation only—my hands are tied by the administration."

"Establishing and developing guidance program and acceptance are very difficult. . . . My greatest problem is establishing rapport with teachers and the principal."

The above comments are actual and typical ones of the new counselors about their first-year jobs.

The new counselor is very much in evidence in the field of education today. Since many inexperienced counselors are appearing on the guidance scene, the problems and difficulties they encounter in their introduction to their jobs are of great concern not only to them but to their employers, their former instructors, and the public they serve. It would be helpful to know what professional problems tyro counselors typically experience in their first year on the job. Subsequent modifications in training or in in-service arrangements can, hopefully, (1) lead to an elimination of some of the problems, (2) diminish the intensity and/or frequency of others, and (3) provide for recognition of still others as inevitable concomitants of the first year.

PREVIOUS INVESTIGATIONS

The first-year experience of beginning counselors and their in-service education have not to date been accorded much attention. Very few such references on beginning counselors appear in the literature. First-year reports of a diary or impressionistic nature have been made by Rosemary Buchanan [3] and by Dr. Mary Gilbert [5]. Dr. Dugald S. Arbuckle [1] has

*Dr. Kaplan is Associate Director for Ancillary Services, Division of Vocational Education, New Jersey State Department of Education, Trenton. His article appeared originally in the *Personnel and Guidance Journal*, 42:5:472 (January 1964), and is reprinted with permission of the author and of the journal.

considered problems common to beginning counselors, but these are limited exclusively to the counseling process and do not encompass the counselor's other duties. Dr. Wilbert Berg'[2] has attempted to define some aspects and levels of a counselor's development.

Educators commencing professional assignments in other fields have not, on the contrary, been overlooked. Many studies have been reported that focus on the professional problems of beginning teachers in general [11, 13], and in specific: beginning elementary teachers [4, 10], beginning secondary teachers [14, 16], beginning industrial arts teachers [7], and beginning science teachers [6]. The difficulties of the school administrator's first year have been treated by Dr. Ben Horton [8] and by Adolph Unruh [15].

However, the beginning counselor and his first-year professional problems constitute a relatively unexplored area.

THE STUDY

The writer investigated the professional problems encountered by beginning full-time counselors in New York State secondary schools during the school year 1958–1959 [9]. For purposes of the study, the following definition of "problem" was adopted: an area or matter of professional difficulty and concern deriving from a lack of skill and/or knowledge. According to Dr. Frederick J. McDonald [12], a problem is defined as follows: "A problem exists when there is a goal to be attained, but the individual sees no well-defined, well-established means of attaining it, or when the goal is so vaguely defined or unclear to the person that he cannot determine what are the relevant means for attaining it." According to this definition, the counselor was adjudged to have a problem when he lacked the skills to attain certain desired guidance goals or lacked the knowledge to determine specific means or ends. The skills and knowledges were stipulated as those which are usually gained as a result of previous preparation or experience.

Problems were limited to professional difficulties experienced by counselors in the routine performance of their professional duties, and limited to the one school year, 1958–1959. Problems resulting from "lack of time" were excluded.

We are mainly concerned here, then, with problems that are related to lack of competency or proficiency *as perceived by the counselor.*

The investigation considered only *full-time* counselors in public secondary (grades 7–12) schools of New York State exclusive of New York City. Part-time counselors, private or parochial school counselors, and elementary school counselors were excluded. Also omitted were shared-service counselors and guidance directors or pupil personnel coordinators without counseling responsibilities.

COLLECTION OF THE DATA

Using the resources and files of the Bureau of Guidance, in the New York State Education Department, the investigator was able to identify the name and location of all new counselors in New York State for the year selected. One hundred and two (96 per cent) out of a possible 109 new counselors completed questionnaires, and these questionnaires were included in the final analysis.

To ascertain the nature and frequency of the professional problems encountered during the school year and to gather data relevant to these counselors' professional preparations, experience, and operational settings, a special questionnaire was devised. This questionnaire contained a list of 62 typical counselor duties categorized under the following eight general headings:

1. *Obtaining Data About Pupils*
2. *Counseling Students*
3. *Working with Occupation and Educational Information*
4. *Working with Teachers*
5. *Working with Parents*
6. *Working with Youth-serving Workers and Agencies*
7. *Placement and Follow-up*
8. *Administration, Organization, and Promotion Activities*

The counselors were asked to react to each duty (or "guidance task") employing a given degree-of-difficulty scale. Counselors judged each duty as "hardly ever difficult," "occasionally difficult," or "often difficult." Counselors could also note that they did not perform a specific counseling duty during the course of the year or not to an extent sufficient to make judgment possible.

In addition to reactions to specific guidance tasks, the questionnaire also solicited information from counselors concerning their previous training, teaching experience, and their present school settings.

RESULTS

The data obtained from the questionnaires were tabulated so that guidance tasks most frequently mentioned by the new counselors as sources of difficulty could be identified.

Those tasks associated with *Counseling Students* ranked highest in difficulty for new counselors (Table 1). Tasks falling under the general category, *Obtaining Data About Pupils*, ranked second in difficulty. Duties associated with *Working with Teachers* and *Working with Parents*, respectively, were the two next most difficult problem areas for beginning counselors.

Those specific individual guidance tasks, irrespective of general area, reported as difficult by at least 40 per cent of all responding counselors, were

Table 1

Rank Order of Difficulty for Specific
Guidance Areas Reported by New
Counselors

Rank	Category
1	Counseling Students
2	Obtaining Data About Pupils
3	Working with Teachers
4	Working with Parents
5	Working with Occupational and Educational Information
6	Administration, Organization, and Promotion Activities
7	Placement and Follow-Up
8	Working with Youth-serving Workers and Agencies

also determined and are shown in Table 2. The two tasks most frequently reported as difficult dealt with keeping up with professional developments. These two, plus four other tasks (ranking 4, 6, 7, and 11) comprise a total of 50 per cent of the most difficult tasks reported and fall in the general area, *Administration, Organization, and Promotion Activities*. Tasks ranking 3, 5, and 8 in Table 2 pertain to *Counseling Students*. These two categories (1) *Administration, Organization, and Promotion Activities* and (2) *Counseling Students* include three-fourths of all the tasks reported as difficult by at least 40 per cent of the new counselors. The three remaining specific tasks, ranking 9, 10, and 12, are ascribable to three other general categories: *Working with Occupational and Educational Information*, *Working with Parents*, and *Placement and Follow-up*, respectively.

From Tables 1 and 2, it can been seen that when tasks reported as difficult are analyzed by general category, a rank order can be established, but that certain specific tasks reported as most difficult by beginning counselors cut across this category ranking. Thus, while one category, *Administration, Organization, and Promotion Activities*, ranks third in order of difficulty, two specific tasks within that category rank first and second as most frequently reported of all 62 tasks included in the questionnaire.

Other findings produced by an analysis of the questionnaire returns revealed the following:

New counselors who work "alone" as the only counselor on the staff in a school system report a greater number of problems in performing their duties than do other new counselors.

The type of professional problems new counselors face is unrelated to—

a. The number of pupils assigned to them.
b. The grade level of counselees assigned to them.
c. The amount of supervisory assistance received, or

Table 2

Most Difficult Tasks Reported by
New Counselors*

Rank	Guidance Task	% Reporting Difficulty
1	Keep informed of latest professional developments in guidance, education, psychology, and related fields	70
2	"Keep up" on trends and current developments in guidance, education, etc.	60
3	Counsel students with reference to vocational considerations	55
4	Evaluate effectiveness of a particular guidance program	54
5	Counsel students with reference to personal-social problems.	53
6	Evaluate effectiveness of over-all guidance program	48
7	Establish guidance program goals, aims, and priorities	45
8	Counsel students with reference to academic problems	44
9	Utilize films, bulletin boards, etc., on occupations and colleges	43
10	Secure parental participation in guidance activities	43
11	Plan, and arrange sequence of, the year's activities	41
12	Assist school leavers with next steps	40

*Reported by at least 40 per cent of all counselors.

d. Consultants and in-service education resources utilized.

New counselors who participate in an above-average number (five or more) of in-service education activities report fewer professional problems.

New counselors who have permanent certification report fewer professional problems in their first year on the job.

New counselors who are assigned responsibility for students in grades 7–9, rather than grades 10–12, report fewer professional problems; also counselors reporting largest number of problems were found more likely to have as their counselees students in grades 10–12.

Adequate physical facilities, materials, and equipment for guidance purposes were reported by first-year counselors having the least number of professional problems; conversely, new counselors who reported inadequate physical facilities, equipment or materials available for guidance purposes reported greater numbers of professional problems.

New counselors who felt that their own career or college choice as a high school student was a relatively easy one reported significantly fewer professional problems during their first years as counselors; on the other hand, new counselors who reported many problems during their first year also were likely to indicate that they had a difficult time as high school students with their career or college choices.

DISCUSSIONS AND IMPLICATIONS

The findings relate to a counselor's preparation, job assignment, job effectiveness, and job satisfaction. They, therefore, have particular significance for counselor educators, directors of guidance and head counselors, school administrators, supervisors, and state education department personnel engaged in guidance supervision.

PRE-SERVICE EDUCATION

Neophyte counselors indicate that their main areas of difficulty relate to counseling and obtaining data about pupils. These two areas should continue to receive emphasis. The fact that new counselors (1) who work "alone" in a school system, (2) who are assigned students in grades 10–12, and (3) who report inadequate physical facilities, equipment, or materials available for guidance, in each instance, report *greater* numbers of professional problems points up the counselor educator's need to bear in mind the important ramifications of special school situations.

Other specific counselor competencies which command renewed or continued attention on the part of counselor educators, in the light of counselors' reported first-year difficulties, are these: (1) keeping informed of latest professional developments and trends, (2) evaluation of guidance activities and over-all guidance program, (3) establishing program goals, aims, and priorities, and (4) establishing effective relationships with others—pupils, teachers, administrators, and parents. For example, counselors-in-training may need additional practice in how to maintain professional competence once they are on the job. Viewed in connection with the above paragraph this need serves to remind the counselor-trainer to concentrate on developing in his students special effectiveness with specific counselor competencies. In addition, his students must be adequately qualified to handle a variety of different situations and operational demands.

IN-SERVICE EDUCATION

First-year counselors who participated in an above-average number of in-service education activities (five or more *kinds*) reported *fewer* professional problems. A majority of new counselors reported personal supervisory conferences with state education department (Bureau of Guidance) personnel and many specifically mentioned that agency's "Beginning Counselor Workshops." The advisability of continuous and concentrated effort of this general kind, therefore, seem opposite. A variety and diversity of in-service education experiences, readily and consistantly available *throughout* the school year, probably constitute the most practical and effective approach, in view of the findings.

CERTIFICATION

Requirements for New York State Education Department guidance certification are specified in terms of experience and education for two levels: provisional and permanent. It was found that counselors who hold the permanent certificate reported fewer professional problems in their first year on the job. It would seem from this that counselor competency and certification are positively related at least in terms of total *number* of problems recognized.

Other findings which have implication for present certification requirements deal with differences in number of problems that new counselors who work "alone" encounter. This suggests that these counselors have special needs which differentiates them from other counselors. The New York State permanent certification requirements are now designed to recognize the special situation of the experienced counselor, establishing generally broad or basic courses for new counselors but specifying more advanced and more specialized courses for later acquisition (*e.g., Organization and Administration of a Guidance Program*). The findings bear out the wisdom of such an arrangement. However, probably it would be equally desirable for new counselors who expect to work "alone" on their first guidance job also to obtain these advanced courses.

APPOINTMENT OF NEW COUNSELORS

Administrators or supervisors attempting to select a candidate for a counseling position frequently have little to go on concerning the applicant's potential effectiveness as a counselor, except for his previous academic record in guidance preparatory courses, the estimate of counselor educators, their own subjective judgments based on an interview, and the recommendations of previous school administrators—who must necessarily evaluate personal and professional qualifications on the basis of teaching performance. Data which would assist in selecting applicants likely to have minimal first-year difficulty or relatively few professional problems would, therefore, be most helpful.

Since new counselors who work "alone" in a school system experience a greater number of problems it would seem advisable that such positions be filled either with experienced counselors or with "strong" inexperienced candidates, *i.e.*, highly recommended applicants or individuals holding or nearly qualifying for the permanent guidance certificate.

New counselors who participate in an above-average number of in-service education activities generally have fewer professional problems; the applicant's record and attitude as a classroom teacher pertinent to such in-service education participation should not be too difficult to ascertain and to evaluate. Similarly, beginning counselors holding the permanent certificate have fewer problems, as do those who report that their high school choice or college choice was an easy one. Such information can be readily obtained; however, it seems prudent to utilize these in conjuction with other criteria.

New counselors who work with students in grades 7–9 rather than grades 10–12 report fewer professional problems. Therefore, as far as the appointment policy of the administrator or director of guidance is concerned, inexperienced personnel should more generally be started at the junior high school level, whenever this is possible or practicable, and vacancies at the senior high level should be filled by experienced junior high school counselors.

AREAS WARRANTING FURTHER INVESTIGATION

It would be interesting to learn whether the *kind* of problems counselors encounter are related in any way to the *number* of problems they report; that is, do counselors with many (or few) professional problems tend to have the same kinds of problems? Such information would be extremely helpful in determining further what factors are significantly related to the occurrence, prevention, and amelioration of professional guidance problems.

Counselors reporting "easy" personal high school choice of college or career also indicated fewer problems in their first year. This is not only a somewhat unexpected finding, but also one that is rather difficult to explain. We can speculate that counselors who had an "easy" time making their educational-vocational decisions in high school also have a particular personality make-up which precludes difficulty with subsequent job tasks . . . and vice-versa. This, incidentally, raises another interesting question: whether perceived ease of decision-making is related to job success, performance, or satisfaction.

In studying the relationships of various counselor, school, and job factors to the relative difficulty with guidance tasks a study of some of the following would undoubtedly shed some light on the nature of frequency of problems encountered by counselors: the affluence and resources of the counselor's school; the general educational philosophy of the staff; and the school community's readiness for, and expectations from, the guidance program. These may well exert a decisive influence on (a) the kinds of problems encountered by the counselor and (b) the kind of counselor a school attracts in the first place.

CONCLUSION

The public school counselor is operating in a position only recently perceived as having strategic educational and manpower significance, in addition to other justifications, at a crucial time in national affairs. The counselor is an educator whose role, effectiveness and professional competence are consequently receiving growing attention, comment, and investigation from numerous and diverse sources: the general public (including parents), educators, education spokesmen, and counselor educators and supervisors. The adequacy of the counselor's job and the quality of his professional performance are areas which have been of primary concern in this discussion. Moreover, these are areas which have only begun to be explored; they should be subjected to additional investigation.

REFERENCES

1. Arbuckle, Dugald S. *Guidance and Counseling in the Classroom*. Boston: Allyn and Bacon, 1957.

2. Berg, Wilbert A. "Some Aspects of the Counselor's Career Development." In *Frontiers of Secondary Education II*. Syracuse, N. Y.: Syracuse Univ. Press, 1957.

3. Buchanan, Rosemary, & Jones, Worth. "A First-Year Counselor's Soliloquy," *Sch. Counselor* (October 1958), 6, 3–9.

4. Foster, Helen W. "Problems of a Group of Beginning Elementary School Teachers." Unpublished doctoral dissertation, Univ. Pennsylvania.

5. Gilbert, Mary E. "Developing a Guidance Program: A Guidance Counselor's First Year in a New Situation." Unpublished doctoral dissertation, Teachers College, Columbia Univ., 1956.

6. Hammond, Harry F. "Problems of the Newly Appointed and Inexperienced Science Teachers of Northern New Jersey." Unpublished doctoral dissertation, Teachers College, Columbia Univ., 1955.

7. Harrison, Paul E., Jr. "Problems of Beginning Industrial Arts Teachers." Unpublished doctoral dissertation, Univ. Maryland, 1955.

8. Horton, Ben H., Jr. "A Study of the Problems of Beginning Principals as a Basis for Improvement of the Program for the Education of Principals at Appalachian State Teachers College." Unpublished doctoral dissertation, Florida State Univ., 1958.

9. Kaplan, Bernard A. "Professional Problems of Beginning Full-time Counselors in New York State Secondary Schools." Unpublished doctoral dissertation, Cornell Univ., 1961.

10. Lane, Frank T. "A Study of the Professional Problems Recognized by Beginning Teachers and Their Implications For a Program of Teacher Education." Unpublished doctoral dissertation, New York Univ., 1955.

11. Mason, Ward S. "The Beginning Teacher: A Survey of New Teachers in the Public Schools (Preliminary Report)." Washington, D.C.: U. S. Government Printing Office, 1958.

12. McDonald, Frederick J. *Educational Psychology*. San Francisco: Wadsworth Publishing Co., 1959.

13. McNeil, Ralph. "Anticipated and Acutal Experiences of Beginning Teachers." Unpublished doctoral dissertation, Teachers College, Columbus Univ., 1955.

14. Scheller, John. "A Study of the Teaching Difficulties of a Selected Group of Beginning Secondary School Teachers with Implications for a Program of In-service Aid." Unpublished doctoral dissertation, Univ. Buffalo, 1957.

15. Unruh, Adolph, "Administrators Look at Their Preparation." *Phi Delta Kappan* (June 1957), 38, 376–378.

16. Wey, Herbert W. "Difficulties of Beginning Teachers." *Sch. Rev.* (January 1951), 59, 32–37.

24

The Attack on Testing and Counseling

James R. Barclay, Ph.D.*

It is now quite apparent that a major attack is being made on both the practice of counseling and the testing movement. From a variety of sources some very severe charges are being lodged against the consulting psychologist, the school personnel worker, and the professional user of tests. I have seen a number of articles in journals and newspapers and have read a current book attacking testing. My reactions have varied from indignation to sympathy with the charges depending on their nature. As a result, this article is being written in order to analyze some of this literature and to ferret out what would appear to be fallacious from what is possibly true.

I have not been able to make a detailed survey of the literature. But I am including in this analysis five articles and a book which I am inclined to believe may be fairly representative of the movement. These are: (1) "Brainpicking in School," [1]; (2) "The Infamous Blackie Cartoons" (*American Capsule News*, September 15, 1962); (3) "A Note on the Technology of Cynicism" by Dr. Donald Barr [3]; (4) a local column by Pierre Pulling [13] in *Intermountain* (an Idaho weekly newspaper); (5) an article by Fred H. Hechinger [10], education editor of the New York *Times*, entitled "Test Question," and (6) the book, *The Brain Watchers*, written by Martin J. Gross [9].

THE CRITICISMS

Let us first of all take a look at these samples of the literature. Included in them are two publications from what may be fairly called "right-wing" organizations. Barr's article appears in a professional journal, and Hechinger's article appears in the education section of the New York *Times*, Sunday Edition. Pulling's column is typical of small town columnists throughout the country insofar as many local papers do carry columns of this general commentary nature. Finally, the book by Gross represents a major effort to "expose" commercial testing agencies.

What do these articles and this book say? The article on "brainpicking" is written by a U.S. Congressman, Representative John Ashbrook. He picks

°Dr. Barclay is Professor of Education at California State College at Hayward. His article appeared originally in the *Personnel and Guidance Journal*, 43:1:6 (September 1964), and is reprinted with permission of the author and of the journal.

some items from the SRA *Youth Inventory* which relate to attitudes toward sex, religion, and parents. He then slips in some items from an unidentified "Moral Value Inventory," which are equally objectionable or more so. Finally, he mentions the "Wishing Well," a test published by the Bureau of Education Research at Ohio State University. His argument, then, is basically that questions that probe at attitudes toward parents, the Bible, or patriotism plant the seeds of doubt in the minds of youth. He states further that these tests are devised arbitrarily and sold under the seal of scientific infallibility. He quotes Dr. Chisholm, former Director-General of the World Health Organization, as stating that sin and the subjective conviction of sin are the arch-enemies of mental health and progress. Finally, Congressman Ashbrook lumps Freudian psychiatry, UNESCO, and brain-picking tests together as being part of a subversive plot "to detect and indoctrinate." He states categorically that the Dewey or Horace Mann approach to education is tied up with testing and these other movements in an attempt to undermine the traditional values of American democracy and make it easy for America to eventually swing into the Marxist-Communist orbit.

This same line of approach, but in a much more vitriolic manner, is pursued by *American Capsule News.* Here the question of the *Blacky Picture Test* is taken up. Several testing projects in Wichita, Kansas, and Seattle, Washington, were mentioned.[1] This is what was written: "The Reds prepared a panel of 12 cartoons for the Seattle 'project.' These were passed on to teachers, who must be either sex degenerates or sex perverts, to innoculate the minds of their pupils with. The little victims were told to write down what (erotic) thoughts each cartoon put in their heads. Not even the degenerate Freud, with his parential (sic!) incest complex, could have thought up anything as rotten as this 'test.' " The balance of the article is concerned with an "expose" of the *Blacky Picture Test.*

A third article which is reviewed here is not in any way written in the same vein as the above two. This is a rather popular approach to difficulties

---

[1]One of the tests or surveys which inspired a good deal of opposition was a document entitled: "Kansas Junior High School Student Survey." This survey was conducted by the University of Kansas Bureau of Child Research in two Wichita Junior High Schools among students of both sexes, ranging from 11 to 14 years of age. This questionnaire consisted of some 200 items which ask questions such as:

1. Steal goods from warehouses or storage houses?
2. Steal more than $2 from your parents?
3. Fight physically and bodily with an adult relative?

True or False—I have gone further than petting with a person of the opposite sex. I have answered ads in comic books or other magazines which advertised pictures, photography, or stories about sexual matters.

In addition, one section of the test was entitled "Rules We All Break." In this section, children were informed of means of stealing property, damaging cemetery property, destroying road markers, siphoning gas from cars, puncturing tires and similar ideas. (Congressional Record [4]).

in multiple-choice tests. The author, Dr. Donald Barr, is Assistant Dean of the Faculty of Engineering and Applied Science at Columbia University. He attacks multiple-choice tests in American education. He singles out the *Scholastic Aptitude Tests*, the *College Entrance Examination Boards*, and a variety of others. He particularly attacks the large corporations who are making money on these tests. But he also returns to the conflict in values theme which is indicated in the other two articles. Without alluding to a "plot" to undermine the morals of American youth, he does point up some particular items in tests such as the *Minnesota Multiphasic Test of Personality* which could create conflict situations in the minds of people who believe in such things as the "second coming of Christ."

The fourth article is of purely local interest, but may be typical of many columnists who are looking for a good "popular" theme. This article was written by Pierre Pulling, a retired professor of Biology at Idaho State University. Mr. Pulling rambled on about testing being similar to phrenology. He said that his article was occasioned by a desultory contact with *some* child who took *some* test at *some* time in *some* place and was not rated too bright in mathematics. Nonetheless, this particular individual went to *some* college *somewhere* and *somehow* succeeded. All of which proves beyond the shadow of a doubt in Mr. Pulling's logic that *all* testing in *all* places and on *all* levels is similar to the cephalic index of the phrenologists. He further stated that he had always had a confused impression of testing, and that prospective students at Idaho State University at one time took "IQ" tests. He obviously here mixed up percentile norms on an achievement battery with "IQ" scores. Observing that he had never looked at test rosters routinely, he clinched his whole argument by relevant memory flashbacks of what education was like in the private schools of upper New York at the end of the last century.

The article by Fred Hechinger simply reports research done by Dr. Benno G. Fricke, Assistant Chief of the Evaluation and Examinations Division of the University of Michigan's Bureau of Psychological Services. Dr. Fricke's conclusions are about the *College Board Examinations* and the *Scholastic Aptitude Tests*. The objections appear to be well couched and indicate that many aptitude tests measure only general academic ability rather than specific achievement in specific areas. Dr. Fricke's objections center on the fact that the *Scholastic Aptitude Tests* are inbred in that when new items are selected they are designed to measure the same old things as the former items. He suggests that specific examinations be given in each subject matter field.

The book by Martin Gross makes interesting reading. Page after page of information is provided about the use of aptitude testing and projective techniques by big business. Example after example is provided to illustrate the techniques used. One chapter speaks of the school counselor and school psychologist. He criticizes school counselors as untrained people or classroom teachers who have taken a few courses and have "empathy." He suggests that counselors use tests in order to find "something" to talk to students about.

> In most cases, guidance people are woefully untrained to handle the proper interpretation of personality tests, a job as we have seen—that is nearly, if not actually, impossible for the Ph.D. psychologist.

Mr. Gross documents many of his statements by references to specific schools or corporations where problems existed. He winds up his discussions by an examination of whether tests are scientific or a mythology.

THE ISSUES

From these articles and the book reviewed it would appear that certain issues are at the basis of these criticisms. Though the particular reports may be exaggerated or the logic of generalization faulty, the issues would seem to be the following:

1. That counseling practice and the use of testing is a Communist- inspired plot to subvert and pervert the morals of American youth.
2. That testing is being misused by many so-called professionals and some individuals who are far from being professional.
3. That some tests are personally obnoxious to certain segments of the population and contain items which actually inform children of anti-social or law-breaking conduct.
4. That the prediction from some of these tests is nearly null for individuals.
5. That there has been a widespread "invasion" of personal rights through the use of certain types of tests and the dissemination of these test results.

These allegations should be considered one by one to determine whether the charges are valid or not. The first one suggests that the entire counseling and testing movement is of a "pinko" nature and is directly or indirectly inspired by Communism. This is pure nonsense. Moreover, the attempt to draw John Dewey and even poor old Horace Mann into this plot is ludicrous in the extreme. What are these charges really aimed at? Are they not directed against the present philosophy of education and the consequent posture of the schools toward learning? The critics of counseling would seem to be disturbed by the failure of present-day schools to be a staunch mechanism of social control for the perpetuation of their particular set of values. They would wish that the school function solely as a transmitter of that information and those values to which they subscribe rather than as a proving ground for learning problem-solving. They cannot see the value of exploring the consequences of divergent thinking in certain areas of the social and behavioral sciences. Are they not really seeking some kind of absolute criterion whereby all learning processes could be monitored and referred to the "correct" solutions? Is it possible that an exaggerated patriotism may be that criterion?

Certainly the patriotic values of American democracy should be sacred to all Americans. These values need not be identified with some kind of religious canon in order to be respected and upheld. It is precisely in the freedom of inquiry, the comparison of opposing ideologies, and the acquisition of habits of critical and creative thinking that the traditional values of our democracy are most strongly reinforced. But it is quite another thing to insist that Americanism and religion are one and the same thing. In a speech in Los Angeles on September 23, 1963, Ezra Taft Benson [6] made just such a connection.

> Let us remember that we are a prosperous people today because of a free enterprise system founded on spiritual, not material values alone. It is founded on freedom of choice—free agency—an eternal God-given principle.... *It is my firm conviction that the Constitution of this land was established by men whom the God of heaven raised up unto this very purpose. This is a part of my religious faith.*

Admirable as these convictions may be—and I do not deny the right for anyone to hold such views as a part of his religious faith—it is probably true that such an intimate connection between the Providence of God and the Constitution of the United States is a minority view. As long as this view remains a personal religious opinion there is no threat from it. But if the traditional view of democracy becomes altered into a form of divine revelation, it could become the vehicle for abolishing freedom of inquiry in the schools. A curriculum based on the testing of consequences of information, the making of qualitative judgments, and the fostering of habits of individual responsibility may be extremely threatening to those whose political-religious identification has become the fixed criterion against which all learning shall be measured.

THE COUNSELOR AND SOCIAL VALUES

It is also a matter of deep concern for the critics of counseling and testing when they discover that counselors in the public schools actually encourage students to think for themselves. The practice of counseling is designed to personalize the educational problem-solving process. Counseling, though often obscured by a host of routine scheduling and clerical functions, basically has as its primary commitment one of the same major functions that characterizes the school in our society. The counselor helps students consider alternate solutions to a given problem and explore the consequences of present or anticipated behavior. The student brings a problem to the counselor and the counselor's chief role is to help the student explore this problem and arrive at a solution which may be tried out in practice. Obviously the values of the counselor are apparent in any interview, but his purpose in the school is not to impose his own values, his own decisions, but to help a student acquire facility and confidence in his own problem-solving ability. In the interests of this goal, the counselor cannot be an agent of authority, but must be an accepting person to whom the student can go in confidence to ventilate his feelings, seek clarification both of his cognitive and non-cognitive attitudes, and to explore the consequences of alternate proposed patterns of behavior.

Very often this position of the counselor seems to indicate to the critics a stance of ambivalence and the toleration of a drifting value system. On the contrary, the counselor recognizes the social dimension within which this problem-solving process operates. A well-trained counselor knows he cannot allow his commitment to the individual to sanction anti-social and illegal behavior. The counselor in the school is dedicated to the proposition that facility in individual problem solving is both beneficial to society and conducive to the highest personal fulfillment in that society. Thus, through the counseling process individual students can best develop those habits of personal decision making and responsibility which are most essential to the very preservation of a democratic society.

If the schools and counselors in the schools fail to develop this sense of individual responsibility, if they fail to identify social issues or to compare opposing ideologies, and if they blandly disguise controversial issues offering instead simple solutions to complex problems, then a primary goal of the present democratic school system has been lost. The child in our society is not a computer in which facts are to be stored and responses appropriate to certain values programmed. He is an individual of unique personal characteristics who needs to learn how to attack all kinds of problems with the tools of analytic reasoning, scientific resources and organized personal experiences. It is towards the achievement of this goal by as many students as possible and to the extent of their capabilities that the counselor functions in the American public school.

That it is necessary for educators in general, and counselors in particular, to be concerned with developing skills in assessing social problems and understanding the processes of government was amply demonstrated by a ten-year study at Purdue University. This study found in a survey of 12,000 high school graduates that 51 per cent of those interviewed believed in the restriction, in some manner or other, of the freedom of the press; 42 per cent approved of "third degree" methods; 30 per cent opposed to the right of petition; 25 per cent would restrict the freedom of speech in one manner or the other; a shocking 60 per cent would give authorities a strict right of censorship; and an unbelievable 10 per cent would abolish trial by jury in criminal cases [5]. The Constitution and the Bill of Rights are great freedoms which cannot be set up as another ten commandments imposed by the authority of God, but rather as great ideals which impose a moral task on those who live under them. Every generation of man has the responsibility to re-interpret these ideas and make them vital. The way to this individual responsibility must be paved in the public schools through the living example of teachers and counselors who believe in the dignity of the individual and his right to set his own values. To impose a rightist position based on an identification of democracy with the Gospel with crush the spirit of free inquiry.

ALLEGATIONS CONCERNING TESTING

The gist of the charges made against testing and the use of tests does appear to be founded in some very real abuses. We need to recognize that there are some items in some tests which are personally obnoxious. Moreover, on occasions individuals who have been unqualified to use restricted tests have used them. Again, school counselors have often used group achievement and personality tests as material to be discussed with students and their parents. The allegation has been made that many test items referring to personality are formulated from a psychoanalytic viewpoint in which religion is considered to be a form of adolescent psychopathology. This would appear to be a valid complaint. A discussion on the nature of sin held several years ago brought this matter out into clear focus (Mowrer, Ellis, Curran, & Shoben [12]). Dr. Albert Ellis held that there was no room for the concept of sin in psychotherapy. Others, however, such as Dr. Hobart Mowrer, called for a re-examination of the entire area of guilt and sin in terms of psychotherapy. In view of the fact that many of the test items for instruments such as the *MMPI*, the *California Test of Personality*, or other such tests presumably have a psychoanalytic bias, it is understandable that certain items may be personally obnoxious.

There are many types of tests and many varieties of testers. Testing in any form is a scientific attempt to measure some aspect of behavior, achievement, personality, or learning. Teacher-made tests which are used by every teacher possess no real reliability or validity except in terms of the teacher himself. These tests ordinarily measure whether a given student has learned to regurgitate those specific bits of information which a teacher deems important or whether a student can organize his material in such a way that it conforms to the design of the teacher. Standardized tests, on the other hand, are usually composed by individuals who are deemed to have some expert knowledge in the field under consideration. Certain items are selected and tested to learn whether they do measure whatever the characteristic may be. Once the complex areas of developmental variation, environmental differences and adequate sampling have been worked out, large representative populations are included in the norming process. By item analysis the content of the test is screened and re-analyzed. The entire approach is based on a statistical theory relating to large populations and the assumption of normality of distribution. The end result of the test is to provide a measure of some characteristic either in the area of personality, learning, or achievement. Prediction is never postulated of individuals and is seldom postulated of populations without considerable qualifying remarks. Finally, tests of this nature never specify anything about motivation, creativity, or those other intangible personal factors which often spell the difference between success and failure. Thus, a test result does not imply that a given individual is predestined in some quasi-theological manner to the heaven of success, the hell of failure, or the limbo of probation.

Of even more concern are those tests known as projective techniques. The most widely known projective techniques are the Rorschach, the *Thematic Apperception Test*, and the sentence-completion tests. The theory behind projective techniques is basically one founded on psychoanalytic theory. Though the roots of this approach lie in phenomenology and the position that each individual structures reality in a basically unique framework, psychoanalytic theory postulates that each individual represses a good deal of his basic needs and wishes. Through the use of the interpretation of ink blots or pictures, the intent is to tap lower levels of cognition through the analysis of quantity and quality of the responses given to these stimuli. Other projective techniques such as the *Blacky Pictures Test* or the IES Test are frankly psychoanalytic in their design and attempt to tap specific feelings which are postulated on the basis of psychoanalytic theory.

The chief problem in the use of projective techniques centers around the interpretation of the results. Personal resistance to some of the concepts in these tests is invariably interpreted as a sign of rigidity and repressed material. This is particularly so in tests such as the *Blacky* where some of the material presented is frankly sexual in nature and can hardly be disguised. What is lacking in the use of projective techniques are adequate, reliable, and valid norms. Generalizations about school youth which are based on norms developed in hospital settings are very precarious. The same fact would seem to be indicated by the use of these tests in industry for determining who would make a good executive.

The root question in regard to testing seems to be focused on the real problem of predictive validity. Many of the arguments against the achievement batteries and entrance tests are that they are not very good predictive instruments. The best correlations of entrance batteries in college with grade point averages range between the 0.60–0.70 level. Obviously there are many students who score highly and still fail in college level work. There are others who are apparently low in academic promise and may end up in the upper ranks of graduating seniors. The problems are not so much related to the format or content of the test given, since we know that high school grades will predict nearly as well as an entrance battery. They are more immediately related to the instability of the criterion used, *i.e.,* grade point average. Grading practices vary within the institution and among institutions, though it is likely that the grading variation within the institution among departments may be more readily approximated among universities than total comparisons. In other words, Colleges of Education probably grade similarly when compared from institution to institution; and certain liberal arts departments also probably are similar in grading practices.

But the problems of prediction do not stop there. There are obviously differences between high school products and their success at various institutions. E. G. Lindquist [11] has attempted to approach this problem, but at present feels that it is nearly a hopeless task. Moreover, when personality tests are added to entrance battery scores the results in multiple correlation are negligible [8].[2] The problems which face the test constructors in college entrance batteries are not so much a matter of which items should be included, but rather how to obtain a stable, practical and utilitarian criterion to measure success by. This same problem besets the users of individual tests and particularly those who would use individual projective techniques which are currently available to qualified psychologists.

RE-EVALUATION

There are two basic problems which need to be discussed in this section: (1) the question of whether these criticisms of counseling and testing have been justified to any extent, and (2) has the rationale employed by the critics been logical. In answer to the first question, it should be apparent, at this point, that the writer believes some justifiable criticism has been leveled against the practice of counseling and the use of tests. Most of these criticisms center on the problem of poor judgment of counselors and psychologists. Examples have been given of the use of tests which are either inappropriate or offensive in some ways. The allegation that counselors are poorly trained and often use psychological tools in ways that they were not meant to also has some truth in it. For the examples of flagrant misuse that are cited in these various articles and Gross' book, there are many others which counselor-educators know about and which they are glad were not written up. But the rationale which has been used in criticizing the entire movement of counseling and testing is an exercise in

[2]Fishman reports that nearly 500 studies have been done in predicting academic success from entrance batteries. When personality tests are added to the multiple factors the multiple correlation is increased by only 0.01 or 0.02.

faulty logic. Because these abuses of testing have taken place they do not imply that the entire profession is at error or that testing and counseling is a Communist plot. Let us discuss here what we need to do to put our own house in order, and how we can answer some of these critics.

STRENGTHENING PROFESSIONAL COUNSELING AND TESTING

The indictments which have been made regarding testing and counseling point up the need for more detailed and advanced training for counselors. They also underline the need for a strong network of professional identification through national, state, and local levels. The proper place to discipline unethical conduct, to impose and maintain standards is through the professional organization of counselors, the American Personnel and Guidance Association. Studies are under way by various groups in the organization to clarify the role of the counselor, and to make recommendations for training and ethical standards within the profession. Accompanying this objective must be efforts on the part of the counselor educators to do a more effective screening and evaluation of counselor trainees. It would seem that many counselors lack a real understanding of basic psychological concepts including testing theory. From local studies done through the NDEA Institutes at Idaho State University, the writer ascertained that a majority of the enrollees actively dislike statistics and do not really wish to understand testing theory [2]. Unless we can train individuals to understand the tests they use, to recognize that a test score is never an absolute predictor or a tool to use to ferret out additional information, it would be best that counselors not use debatable tests at all.

Counselor trainers also need to work on a variety of other problems. Some of these are merely technical in nature, and the others are of a much more profound nature. Representative of the technical problems are counselor attitudes toward referrals and what may be called, for lack of a better term, naive curiosity. Counselors are often threatened by the referral process. Often insecure and poorly trained counselors feel that a referral to someone else is an implicit acknowledgment of personal inadequacy. As a result, they will often hold on to cases until little can be done by others. In this way, they damage the professional responsibility of the profession. Until counselors are trained to a much more sophisticated level than they presently are, they should make referrals whenever a child is having repeated serious problems in school which are of a long-standing nature and jeopardize the on-going process of education for other children. Curiosity-seeking is also a problem in the naive counselor. Often he probes into areas of personal concern not so much to understand as to satisfy his own needs for vicarious experience. Sometimes he will develop questionnaires or adopt tests which are represented to him through misleading advertisement as panaceas of prediction. Curiosity to pry into personal experiences is an immature aspect of psychological sophistication. In its worst aspect it is akin to voyeurism. Counselors need to recognize that this kind of prying reveals their own adolescent development and need for vicarious experience. If they have this type of need, let them read novels! Where such curiosity in the use of tests springs from a desire to do a better job, or to write a thesis, or investigate some aspects of developmental behavior, then it would be best if they consult with university personnel. Whenever research is undertaken in the public schools it should be a joint concern of both school administrators and university faculty. For the preserving of a good research climate in a community is essential if we are to utilize the community in research activities.

Of more basic concern particularly to counselor educators is the recognition that we have grown from a technique-oriented "how-to-do-it" approach in counseling and testing to a distinct professional group. With the recognition should come both changes in the professional training curriculum and more meaningful research findings. Two trends in the evolution of our role may be noted. The first concerns a move away from emphasis on the concept of guidance to accent on the counseling process. This move is in accord with the gradual abandonment of the "how-to-do-it" approach of earlier times. Guidance as a term -was always hard to define or even describe. It embraced so many dimensions of activities, including everything from keeping records to going on field trips with youth, that it was difficult to assess this activity in any precise manner. With the concern about the counseling process becoming paramount in the field, it is now more possible to seek concrete research outcomes about human behavior as effected by counseling. Whereas it was nigh impossible previously to obtain adequate answers to what constitutes guidance, it is now possible to formulate good questions about what is counseling. And in conjuction with this evolution of a more precise research methodology it may be time now to lay to permanent rest that hoary old argument about directivity and non-directivity. It sold a good many books and provided much ammunition for great polemics in which the dogmatic non-directivists could condemn and challenge the authoritarian directivists.

Perhaps now we need to determine a basic question about the counseling process. Is counseling designed to first change attitudes and then through this change of attitudes result in behavioral modifications which are more suitable to the individual? Or is it possible that counseling ought first to bring about changes in behavior which then may result in changes of attitudes? Much of our present counseling theory seems to be postulated on the development of insight and understanding which in turn is conceptualized as the reason for bringing about changes in behavior.[3]

From the point of view of research the evaluation of counseling might be more meaningfully assessed by noting the facility shown by clients in problem solving and the effectiveness of these decisions in producing more stable and personally satisfying results. This point of view would ignore as irrelevant all those clinical assumptions about early developmental treatment, such as maternal rejection, etc., which presumably have brought about patterns of unsuitable behavior. On the other hand, this research orientation might conceivably overlook the long-range effects of attitudes. Is it sufficient to facilitate problem-solving resulting in temporary positive reinforcement without concomitant explorations into the earlier causes of unsatisfactory behavior?

Perhaps a further goal of exploration beyond these problems is an investigation into possible differences between counseling practices based on a phenomenological viewpoint, psychoanalytic theory, a Thomistic-Realist conception of the universe, and the philosophy of experimentalism. One of the most important gaps in counselor training is the failure to explore the possible relationship which exists between philosophical theories about the nature of reality, the extension and validity of knowledge, the nature of values, and the nature of man as they relate to counseling practices, Admittedly, few counselors may advert to the explicit views which they may hold regarding the nature of reality, the nature of man, and axiology. May we not question, however, whether they do not implicitly operate on the basis of a system which they have either acquired unconsciously from their life experiences or which they have constructed in one manner or another from their training? One may find real differences in an investigation of this area relating various approaches to the outcomes of counseling. For phenomenological theory holds that the responses of individuals are unique and acceptable on that basis alone. Freudian and Neo-Freudian approaches implicitly assume an approved theory about the nature of reality and culture values. These positions long discussed in counseling theory classes are assumed to result in different counseling outcomes. But do we know this? Finally, another philosophical base should be closely scrutinized as a theory for counseling. I refer to Dewey's experimentalism and his conception of all human relations as being a transaction in experience. It would be interesting to learn whether experimentalism might not be the *de facto*, if not *de jure*, philosophical basis of those who embrace eclecticism in counseling.

Another important task which counselor educators need to face up to is

---

[3] I am indebted to Dr. John Krumboltz and Dr. Stanford Glazer for their contribution to the thoughts expressed here.

the basic orientation which counselors take toward problems in the school. The orientation of clinical psychology, particularly the clinical psychology of the 1940's and 1950's, was toward the abnormal. The basic postulate was that a person was abnormal until proved normal. I do not imply that this was ever taught as such, but rather that with the tremendous variety of diagnostic categories, and the need which clinicians had to diagnose, this became a by-product of their education. This same procedure was transferred into areas of educational, school, and counseling psychology. There is no question that knowledge about abnormal people is needed, but there is a real question as to whether the diagnostic categories of the clinician have any validity outside the hospital setting. There is a parallel between procedures in law and this attitudinal posture. In Continental law, which is derived ultimately from the Napoleonic and Justinian Codes, an individual is considered guilty when charged until proved innocent. In the British Common Law and the American courts, an individual is considered innocent until proved guilty. What I am suggesting is that we change our orientation to recognize that the vast majority of individuals manifest abnormal adjustment symptoms on occasion. But the criterion of their efficiency is whether they can live and work meaningfully in society. When they cannot do so, they need institutional structure and help. In the school situation, we should consider all children as normal until it is absolutely imperative to remove the child from the setting for his own good and the good of others. Labels of maladjustment and delinquency merely make it difficult to work with the child, the teacher and the parents.

That we need to set our own house in order is apparent, not only by these criticisms, but by their results. In the 1962 article by Congressman John Ashbrook the following legislative suggestions were made:

> Be it enacted by the Senate and House of Representatives of the United States of America in Congress assembled, That, notwithstanding any other provision of law, no funds appropriated or otherwise made available to the Department of Health, Education and Welfare shall be expended, granted, or otherwise used for the purpose of giving an examination to any student in an elementary or secondary school or to pay or supplement the salary of an individual administering an examination taken by any such student, if any information is to be *requested or obtained by means of such examination which relates to such student's personality, environment, home life, parental or family relationships, economic status, religious beliefs, patriotism, sexual behavior or attitudes, or sociological or psychological problems,* unless (1) reasonable notice is given to parents of students to whom such examination is administered of the giving of such examination and of the right of each parent (A) to see or hear each question that will be given or asked during such examination, and (B) to refuse to permit the giving of such examination to his child; and (2) the rights described in subclasses (A) and (B) of clause (1) are accorded to each such parent.

This approach suggested by Congressman Ashbrook actually was incorporated in the Senate amendment of H.R. 4955 [5] passed in October 1963. This amendment read:

> Provided that no such program shall provide for the conduct of any test or the asking of any questions in connection therewith, which is designed to elicit information dealing with the personality, environment, home life, parental or family relationships, economic status, or sociological or psychological problems of the pupil tested.

Although this amendment was not part of the final bill, it clearly indicates that unless counselors and counselor educators come to recognition of the need for self-discipline and reappraisal of training techniques we may find the Federal Government monitoring the entire counseling and testing field.

ANSWERING THE CRITICS

The second major problem mentioned under the heading of "Re-evaluation" is the rationale of the critics. In general, it is very difficult to argue against these critics. But it may be said that the critics generally divide themselves into two major camps: (1) those who are emotionally involved, having some kind of "hidden agenda," or who simply wish to get a little mileage out of attacking a popular subject, and (2) those critics who point up a serious problem which needs to be considered objectively.

We need not concern ourselves about critics of the second variety. If their observations are based on genuine research findings they should be studied and analyzed accordingly. But critics of the first category usually level their criticisms in the most offensive generalizing language. There is a tendency seemingly universal to a form of absolutist thinking which is really a decadent form of Aristotelianism. This approach to reality requires a dichotomous relationship in all things. Academic individuals often wish to see matters of other fields in the same black and white, true or false, good or evil categories as unsophisticated journalists. This view implicitly subscribes to a Ptolemaic configuration of the universe in which these individuals see themselves at the hub of the wheel and everybody else beyond the spokes. It is extremely difficult to debate complex issues involving interpersonal theories of perception, probability and the normal curve, statistical methods of reliability and validity, item analysis and the concept of prediction on the same plane with irrational arguments, ingrained prejudice, and personal hostility reinforced by many decades of myopic perspective. Their usual argument boils down to this, that because abuses or problems are found in a few instances the entire movement is discredited. They wish to abolish all counseling and testing or to change it so radically that it loses its identity. But for the moment, let us adopt the position of these critics and throw out both counseling and testing. What then are the alternatives? In the area of counseling, this would mean an abandonment of the conviction that students need someone to whom they can turn independently for help and clarification of their ideas. Without testing, the only alternative would be to return to judgment based on subjective criteria whether empirically derived from individuals or groups of individuals or simply by personal intuitive means. The history of the mental hygiene movement is replete with case histories of individuals who spent their lives in mental hospitals or institutions for the mentally ill or mentally retarded because someone made a subjective judgment about them. The case is exactly parallel to medicine. Should medical doctors not try to save lives even though their present tools, skills, and drugs are inadequate? Because there have been a few medical quacks and a few proved cases of medical malpractice does this mean that we should all go back to the witch doctors? The answer must be a resounding "no." In testing and the field of interpersonal relations our tools and techniques are still quite crude. We are at the state of development in the social sciences that Newton represented in the physical sciences. We know certain basic facts, but we are still incapable of assessing the total complexity of the phenomena we deal with in a way meaningful for prediction and control.

As individuals we may not be able to answer critics on a written level. But we can do a good deal by informing teachers, speaking to parent-teacher's associations about the nature of testing and counseling, and by addressing local business groups on the same subject. We can never underestimate the need for maintaining a favorable community attitude toward these subjects.

SUMMARY

This article has been concerned with an evaluation of various kinds of criticism leveled against the practice of counseling and testing procedures. Five articles and a book criticizing counseling or testing were reviewed. The analysis of the articles and the book indicates that some charges do represent deficiencies in present professional conduct and training programs. Nonetheless, the critics of counseling and testing procedures often show a personal bias and use faulty logic. It is the conviction of the writer that these criticisms are evidences of some real weaknesses in counseling practice and counselor training. Membership in professional organizations, a clearer understanding of the use of testing, some new considerations in counselor training, and a systematic program to inform the public are suggestions for answering the critics and improving both the practice of counseling and the use of testing procedures.

REFERENCES

1. Ashbrook, John. "Brainpicking in School," *Hum. Events,* Section. 4, November 17, 1962.

2. Barclay, James R. "Evaluation Studies of NDEA Enrollees." Unpublished study, Idaho State Univ., Pocatello, Summer, 1963.

3. Barr, Donald. "A Note on the Technology of Cynicism." *Columbia Univ. Forum* (Summer 1963), *6*, 3.

4. Congressional Record, Calendar No. 627, 87th Congress National Defense Education Act Amendment of 1961, p. 131 and Appendix F, pp. 164–176.

5. Congressional Record, September 30, 1963a, No. 109, No. 155, p. A6105.

6. Congressional Record, November 4, 1963b, pp. A6856 and A6858.

7. Congressional Record, Calendar No. 531, H.R. 4955, 88th Congress, pp. 65–65.

8. Fishman, Joshua A., & Pasanella, Ann K. "College Admission-Section Studies," *Rev. Educ. Res.* (October 1960), *30*, 4.

9. Gross, Martin J. *The Brain Watchers.* New York: Random House, 1962.

10. Hechinger, Fred H. "Test Question," *New York Times* (October 27, 1963).

11. Lindquist, E. G. "Special Report on ACT Study of a Method of Scaling High School Grades to Improve the Prediction of College Grades." Mimeographed report, May 12–14, 1963.

12. Mowrer, O. Hobart, Ellis, Albert, Curran, Charles A., & Shoben, Edward Joseph, Jr. "The Role of Sin in Psychotherapy," *J. Counsel. Psychol.* (1960), *7*, 3.

13. Pulling, Pierre. Article in *Intermountain* (November 7, 1963), *12*, 43.

25

*A Bill of Rights for Teachers**

THE TEACHER IS ENTITLED TO A LIFE OF DIGNITY EQUAL
TO THE HIGH STANDARD OF SERVICE THAT IS JUSTLY
DEMANDED OF THAT PROFESSION. THEREFORE,
WE HOLD THESE TRUTHS TO BE SELF-EVIDENT:

I

Teachers have the right to think freely and to express themselves openly without fear. This includes the right to hold views contrary to the majority.

II

They shall be entitled to the free exercise of their religion. No restraint shall be put upon them in the manner, time, or place of their worship.

III

They shall have the right to take part in social, civil, and political affairs. They shall have the right, outside the classroom, to participate in political campaigns and to hold office. They may assemble peaceably and may petition any government agency, including their employers, for a redress of grievances. They shall have the same freedom in all things as other citizens.

IV

The right of teachers to live in places of their own choosing, to be free of restraints in their mode of living and the use of their leisure time shall not be abridged.

V

Teaching is a profession, the right to practice which is not subject to the surrender of other human rights. No one shall be deprived of professional status, or the right to practice it, or the practice thereof in any particular position, without due process of law.

°Authorship of the American Federation of Teachers' Bill of Rights is attributed in the document to Carl J. Megel, Washington Representative, American Federation of Teachers, in collaboration with John Ligtenberg, general counsel. The AFT has no code of ethics, as such. The AFT Bill of Rights is reprinted with permission of the American Federation of Teachers.

VI

The right of teachers to be secure in their jobs, free from political influence or public clamor, shall be established by law. The right to teach after qualification in the manner prescribed by law, is a property right, based upon the inalienable rights to life, liberty, and the pursuit of happiness.

VII

In all cases affecting the teacher's employment or professional status a full hearing by an impartial tribunal shall be afforded with the right to full judicial review. No teacher shall be deprived of employment or professional status but for specific causes established by law having a clear relation to the competence or qualification to teach, proved by the weight of the evidence. In all such cases the teacher shall enjoy the right to a speedy and public trial, to be informed of the nature and cause of the accusation; to be confronted with the accusing witnesses, to subpoena witnesses and papers, and to the assistance of counsel. No teacher shall be called upon to answer any charge affecting his employment or professional status but upon probable cause, supported by oath or affirmation.

VIII

It shall be the duty of the employer to provide culturally adequate salaries, security in illness and adequate retirement income. The teacher has the right to such a salary as will: (a) Afford a family standard of living comparable to that enjoyed by other professional people in the community; b) To make possible freely chosen professional study; c) Afford the opportunity for leisure and recreation common to our heritage.

IX

Teachers shall not be required under penalty of reduction of salary to pursue studies beyond those required to obtain professional status. After serving a reasonable probationary period a teacher shall be entitled to permanent tenure terminable only for just cause. They shall be free as in other professions in the use of their own time. They shall not be required to perform extracurricular work against their will or without added compensation.

X

To equip people for modern life requires the most advanced educational methods. Therefore, the teacher is entitled to good classrooms, adequate teaching materials, teachable class size and administrative protection and assistance in maintaining discipline.

XI

These rights are based upon the proposition that the culture of a people can rise only as its teachers improve. A teaching force accorded the highest possible professional dignity is the surest guarantee that blessings of liberty will be preserved. Therefore, the possession of these rights imposes the challenge to be worthy of their enjoyment.

XII

Since teachers must be free in order to teach freedom, the right to be members of organizations of their own choosing must be guaranteed. In all matters pertaining to their salaries and working conditions they shall be entitled to bargain collectively through representatives of their own choosing. They are entitled to have the schools administered by superintendents, boards or committees which function in a democratic manner.

26

Counselor Competence: Some Proposals in Search of Advocacy

Richard S. Dunlop, Ed.D.*

INTRODUCTION

When the new counselor comes to a school, several assumptions are made. It is assumed that he has been competently trained, that his application for employment has been screened in a meaningful way, that when he goes to work with clients his performance will be one of a helping nature, that he will be ethical, and that he will continue to function in these and other satisfactory ways through the remainder of his career.

But we cannot guarantee the validity of our assumptions. They may be unsupportable, in whole or in part. As a profession we have taken inadequate steps to police ourselves and have not yet arrived at the mechanics whereby public protection and professional confidence in the practitioner might best be assured.

The fully certified counselor is assumed competent by virtue of his extensive training, yet in-service opportunities are not made universally available in order that the profession might be assured that competent services are provided in its name. Quality control of guidance efforts is apt to reside exclusively with building principals, whose skills in our area of specialization may be marginal, at best. Employment and retention of counselors is typically regarded as the special province of administrators, rather than of persons better able to make judgments related to individuals' potential for and demonstrated ability in professional practice. The first several months of a new counselor's school experiences are apt to be harrowing indeed, and efforts to help him are typically informal if not casual in nature. A structured initiatory experience under more formalized on-the-job supervision might well prove to be superior and of value to the new counselor's clients. The lay public should have assurance (other than blind faith or confidence in the principal's good will) that the school counseling and guidance services provided in its behalf are competent, and appropriate avenues should be open for the lodging and investigation of complaints.

It would seem that approaches should be sought to the solution to these limitations of quality control, whether or not we hope one day to assume

Dr. Dunlop is Associate Professor of Education at the University of Missouri at Kansas City. His article appeared originally in the *Personnel and Guidance Journal*, 46:7:655 (March 1968) and is reprinted with permission of the author and of the journal.

for ourselves the qualified autonomy which is granted by a trusting public to practitioners of accepted professions: the freedom of the professional person to practice on his own responsibility, subject to judgment and evaluation by his occupational peers, under a generally held assumption of the practitioner's competence in the performance of some helping service. If we ourselves fail to provide public protection we are in no position to complain when school administrators and laymen assess our work and determine which of us will practice, with whom, in what ways, and for how long.

The problem is how to go about assessing competence. Quantitative evaluation of the counselor's success is an elusive proposition, and qualitative assessments are fraught with difficulty. Nonetheless, the responsibility for making the attempt cannot properly be left, by default, to persons whose competence to make such judgments is even more crude and subject to irrelevancies than our own.

It is postulated that (a) quality control exercised by the practitioner's peers precedes autonomy, (b) high levels of autonomy precede true professionalism, and (c) professionalism precedes the assurance of fully competent service. With these thoughts in mind as background, I should like to suggest three broad methods and several implementations of each by which school counselors might undertake to judge their own competence and that of colleagues. Perhaps these methods are inadequate; perhaps other provisions would be superior. But with hope that these procedures might lend themselves as a means toward assuring competence, they are submitted for consideration by practicing school counselors—and perhaps for advocacy among them.

I. PRACTITIONERS SHOULD BE INVOLVED IN THE TRAINING EFFORT

The school counselor's work includes much more than counseling. Counseling takes place, to be sure. Also, though, counselors are presumed to be guidance experts who must be knowledgeable concerning curricula and the many sorts of educational opportunities available to their clientele. They must be able to provide help to students with poor study habits, overinvolvement, underinvolvement, underachievement, and so forth. The counselor must know how to supervise clerical personnel and the work properly done by them. He must be adept at operating within the power structure of the school. He must know the sorts of trouble he can encounter with the faculty, administration, and custodial and secretarial staffs—and with parents. He should know in advance what sorts of public relations activities he may stumble into simply by having a telephone in his office. He must be prepared to deal with the Clerical *Coup*: the evident law of behavior which compels secretaries in schools to pass on to educators those tasks which are beneath the dignity of the typist. The counselor must be prepared to deal with the unusual, the unheard of, the grotesque—all of those things which school counselors are somehow supposed to know how to handle, so that from anticipation they might be prepared to protect themselves to do their real work.

To gain these advantages for candidates in training, practitioners should be more actively involved in counselor education than they typically are at present. Through employment of practicing school counselors as "clinical professors," a fusion of theory and the real world might better be realized than under circumstances more often observed in which the entire training experience is managed nearly exclusively, in most places, by professors of education and of psychology. By no means am I suggesting that the highly trained people available to counselor candidates in schools of education should be phased out of the preparation program; rather, the suggestion is that practitioners, who have *another kind* of important expertise, should be more actively phased *in*.

I would suggest that, for every 250 to 300 graduate students in counselor training, the salary of a full professor be made available every academic year to support the part-time paid involvement of as many as ten clinical professors, as here defined: that is, one part-time clinical professor for every 25 to 30 candidates. The usefulness of clinical professors could easily extend across the entire training process, and for an annual retainer on the order of perhaps $1000 each, their part-time participation could be extensive. This expansion of quality in training would reap profound dividends in practice, and the profession might thus be in a better position to assert that the graduates of approved training programs are, indeed, as competent for school employment as the profession can make them prior to practice.

II. COUNSELORS IN PRACTICE SHOULD BE THEIR OWN EVALUATORS AND JUDGES

Counselors hold routine staff meetings. What is needed is another series of meetings, "professional conferences," held perhaps every other week, the purpose of which would be to promote self-improvement rather than to deal with administrative routine. Membership in these meetings should be restricted to practicing counselors.

PROFESSIONAL CONFERENCES

Several types of professional conferences might be undertaken. Four will be considered here.

Case Presentation Conference. Practicing counselors might continue as they did in training, holding meetings devoted to the presentations of routine or especially interesting cases by staff members. Two counselors might be called upon to "present" at each meeting. Each could be expected to play a tape recording of an interview or series of interviews, and provide appropriate background data, procedural explanation and defense, statement of proposed future procedures, and so on. Adequately trained counselors should be accustomed to the procedure and in an atmosphere of helpful cooperation the element of threat should not be impossible to live with.

I would suggest in addition that three sorts of *specialized* conferences be set up, each to last for at least half a day, and each to occur at the end of the first semester and during the fourth quarter of the school year.

Academic Failure Conferences. One would be a modification of the mortality conference common to the experience of physicians, in which the medical man is called upon by his peers to justify his treatment of a deceased patient. The physician does not retain hospital privileges long if many of his patients die because of improper medical management—and the determination of his fitness to practice is made by fellow physicians and not by the insurance agents, farmers, bankers, and plumbers who may sit on the hospital's board of directors. Counselors could emulate this custom to the betterment of our profession.

The academic failure conference would focus on students who had received failing grades during the most recent marking period. A random sample of perhaps ten per cent of each counselor's clientele who received failing grades could be reviewed, with the counselor called up to report from his records what steps he had taken to be of assistance to each of the students in the sample. Evidence of counseling contacts with the students, conferences with their parents where indicated, consultations with the teaching faculty, provision of assistance in the development and utilization of appropriate study skills, and similar procedures assuring that all possible assistance was given the students would seem to be among the techniques which counselors might perform in their educational guidance role. Colleagues might be expected to look for such evidence as the academic failure conference proceeds. One's colleagues might accept that everything reasonable or potentially fruitful had been done. On the other hand, they might feel that greater efforts of specified kinds might have been extended or better procedures employed.

Academic Success Conferences. Another specialized conference is perhaps necessary in the unique circumstances and demands of the education profession. This I would call the "academic success conference." Like the failure conference, it would occur at about the same times during the school year, and would be given equal time. In this setting, a random sample of each counselor's clientele who have demonstrated academic strength (or potential) would be reviewed, with the counselor expected to give detailed reports on such things as precisely what he had done during the marking period by way of developing appropriate pre-college admissions testing programs with them, going over admissions requirements and opportunities associated with various colleges and other post high school educational institutions, and in other ways orienting strong students and their parents toward the ultimate day of decision when the final choice regarding later education must be made.

Maladaptive Conference. The third proposed specialized conference, again to occur twice yearly, might be called the "maladaptive conference." Its operation would be similar to the two proposed above, but the focus of attention would be upon students identified by the vice principal, dean, or faculty as being atypically disruptive or hostile, acting-out, aggressive sorts of disciplinary cases. Each counselor would be expected to report on his own efforts with those students for whom he had responsibility on whatever remedial procedures he had undertaken.

ANNUAL COLLEAGUE EVALUATIONS

The second major kind of evaluation would take the form of annual written assessments of counselors by one another. This function might well be performed shortly before the spring vacation, and would be reported by local counselors to their District (or Area) Committee on Ethics and Standards (see below) in one of the following ways, based upon the combined judgment of each counselor's peers:

1. Throughout the year counselors at this school have engaged in periodic review of the professional services offered by the counselor named above. In our opinion he is competent in his work, demonstrates a high sense of ethics, serves his clientele and our school well, and should continue in employment as a counselor.

2. Throughout the year counselors at this school have engaged in periodic review of the professional services offered by the counselor named above. In our opinion, with intensified attention to the standards of our profession he should be able to meet fully our standards for competence, and it is our recommendation that he continue in employment as a counselor for another school year, during which time continued review of his performance and efforts at assisting him toward desirable levels of competency may be undertaken.

3. Throughout the year counselors at this school have engaged in periodic review of the professional services offered by the counselor named above. In our opinion the counselor named above is deficient in competence within our meaning of the term. We have recommended to him that he seek reassignment within this District to a non-counseling position, and request that in the event he does not make this request that the Committee on Ethics and Standards follow customary procedures.

A fair question arises as to whether counselors would be willing to subject themselves to the sort of evaluative behavior which has been discussed.

Further, would counselors be prepared to enforce high standards on one another, particularly when in doing so they might very well be affecting the careers of friends? The answer to this must be speculative. But if counselors are willing to say, as do other professional workers, that the profession and the welfare of its clientele must come before the needs of any given practitioner, they just might be able to assume this kind of responsibility.

This is not to say that school counselors should be expected to leap into an advanced level of professional conduct alone. Perhaps they could; however, many could very easily use help. To provide such help they might want to call upon an outside consultant (counselor educator, guidance worker from the county office, State Department of Education worker) to meet with them at each of the conferences recommended, perhaps to assume a leadership role. Such a person would, to be sure, have to be one in whom the counselors could place confidence and regard as a colleague. He should be at least as well trained as they, have had appropriate experience, and be fully certified—in effect, an outside-insider. He should emphatically not be a local school administrator.

Another legitimate question might be raised concerning the size of the professional conference groups. Clearly it would be ludicrous for a school with two counselors to sit in judgment of each other, or for a single counselor to behave in the ways suggested toward himself. It would seem, at this admittedly primitive and "in search of advocacy" level that groups of not less than four nor more than ten counselors would be appropriate. This might mean that the counselors associated with two high schools might, in some areas, need to meet together; that more commonly the counselors working in three or four junior high schools might meet in common; and that counselors from several elementary schools could form a professional conference group. Given four high schools, each with four counselors, it might even be desirable to create four professional conference groups, each consisting of counselors from each of the schools. The mechanics would not be simple, but could be surmountable.

III. COMMITTEES ON ETHICS AND STANDARDS SHOULD BE CREATED

As a further means of promoting and maintaining competent performance among counselors associated with a school district, committees on ethics and standards should be established. The basic committee could well be developed at the building level, and consist of counselors offering services there. It might be desirable under some circumstances for the basic committee to be a group consisting of perhaps eight to ten counselors from neighboring schools. A senior committee consisting of representatives from building-level groups could be organized at the school district level, or, in very large districts, on a high school attendance area basis or according to some other criterion. The functions of these committees would be, essentially, four.

THE SELECTION FUNCTION

Candidates for counseling positions should be engaged for practice only upon the recommendation of counselors. Candidates might well be interviewed by a school's committee on ethics and standards and, subsequently, by the district (or area) committee, assuming that a positive recommendation was forwarded by the building-level group. Selection procedures could include interviews, review of academic records, written recommendations, locally devised tests (or nationally standardized tests, should appropriate instruments ever be available), and determination that candidates subscribe to the APGA Code of Ethics. Selection of counselors by specialists in school administration seems an unlikely means of securing the services of the best qualified. Too often professional competence is seen by administrators as reflecting less the promise of success in the guidance office than such irrelevant factors as past teaching performance, skill at public relations, and absence of any history of boat-rocking behavior. Counselors, on the other hand, might be predicted to place more faith in the training of the candidate, his performance in oral interviews where responses might reflect counseling rather than administrative attitudes, and so on.

THE RETENTION FUNCTION

Evaluation of counselors is traditionally left to school administrators and it is suggested that counselors assume this responsibility in order that more meaningful evaluation of professional competence might be maintained. Local, area, or district counselors, working from their professional conferences, might determine that a colleague should no longer be permitted to perform counseling services in the school. This recommendation would be passed on, perhaps in the manner suggested above, to the district or area committee on ethics and standards. The committee could serve as an appeal board for the counselor concerned and would be expected to review judgments of the lower-level group. Should its decision be that the public and professional interest would best be served by removal of the counselor from practice, a letter to that effect would be sent to the director of personnel with carbons to the district superintendent and building principal. Should a history develop of administrators typically ignoring committee recommendations and maintaining incompetent persons in practice, consideration might be given to forwarding copies of future recommendations to the school board president or possibly to all members of the board.

Continued failure of counselors to receive adequate attention to their recommendations could be met by notifying placement offices and colleges of education of the difficulties encountered, and, lastly, by resignations.

THE BEGINNING COUNSELOR SUPERVISION FUNCTION

A third function of the proposed committee on ethics and standards could be the provision of supervision and assistance to new counselors, entering the profession at the beginner level. Consideration might be given to reserving the title, "counselor," for those workers who had not only completed their full academic preparation but who had also met with success during a two year on-the-job period of apprenticeship as "counseling associates." Counseling associates might fulfill most functions of fully-accepted counselors but would be responsible to a senior colleague who would, in turn, be responsible for the beginner. The experienced counselor would be expected by his colleagues to work closely with the beginner during his first year or two until the associate had earned admission to counselor ranks. An extension of this proposal might involve limiting membership in the ethics and standards committee to counselors, and withholding the vote from associates in professional conferences.

THE COMPLAINT INVESTIGATION FUNCTION

A final role of the ethics and standards committees might be found in the realm of reviewing complaints from professionals, students, or the lay public concerning the practice of colleagues. Such complaints are made, day in and day out, with good reason and without—but they are made to building principals. This traditional practice is both ludicrous and anti-professional. The principal should be enabled to tell complainers that their best means of lodging a grievance would be to reduce allegations to writing and submit them to the committee on ethics and standards. Such complaints should receive prompt attention at the local level, and be responded to by the area or district committee chairman after full details of the incident had been thoroughly investigated.

SUMMARY

It has been postulated that as counselors we have not adopted adequate procedures to assess the competence of those who practice our craft—that we assume quality but don't control for it. The suggestion has been made that we must be self-disciplining before we achieve autonomy; that we must enjoy a large measure of autonomy before we can meaningfully call ourselves a profession; and that we must have the status, responsibility, authority, and the assumption of competence typically associated with the accepted professions in order that we may best fulfill our unique helping role in human relationships.

Several methods of quality control have been suggested. Others might be considered (evaluation of guidance programs by counselors and counselor educators from outside of the specific school, employing the free-choice method in assignment of students to counselors, establishing a random-check system in professional conferences rather than the specific orientations discussed, requiring the periodic return of counselors to supervised practicum in university settings, and so on). But no methods of improving and maintaining competence will be successful if they exist only on paper. If these thoughts have merit in theory, their workability will depend first upon advocacy among those who share these several convictions, and secondly upon implementation. The ways await the will, and the will precedes the fact.

Catharsis

18A. Should the counselor be held legally responsible for the quality of care he provides, or is he properly judged in the same context as other prudent men? How do we feel about ourselves as experts who may be called upon to defend the expertness of our professional behavior?

18B. Does the desire of counselors to provide a social service rule out their insistence upon economic rewards comparable with those available to others with similar education and responsibility (or substantially less)? Discuss some of the implications of continued economic medicocrity for educators.

18C. What is your reaction to the thought that evidence of APGA membership should be given by graduate students prior to their admission to practicum, and that such membership should be expected of newly appointed counselors by their senior colleagues prior to beginning professional practice?

19A. Who constitute the "Education Establishment" referred to by Mr. Fulks? Where stand practitioners in the Establishment? Where *should* they stand?

19B. If professional training in education is as mediocre as 'Mr. Fulks suggests, why don't practitioners do something about it? (How about school district committees of practitioners to grant or deny salary schedule credit for graduate study, upon teacher application—and the withholding of such credit for specific courses taken with specific professors when those courses and professors are adjudged by practitioners to be mediocre?)

19C. Is there any good reason why professional training in education should not be rigorous? What might added rigor contribute? *Are teachers and other specialists really prepared to undergo such training and subject themselves to high standards of evaluation?*

19D. Prepare a brief statement suggesting what our profession might be like if views expressed by Mr. Fulks (an administrator) were accepted and acted upon vigorously by all educators in positions of leadership.

20A. Dr. Stefflre mentions that "Former counselors who are now administrators, supervisors, or college instructors are all evidences of 'waste' recruitment in the sense that they did not have a lasting and firm identification with the occupation of the school counselor." What procedures might be available to promote closer counselor identification with his profession (or specialty)?

20B. Dr. Stefflre dichotomizes between those who emphasize the "school" in school counseling and those who emphasize the "counseling." Readers might react to the proposition that the school counselor's unique situation is such that he can properly emphasize *both*.

20C. The counselor feels more professional, Dr. Stefflre feels, because he has a code of ethics. But we have evolved no way of enforcing our code of ethics; thus, can the possession of such a code really be viewed as pertinent?

20D. The reader should be very honest with himself, and indicate who his "hidden audience" is. Does he seek the approval of educators? Of psychologists? Social workers? Parents? If, in a given circumstance, he had to choose between pleasing a parent and pleasing an internalized notion of what psychologists would expect, whom would he try to please? Suppose the choice were between pleasing a *teacher* or a psychologist? Is there something about *school* counseling which requires the practitioner to constantly try to please *various* hidden audiences?

20E. It is pointed out by Dr. Stefflre that "Our professional identification is so diffuse that we cannot select a model for ourselves from among ourselves but rather must look elsewhere for significant professional others." Who are some of the "significant professional others" after whom we might successfully model ourselves?

20F. Dr. Stefflre says, "There may be a conflict . . . within a professional association between its leaders who are very concerned about advancing professionalization and the rank and file members of the association who are less eager for changes." With reference to counseling, could it be the other way around? Might true professionalization of counselors pose too many threats for guidance directors and counselor educators? What about true professionalization of teachers? How might that be viewed by department chairmen, principals, superintendents, school board members? Professionalization is only a means toward the end of better service to people—but is the public prepared for all that would be involved in the professionalization of education?

20G. Dr. Stefflre tells us that "School administrators in some states have effectively blocked or weakened regulations requiring certification of counselors." Why do we permit this?

20H. We often use the physician as our model of "The Professional Man," in admiration of his occupational skills, organizational arrangements, enviable financial circumstances, and status, although we may be appalled at the social points of view broadcast by groups with which he affiliates. The physician has an idealized view of *himself* as an effective model. The physician employed by the Public Health Service probably sees himself as a Man in White, marching purposefully here and there, brandishing knives and comforting children, all-adangle in stethoscopes, never sleeping, and living in financial squalor. However, his real situation is notably different. But how does the school counselor see himself? Have we an ideal professional model within our own ranks?

20I. Dr. Stefflre asks, "What price professionalization?" Let the reader react to the question, "What price non-professionalization?"

21A. The suggestion has been made that organized counseling "bring pressure upon commercial enterprises to employ occupational titles which do not imply expertise" in counseling. What pressures might counselor organizations bring? Is this too much akin to power politics? Have we a right to assert "ownership" of the title "Counselor"?

21B. What local steps might be taken by counselors to insure that persons employed to work as counselors are fully trained?

21C. The suggestion is made that educators who hold masters' and doctors' degrees place the initials of the degrees after their names in correspondence, that diplomas and certificates be displayed on the office wall, that special diplomas be awarded for advanced study and professional contributions, and so on. Some school people would flatly reject such proposals as being "show offy," "pretentious," or, horrors, "undemocratic." But is it pretentious to demonstrate respect for one's profession and to communicate to others that school people possess high levels of training? Does not the public have a right to know the qualifications of those who undertake to serve it? How does the reader feel? If the reader holds an M.A., M.Ed., Ed.D., or similar evidence of advanced training and competence in his profession is he prepared to employ some of the techniques suggested? Is he *really* ready *to be a little bit different*?

21D. It is suggested that counselors undertake to police themselves. Are counselors ready for all that this implies? What problems might be involved?

21E. Would counselors be prepared to report regularly to the state and national organizations on conditions-for-counseling as they exist in their own schools? What difficulties suggest themselves?

21F. A proposal is made for a separate graduation program for new counselors—or, at least, an Event of some magnitude. What might be included in such a program? Unfortunately, no deceased Greek ever had kind things to say about counselors so we don't have an oath to repeat. Would the reader like to play Dead Greek Scholar and make a pass at devising an appropriate verbal commitment for new counselors to subscribe to?

21G. Rather specifically, what sorts of public relations programs might be developed at local levels to inform the public of the school counselor's professional role as a means toward promoting autonomy for the practitioner and acceptance among members of the public?

22A. Dr. Dunsmoor draws attention to some of the attacks which counselors and other mental health workers live with. In what sorts of ways might counselors become more vigorous in telling our story and putting half-baked critics on the defensive? What implications does the reader find *vis-a-vis* rational, enlightened, and purposefully helpful critics of education?

23A. With reference to Dr. Kaplan's paper, what are some of the things the profession might do to make the initial years of practice better and more productive for the beginner and for his clientele?

24A. With reference to Dr. Barclay's article concerning the attack on testing and counseling, have teachers characterized as "sex degenerates or sex perverts" no avenues for legal relief? Neurotics and psychotics will continue their vitriolic attacks on education, educators, and on the tools some educators see fit to employ as long as they may do so with impunity. Has the reader any concrete suggestions as to what individual counselors and the associations which represent them can do to protect the practitioner and the profession from irresponsible smear campaigns? What might teachers do?

24B. Should counselors and other mental health workers be autonomous in their practices to the extent that they are permitted to use those techniques which, in their judgment, are appropriate to the circumstances at hand; or should their professional behavior be subjected to the attacks of any uninformed person who is able to find his way into print? What are some ways in which autonomy might be achieved, within a socially desirable framework?

24C. Disregarding the psychoceramic critics of our profession (who will never be convinced by rational methods), are there ways in which counselors and school psychologists can educate the overwhelmingly sensible and fair American public as to what our work is and how we go about doing it?

24D. Simply because a test may include *some* items which may be obnoxious to *some* people, is this sufficient justification to abandon its use? Is the counselor prepared to abandon a test which he knows to be unreliable or invalid, even if abandonment of the test would put him in direct conflict with an administrator who wants the test given? Which is the criterion by which a test should be measured: its relative technical integrity and utility, or the manner in which hypersensitive members of the community or poorly informed members of the profession might view it?

24E. If the use of any test has been demonstrated to be useful in the educational process, may that test be employed by professional specialists in schools when, in their judgment, its use is indicated; or should such usage rest upon the consent of minority groups in the community? Suppose a *majority* of the community opposes a particular test? What if school board members are in opposition to some psychometric instrument? Is professional judgment subject to lay control? Should it be? Where should the line be between public control of public institutions and professional autonomy?

24F. What is the appropriate behavior for a counselor when confronted with a fanatical parent or student condemning a particular teacher for "communist leanings"? Can we as counselors undertake serious discussions of our own needs for autonomy unless similar professional protections are extended to teachers as well? How does it happen that academic freedom, so honored in the college setting, is so shaky in its extension into the secondary and elementary school?

24G. Dr. Barclay says, "Counselors need to recognize that . . . prying reveals their own adolescent development and need for vicarious experience." Is this a fair generalization? Do well-trained counselors "pry"? Who defines what "prying" is? Simple reflections of verbal content could be seen as "invasion of the sanctity of the family" by some of the more glandular types of mental health critics.

24H. According to Dr. Barclay, "Whenever research is undertaken in the public schools it should be a joint concern of both school administrators and university faculty." Can the reader suggest reasons why the involvement of administrators in guidance research is indicated? What might the role of university consultants be?

25A. The American Federation of Teachers' statement says much of teacher rights, which are related directly to the question of autonomy and presumably extend to include the school counselor. But the statement says nothing of the educator's *responsibilities*. May it be assumed that the educator whose rights are protected will behave responsibly without some sort of quality control?

25B. AFT's "Bill of Rights" calls for an "impartial tribunal" to adjudicate problems affecting teacher (educator?) employment, with the implication of judicial procedure. Does this rule out teacher assessment by groups of peers? Might the counselor who is affiliated with AFT experience a professional conflict if counselors were to establish means of assessing themselves as to competence?

25C. AFT opposes requirements that educators pursue studies "beyond those required to obtain professional status," when such requirements are hinged to threats of salary reduction. Suppose that counselors in a building were to notify a colleague that in their judgment he should either retire from counseling or return to college for advanced training to improve his competence, and suppose the incompetent counselor belonged to AFT. Where might his allegiance lie? What position might his AFT colleagues take?

25D. Using the AFT "Bill of Rights for Teachers" as a base, the reader should try drawing up a "Bill of Rights for Counselors," trying, if he can, to make it consistent with his specialty's Code of Ethics and possibly, too, with the NEA Code of Ethics, which deals in part with professional responsibilities (but says little of rights!). The result should be a document relating successfully to autonomy, competence, responsibility, and the spirit of professionalism. This may be a tall order, but one would hope it might introduce readers to some of the very complex value judgments implicit in such an undertaking.

26A. Does competence precede autonomy? Does autonomy precede professionalism? Is professionalism basic to the best public interest insofar as the counseling effort is concerned? The reader might want to take a stand on each of these questions, and defend his stance.

26B. Administrators have been evaluating teachers and counselors for years and years. What's wrong with continuing this practice?

26C. The reader might consider in detail the possible problems a counseling staff could encounter in establishing (a) Professional Conferences, (b) Case Presentations, (c) Failure, Success, and Maladaptive Conferences, (d) evaluation procedures relating counselors to one another, (e) Committees on Ethics and Standards to fulfill the responsibilities discussed, and (f) involving themselves in the counselor education effort.

Ethical Considerations for the
School Counselor

PRESENTING PROBLEM

The counselor is faced regularly with ethical problems.

Efforts to codify behaviors which are appropriate in the face of difficulties commonly faced by educators have been made by the National Education Association, with degrees of success which may best be evaluated by the reader. The NEA Code occurs first in Part IV. Ethical standards of the American Personnel and Guidance Association are included as well for their specific application to the professional specialty in which we engage. Both should be given serious attention by the practicing counselor, as their implications are many.

(It should be noted that the American Federation of Teachers has no code of ethics, for reasons best known to the membership of that organization. The AFT's "Bill of Rights" has ethical implications, however, and perhaps the reader would want to turn back to Part III for a review of that document before proceeding.)

Papers relating broadly to the question of ethical practice are included as prepared by Dr. James Adams, of Temple University, and by Ohio University's Dr. Lyle Schmidt. Particular attention is directed to the hazy matter of privileged communication by Dr. Robert Geiser, a psychologist, and Paul D. Rheingold, an attorney. Examples and discussions of unethical practice are provided by Dr. Milton Schwebel.

Dr. Charles Clark endeavors to relate the whole question of confidentiality and ethical behavior to the world of the school counselor, and two practicing school counselors, Robert F. Cox, of Pennsylvania, and Elizabeth T. Burianek, of Iowa, turn their attention, respectively, to first obligations of the school counselor and to the confidential nature of school records. In conclusion, a statement of the American Council on Education is presented which relates primarily to the safekeeping of college students' records but which is equally applicable at other school levels.

As before, it may be well for the reader to attend throughout to several questions which seem basic to the considerations presented in the articles.

If codes of ethics exist, they should be enforceable. Whose responsibility is enforcement?

Can school counselors behave according to APGA's ethics code? What problems might arise for the ethical practitioner?

If counselors are psychologists or sociologists or unique professionals rather than educators, does the NEA Code have relevance to them in their work?

If counselors are specialized educators, are there conflicts between the NEA and APGA Codes of Ethics?

What about the counselor as recommender of applicants for college, employment, scholarships, etc.?

What of the counselor and privileged communication? Is it needed in our work?

If counseling can be therapeutic, are counselors engaged in therapy?

Who are the "professionals" among the school staff?

What of the counselor, ethics, and conflicts of interest; his obligation to serve the interest of each among his clientele, among whom interests may be in conflict?

27

Code of Ethics of the Education Profession*

ADOPTED BY THE NEA REPRESENTATIVE ASSEMBLY
DETROIT, MICHIGAN, JULY 1963

PREAMBLE

We, professional educators of the United States of America, affirm our belief in the worth and dignity of man. We recognize the supreme importance of the pursuit of truth, the encouragement of scholarship, and the promotion of democratic citizenship. We regard as essential to these goals the protection of freedom to learn and to teach and the guarantee of equal educational opportunity for all. We affirm and accept our responsibility to practice our profession according to the highest ethical standards.

We acknowledge the magnitude of the profession we have chosen, and engage ourselves, individually and collectively, to judge our colleagues and to be judged by them in accordance with the applicable provisions of this code.

PRINCIPLE I

Commitment to the Student

We measure success by the progress of each student toward achievement of his maximum potential. We therefore work to stimulate the spirit of inquiry, the acquisition of knowledge and understanding, and the thoughtful formulation of worthy goals. We recognize the importance of cooperative relationships with other community institutions, especially the home.

In fulfilling our obligations to the student, we—

1. Deal justly and considerately with each student.
2. Encourage the student to study varying points of view and respect his right to form his own judgment.
3. Withhold confidential information about a student or his home unless we deem that its release serves professional purposes, benefits the student, or is required by law.
4. Make discreet use of available information about the student.
5. Conduct conferences with or concerning students in an appropriate place and manner.

° Reprinted with permission of the National Education Association.

6. Refrain from commenting unprofessionally about a student or his home.
7. Avoid exploiting our professional relationship with any student.
8. Tutor only in accordance with officially approved policies.
9. Inform appropriate individuals and agencies of the student's educational needs and assist in providing an understanding of his educational experiences.
10. Seek constantly to improve learning facilities and opportunities.

PRINCIPLE II

Commitment to the Community

We believe that patriotism in its highest form requires dedication to the principles of our democratic heritage. We share with all other citizens the responsibility for the development of sound public policy. As educators, we are particularly accountable for participating in the development of educational programs and policies and for interpreting them to the public.

In fulfilling our obligations to the community, we—

1. Share the responsibility for improving the educational opportunities for all.
2. Recognize that each educational institution may have a person authorized to interpret its official policies.
3. Acknowledge the right and responsibility of the public to participate in the formulation of educational policy.
4. Evaluate through appropriate professional procedures conditions within a district or institution of learning, make known serious deficiencies, and take any action deemed necessary and proper.
5. Use educational facilities for intended purposes consistent with applicable policy law, and regulation.
6. Assume full political and citizenship responsibilities, but refrain from exploiting the institutional privileges of our professional positions to promote political candidates or partisan activities.
7. Protect the educational program against undersirable infringement.

PRINCIPLE III

Commitment to the Profession

We believe that the quality of the services of the education profession directly influences the future of the nature and its citizens. We therefore exert every effort to raise educational standards, to improve our service, to promote a climate in which the exercise of professional judgment is encouraged, and to achieve conditions which attract persons worthy of the trust to careers in education. Aware of the value of united effort, we contribute actively to the support, planning, and programs of our professional organizations.

In fulfilling our obligations to the profession, we—

1. Recognize that a profession must accept responsibility for the conduct of its members and understand that our own conduct may be regarded as representative.
2. Participate and conduct ourselves in a responsible manner in the development and implementation of policies affecting education.
3. Cooperate in the selective recruitment of prospective teachers and in the orientation of student teachers, interns, and those colleagues new to their positions.
4. Accord just and equitable treatment to all members of the profession in the exercise of their professional rights and responsibilities, and support them when unjustly accused or mistreated.
5. Refrain from assigning professional duties to non-professional personnel when such assignment is not in the best interest of the student.
6. Provide, upon request, a statement of specific reason for administrative recommendations that lead to the denial of increments, significant changes in employment, or termination of employment.
7. Refrain from exerting undue influence based on the authority of our positions in the determination of professional decisions by colleagues.
8. Keep the trust under which confidential information is exchanged.
9. Make appropriate use of time granted for professional purposes.
10. Interpret and use the writings of others and the findings of educational research with intellectual honesty.
11. Maintain our integrity when dissenting by basing our public criticism of education on valid assumptions as established by careful evaluation of facts or hypotheses.
12. Represent honestly our professional qualifications and identify ourselves only with reputable educational institutions.
13. Respond accurately to requests for evaluations of colleagues seeking professional positions.
14. Provide applicants seeking information about a position with an honest description of the assignment, the conditions of work, and related matters.

PRINCIPLE IV

Commitment to Professional Employment Practices

We regard the employment agreement as a solemn pledge to be executed both in spirit and in fact in a manner consistent with the highest ideals of professional service. Sound professional personnel relationships with governing boards are built upon personal integrity, dignity, and mutual respect.

In fulfilling our obligations to professional employment practices, we—

1. Apply for or offer a position on the basis of professional and legal qualifications.
2. Apply for a specific position only when it is known to be vacant and refrain from such practices as underbidding or commenting adversely about other candidates.
3. Fill no vacancy except where the terms, conditions, policies, and practices permit the exercise of our professional judgment and skill, and where a climate conducive to professional service exists.
4. Adhere to the conditions of a contract or to the terms of an appointment until either has been terminated legally or by mutual consent.
5. Give prompt notice of any change in availability of service, in status of applications, or in change in position.
6. Conduct professional business through the recognized educational and professional channels.
7. Accept no gratuities or gifts of significance that might influence our professional duties.
8. Engage in no outside employment that will impair the effectiveness of our professional service and permit no commercial exploitation of our professional position.

28

Ethical Standards of the American Personnel and Guidance Association*

PREAMBLE

The American Personnel and Guidance Association is an educational, scientific, and professional organization dedicated to service to society. This service is committed to profound faith in the worth, dignity, and great potentiality of the individual human being.

The marks of a profession, and therefore of a professional organization, can be stated as follows:

1. Possession of a body of specialized knowledge, skills, and attitudes known and practiced by its members.

2. This body of specialized knowledge, skills, and attitudes is derived through scientific inquiry and scholarly learning.

3. This body of specialized knowledge, skills, and attitudes is acquired through professional preparation, preferably on the graduate level, in a college or university as well as through continuous in-service training and personal growth after completion of formal education.

4. This body of specialized knowledge, skills, and attitudes, is constantly tested and extended through research and scholarly inquiry.

5. A profession has a literature of its own, even though it may, and indeed must, draw portions of its contents from other areas of knowledge.

6. A profession exalts service to the individual and society, above personal gain. It possesses a philosophy and a code of ethics.

7. A profession through the voluntary association of its members constantly examines and improves the quality of its professional preparation and services to the individual and society.

8. Membership in the professional organization and the practice of the profession must be limited to persons meeting stated standards of preparation and competencies.

9. The profession affords a life career and permanent membership as long as services meet professional standards.

10. The public recognizes, has confidence in, and is willing to compensate the members of the profession for their services.

The Association recognizes that the vocational roles and settings of its members are identified with a wide variety of academic disciplines and

*Reprinted with permission of the American Personnel and Guidance Association.

levels of academic preparation. This diversity reflects the pervasiveness of the Association's interest and influence. It also poses challenging complexities in efforts to conceptualize:

   a. the characteristics of members;
   b. desired or requisite preparation or practice; and
   c. supporting social, legal and/or ethical controls.

The specification of ethical standards enables the Association to clarify to members, future members, and to those served by members the nature of ethical responsibilities held in common by its members.

The introduction of such standards will inevitably stimulate greater concern by members for practice and preparation for practice. It will also stimulate a general growth and identification with and appreciation for both the common and diverse characteristics of the definable roles within the world of work of Association members.

There are six major areas of professional activity which encompass the work of members of APGA. For each of these areas certain general principles are listed below to serve as guide lines for ethical practice. These are preceded by a general section which includes certain principles germane to the six areas and common to the entire work of the Association members.

SECTION A: GENERAL

1. The member exerts what influence he can to foster the development and improvement of the profession and continues his professional growth throughout his career.

2. The member has a responsibility to the institution within which he serves. His acceptance of employment by the institution implies that he is in substantial agreement with the general policies and principles of the institution. Therefore, his professional activities are also in accord with the objectives of the institution. Within the member's own work setting, if, despite his efforts, he cannot reach agreement as to acceptable ethical standards of conduct with his superiors, he should end his affiliation with them.

3. The member must expect ethical behavior among his professional associates in APGA at all times. He is obligated, in situations where he possesses information raising serious doubt as to the ethical behavior of other members, to attempt to rectify such conditions.

4. The member is obligated to concern himself with the degree to which the personnel functions of non-members with whose work he is acquainted represent competent and ethical performance. Where his information raises serious doubt as to the ethical behavior of such persons, it is his responsibility to attempt to rectify such conditions.

5. The member must not seek self-enhancement through expressing evaluations or comparisons damaging to other ethical professional workers.

6. The member should not claim or imply professional qualifications exceeding those possessed and is responsible for correcting any misrepresentations of his qualifications by others.

7. The member providing services for personal remuneration shall, in establishing fees for such services, take careful account of the charges made for comparable services by other professional persons.

8. The member who provides information to the public or to his subordinates, peers, or superiors has a clear responsibility to see that both the content and the manner of presentation are accurate and appropriate to the situation.

9. The member has an obligation to ensure that evaluative information about such persons as clients, students, and applicants shall be shared only with those persons who will use such information for professional purposes.

10. The member shall offer professional services only through the context of a professional relationship. Thus testing, counseling, and other services are not to be provided through the mail by means of newspaper or magazine articles, radio or television programs, or public performances.

SECTION B: COUNSELING

This section refers to practices involving a counseling relationship with a counselee or client and is not intended to be applicable to practices involving administrative relationships with the persons being helped. A counseling relationship denotes that the person seeking help retains full freedom of choice and decision and that the helping person has no authority or responsibility to approve or disapprove of the choices or decisions of the counselee or client. "Counselee" or "client" is used here to indicate the person (or persons) for whom the member has assumed a professional responsibility. Typically the counselee or client is the individual with whom the member has direct and primary contact. However, at times, "client" may include another person(s) when the other person(s) exercise significant control and direction over the individual being helped in connection with the decisions and plans being considered in counseling.

1. The member's *primary* obligation is to respect the integrity and promote the welfare of the counselee or client with whom he is working.

2. The counseling relationship and information resulting therefrom must be kept confidential consistent with the obligations of the member as a professional person.

3. Records of the counseling relationship including interview notes, test data, correspondence, tape recordings, and other documents are to be considered professional information for use in counseling, research, and teaching of counselors but always with full protection of the identity of the client and with precaution so that no harm will come to him.

4. The counselee or client should be informed of the conditions under which he may receive counseling assistance at or before the time he enters the counseling relationship. This is particularly true in the event that there exist conditions of which the counselee or client would not likely be aware.

5. The member reserves the right to consult with any other professionally competent person about his counselee client. In choosing his professional consultant the member must avoid placing the consultant in a conflict of interest situation, *i.e.*, the consultant must be free of any other obligatory relation to the member's client that would preclude the consultant being a proper party to the member's efforts to help the counselee or client.

6. The member shall decline to initiate or shall terminate a counseling relationship when he cannot be of professional assistance to the counselee or client either because of lack of competence or personal limitation. In such instances the member shall refer his counselee or client to an appropriate specialist. In the event the counselee or client declines the suggested referral, the member is not obligated to continue the counseling relationship.

7. When the member learns from counseling relationships of conditions which are likely to harm others over whom his institution or agency has responsibility, he is expected to report *the condition* to the appropriate responsible authority, but in such a manner as not to reveal the identity of his counselee or clients.

8. In the event that the counselee or client's condition is such as to require others to assume responsibility for him, or when there is clear and imminent danger to the counselee or client or to others, the member is expected to report this fact to an appropriate responsible authority, and/or take such other emergency measures as the situation demands.

9. Should the member be engaged in a work setting which calls for any variation from the above statements, the member is obligated to ascertain that such variations are justifiable under the conditions and that such variations are clearly specified and made known to all concerned with such counseling services.

SECTION C: TESTING

1. The primary purpose of psychological testing is to provide objective and comparative measures for use in self-evaluation or evaluation by others of general or specific attributes.

2. Generally, test results constitute only one of a variety of pertinent data for personnel and guidance decisions. It is the member's responsibility to provide adequate orientation or information to the examinee(s) so that the results of testing may be placed in proper perspective with other revelant factors.

3. When making any statements to the public about tests and testing care must be taken to give accurate information and to avoid any false claims or misconceptions.

4. Different tests demand different levels of competence for administration, scoring, and interpretation. It is therefore the responsibility of the member to recognize the limits of his competence and to perform only those functions which fall within his preparation and competence.

5. In selecting tests for use in a given situation or with a particular client the member must consider not only general but also specific validity, reliability, and appropriateness of the test(s).

6. Tests should be administered under the same conditions which were established in their standardization. Except for research purposes explicitly stated, any departures from these conditions, as well as unusual behavior or irregularities during the testing session which may affect the interpretation of the tests results, must be fully noted and reported. In this connection, unsupervised test-taking or the use of tests through the mails are of questionable value.

7. The value of psychological tests depends in part on their novelty to persons taking them. Any prior information, coaching, or reproduction of test materials tends to invalidate test results. Therefore, test security is one of the professional obligations of the member.

8. The member has the responsibility to inform the examinee(s) as to the purpose of testing. The criteria of examinee's welfare and/or explicit prior understanding with him should determine who the recipients of the test results may be.

9. The member should guard against the appropriation, reproduction, or modifications of published tests or parts thereof without express permission and adequate recognition of the original author or publisher.

Regarding the preparation, publication, and distribution of tests reference should be made to:

"Test and Diagnostic Techniques"—Report of the Joint Committee of the American Psychological Association, American Educational Research Association, and National Council of Measurements used in Education. Supplement to *Psychological Bulletin* (1954) 2, 1–38.

SECTION D: RESEARCH AND PUBLICATION

1. In the performance of any research on human subjects, the member must avoid causing any injurious effects or after-effects of the experiment upon his subjects.

2. The member may withhold information or provide misinformation to subjects only when it is essential to the investigation and where he assumes responsibility for corrective action following the investigation.

3. In reporting research results, explicit mention must be made of all variables and conditions known to the investigator which might affect interpretation of the data.

4. The member is responsible for conducting and reporting his investigations so as to minimize the possibility that his findings will be misleading.

5. The member has an obligation to make available original research data to qualified others who may wish to replicate or verify the study.

6. In reporting research results or in making original data available, due care must be taken to disguise the identity of the subjects, in the absence of specific permission from such subjects to do otherwise.

7. In conducting and reporting research, the member should be familiar with, and give recognition to, previous work on the topic.

8. The member has the obligation to give due credit to those who have contributed significantly to his research, in accordance with their contributions.

9. The member has the obligation to honor commitments made to subjects of research in return for their cooperation.

10. The member is expected to communicate to other members the results of any research he judges to be of professional or scientific value.

SECTION E: CONSULTING AND PRIVATE PRACTICE

Consulting refers to a voluntary relationship between a professional helper and help-needing social unit (industry, business, school, college, etc.) in which the consultant is attempting to give help to the client in the solving of some current or potential problem.[1]

1. The member acting as a consultant must have a high degree of self-awareness of his own values and needs in entering a helping relationship which involves change in a social unit.

2. There should be understanding and agreement between consultant and client as to directions or goals of the attempted change.

3. The consultant must be reasonably certain that he or his organization have the necessary skills and resources for giving the kind of help which is needed now or that may develop later.

4. The consulting relationship must be one in which client adaptability and growth toward self-direction are encouraged and cultivated. The consultant must consistently maintain his role as a consultant and not become a decision maker for the client.

5. The consultant in announcing his availability for service as a consultant follows professional rather than commercial standards in describing his services with accuracy, dignity, and caution.

---

[1]This definition is adapted from "Dimensions of the Consultant's Job" by Ronald Lippitt, *The Journal of Social Issues*, Vol. XV, No. 2 (1959).

6. For private practice in testing, counseling, or consulting the ethical principles stated in all previous sections of this document are pertinent. In addition, any individual, agency, or institution offering educational and vocational counseling to the public should meet the standards of the American Board on Professional Standards in Vocational Counseling, Inc.

SECTION F: PERSONNEL ADMINISTRATION

1. The member is responsible for establishing working agreements with supervisors and with subordinates especially regarding counseling or clinical relationships, confidentiality, distinction between public and private material, and a mutual respect for the positions of parties involved in such issues.

2. Such working agreements may vary from one institutional setting to another. What should be the case in each instance, however, is that agreements have been specified, made known to those concerned, and whenever possible the agreements reflect institutional policy rather than personal judgment.

3. The member's responsibility to his superiors requires that he keep them aware of conditions affecting the institution, particularly those which may be potentially disrupting or damaging to the institution.

4. The member has a responsibility to select competent persons for assigned responsibilities and to see that his personnel are used maximally for the skills and experience they possess.

5. The member has responsibility for constantly stimulating his staff for their and his own continued growth and improvement. He must see that staff members are adequately supervised as to the quality of their functioning and for purposes of professional development.

6. The member is responsible for seeing that his staff is informed of policies, goals, and programs toward which the department's operations are oriented.

SECTION G: PREPARATION FOR PERSONNEL WORK

1. The member in charge of training sets up a strong program of academic study and supervised practice in order to prepare the trainees for their future responsibilities.

2. The training program should aim to develop in the trainee not only skills and knowledge, but also self-understanding.

3. The member should be aware of any manifestations of personal limitations in a student trainee which may influence the latter's provision of competent services and has an obligation to offer assistance to the trainee in securing professional remedial help.

4. The training program should include preparation in research and stimulation for the future personnel worker to do research and add to the knowledge in his field.

5. The training program should make the trainee aware of the ethical responsibilities and standards of the profession he is entering.

6. The program of preparation should aim at inculcating among the trainees, who will later become the practitioners of our profession, the ideal to service to individual and society above personal gain.

29 | Ethical Responsibilities of Counselors

James F. Adams, Ph.D.*

One of the marks of the professional status of counseling is an increasing concern with ethical problems. This old adage about an ounce of prevention being worth a pound of cure is particularly apropos in this area. Many of the ethical problems which arise in counseling could have been either avoided or settled with a minimum of concern if the counselor had considered them in advance or had been aware of his ethical responsibilities [12]. Hence the need for some general guidelines and considerations.

COUNSELOR'S LEGAL STATUS

Dr. C. Gilbert Wrenn [16] has pointed out that the counselor actually has more legal protection, in a broad sense, than he may realize. A counselor does not have to release confidential information, personnel or counseling records, upon the *request* of a police officer, an officer of the court, or any other court official. Quite the contrary, the counselor should probably not release such information, for the counselee would then have every right to bring legal action against him. An exception to this statement may be found in those states, e.g., California, where the counselor may legally release information to certain public agencies and is protected under the law in such release. However, in general, the only legal way in which a court can gain access to a counselor's records is by serving a warrant for release of the records. Further, if the counselor keeps personal records which are not a part of the official records of the institution which he serves, these records do not have to be released when the official records are taken into custody. They would need to be mentioned specifically in the original subpoena or subpoenaed separately.

Dr. Lyle D. Schmidt [11] discusses the problems of the counseling and clinical psychologist with respect to professional recognition, privileged communication, libel, slander, the right of privacy, malpractice, and criminal liability. Gradually psychologists are gaining certification in a number of states. This certification usually affords the psychologist the same rights for "privileged communication" as is given to ministers,

°Dr. Adams is Professor of Psychology, Temple University, Philadelphia, Pennsylvania. His article appeared originally in *The School Counselor*, 12:191 (May 1965), and is reprinted with permission of the author and of the journal.

lawyers, and physicians. Insofar as counselors meet the requirements for certification, they would of course have the same protection under the law. However, for those counselors who are not certified or do not reside in states which have certification, the problem remains.

The last comprehensive survey of the counselor's right to "privileged communication" was conducted by Dr. Carol E. Smith [14]. At that time Michigan was the only state in which the counselor was protected under the law. A California attorney general's opinion suggests that confidential communication, since it is information not required by law, *might be privileged*. While this is hardly a satisfactory state of affairs, it does suggest the possibility that in California, if the issue were to arise, counselors would have legal protection. Montana specifies privilege in civil proceedings only for any information obtained "in the study and observation of child mentality." Oklahoma makes it a misdemeanor for a teacher to reveal any information concerning a child, "except as may be required in the performance of his contractual duties." It would seem that Oklahoma counselors, if they are also considered teachers, should take a close look at their "contractual duties." Seven states empower the local board of education to rule on the disposition of information as long as there is no legislation to the contrary. Thirty-seven states have no laws or rulings which are of any help to a counselor in the withholding of confidential information. Information on this problem was not available for Hawaii or Alaska.

Counselors should note that where they do not have privileged communication, they do not have an obligation to reveal confidential information unless they are under oath before a court of law. The mere request for the information on the part of an officer or court official does not obligate a counselor to reveal the information. If under oath a counselor refused to reveal confidential information, he could be cited for contempt of court. It would behoove counselors to be very certain that they are justified in withholding such information. It is likely that if the counselor's case for the withholding of such information were very strong, his professional societies, such as the American Psychological Association or the American Personnel and Guidance Association, would come to his aid. However, the counselor should make his decision to withhold legally requested information on the basis of his own personal and professional ethics and should not count on receiving aid from an outside source. It will take a number of favorable court decisions to establish precedent, and it is the writer's opinion that tests of a counselor's right to privileged communication should very clearly concern a violation of counseling ethics since unfavorable decisions will not strengthen the counseling profession's position [4].

Another point to consider is the possession of "hearsay evidence" [16]. When a counselor possesses information that a counselee has broken a law and this information has been gained in a counseling session, it is likely to be considered as "hearsay evidence." This type of evidence is not generally admissible in a court of law. Certainly an objection by an attorney as to the admissibility of the evidence would rule out the information in most cases. As much of what is gained in a counseling interview is "hearsay evidence," the possession of such information will not normally be a legal problem, although it may be an ethical problem for the counselor. Further, the possession of such information, while an ethical problem, is not a legal problem *until* the counselor is under oath. Many problems of this nature can be readily solved by encouraging the counselee to go to the proper authorities himself. The fact that a counselee reveals something of this nature to his counselor frequently indicates that he is asking for support and encouragement in making restitution.

In a juvenile court case, "hearsay evidence" may carry more weight. Attorneys are usually not present and the admissibility of evidence is left to the discretion of the judge. In an instance of this nature the counselor will have to decide for himself whether or not his testimony is a violation of counseling ethics and in the best interest of the counselee and society.

None of the foregoing should be interpreted to mean that the counselor will not cooperate with any agent of society. The intent of what has been said is only to point out that counselors may have more protection under the law than they realize and the counselor is not under an obligation to "reveal all" upon request but should use caution and discretion.

ETHICAL PRINCIPLES IN COUNSELING

Ethical standards which are of importance for counselors have been proposed from a number of sources and discussed in many more [7, 16, 5, 8, 14, 6, 1]. Many of these standards are equally applicable to all of those who are in the helping professions. Some of the more pertinent of these standards will be discussed within this section.

Counselors in all areas of work should clearly recognize the limits of their competence and should not offer services which fail to meet the professional standards of recognized specialists in the fields in question. Furthermore, a counselor should not attempt to diagnose, treat, or advise a counselee with reference to problems which are not within the counseling domain. There are times when it is very difficult or impossible to obtain the aid which is necessary for the counselee. To be realistic, there are also situations which occur when there are mandatory professional referral sources available which, in the counselor's opinion, may do more harm than good, i.e., there are "professionals" in all fields who are incompetent in their profession but who are "available." There are then, two separate problems, the first one that of no available referral source. Dr. Leona Tyler [15] states that there are some individuals whom the counselor, by virtue of his training, cannot help and that good intentions do not guarantee good results. While this is quite true, this writer cannot help but feel that the *skilled* counselor has the responsibility in this situation to act in a supportive role, i.e., be aware that he is *not* conducting therapy but at the same time realizing that by being an empathic listener he may give the individual the time he needs to resolve his own problems. It would be quite easy to become diverted into a discussion of whether or not, in fact, this isn't therapy and, perhaps, the best type of therapy [10]. In any case, the counselor will need to carefully weigh the pros and cons for continuing the relationship, and if there is any question of his being able to conduct the type of support necessary, he should follow Tyler's advice and terminate the relationship.

The second problem, i.e., referring, when in the counselor's opinion there is substantial evidence that a mandatory referral source is not a good one, is not an easy one to resolve. However, it occurs frequently enough that the issue is one which must be faced, although the writer does so with some trepidation. As an opinion which is neither supported nor negated from other sources, it would seem that the ethical thing to do would be to continue to refer individuals to this "professional" when absolutely necessary, even though in the counselor's opinion little of a beneficial nature for the counselee may be accomplished. At the same time, the counselor has a very real responsibility to sensitize his administrators and fellow counselors to the problem. Incompetency is much more difficult to document than unethical behavior; yet the counselor should do everything he can to remedy a situation of this type through documentation and through enlisting the aid of other professionals if possible.

A counselor should not normally accept a counselee who is receiving psychological assistance from another professional worker unless an agreement has been reached as to the respective areas of help being offered or unless the counselee's former professional relationship has been terminated. This principle has both ethical and practical implications. Counselors should work in cooperation with other agencies and professional workers far more than they do at the present time [9, 13]. Without this cooperation there can be much duplication of effort as well as a loss of valuable information. If counselors wish to consider themselves as professional people, they will need to develop professional relationships.

The counselor should also insist on ethical standards with respect to his associates. As a general rule, the counselee's permission should be gained before communicating any information to another person or agency. A counselor in a school setting should assume, until proved wrong, that other school personnel are capable of maintaining confidences. He should be quite sure that they are aware of the need and the reasons for maintaining this confidence. It is the counselor's responsibility to help develop this awareness. Many problems in this area could have been avoided if counselors had assumed this responsibility, or educative function, prior to expecting its automatic occurrence. If the counselor finds that his professional colleagues are not able to act in a professional manner, he should withhold confidences even though their knowledge of the counselee's problem might benefit the counselee. Many times a counselor can sensitize teachers to the fact that a child has a problem without being specific about what has been told the counselor in confidence. The welfare of the counselee is a primary consideration, and considerable thought should be given to this before a confidence is revealed (without the counselee's permission) to teachers or other professional people.

The counselor should guard confidences which are extended to him in respect to a counselee. When information is gained from other professional workers or parents, it is not wise in most instances to inform the counselee that the information has been obtained. This is not to say that the counselee should be unaware of the fact that the counselor has contacted and is working with the pertinent outside agencies (although it is desirable to get the counselee's permission to make this contact); but rather that by telling the counselee of the information obtained, the counselor may be destroying another very essential relationship. As a rule, the only time a counselor should reveal a confidence received from another professional or, for that matter, a confidence received from counselee or his parents, is when it is quite clear that there is imminent danger to the counselee or to society. Of course, if permission is given to release the confidence, it ceases to be an ethical problem and becomes one of wisdom.

A counselor should present or report his findings with respect to a counselee accurately and simply to facilitate understanding. It should not be assumed that the referral source or the recipient of the report understands complicated psychological jargon unless this is known to be true. In many instances the counselor does not have the professional training to make a diagnostic judgment (e.g., schizophrenic behavior), and typing a counselee with such a term can have deleterious effects. If the counselor feels that the counselee has an emotional problem, he can state it just as simply as that, i.e., "I feel that the counselee has an emotional problem which needs attention." Psychological nomenclature which is misused, and even sometimes when correctly used, can be harmful. The rule is that any communication concerning a client should promote the welfare of the client. It should be insured that any recipient of a communication (or possible future recipient) concerning a counselee can understand and profit from that communication. With respect to this, the professional training and experience of the recipient, if known, should be considered.

The counselor should refuse to suggest or support unwarranted assumptions, invalid applications, or unjustified conclusions with respect to psychological instruments or techniques. This is frequently done with the individual intelligence test when questionable clinical conclusions are drawn from very meager evidence. Many counselors have had an introductory course in the use of projective techniques. While this experience is valuable in sensitizing the counselor to an area of personality evaluation, the use of these same tests for diagnosis, without much more extensive training, is most unethical and may be harmful to the counselee.

Occasionally a counselor is found who has been oversold on a personality theory. Psychoanalytic personality theory seems to produce this result quite frequently. It should be remembered that there is *no* personality theory to the present time which has been sufficiently validated to warrant unrestrained enthusiasm. In any case, diagnosis of this type is seldom a function of the school counselor, and it seems to this writer that many counselors verge on being unethical in their diagnoses which are based on personality theory and which are largely unsupported from objective evidence.

As a member of a helping profession a counselor should be willing to devote part of his services to work not included in his duties or for which he will receive little, if any, financial return. School counselors occasionally will have students come back to them after they have graduated from school. Within limits the school counselor and other counselors have a continuing responsibility for past counselees. The problem of performing counseling without financial remuneration when the counselee is unable to afford a fee is not as simple as it seems. In our society a premium is placed on that for which we pay financially. Frequently services which are offered for nothing are evaluated at the same level. Consequently the counselor should be very sure that the counselee cannot pay at least a token fee if this is the customary practice.

A cardinal obligation of the counselor is to respect the integrity and to protect the welfare of the counselee. A counselor's ultimate responsibility is to society, and his professional behavior should reflect his awareness of this. The welfare of the counseling profession and of the counselor are clearly subordinate to the welfare of society. In most instances the welfare of society can be best served by protecting the welfare of the counselee. Only when it is quite clear that either society or the counselee is in imminent danger should a counselor consider breaking a counseling confidence.

Dr. Edward S. Bordin [3] notes four areas of counselor responsibility to be considered in ethical decisions: to society, to his sponsoring unit, to his client, and to his profession. Another source for ethical consideration is the counselor himself. Most certainly a counselor's values will enter into his ethical decisions. It is impossible to state precisely what personal ethical standards a counselor should hold, particularly in a constantly shifting environment and society. About all that can be said is that a counselor should be aware of his values and his reasons for holding them. A counselor should not insist that all individuals hold the same standards that he personally holds. This is not to imply that a counselor must compromise his personal standards, but it should be remembered that they are *personal* standards. A statement from Ethical Standards of Psychologists [5] is worthy of note as it applies equally well to counselors.

> "Very often the resolution of ethical problems requires that the psychologist choose between two or more interests that are in conflict. Are the psychologist's obligations primarily to the social group, or to his individual client, or to his profession, or to himself? There is, of course, no simple answer to this question. Most situations where ethical decisions are necessary involve an implicit hierarchy of values, and this hierarchy has to be redefined for each situation. The equation of ethical responsibility is a complex one: weights for the variables must be computed anew as each new ethical problem is solved."

HOW DO COUNSELORS FEEL ABOUT ETHICAL PROBLEMS

A study by Smith [14] will be considered in some detail because of its pertinence to this topic and because of the large number of counselors found in the secondary schools. In this study professional members of the National Vocational Guidance Association submitted critical incidents in which ethical decisions were involved. From these incidents an ethical questionnaire was constructed. This, in turn, was sent to 1,225 professional members of NVGA. Six hundred questionnaires, or approximately 50 per cent, were returned. The questionnaire was scored to indicate the degree to which the respondents would favor revealing confidential information to some authorized agency or person. A near normal distribution of scores was found. A high score on the questionnaire indicated that the respondent favored revealing confidential information to an authorized agency or person; a low score indicated the converse. In other words, a high score indicated that the respondent's major loyalty was to society; a low score indicated that the respondent's major loyalty, or feeling of responsibility, was to the counselee. The group most closely associated with secondary school counseling showed the greatest preference for social obligation choices. Public school employees emphasized civic responsibility more than did any other occupational field. All educational counselors below the college level were significantly higher in social obligation choices than were college counselors. The greater the amount of public school teaching experience the respondent had, the greater was his degree of loyalty to society, and the lesser was his feeling of loyalty to the counselee.

One hopeful sign found was that the more graduate units in guidance, psychology, and related subjects, the greater was the loyalty of the respondent to the counselee. Respondents with the doctorate had the lowest mean scores on the questionnaire or were the highest counselee-centered group. Neither amount of counseling experience nor amount of time devoted to counseling proved to be a significant factor when comparing responses to the questionnaire.

A comparison of related items concerning access to cumulative records ranked administrators, other counselors, parents, teachers, social welfare agencies, law enforcement agencies, and employers—in decreasing order —for accessibility to records. Availability of records to the latter two groups was considered extremely debatable. Respondents tended to agree that personal problem information should not be available, but they tended to disagree as to whether administrators, other counselors, welfare agencies, or the counselee himself should have access to this information. Three fourths of the respondents agreed that when information was received directly from the counselee, the counselor had a responsibility to maintain the confidence.

Dr. Smith concludes that, with the exception of imminent harm to the counselee or others, respondents tended to place loyalty to the counselee above loyalty to society, although there was a tendency for public secondary school counselors not to share this direction of loyalty. Based upon the concurrence of at least 70 per cent of the respondents, Smith proposes that the following ethical standards be considered by counselors:

1. The counselee commands the primary loyalty of the counselor under ordinary conditions.
2. A counselor is justified in revealing confidential information to selected individuals when the counselee or others are in imminent physical danger.
3. A counselor should not voluntarily, nor upon request of the police, reveal counselee information of any offense short of guilt of a major crime.
4. A counselor should not voluntarily, nor upon request of administrators or parents, reveal any information about a counselee or former counselee received in confidence.
5. A counselor is not released from maintaining a confidence because others have the same knowledge.
6. A counselor is released from maintaining a confidence if he gains the counselee's consent to reveal such information.
7. When two counselees are seeking help on a mutual problem, a counselor should not reveal either counselee's confidence to the other.
8. When two counselors are working with the same counselee, it is ethical for them to share confidential information.
9. Confidential information may be revealed to another counselor if the counselee's anonymity is maintained.

Smith also proposes the following standards relating to the confidentiality of cumulative records:

1. Cumulative records should contain a conselee's transcript of grades, achievement test results, mental ability and other aptitude test results, interest inventories, personal problem information, and discipline records.
2. Teachers and other counselors who are directly concerned should have routine access to all cumulative record data except discipline and personal problem information.
3. All data concerning a counselee except personal problem information should be available to school administrators.
4. Parents and social welfare agencies should have access to achievement test results, interest inventories, and transcripts of grades.
5. A counselee should have access to his own transcript of grades and all test data except mental ability test results.

It might be said, as a practical criticism of these cumulative record proposals, that most schools have extremely lax filing systems. It is possible for almost any determined person to obtain access to cumulative record files with little difficulty. Furthermore, withholding materials from the files before handing them to a responsible person seems a little like questioning a person's patriotism. A more practical proposal might be for the counselor to keep two sets of records. In one set of files would be kept materials on the student to which authorized personnel would have access. In the counselor's personal file would be kept the confidential materials on the counselee.

Lastly, Smith proposes several standards relating to other aspects of counseling:

1. A counselor should not intervene in a counselee's curriculum choice despite predictive evidence of academic or emotional outcomes.
2. A parent who has given information about a counselee's problem should be promised confidence.
3. A counselor's record of a counselee's psychotic behavior should be made available to other schools.
4. It is ethical for a counselor to gather information about a counselee from other schools without the counselee's consent.

It will be noted that almost all of Smith's proposals can be subsumed under the heading of counseling in a manner which will do the most to promote the counselee's welfare. It is also apparent from her study that there is a further need for school counselors to consider their ethical responsibilities with respect to their own school and their personal professional status. Lack of agreement of these counselors on many ethical problems highlights the need for continuing thought in this area. Perhaps the school counselor could sensitize his administrative and teaching colleagues by an open discussion of ethical problems and communicate his ethical responsibilities to those with whom he works.

CONCLUSION

Dr. Milton Schwebel [12] believes that the causes of unethical behavior can be categorized into three areas: "The overpowering self-interest of the professional worker as expressed in personal profit, self-enhancement, and the maintenance of security and status; poor judgment, due in part at least to inexperience in problem solving in counseling; ignorance of technical knowledge and of one's own values." It may be that not much can be done to help the counselor in the first of Schwebel's categories; however, by being familiar with the problems which are likely to arise in the ethical area and by being adequately trained in counseling, the counselor should have little excuse for violations of ethical principles because of the last two categories.

Many of the considerations which have been discussed here are common problems for counselors. The theme running through almost every ethical consideration is that the goals and purposes of society can be best served by keeping the welfare of the individual counselee as the paramount concern.

REFERENCES

1. Adams, J. F. *Problems in Counseling: A Case Study Approach.* New York: Macmillan Co., 1962.

2. American Personnel and Guidance Association. "Ethical Standards," *Personnel Guid. J.* (1961), 40, 206–209.

3. Bordin, E. S. *Psychological Counseling.* New York: Appleton-Century-Crofts, Inc., 1955.

4. Carter, T. M. "Professional Immunity for Guidance Counselors," *Personnel Guid. J.* (1954), 33, 130–135.

5. Committee on Ethical Standards for Psychologists. *Ethical Standards of Psychologists.* Washington, D. C.: The American Psychological Association, 1953.

6. Committee on the Preparation of Ethical Standards. "A Proposed Code of Ethics for A.P.G.A., *Personnel Guid. J.* (1959), 38, 168–170.

7. Gluck, S. et al. "A Proposed Code of Ethics for Counselors," *Occupations* (1952), 30, 484–490.

8. Hahn, M. E. and MacLean, M. S. *Counseling Psychology.* New York: McGraw-Hill Book Co., 1955.

9. Mitchell, H. E. "A Brief History of an Interdisciplinary Relationship," *J. Couns. Psychol.* (1955), 2, 201–204.

10. Rogers, C. R. "The Characteristics of a Helping Relationship," *Personnel Guid J.* (1958), 37, 6–16.

11. Schmidt, L. D. "Some Legal Considerations for Counseling and Clinical Psychologists," *J. Couns. Psychol.* (1962), 9, 35–44.

12. Schwebel, M. "Why Unethical Practice?" *J. Couns. Psychol.* (1955), 2, 122–128.

13. Shoben, E. J., Jr. "Some Thoughts on Interprofessional Relationships," *J. Couns. Psychol.* (1955), 2, 196–201.

14. Smith, Carol E. "Development of Ethical Standards in the Secondary School Counseling Relationship for the Use of Counseling Information." Unpublished Doctoral Dissertation, University of Southern California, 1956.

15. Tyler, Leona E. *The Work of the Counselor*. New York: Appleton-Century-Crofts, Inc., 1961.

16. Wrenn, C. G. "The Ethics of Counseling," *Educ. Psychol. Measmt.* (1952) 12, 161–177.

30

Some Ethical, Professional, and Legal Considerations for School Counselors

Lyle D. Schmidt, Ph.D.*

It is generally believed that most of what clients talk about with counselors is rather personal in nature. It may not always be the sort of information that a client would purposely conceal from other people but many times he would. As a matter of fact, the very secrecy of the information may sometimes be the reason he has come to the counselor.

The more one works with people in a counseling capacity the more he realizes how significant the private or personal aspects of the clients' lives and experiences are to them. Even as psychologically "open" as children are, they soon learn the concept of having secrets and learn, too, that all things they see or do or think or feel are not to be shared with others. Sometimes if they do they may be punished; sometimes they may be embarrassed; sometimes they may be ashamed; sometimes they may be disappointed because the other person simply does not understand or appreciate what they try to share with him.

These privacies can affect everyone in unlimited ways, as we all know. To experience something "bad" and not feel safe to tell someone about it can certainly be a conflicting situation and may even be traumatic. To experience something of great joy only to realize how comparatively unmoved another person is by your best attempt to explain your joy can be a severe disappointment. The tremendous variety of events and consequences is apparent—as are the many developmental effects a series of these events might have on one's life.

One implication of all this seems to be that a large part of our life experience is essentially private—whether or not one desires it to be so. Some things cannot quite be told to others, even though one tries. This being the case, and if these are some of the things that clients seek to discuss in a counseling relationship, then how a counselor receives them and what he does with them is of real concern—to a client because these revelations are basic to his status as a person and if they are treated disrespectfully, he is treated disrespectfully; to a client's family and friends because of

*Dr. Schmidt is an Associate Professor of Educational Psychology, University of Minnesota, Minneapolis. His article appeared originally in the *Personnel and Guidance Journal*, 44:4:376 (December 1965), and is reprinted with permission of the author and of the journal.

their interest in and responsibility for the client, and, as a result, what happens to him affects them; to the community at large indirectly since it countenances the counseling act and directly since anyone may be the next to become a client; to a counselor's colleagues because whatever he does in his work will reflect on what they claim to do and on how individuals and the community regard counselors and counseling; to the counselor himself since he, too, is a person with needs involving others and expectations or feelings about what is "good" and "proper" for interpersonal relations.

Is it any wonder that so much attention is focused on the behavior of the counselor by the public as well as by counselors themselves? It certainly seems to be partial explanation for the emphasis in counselor training programs on "the dignity of the client," "the right of self-determination," and "the avoidance of client manipulation." It is also true that protection of the individual and his privacy represents a basic feature of our entire legal and governmental system. We learn in high school that the Fourth Amendment to the Constitution provides that:

> The right of the people to be secure in their persons, houses, papers, and effects, against unreasonable searches and seizures, shall not be violated, and no warrants shall issue, but upon probable cause, supported by oath or affirmation, and particularly describing the place to be searched, and the persons or things to be seized.

It would seem to be of interest to examine some of these sources of interest in or concern about the activities and behavior of counselors in their professional work. First, three general sources of such interest or concern will be suggested and briefly described. Then an attempt will be made to discuss the implications of each in greater detail.

One general type of concern might be termed *legal*. "Legal" means "according to law or lawful," and "law" in turn, refers to a body of rules recognized by a state or community as binding on its members. "Law" can also refer to the condition of society brought about by observance of these rules. For purposes of this paper, then, let us think of the "legal" concern over counseling as *what society expects from the counselor or limits him to in his work with clients*.

A second general type of concern might be termed *professional*. "Professional" is defined as "pertaining to a profession or appropriate to a profession." Without a detailed consideration at this time of how "profession" is determined, let it be assumed temporarily that counseling either is now a profession or will eventually become one. It should also be noted that one of the dictionary meanings of "ethical" was found to be "in accordance with formal or professional rules of right and wrong." Such rules typically are in the form of professional codes of ethics which may be either written

or implied. Within this paper let us think of "professional," then, as relating to *what one's colleagues expect from him as a counselor or limit him
to in his work with clients.*

A third type of concern might be termed *ethical.* In addition to the
meaning of this word stated above, "ethical" also has to do with standards
of right and wrong; of ethics and morality. "Ethics" is defined as "the
standards of right and wrong; that part of science and philosophy dealing
with moral conduct, duty, and judgment." This term might be used in a
variety of ways, but for our present purposes let us think of "ethical" as
relating to *what the counselor, morally, philosophically, and otherwise,
expects from himself as a counselor or limits himself to in his work with
clients.*

LEGAL

One source of interest in or concern about the behavior of counselors is
the community or society within which they function. The community is
concerned about most professional functions and the more powerful or influential the function is, the more the concern is demonstrated. Teaching,
for example, is an extremely powerful and influential function. Teachers
can teach children ideas, values, and behavior that may be "good" but at
the same time antithetical to what their parents think, believe, and do.
This fact probably leaves many parents suspicious if not fearful of teachers
and may partially explain why communities try to keep teachers subjugated
and dependent. The same is true of counseling since it, too, is influential
in regard to client belief and behavior.

Community concern is usually shown in at least two ways. One is
through public opinion, for the most part a diffuse and generally ineffective
expression unless it is somehow organized or focused. Some focusing occurs
politically and electorally, and occasionally, for example, through the influencing of hiring practices and salary schedules within public institutions.
A more pointed expression of community concern about professional
activity is through its legal system and its laws. Although generally designed to provide the greatest good for the greatest number, laws sometimes are established for the control or protection of specific groups. The
medical practices acts would be one example. Laws licensing psychologists
in some states would be another. As yet there are few if any laws aimed
directly at counselors, but some enacted concerning other professions
might apply to them.

It is becoming less and less unusual for counselors to be confronted with
a legal problem. It also seems safe to predict that in the future we will be
hearing more and more about lawsuits and other legal matters wherein one
of the parties is an educational institution or a person who has acted in the
capacity of counselor. Guidance and counseling services are becoming so

widespread in existence, provide such inclusive services, and are developing such increasingly intensive and intimate contacts with students that,
if for no other reason than sheer numbers and statistical probability, an
increasing number of legal incidents can be expected to occur.

It is quite possible that courts may seek with greater frequency the use
of personnel records of college and high school students involved in litigation because of the wider existence of such records and their more personal
and psychological nature. It is also conceivable that parents of a student
could claim that information contained in personnel records was damaging
to the student's reputation or standing and therefore libelous. It is even
possible that a parent or group of parents could attempt to show that certain
information obtained on students or the manner of obtaining this information, which was then placed in the record, involved an invasion of the student's privacy.

Obviously, there is a wide variety of *potential* problems in the legal
area. It would seem that counselors might benefit from having more information about laws that affect them and more knowledge about legal
procedures. At a practical level counselors might be interested in general
information on legal terminology, legal concepts, and legal practices.
Publications of T. M. Carter [2], Dr. Thomas B. Shrewsbury [8], Dr. Lyle D.
Schmidt [7], M. L. Ware [11], and especially D. W. Louisell [4] and Dr. R. L.
Geiser and P. D. Rheingold [3],° could be of help here. Counselors might
want to know what legal basis there is for their work, what have been the
legal influences in the development of their profession, what legal rights
and obligations are associated with their services, and what to do if they
become involved in a lawsuit or other legal matter.

Finally, although it is unlikely that any particular school counselor
ever will be involved in a legal situation because of his work, there is
something to be said for his anticipating the possibility. It would seem
helpful for school counselors to invite lawyers to speak at local or state
guidance meetings, from time to time, on the relation of the law to counseling and guidance practices. It might even be helpful to discuss with a
school or city attorney, or with an interested local attorney, just what a
counselor should do if some legal problem developed in his work. To wait
until something actually happens may be too late.

PROFESSIONAL

A second important source of interest in and concern about a counselor's behavior would be found in his colleagues—other counselors. They
have a vested interest since public reactions to a counselor's activities reflect on them as similar practitioners and may raise or lower their standing

°This article follows [Text Editor].

in the eyes of their clientele and others. As a result they tend to strive to enhance the status and function of counseling as much as possible, to assist and support each other in what they do as counselors, and at times to try to influence or control, within broad limits, the nature and type of official activities carried on by individual counselors.

As part of the desire of counselors as a group to enhance the status and function of counseling as much as possible, much interest has been shown in the matter of professionalization. Dr. C. Harold McCully [5] has examined this problem for school counselors in some detail and discusses six of the "developmental tasks" that must be achieved if school counseling is to become a profession. They are:

1. The unique social service the school counselor performs must be identified in a manner which will differentiate it from the services properly provided by all other staff in the school setting.

2. Standards for the selection and training of school counselors must be developed and such standards must be acceptable to the corporate group of qualified school counselors as well as to those professional schools offering counselor preparation of high quality.

3. In order to make selection and training standards functional it will be necessary to develop a means of accrediting those institutions which meet such standards on at least a minimum basis.

4. In order to assure the public and prospective employers that entering school counselors possess at least minimum competence to perform their tasks, certification must be based on more valid estimates of minimum competence.

5. Qualified practitioner school counselors, severally and as a corporate group, must actively involve themselves in winning and maintaining sufficient autonomy to permit them to perform their unique service in a professional manner; they must severally assume responsibility for their individual judgments and action in the performance of their unique service, and as a corporate group assume responsibility for safeguarding the interests of the public they serve.

6. The corporate group of qualified school counselors must possess and enforce a code of ethics governing the professional conduct of its members.

When or if these "tasks" are satisfactorily accomplished seems to be a matter of group consensus. No agency exists whose function it is to certify the professionalization of occupational groups. Some people say school counseling is already a profession. Many say it is not and may never be one. Still others feel the question is not worth wasting time on since the matter is irrelevant anyhow—"counseling is as counselors do."

The profession also attempts to assist and support its practitioners as much as possible in their day-by-day activities. One major effort in this regard is the establishment and maintenance of quality training programs through which the knowledge and skills necessary for practice are transmitted to potential colleagues. A second major effort here would be various attempts to provide support to colleagues as they face problems in assuming difficult professional responsibilities and maintaining their morale.

Once a counselor agrees to counsel with a client he must also accept the obligation of seeing this person through at least some initial or contributing solution to his difficulty, no matter how unpleasant or stressful the situation may become. This often entails the responsibility of making professional judgments that may have far-reaching consequences both for the client and for the counselor. Frankly, it seems that too many counselors enjoy the benefits and satisfactions of their work but sometimes abandon their professional responsibilities when the going gets rough. Many times by seeking consultation in difficult cases from colleagues and professional groups, the counselor can get perspective on his situation and ideas and support on what he might do.

Morale can also become a problem to counselors at times and can seriously hamper a counselor's productivity or his counseling skills. Dr. C. Gilbert Wrenn [12] has discussed a number of difficulties that are related to this problem. They have been modified slightly to apply to counselors.

> 1. A fundamental lack of assurance of the status and importance of counseling and of his own position can lead to the development of compensatory behavior such as belligerence or apologetic attitudes.
> 2. A blunting of one's psychological sensitivities because of constant and repetitive human contact.
> 3. The tendency toward smugness in some counselors as a result of client dependence and gratitude.
> 4. The possibility of discouragement and self-disparagement from a relization of the complexity of human behavior.
> 5. The liability of the strain of indecision and uncertainty as to the most constructive course of action in dealing with a client or staff member.

Wrenn [12] also mentions some ways in which the counselor might use his own resources to prevent the development of such difficulties or to help reverse them if they already exist.

> 1. He might, in general, attempt to have more fun from his associations with people.
> 2. He should try to recognize his fatigue points and deliberately avoid any extensive contact with people once that point has been reached.
> 3. He should stop setting impossible goals for himself in terms of the amount of work to be accomplished each day.
> 4. He should block out a small amount of professional reading each day and thereby help reduce the feeling of frustration that might develop over not making any professional progress.
> 5. He might try to deliberately practice small courtesies in his relations with other people. The effect could be surprisingly circular.
> 6. He can remember that ultimate values persist regardless of what might happen in our personal lives.

Counselors also have professional resources to turn to for support in situations like these and others that might arise. Consultation and discussion with understanding colleagues in his school or in professional organizations who have worked out similar problems of their own can be of tremendous help. Local, state, and national meetings and conferences of professional organizations provide many opportunities for this also.

Finally, the profession tries to influence or control, within broad limits, the nature and type of activity that is carried on by a counselor in his professional work. Most prominent here are attempts to develop and establish codes of ethical conduct. One of the first attempts to formulate such a code for counseling was made by A. J. Sutich in 1944. It was followed during the next few years by reactions of others to his statements and by further attempts to develop an ethical code for counselors. Wrenn [13] made specific application to counselors of early statements on ethics for psychologists. In 1953 the American Psychological Association [1] established a code of ethics for psychologists, and in 1961 the American Personnel and Guidance Association approved a code of ethics for its members (*Personnel and Guidance Journal,* October 1961).°

It would seem clear that there are available to counselors both official and unofficial ethical standards to which he can refer for guidance. A final word should be said about the value that counselors might derive from such ethical codes. Dr. John McGowan and Schmidt [6] mention these:

> 1. They provide a position on standards of practice to assist each member of the profession in deciding what he should do when situations of conflict arise in his work.
> 2. They help clarify the counselor's responsibilities to the client and protect the client from the counselor's violation of, or his failure to fulfill, these responsibilities.
> 3. They give the profession some assurance that the practices of members will not be detrimental to its general functions and purposes.
> 4. They give society some guarantee that the services of the counselor will demonstrate a sensible regard for the social codes and moral expectations of the community in which he works.
> 5. They offer the counselor some grounds for safeguarding his own privacy and integrity.

ETHICAL

A third source of concern about a counselor's behavior would seem to come from the counselor himself, concern for what he—morally, philosophically, and otherwise—expects from himself as a counselor or limits

---

°Also, see Dr. Carol F. Smith's recommendations, summarized in Dr. James F. Adams' article, preceding. These recommendations were included in Dr. Schmidt's original article, but are deleted here to avoid repetition [Text Editor].

himself to in his work with clients. This is related to the matter of professional ethics as discussed above, but in the last analysis such codes are always subject to the interpretation of each individual counselor. That interpretation, in turn, is a function of the individual's personal needs, values, attitudes, and past experiences. It might therefore be of interest to look at some of the ways the personality of the counselor can affect or even control his work with clients.

It is questionable whether most students entering a graduate program in counseling have any idea what *really* will be demanded of them in a counseling situation. Actually, there is little reason why they should since this aspect of counseling is seldom discussed. The "why" of this seems to be that the personal demands of counseling practice tend to be in that category of experience where "if you don't know, I can't tell you."

Neither do most trainees discover much about these demands during the more or less didactic phases in the early part of their training. There one reads and listens and discusses what counseling is about but it does not seem to have much reality, even in the most interesting and inspiring moments of theoretical or philosophical discovery.

It probably is not until a trainee sits down for the first time with a client, perhaps in practicum, that he begins to discover what personal demands counseling will make on him and whether or not, subjectively, he is "up to it." The sharp pain in his stomach when a client describes a seemingly impossible situation; the lump in his throat when a client tells of a humiliating incident; the feeling of fear or uncertainty aroused by a client's telling that he is contemplating suicide; or the anxiety of not knowing what to do or say next when the client seems to be waiting for an answer—all these reactions help the trainee to discover something about what counseling will demand from him.

Sometimes even the practicum is merely an introduction to this necessary self-discovery. It is, after all, a protected situation. Having but one or two clients to cope with at any one time and the support and understanding of a competent and experienced supervisor constantly available, a counselor might often muster enough psychological "strength" to rise up to whatever demands occur. Later on, with 20 or more clients in various stages of counseling, and consultation available only if he makes the effort to seek it out, the counselor's reactions may become somewhat more vivid.

What might be some of the personal demands that counseling can make on a counselor that will test his limits? For one thing it demands an ability and a willingness to tolerate intimate interpersonal relationships over extended periods of time. It also demands that he strive to be at his best in relating to the client and attending to what he says and does, like being *en garde* socially at all times. I think these two demands may account for the realization most counselors have sooner or later that counseling is hard and fatiguing work. If a counselor finds himself becoming reluctant toward such situations, or becoming generally irritable because of them, perhaps he is coming face to face with certain limits he is imposing on himself or his clients, not because he wants to but because that is the way he is.

Counseling demands that you be exposed to the worst as well as the best in other people. It also demands that you learn how to live with these awarenesses without being calloused by them. It involves the discovery that other people's tragedies are the counselor's daily business. It expects the mature counselor to recognize that human beings are, under the right conditions, capable of anything, and that he will seek to aid his clients to understand and cope with their experiences, whatever they may have been.

Counseling demands self-disclosure from counselors in spite of occasional directives to the contrary. If you relate to a client you are bound to reveal aspects of yourself to him. If you conceal your "self," even that is a revelation. At times a client will respond to his awareness of you in an open and direct way you might effectively capitalize on in furthering the counseling progress. At other times he might use such knowledge about you to stall the counseling process or reduce your status in the relationship because the counseling experience has grown so difficult or threatening for him. He may want very much to continue but cannot prevent himself from interfering.

In view of this, one wonders sometimes if, because of what counselors are and have not been able to change, they might want or need clients to behave in certain ways if they are to be able to counsel with them. Some counselors seem to demand that their clients ask them questions. Some desire them to be introspective. Some need them to be sociable, or insightful, or talkative, or grateful. The things that counselors need their clients to be or the ways in which they desire them to behave in order to be able to counsel with them are examples of how counselors limit themselves or of what they expect from themselves in counseling.

How they cope with these self-imposed demands or limitations is primarily a function of their personalities and certain fortunes of their life and training. Some find counseling to be personally intolerable and either develop a technique of counseling that reduces these demands, structure their jobs so as to avoid having the demands occur, or leave the field of counseling entirely. Others discover that in spite of the pain and difficulty of facing up to their feelings of stress and avoidance, to do so under favorable conditions can be personally rewarding and can at the same time improve their counseling and their feelings of adequacy toward it.

CONCLUSION

This has been a brief examination of three sources of interest in or concern about the counselor's behavior regarding client privacy—the community at large, the counselor's colleagues, and the counselor himself. Perhaps this initial consideration might encourage some continued interest; an interest many regard as a necessary aspect of the counselor's professional development.

REFERENCES

1. American Psychological Association. *Ethical Standards of Psychologists.* Washington, D. C.: American Psychological Association, 1953.

2. Carter, T. M. "Professional Immunity for Guidance Counselors," *Personnel Guid. J.* (1954), *33*, 130–135.

3. Geiser, R. L., & Rheingold, P. D. "Psychology and the Legal Process: Testimonial Privileged Communications," *Amer. Psychologist* (1964), *19*, 831–837.

4. Louisell, D. W. "The Psychologist in Today's Legal World: Part II; Confidential Communication," *Minn. Law Rev.* (1957), *41*, 731–750.

5. McCully, C. H. "The School Counselor: Strategy for Professionalization," *Personnel Guid. J.* (1962), *40*, 681–689.

6. McGowan, J. F., & Schmidt, L. D. *Counseling: Readings in Theory and Practice.* New York: Holt, Rinehart, and Winston, 1962.

7. Schmidt, L. D. "Some Legal Considerations for Counseling and Clinical Psychologists," *J. Counsel. Psychol.* (1962), *9*, 35–44.

8. Shrewsbury, T. B. "Legal Implications for Student Personnel Workers." In Esther Lloyd-Jones & Margaret Smith (Eds.), *Student Personnel Work as Deeper Teaching.* New York: Harpers, 1954, 295–323.

9. Smith, Carol E. "Development of Ethical Standards in the Secondary School Counseling Relationship for the Use of Counseling Information." Unpublished doctoral dissertation Univ. Southern California, 1956.

10. Sutich, A. "Toward a Professional Code of Ethics for Counseling Psychologists," *J. Abnorm. Soc. Psychol.* (1944), *39*, 329–350.

11. Ware, M. L. (Ed.) *The Law of Guidance and Counseling.* Cincinnati, Ohio: W. H. Anderson, 1965.

12. Wrenn, C. G. "The Fault, Dear Brutus . . ." *Educ. Psychol. Measmt.* (1949), *9*, 360–378.

13. Wrenn, C. G. "The Ethics of Counseling," *Educ. Psychol. Measmt.* (1952), *12*, 161–177.

31

Psychology and the Legal Process: Testimonial Privileged Communications

Robert L. Geiser, Ph.D.

Most of us during our lifetime will encounter situations with which we are unable to cope by ourselves because we lack the necessary knowledge and training. In our complex society there are many professional people who offer their help to others in dealing with specific problems. The roles of a lawyer, clergyman, phsyician, accountant, and various mental health specialists, for example, are familiar to us all. A professional and his client usually form an intimate relation in which the client reveals the things which concern him in order to receive the special help with his problems which the professional can provide. Often the matters of which the client speaks are of a highly personal and private nature such that he does not want other people to know of them. In some instances, the revelation of these matters might cause the client to be embarrassed or ridiculed.

In consulting a professional person, the client usually assumes that his disclosures will not be passed to others without his knowledge and consent, and then only for the specific purpose of further assisting him with his problem. When such an assumption is made by the client, a confidential relation exists and the professional person is obligated to secrecy in matters concerning his client.

Confidentiality is both an ethical and a legal issue. Professional ethics obligate the professional person to maintain his client's confidential communications. The legal doctrine of privileged communications is concerned only with guarding the client's confidences in a courtroom, in the relatively rare case where a professional person is called to testify. It is our intent to discuss the interesting and complex area of confidentiality outside of the courtroom in detail elsewhere. This paper is concerned with one special aspect of confidentiality: the matter of testimonial privileged communications.

°Dr. Geiser is associated with the Tufts-New England Medical Center, Tufts University, Boston. Paul D. Rheingold is a practicing attorney in New York. Their article appeared originally in *American Psychologist*, 19:11:831 (November 1964), and is reprinted with permission of the authors and of the journal.

Privileged communication is the legal right which exists either by statute or common law (nonstatutory law) that protects the client from having his confidences revealed publicly from the witness stand during legal proceedings. It means that certain professionals cannot be legally compelled to testify to the content of the confidential relation they entered into with their client. The privilege protects the client, and the right to exercise the privilege, i.e., the "ownership" of it, belongs to the client or lay person, not to the professional. The client's privilege imposes the legal obligation of secrecy upon the professional person in court, in those cases where the law recognizes a privilege. That is, if the client wishes, he may bar the professional person from testifying. Under certain conditions, the client may waive his privilege, and then the professional person has no legal right to withhold his testimony: He must testify.

The foundation for the legal concept of a privilege is to be found in the explicitly recognized confidential relation at common law between the attorney and his client, dating back to the late sixteenth century. It is from the lawyer's confidential relation with his client, and the broad protection for privileged communications granted that relation, that the privilege has been extended to the clients of other professional people. It has only been possible to make this extension, however, through legislation (statutory law). Lawyers remain the only professional group whose clients clearly have the privilege at common law. It should be noted that the only other relationship clearly privileged at common law is the husband-wife relation.

The rationale for the lawyer-client privilege has undergone much change, and even today legal theorists disagree as to the justification for the privilege. It has been justified on the grounds that it was necessary to insure full disclosure by the client to the attorney, without which the attorney would be unable to defend his client adequately. Not all legal theorists agree with this rationale, and there are those who would argue that the need for the privilege stems from the necessity to protect a person's right of privacy in certain vital human relations. The individual's right to privacy is protected by the Constitution against unlawful invasion by the government. It is under the threat of adverse exercise of governmental powers that the lawyer-client relation assumes its greatest importance. Privilege is essential to protect the individual's freedom and privacy in vital human relations from governmental infringement.

Appealing though the protection of the individual's rights may be, still other legal scholars would subordinate the protection of these rights to what they believe is a more important social value, accurate fact finding in litigation. The existence of the privilege operates to exclude the judge and jury from hearing good, material, relevant evidence which otherwise would be admissible. These scholars have, in a sense, partially abandoned the notion of privileged communications. They believe that confidentiality in practically all relations, when it is an obstacle to the ascertainment of truth in legal proceedings, must be repudiated. There has been a growing tendency within the legal profession toward limiting the scope of the attorney-client privilege, largely through the action of the judiciary.

However, many other professional relations are protected today from courtroom disclosure by special statutes. Nearly two-thirds of the states have adopted the privilege for physician-patient relations, while 17 states have specifically refused to recognize the privilege for the patients of physicians. As will be discussed later, 11 states have granted privilege to the clients of psychologists, giving this privilege a status equivalent to that enjoyed by client-attorney communications. By law, 15 states grant the privilege to client-accountant relations. In at least 12 states statutes have been enacted allowing journalists to withhold their sources of information.

The attorney-client privilege has often served as the model for the privilege demanded by these other professional groups. Any serious re-evaluation of the ancient and honored client-attorney privilege is bound to lead to closer scrutiny of the desirability of the privilege for the clients of other professional groups. It might be prudent for psychologists to re-examine their need for the privilege.

Among many professional groups, obtaining the privilege for their clients has often been construed as a sign that the profession has obtained a degree of legal recognition. Obtaining a privilege, equal under the law to that granted the attorney-client relation, has become a professional status symbol. In some cases, the granting of the privilege has probably been unnecessary, perhaps even detrimental to the legal process. To some degree, the attempts of psychologists to obtain the privilege for their clients probably has been so motivated.

Since the 1948 Kentucky legislation, there has been a growing trend for state regulation of psychologists through certification or licensing. It has been generally true that the question of whether or not to grant the privilege to the clients of psychologists has usually arisen at this time. In the 17 states which presently provide for the statutory certification or licensing of psychologists, 11 also contain in their acts a section granting the privilege. These states are: Arkansas, California, Colorado, Georgia, Kentucky, Michigan, New Hampshire, New York, Tennessee, Utah, and Washington.

As an example of a privilege section in a state law, the following is presented from the certification statute of New York State (N.Y. Education Law Sec. 7611).

> The confidential relations and communications between a psychologist registered under the provisions of this act and his client are placed on

the same basis as those provided by law between attorney and client, and nothing in this article shall be construed to require any such privileged communications to be disclosed.

It should be clear that in those 11 states which have the privilege, the only clients protected are those who consult psychologists qualified to be registered under the various acts. Thus, in any of these states, the client of a nonlicensed or noncertified psychologist does not have the privilege. Hence, how the term "psychologist" is defined for the purposes of certification or how the practice of "psychology" is delineated for licensing is the crucial issue, because it determines which psychologists are granted the privilege.

Even in those states which have the privilege, the psychologist's client cannot be absolutely certain that his confidences will be protected in the courtroom. One cannot place too much faith in a law simply because it exists. The important thing is what happens in practice. For example, the whole issue of the constitutionality of any particular state's certification or licensing statutes is open to question. If they should be challenged, and the courts refuse to uphold them, then statute, privilege, and all are invalid (as long as granting the privilege is part of these statutes). This is not just idle speculation: Precisely this happened to Florida's certification statute though it contained no section granting privilege. The law was held unconstitutional and had to be amended and repassed by the legislature (Husband v. Cassel, 130 S.2d 69, Fla. 1961). Three years ago the validity of the New York certification law was tested and upheld (Nat. Psychol. Assoc. for Psychoanalysis, Inc., v. Univ. of State of N.Y., 8 N.Y. 2d 197, 1960).

One must remember too, that statutes are not fully developed in their meaning until the courts begin to interpret them. Gradually over a period of years the bones of the statute are given the flesh and blood of judicial interpretation. For example, a prisoner was committed by a court for a pretrial psychiatric examination and diagnosis. In the course of hospitalization, a psychiatrist commenced treating the patient in therapy. At the hearing on the accused's capacity to form a criminal intent, the psychiatrist was compelled to testify about the treatment relationship. A Federal Court of Appeals held the psychiatrist should not have been forced to testify, since he was functioning in a therapeutic capacity, and thus covered by the privilege. The case was remanded for retrial, the court having thus spelled out a fine distinction between diagnosis and therapy (Taylor v. United States, 222 F.2d 398, D.C. Cir. 1955). Pretrial psychiatric examinations of accused criminals are usually not privileged, since no confidential relation is assumed to exist. Since most certification or licensing statutes for psychologists are of fairly recent origin, judicial elaboration of them and of the privilege for psychologist's clients are relatively rare.

Some other possible issues which might arise around the client-psychologist privilege, which a court would have to decide, are as follows:

1. A client may waive his privilege, but what if he is a minor or incompetent (mentally ill or senile, for example)?

2. What happens to the privilege when the client dies?

3. What is the psychologist's responsibility to insure the secrecy of his records of the client's confidences when the psychologist himself dies?

4. Does the privilege extend to the psychologist's typist and/or his records? If he indiscreetly tells a fellow colleague, can the colleague be called as a witness?

5. If an eavesdropper overhears a client's confidences to a psychologist, could he be called as a witness?

6. If a psychologist represents himself to be licensed when he is not, does the client who consults him in good faith, assuming the protection of the privilege, have the privilege or not?

7. What of a psychologist asked to testify in a state without a privilege about matters obtained by him in another state where they were privileged? A recent case involving a New York psychologist (privileged) held he could not be compelled to testify in a custody suit in Massachusetts, which has no privilege (Queen v. Ortmeyer, 233 N.Y. S.2d 798, Sup. Ct. 1962).

8. A physician (privileged) refers a patient to a psychologist for consultation and testing. He provides certain necessary information to the psychologist about the patient. Could the psychologist be called to testify about what the physician told him, or is he covered by an extension of the physician-patient privilege?.

One final word on this issue. The trial judge has absolute discretion, at the time, about what goes on in his courtroom. A psychologist witness may be covered by the privilege but the judge may refuse to recognize it and order the witness to testify. The judge may be in error and may well be overruled in a subsequent appeal of the case. However, the knowledge is of little consolation to the psychologist who then and there has to decide if he will follow the dictates of his conscience and not testify, thus exposing himself to contempt of court.

In those states without the privilege, does the psychologist have no recourse but to testify? It should be noted that in the absence of the privilege, all of the psychologist's records, such as therapy notes, records of payment, appointment books, tape recordings, etc., can be subpoenaed. There are, however, other alternatives in the absence of the privilege. The psychologist could fall back on his ethical commitment of confidentiality. In matters of conscience, many courts are hesitant to force witnesses to testify. One reason for their reluctance is because to do so is to seriously tempt the witness to perjure himself. After all, there probably is no other source of information to the content of the confidential relation which can be used to verify the testimony of the professional witness. If the court should force the matter, then the whole issue becomes a matter of conscience for the individual psychologist. Early discussions in the development of the APA Code of Ethics recognized this by saying, in effect, that forced to such a choice it was ethical either to accede to the court or to refuse to testify [1].

But there is still another alternative. In the absence of a privilege, the court itself could create one. This happened in a court in Illinois (Binder v. Ruvell, Civil Docket 52C2535, Circuit Court Cook County, Ill., 1952). This state has no physician-patient privilege, but a trial court granted a privilege to the patient of a psychotherapist, a psychiatrist. The court felt that psychiatric treatment could be distinguished from general medical care. It would remain to be tested in further cases whether or not the courts would uphold the privilege for any qualified nonpsychiatric psychotherapist. Unfortunately, the case was never appealed, so the judge's action in this case was never reviewed by a higher court.

Similarly, in an alimony hearing, an Ontario Supreme Court justice excused a psychiatrist from testifying as to what the estranged wife had told him (reported in *A.M.A News*, July 8, 1963, p. 12). This ruling was made even though Canadian law recognizes no physician-patient privilege. In another Canadian decision, a Saskatchewan magistrate accorded a privilege to information obtained by a social worker (re Kryschuk and Zulynik, 14 D.L.R. 2d 676–677, Sask. Magis. Ct. 1958).

One state, Montana, which neither licenses nor certifies psychologists and thus has no broad privilege for their clients, nevertheless has a narrow privilege in its general statute on confidential communications. This provision provides as follows.

> Any person engaged in the teaching of psychology in any school, or who acting as such is engaged in the study and observation of child mentality, shall not without the consent of the parent or guardian of such child being so taught or observed testify in any civil action as to any information so obtained [Mont. Rev. Codes Ann. Sec. 93-701-4(6) 1947].

In brief, this is the status of psychologists and the privilege today. It is necessary to look more closely at some of the implications and consequences of granting the privilege to psychologists and at the manner in which this has been done. This is necessary in order to consider if the privilege for clients of psychologists should be adopted as is by all other states, or if those states which now have privilege should expand or amend it.

In particular, we would like to explore whether the practice of granting privilege in the context of licensing or certification is a sound one. The purpose of the privilege is supposedly to protect the confidences of the client from public exposure. Why, then, does not the client of a nonlicensed or noncertified psychologist have the privilege? Surely if any one is to have the privilege, his clients deserve it too. At the present time, a noncertified psychologist can lawfully practice psychology (as long as he does not call himself a "certified" psychologist) and can be just as well trained and competent as his certified colleagues.

It would seem to us that this inequitable state of affairs is an outgrowth of confused thinking about privilege, due to a failure to clearly recognize that the privilege belongs to the client for his protection. We see no logical reason why licensing or certification statutes and the granting of privilege should go together. This practice seems to be emphasizing the grating of the privilege to meet professional interests (as if the professional "owned" it) and not to meet the client's interests. The privilege logically should be granted to the client seeking services, regardless of what professional person he consults, and not to the professional offering services, regardless of who his client is.

A further inequality is that the clients of other professionals equally interested in mental health are not protected. For example, in Georgia, Tennessee, and New Hampshire, the granting of privilege to psychologists results in a curious dilemma. These states have no statutory privilege for physician-patient relations, and since common law does not recognize such a privilege, the patient of a psychiatrist would probably not have the privilege. In all fairness to the patient, such an inequity ought not exist. It is of interest to note that, in 1959, the legislature of Georgia rectified this situation by passing a statute granting the privilege for communications between psychiatrist and patient (Ga. Code Ann. Sec. 38–418 Supp. 1960).

In some states, patients of physicians have the privilege only in civil cases. Clients of psychologists, if granted a privilege as broad as that of the attorney, would have the privilege in both civil and criminal proceedings. Perhaps the greatest inequity of all is that no American jurisdiction grants a privilege to social workers.

One final consequence of linking privilege with certification or licensing statutes is that the privilege probably embraces—because the statutes are usually so broad—the clients of all psychologists qualified to be registered under the various acts. Basically these statutes attempt to regulate those psychologists who offer services to the public for a fee. Consequently the privilege has been granted to a very wide range of functions performed by psychologists, many of which do not need to be and probably should not be privileged.

Dean Wigmore, an eminent legal scholar, tried to derive a rationale for the granting of the privilege and has set forth four conditions which he believes should be met for legitimate privilege (8 Wigmore, Evidence 3d. ed. 1940, Sec. 2285). The communications must arise in a confidence that they will not be disclosed. This element of confidentiality must be essential to the full and satisfactory maintenance of the relation between parties. The relation must be one which in the opinion of the community ought to be sedulously fostered. Finally, the injury which would inure to the relation by the disclosure of the communications must be greater than the benefit thereby gained for the correct disposal of the litigation. Many lawyers feel that these conditions neither explain nor justify the rule for granting privilege. Wigmore himself in applying these conditions concluded that statutory enactments of patient-physician privilege were unsound and unjustified.

Nevertheless, with these conditions in mind, it would not seem desirable to protect the confidences of the client of the industrial consulting psychologist, or those of psychologists engaged in market research, survey research, advertising, contract research (in social or experimental psychology), administration, etc. These functions do not meet Wigmore's criteria and do not involve vital human relations, whose inviolate privacy benefits society. Including these functions under a privilege to clients of psychologists needlessly impedes fact finding in litigation.

We have mentioned a number of reasons why it would seem to be undersirable and unwise for psychologists to continue to advocate the granting of the privilege in the context of certification or licensing statutes. It should be clear that granting the privilege in this manner bestows it upon the client of a psychologist irrespective of the functions performed by the particular psychologist. Psychologists do too many things, and their activities overlap with too many other professions, to justify all their clients being covered by the privilege.

One can certainly raise the question of whether or not the clients of psychologists need the privilege at all. A recent survey by the *Yale Law Journal* asked lawyers and judges their opinions on the need for a privilege for various professional groups [5]. Of 125 lawyers surveyed on the question of privilege for psychologists' clients, 42 favored it; 50 opposed it; and 33 had no opinion. By contrast, 83 favored a privilege for psychiatrists; 49 for marriage counselors; and 24 for social workers. Of 47 judges surveyed, 20 favored the privilege for clients of psychologists; 13 opposed it; and 14 were undecided. The comparable figures for clients of psychiatrists were: 29, 10, and 8.

Generally psychologists and marriage counselors each endorsed a privilege for their own profession (of 51 psychologists, 43 favored privilege, 1 opposed it, and 7 were undecided); a position supported generally by laymen and judges but narrowly opposed by lawyers. On the other hand, legal commentators, psychiatrists, professional psychiatric organizations, lawyers and judges, as well as laymen, enthusiastically supported a psychiatrist-patient privilege.

Perhaps some of the less than enthusiastic support for a privilege for the clients of psychologists stems from confusion in the minds of the legal profession as to what a psychologist does with clients that would need to be privileged. Others have suggested [3, 5], and we concur, that there are two main functions which a psychologist performs which do involve vital human relations and in which the client's privacy should be respected and protected. If there is to be a privilege at all, it is needed when a psychologist functions as a psychodiagnostician and as a psychotherapist.

One of the rationales for the privilege is that it supposedly promotes the full disclosure by the client necessary for the professionals' adequate functioning. There can be no question that full disclosure is a prerequisite for adequate, effective diagnosis and treatment. The Yale article further suggests that there is no substantial evidence suggesting that the treatment of patients is actually more hindered in states with no privilege for confidential communications with psychiatrists or psychologists than in states which extend such a privilege. Many explanations for this suggest themselves. Perhaps patients mistakenly assume they have a privilege. In the Yale study, when psychologists were asked if their clients believed psychologists could not be forced to testify in court, the majority answered they thought their clients believed this to be so. Other possibilities are that clients never heard of the privilege; clients seeking help will tell professionals what they think is necessary regardless of the law; psychologists at present are rather rare witnesses in court since few of their clients become involved in litigation, and hence the whole issue of privilege is partly academic at this time.

If the privilege has no effect on the treatment of patients, but serves only to protect the client's confidences on the rare chance that he may someday appear in court and his psychologist may be called as a witness, is there any compelling reason to retain the privilege? After all, those who believe that fact finding in litigation is the most important issue, and since privilege obstructs this it should be done away with, have a valid position which needs to be countered.

We believe that a privilege should exist for the clients of psychologists functioning as diagnosticians or therapists, but in this connection we would like to recall an earlier statement that we made. The privilege logically should be granted to the client seeking services, regardless of what professional person he consults, and not to the professional offering services, regardless of who his client is. Thus, it would be our position that a privilege should exist for any person who consults a recognized professional (psychiatrist, psychologist, social worker, marriage counselor) for the purpose of the diagnosis of a mental, emotional, or adjustment difficulty, or for the treatment by psychotherapy, counseling, casework, etc., of said condition. We would give the following justifications for such a privilege, which we believe to be valid for the functions of diagnosis and/or treatment, but not for other functions these specialists may perform.

1. The community has a vested interest in the mental health of its members, and as such, diagnostic or therapeutic relationships with mental health professionals should be fostered as a desirable social policy.

2. Diagnostic and therapy relations are typically of the most personal, private, and intimate nature and a person's right to privacy in these vital human relations should be protected.

3. In order to effectively carry on diagnosis and/or therapy, and only these functions, an attitude of privacy and confidentiality is essential.

4. To violate these relationships in legal proceedings would be tantamount to asking the individual to testify against himself.

5. It is seldom that the only proof of events which transpired outside of the confidential relation, but revealed therein, is to be obtained by violating these relationships. The litigant should be forced to look elsewhere for his evidence.

6. As judicial distrust of social scientists decreases, we may look forward to the increasing appearance of professionals in court as witnesses. Hence it is imperative that the client's rights be protected and the privilege retained or granted for the functions of diagnosis and treatment.

To this end, therefore, we would like to propose the following model statute, intended to exist independently of licensing or certification statutes:

> A client, or his authorized representative, has a privilege to prevent a witness from disclosing, in any judicial, administrative, or legislative proceeding, communications pertaining to the diagnosis or treatment of the client's mental or emotional disorder, or difficulty in personal or social adjustment between the client and any of the following: a member of a mental health profession, any other professional or lay person who participates with such a member of a mental health profession in the accomplishment of individual or group diagnosis or treatment, or members of the client's family, or between any of these persons as concerns diagnosis or treatment.

We believe this model statute is a more realistic and sound approach to the question of privilege than the licensing or certification method because it does not grant the privilege to the clients of a professional group but instead puts the "ownership" of the privilege where it clearly belongs, in the client's hands, protecting his interests. It sees the problem through the client's eyes, in effect treating all professions with identic interests equally, as well as treating all members of the same profession performing the same functions equally. Further, it does not associate the privilege with licensing or certification statutes which might be held unconstitutional if challenged. It also avoids needlessly privileging certain professional functions as licensing and certification statutes probably have done.

Another definite advantage to this statute is that it does not tie the privilege to the vague and amorphous attorney-client privilege, as many certification or licensing statutes have tended to do. This latter privilege contains some exceptions probably not applicable to the client-mental health professional relationship. It is also questionable whether the attorney-client privilege is valid in legislative and administrative proceedings. An entire new area of conflict of individual rights has appeared recently in the attempts by legislative and administrative agencies concerned with national security to utilize information obtained by mental health specialists in evaluating individuals as "security risks." (For a further discussion of this issue, see [2, 4].

Finally, this statute explicitly recognizes the modern trend toward the team approach on the professional side, and the group approach on the client's side, in treatment and diagnosis. It privileges the client's communications to team members and the team's discussions among themselves, as well as confidences revealed by a client in a group setting. Traditionally, all confidential relations, with only a few technical exceptions, have been viewed by the law as essentially two-person relationships. It is very unlikely that confidences disclosed to a team member or revealed in a group setting are privileged under present statutes. The suggested model statute is an attempt to bring legal thinking more in line with accepted advances in mental health techniques.

It is the hope of the authors that this paper will generate some re-evaluation by psychologists on the issue of privileged communication and the protection of their client's interests.[1]

REFERENCES

1. American Psychologicial Association. *Ethical Standards for Psychologists*. Washington, D.C.: APA, 1953.

2. Group for the Advancement of Psychiatry. *Confidentiality and Privileged Communication in the Practice of Psychiatry*. (Report No. 45) New York: GAP, 1960.

3. Louisell, D. W. "The Psychologist in Today's Legal World: Part II. Privileged Communications." *Minn. Law Rev.* (1957), 41, 731–750.

4. Slovenko, R., & Usdin, G. L. "Privileged Communication and Right of Privacy in Diagnosis and Therapy." In, *Current Psychiatric Therapies*. Vol. 3. New York: Grune & Stratton (1963), pp. 277–319.

5. Yale Law Journal. "Confidential Communications," *Yale Law J.* (1962), 71, 1226–1273.

[1]Since this article was written, seven additional states have passed legislation to regulate psychologists, and in each case the privilege has also been granted. These states are: Alabama, Delaware, Idaho, Illinois, Nevada, New Mexico, and Oregon.

32

Why Unethical Practice?

Milton Schwebel, Ph.D.[*]

The counseling and psychological professions have established codes of ethical practice and provided machinery to deal with violations; but they have not as yet attempted to find the causes of unethical practice. The literature includes numerous codes and descriptions of the right kind of professional behavior, but there are no published data on the kind of personal qualities that are associated with ethical practice and the kind of training program that facilitates such practice. This paper is a first step toward identifying the causes of unethical practice and behavior.

The criteria for the selection of counseling psychologists cannot be adequate until the correlates of ethical practice and behavior are known. Is ethical behavior correlated with a personality trait? A configuration of traits? A character type? A pattern of values? A pattern of interests? Is there such a creature as an ethical person, or does the ethical quality of behavior vary with the situation? In either case, what changes in curriculum and in teaching approaches will contribute to ethical practice?

Such information on selection and training is not available in the codes of practice devised by counselors and psychologists. These codes have other purposes. Some of them are *professional* codes, for example the work of the American Personnel and Guidance Association and earlier the National Vocational Guidance Association in developing minimum standards for vocational guidance services and in listing approved agencies that meet those standards [25, 26]. Others are *technical* codes, for example, the technical recommendations for the preparation and publication of psychological tests and diagnostic techniques, developed by a joint committee of three organizations [29]. Still other codes deal with *ethical practice* such as those proposed by counselors in recent years [10, 11] and *The Ethical Standards of Psychologists* of the American Psychological Association [27]. Application of the APA code to counseling have been indicated by Dr. C. Gilbert Wrenn [23].

[*]Dr. Schwebel is Professor of Education and Chairman of the Department of Guidance and Personnel Administration, New York University. His article appeared originally in the *Journal of Counseling Psychology*, 2:122 (1955), and is reprinted with permission of the author and of the journal.

THE APA DATA

While not designed for this purpose the published data of the APA code are a source of information on the causes of unethical behavior and practice, and will be used in this paper for the formulation of hypotheses. These data were obtained from the members of the APA who "were asked by letter to describe a situation they knew of first-hand, in which a psychologist made a decision having ethical implications, and to indicate what the correspondents perceived as being the ethical issues involved." The limitations of these data should be recognized. Although the published statements are representative of the "more than a thousand" reports received from APA members, these reports represent no more than one-seventh of the total population of the APA membership at the time. Furthermore, "the incidents cannot be thought of as an accurate sampling from the universe of ethical problems of psychologists." Nor can the hypotheses be thought of as an accurate sampling from the universe of causes of ethical problems.

DEFINITIONS

In order to understand the terminology of this paper the reader should understand the different meanings that are assigned to the terms "practice" and "behavior." Practice refers to an act but not to the motivation of the practitioner. Behavior, on the other hand, refers to the motivation and the underlying values of the person. Thus, an unethical practice is an act by a psychologist that is not in accord with the accepted standards of ethical practice; unethical behavior occurs only when conflicting personal interests of the psychologist lead to the unethical practice. A psychologist who commits an unethical practice as a result of ignorance or inadequate training or supervision is not behaving unethically. While this seemingly academic distinction in no way alters the effect of unethical practice on the client, it does have significance for the selection and training of psychologists.

THE HYPOTHESES

1. SELF INTEREST CAUSES UNETHICAL BEHAVIOR AND UNETHICAL PRACTICE.

A. Personal profit motive as a cause.

An adolescent boy sought vocational guidance and personal counseling from the consulting psychologist. As a "come on" tactic the psychologist told him at the end of an hour that if he wanted to hear more he would have to pay more.

A consulting psychologist in private practice, mainly in vocational counseling, was visited by a representative of a private trade school, who set forth the merits of the school, and then stated that the school would of course pay the psychologist a commission on the tuition of any student referred by the psychologist as a result of counseling. The psychologist stated that he was not interested in such an arrangement. . . .

The profit motive provides a conflict for workers whose dominant professional purpose is service to people. It can serve well as a standard for wise decision in many occupations where success is measured by the profits of the organization, but for the psychologist, school counselor, social worker, and others, in agencies or in private practice, this motive can impair professional judgment.

The profession wants to exclude those among its candidates whose character would make them susceptible to temptations of profit at a cost to the welfare of the client. The need is for research that will determine the identifiable correlates of the ethical character in counseling psychology and that will develop instruments and techniques for the recognition of these correlates in an individual.

B. The need for self-enhancement as a cause.

Several months ago, a female student left the university campus and was not heard of for approximately two weeks. The newspapers made a big story out of the incident, and a psychologist on the university staff told the newspapers that the girl was in his class and that he had had several talks with her. He gave out considerable information that seemed of confidential nature.

A successful professional man arranged to have a college counselor provide vocational guidance for his son. He implied strongly that he would like the counselor to persuade his son to enter his profession and to join his business as a partner. The counselor sensed the direction of the father's thinking and explained to him that these considerations would probably be discussed but that the son would have to work out his own decisions.

It is assumed that psychologists know that the content of a professional conference should not be publicized. How then account for the behavior of the psychologist?

The inadequate self seeks for enhancement, sometimes at a cost to others. The psychology instructor may have been motivated in his unethical behavior by such a need which could be fed by publicity. The college counselor, on the other hand, was free from the need to please the "successful professional man."

Feelings of inadequacy obviously can impede counseling and contribute to unethical behavior. Such feelings are common in our culture. To exclude all candidates who are infected with them would eliminate many potentially effective counselors. How intense, then, must these inferiority feelings be before they lead to violations of accepted standards? Are they destructive only when they remain unconscious? While investigators seek answers to these and other questions, the profession can remain alerted to the "inadequacy syndrome" in its screening and training of candidates.

Some reported practices, like the following, are blatant violations of good professional behavior.

A member of a clinic staff pointed to a fourteen-year-old lad and said (after viewing the report handed him by the staff psychologist), "You are a feebleminded boy. . . ." The boy as well as the parents were very much disturbed and sought counsel elsewhere.

It seems that such gross insensitivity can be recognized in candidates even now, without further research.

C. The need to maintain security and status as a cause.

An earnest but inexperienced young psychologist on a hospital staff examined a man who showed some schizophrenic characteristics although there were also some indications that were not consistent with this diagnosis. Instead of indicating the uncertainty of diagnosis, he firmly recommended a diagnosis of schizophrenia. The discrepancy was noticed later. The young psychologist felt it would be a weakness to admit error and clung tenaciously to his conclusion. . . .

A lieutenant (jg) psychologist in a naval training center was ordered by his senior officer, a psychiatrist, to change the wording and omit certain items on certain standardized tests being used in screening recruits. The psychologist refused on grounds that this was an improper order. The psychiatrist initiated disciplinary proceedings with the senior medical officer who, however, sided with the psychologist and refused to entertain the charge of "disobedience of military orders," maintaining that the psychologist alone was responsibile for decision within the clear limits of his own specialty.

The young psychologist on the hospital staff was aware of the uncertainty of his diagnosis. Yet he could not risk what he regarded as weakness and threat to his status in revealing uncertainty. The naval officer on the other hand seemed to have taken a far greater risk in maintaining a fundamental principle of test procedure.

What accounts for the difference in behavior? In part it appears to be attributable to the character of the professional worker. The adequate individual is willing to risk suffering some loss of status or security rather than work in an unethical manner. The inadequate person will tend to see threat to his security even when none exists.

In part the difference in behavior may be attributable to the climate in the organization and the character of the leader. If the climate is threatening, perhaps in being highly competitive, the counselor may choose unethical practice rather than admit to uncertainity and expose himself to real or imagined retaliation. The autocratic leader bestirs the anxieties of the "marginal" worker and leads him in self-defense to behavior that he might not otherwise engage in.

2. UNSOUND JUDGMENT DUE TO INADEQUATE TRAINING AND/OR SUPERVISED EXPERIENCE, OR DUE TO INEFFECTIVE SELECTION, CAUSES UNETHICAL PRACTICE; SINCE SELF-INTEREST IS NOT A PRIMARY FACTOR, THE BEHAVIOR OF THE PSYCHOLOGIST IS NOT UNETHICAL.

A. Unsound judgment in maintaining confidences in staff relations.

In an industrial testing situation, where interviews were conducted for research purposes, with the assurance that the results would be treated in confidence, it was revealed that a foreman was regarded by his men as being particularly incompetent. Management was informed and steps were taken to train the foreman in more effective ways of doing his job. This was considered to be a breach of ethics on the grounds that information received in confidence as a professional worker must not be revealed under any circumstances even to achieve desirable ends.

In a high school guidance program there has been some discussion of how much of the information given by a student should be divulged to the principal, to the classroom teacher, to the school nurse, or to anyone else present when the case is staffed. The counselors are acting as consultant in matters of guidance to the rest of the staff, and find it difficult to know to what extent students' confidences may be discussed in a staff meeting.

What makes for wise judgment? This could be restated: What kind of training, of supervised experience, will enable the counselor to find in many such situations that no conflict exists because the right, the ethical, course of action is obvious? Problems cannot be entirely eliminated but their number and intensity can be significantly reduced.

Additional factors may operate in cases like these. The counselor's need to impress the staff could interfere with his judgment in determining the limits of sharing information about a client.

B. Unsound judgment in maintaining confidences about anti-social behavior.

A student whose apparent classification should be nymphomania came voluntarily to a school psychologist for assistance. Her behavior was a record of repeated violations of the standards of conduct prescribed by the institution. The psychologist decided against reporting her to school authorities and instead persuaded her to go to a psychiatrist in a neighboring city for treatment. The psychologist concluded, "Confidences of clients must be kept inviolate. However, every effort to protect the group should be exerted. In this case, protection will be afforded, we hope, by the fact that the client is having psychiatric treatment and may improve."

A child of a guard in a hospital for the criminally insane was refered to me as an emotionally disturbed child. In an interview, she described in detail an incident relating to the subduing of a prisoner with a blunt instrument which resulted in the prisoner's death. There was a question in my mind whether or not I was obligated to turn this information over to the hospital authorities for further investigation. My personal feeling is that any information divulged by a patient should be held in strictest confidence. On the other hand, there is also the responsibility for protecting prisoners from the possibility of such treatment.

No rule of thumb can be applied to such problem solving. The easy way is to decide that the group comes first. This is a tempting rationalization. While it can protect the insecure psychologist from possible anguish, it can defeat the very purposes of counseling and therapy, one of them being the protection of society by changing the behavior of the client. It can make the counselor's office a very unpopular place, "off-limits" for those who need to speak freely of anti-social behavior.

The comments about training and experience in the previous section (2A) apply here too.

3. IGNORANCE CAUSES UNETHICAL PRACTICE. SINCE SELF-INTEREST IS NOT A PRIMARY FACTOR, THE BEHAVIOR OF THE PSYCHOLOGIST IS NOT UNETHICAL.

A. Ignorance of technical information as a cause.

I received a Rorschach from a therapist in another city requesting that I help in the interpretation. This I did. Some time after, I received a letter from a woman, the patient for whom the Rorschach record had been obtained. It developed that the therapist had passed on information directly to her which was intended entirely for him, including apparently an interpretation of schizophrenia. From the woman's letter, I judged that a distressing, and unwarranted, situation had been set up . . . I believe it was a sin of ignorance rather than of deliberate abuse.

Ignorance plays no small part in producing undesirable professional practice. An experienced school counselor, certified by his state education department, informed one student that his low Social Welfare score on the Kuder signified that he was selfish. The Kuder and Strong are cited to document the client's possession or lack of "aptitudes." Students are encouraged by counselors to go to college or enter professions so that they will lead "fuller, richer lives."

To the client it is little comfort to learn that the professional blunders may have been due primarily to ignorance. But to the profession it is important because ignorance is remediable. A student with sufficient intelligence for graduate work has the capacity to learn to avoid such "a sin of ignorance."

B. Ignorance of his values, especially those that are incompatible with respect for the integrity of the individual, as a cause.

A vocational advisor projected his stereotype of a minority group into the advisement procedure, thereby attempting to persuade a Negro client to accept a lower level objective than the client was capable of reaching even with a realistic social handicap. I believe that if a psychologist agrees to accept a human being as a client he should be expected to give as objective and as high quality professional service as possible, regardless of race, color, creed, or fee involved.

This person is not yet ready for the profession. To say that such practices are a product of early learning, of values rooted in an individual in his early years, does not remove responsibility from the profession and the universities for their prevention. The problem becomes one of introducing learning experiences that make the psychologist fully aware of his values.

SUMMARY

The ethical problems of psychologists throw some light on the origin of unethical practice and behavior. Practices that are contrary to the best interests of the client appear to stem from (a) the overpowering self-interest of the professional worker as expressed in personal profit, self-enhancement, and the maintenance of security and status; (b) poor judgment, due in part at least to inexperience in problem solving in counseling; and (c) ignorance of technical knowledge and of one's own values. Only the first type of behavior is unethical in origin, and only in this case is the psychologist motivated primarily by self-interest.

IMPLICATIONS

Since the hypotheses were derived by induction from the experiences of psychologists, and by less conservative interpretation would rate as conclusions, it seems justifiable to present implications.

SELECTION

The introduction of more rigid personality criteria in the selection of counselors can be expected to promote ethical practice. The dangers inherent in such action are recognized by the APA in its policy on entrance requirements: "Exclusion on the grounds of . . . vague unvalidated considerations of an applicant's personality is never warranted" [28, p. 7]. This emphasizes the need for research on personality criteria. The prediction studies of Dr. E. L. Kelly and Dr. D. W. Fiske [13] on the performance of clinical psychologists have not been encouraging.

Knowledge of the qualities that make for the effective counselor is incomplete. According to a recent study [22] less than half of thirty-three universities that train counseling psychologists felt satisfied that they knew the essential traits and more than half were "actively dissatisfied" with their present selection methods. Yet progress is being made. Dr. F. E. Fiedler's [8] study of therapist characteristics has been an important forward step. So has Dr. A. T. Dittman's [7] development of a research method. Dr. William C. Cottle [4, 5, 6] has reviewed studies on the personal characteristics of counselors and has devised an experimental scale for the differentiation of counselors from other groups. The writer and two associates are developing an instrument to identify "good counselor" traits which will be used to test the effects of various aspects of counselor training. Until such time as the desired qualities can be more precisely identified the profession can protect itself from gross violations by excluding those who in their relations with other persons are extremely autocratic, exploitative, and narcissistic.

TRAINING

Several causes of undesirable behavior appear to be susceptible to change through training. In some cases the counselor's conflict is due to his inexperience in facing problems, in making independent judgments. What seem to be indicated are functional training programs that focus on problems and that utilize theory as an instrument of problem solving rather than as an end of learning. The professional case conference and various workship procedures are especially appropriate both in the universities and on the job in agencies, schools, and hospitals. Some teaching approaches such as role-playing [20] confront the student with realistic problems and with practice at solving them from the earliest training experience. There is no substitute for the well-supervised practicum [3, p. 182] and continued supervision on the first job.

Some violations seem to breed in a threatening atmosphere created by poor training leadership. Greater emphasis in training programs on the use of dynamic group processes in staff, faculty, and committee meetings would probably make for healthier climate and for greater security of the administrator as well as his staff.

In other instances professional indiscretions are due to ignorance of some of the "facts of life," a situation that counselor training institutions can seek to correct by increased use of evaluative devices that measure understanding and competency rather than memory and industry. One example of a device of this type for use particularly in lower level graduate work is the set of tests developed by Axline and Porter [16, p. 41, 190]; another example, for use with advanced graduate students, is the joint evaluation by supervisor and trainee of the latter's interview recording, a procedure recommended by Dr. F. P. Robinson [17, p. 159].

The conflicts in many cases stem from the subtle intrusion of the counselor's values. His values are important to good counseling as well as to ethical practice. Hiltner [12] demonstrated by use of interview material the ways in which personal attitudes affect the counseling process. Dr. Carl R. Rogers [18] reported on recent research suggesting that the counselor's liking and respect for the client are factors in the success of counseling; and in a review of studies, Fiedler [9] indicated the need for certain feeling on the part of the therapist. Because learning about his motivation is so important, the graduate student in counseling needs to experience some form of personal counseling, perhaps in small classes designed for that purpose. Wrenn [24] emphasized the value of such an experience in an article on the training and selection of student personnel workers. Division 17's Committee on Counselor Training described it as a way "by which the student may gain an enlarged basis for understanding the counseling process" [2, p. 178], yet it did not recommend personal counseling as a requirement on the grounds that it is of the greatest value when it comes as a result of the student's motivation. Undoubtedly this is true, but surely the student's motivation is equally desirable for the entire program. Another writer [1] pointed to the danger of ignoring the importance of counseling techniques in the growing awareness of the importance of counselors' attitudes. At a time when courses in counselor training focus either on techniques or on dynamics of the *client*'s behavior this fear seems groundless.

In its report on practicum training the Committee on Counselor Training [3, p. 186] said that "self-understanding and self-discipline" were needed at the point of entering internship. Changes in self-knowledge achieved by a course in counseling techniques were studied by Dr. Walter M. Lifton [15] and are now being studied by Dr. M. Slomowitz [21]. Lifton [14] also made a preliminary study of some effects of supervision on empathic ability; and Blocksma in a pioneer investigation reported by Rogers [19, pp. 452–458] studied the effectiveness of an intensive course in client-centered therapy which achieved changes in the counselor's concept of his role. By one means or another, either as an integral part of existing courses or as an addition to the curriculum the profession will want to provide increased opportunity for "self-understanding and self-discipline."

REFERENCES

1. Berdie, R. F. "Counselor Attitudes," *Educ. Psychol. Measmt.* (1951), 11, 349–354.

2. Committee on Counselor Training, APA Division 17. "Recommended Standards for Training Counseling Psychologists at the Doctoral Level," *Amer. Psychologist,* 7 (1952), 175–181.

3. Committee on Counselor Training, APA Division 17. "The Practicum Training of Counseling Psychologists," *Amer. Psychologist,* 7 (1952), 182–188.

4. Cottle, W. C. "Personal Characteristics of Counselors: I," *Pers. and Guid. J.* (1953), 31, 445–450.

5. Cottle, W. C. & Lewis, W. W., Jr. "Personal Characteristics of Counselors: II. Male Counselor Responses to the MMPI and GZTS," *J. Counsel. Psychol.* (1954), 1, 27–30.

6. Cottle, W. C., Lewis, W. W. Jr., & Penny, M. M. "Personal Characteristics of Counselors: III. An Experimental Scale," *J. Counsel. Psychol.* (1954), 2, 74–77.

7. Dittman, A. T. "The Interpersonal Process in Psychotherapy: Development of a Research Method," *J. Abnorm. Soc. Psychol.* (1952), 47, 236–244.

8. Fiedler, F. E. "A Comparison of Therapeutic Relationships in Psychoanalytic, Nondirective and Adlerian Therapy," *J. Consult. Psychol.* (1950), 12, 436–445.

9. Fiedler, F. E. "Quantitative Studies on the Role of Therapists' Feelings Toward Their Patients." In O. H. Mowrer, *Psychotherapy: Theory and Research.* New York: Ronald Press Co., 1953.

10. Gluck, S., *et al.* "A Proposed Code of Ethics for Counselors," *Occupations* (1952), 30, 484–490.

11. Hawkes, A. L., Mills, T., & Hoppock, R. "A Proposed Code of Ethics for Counselors Using Occupational Information," *Occupations,* 28 (1950), 466.

12. Hiltner, S. *The Counselor in Counseling.* New York: Abingdon-Cokebury, 1952.

13. Kelly, E. L. & Fiske, D. W. *The Prediction of Performance in Clinical Psychology.* Ann Arbor: Univ. of Michigan Press, 1951.

14. Lifton, W. M. *A Pilot Study to Investigate the Effect of Supervision on the Empathic Ability of Counseling Trainees.* Urbana, Ill.: Bureau of Educational Research, Univer. of Illinois, 1952.

15. Lifton, W. M. "A Study of the Changes in Self-concept and Content Knowledge in Students Taking a Course in Counseling Techniques." *Microfilm Abstr.,* 1951, II (1), 55–56. (Doctoral thesis, New York Univer., 1950.)

16. Porter, E. H. Jr. *Introduction to Therapeutic Counseling.* Boston: Houghton Mifflin, 1950.

17. Robinson, F. P. *Principles and Procedures in Student Counseling.* New York: Harper and Bros., 1950.

18. Rogers, C. R. "An Overview of the Research and Some Questions for the Future." In C. R. Rogers and R. F. Dymond, *Psychotherapy and Personality Change.* Chicago: Univer. of Chicago Press, 1954.

19. Rogers, C. R. *Client-centered Therapy.* Boston: Houghton Mifflin, 1951.

20. Schwebel, M. "Role-playing in Counselor Training," *Pers. and Guid.* J. (1953), 32, 196–201.

21. Slomowitz, M. "A Comparison of the Changes in Personality and Content Achievement Gains in Two Modes of Instruction." Doctoral thesis, New York Univer., in process.

22. Subcommittee on Counselor Trainee Selection, APA Division 17. "An Analysis of Practices in Counselor Trainee Selection," *J. Counsel. Psychol.*, I (1954), 174–179.

23. Wrenn, C. G. "The Ethics of Counseling," *Educ. Psychol. Measmt.* (1952), 12, 161–177.

24. Wrenn, C. G. "The Selection and Education of Student Personnel Workers," *Pers. and Guid. J.* (1952), 31, 9–14.

25. 1951 *Directory of Vocational Counseling Services.* Ethical Practices Committee, National Vocational Guidance Association, Washington, D.C. 1951.

26. *Directory of Approved Vocational Counseling Agencies.* American Personnel and Guidance Association, Washington, D.C. 1954.

27. *Ethical Standards of Psychologists.* Committee on Ethical Standards for Psychologists, American Psychological Association, Washington, D.C. 1953.

28. *Psychology and Its Relations with Other Professions.* Ad hoc Committee on Relations with Other Professions, American Psychological Association, Washington, 1954.

29. *Technical Recommendations for Psychological Tests and Diagnostic Techniques.* Joint Committee of the American Psychological Association, American Educational Research Association, and National Council on Measurements Used in Education. Supplement to *Psychol. Bull.* (1954), 2, 1–38.

33

Confidentiality and the School Counselor

Charles M. Clark, Ph.D.°

Maintaining appropriate confidentiality of the information received in a counseling interview is one of the most complex and pervasive problems confronting the school counselor. The problem of confidentiality brings into sharp focus the nature of the loyalties of the school counselor; to himself, to the profession of psychology, to the school system which employs him, and to the individual in counseling. The code of ethics of each of the professional groups involved outlines the counselor's responsibilities to the school and to the individual seeking his assistance but does not indicate which of these is to take precedence when there is a conflict of interests (APGA [1]; APA [2]; NEA [7]).

POSITIONS REGARDING CONFIDENTIALITY

Dr. Edward S. Bordin [3], Dr. C. Gilbert Wrenn [9], and the American Psychological Association [2] state that the counselor working in an organizational setting must decide for himself the nature and direction of his loyalties and responsibilities. Bordin [3] further states, however, that the counselor ". . . must operate within the limitations implied by the institution and by the amount of freedom it is willing to give him, fitting his behavior to the ethics of the sponsoring unit. . . ." The sponsoring unit for the school counselor is the school. The official spokesman for the school is the administrator; his position regarding confidentiality is therefore critical to the school counselor. B. S. McRae [6] reported the position on confidentiality of a representative cross section of the administrators of the State of Texas (representative in terms of geographical distribution and size of school). The population of the survey was comprised of 40 superintendents and 87 secondary school principals. The writer conducted a survey of the attitudes of counselors toward these same statements. The 80 counselors polled were enrolled in three advanced level National Defense Education Act Counseling and Guidance Institutes. They were from 27 states (13 from Texas) and had been counselors from zero to 11 years with a mean of 3.4 years.

°Dr. Clark is an Assistant Professor of Educational Psychology at California State College, Hayward. His article appeared originally in the *Personnel and Guidance Journal*, 43: 482 (January 1965), and is reprinted with permission of the author and of the journal.

The majority of the administrators (68 percent) and almost all of the counselors (95 percent) *agreed* a counselor should treat information obtained in a counseling interview (and the records of such information) as confidential to be discussed with no one except the student in counseling. A majority of the administrators *agreed* (76 percent) and almost all of the counselors *disagreed* (92 percent) with the position that a counselor should furnish any information obtained in a counseling situation to parents or the principal upon legitimate request. The administrators were *divided* in their opinion (52 percent agree, 43 percent disagree, 5 percent unusable responses) and the counselors united in their *disagreement* (93 percent disagree) regarding the position that a counselor should report to the principal infractions of school rules or civil laws discussed by a student in a counseling interview.

The position of these administrators regarding confidentiality appears, on the surface at least, to lack internal consistency. A better interpretation of their position might be, however, that the counselor should guard the privacy of the client but not have complete confidentiality of communication. The counselors, on the other hand, take the position that they should maintain complete confidentiality of information received in a counseling interview. The position of these counselors clearly is not congruent with that of the administrators who are the official spokesmen for the sponsoring unit, the school.

The *Code of Ethics* of the American Personnel and Guidance Association [1] contains several passages of significance to the problem of confidentiality. The general statement that introduces the pertinent section—Section B, Counseling—contains these two sentences: "Typically the counselee or client is the individual with whom the member has direct and primary contact. However, at times, the "client" may include another person(s) when the other person(s) exercise significant control and direction over the individual being helped in connection with the decisions and plans being considered in counseling." The general introduction is supplemented by nine statements from which the following pertinent information has been extracted. The *primary* obligation of the school counselor is to *respect* the *integrity* and *promote* the *welfare* of the client with whom he is working. Information obtained in a counseling interview (and the records of such information) must be kept confidential *consistent with the obligations of the counselor as a professional person*. Conditions under which such information may be revealed to others for professional purposes are delineated with a general condition that the identity of the client be concealed and with precautions to protect him from harm. When the counselor ". . . learns from counseling relationships of conditions which are likely to harm others for whom his institution or agency has responsibility, *he is expected to re-*

port the condition to the appropriate responsible authority but in such a manner as not to reveal the identity of his counselee or client. In the event that the counselee or client's condition is such as to require others to assume responsibility for him or when there is clear and imminent danger to the counselee or client or to others, the member is expected to report this fact to an appropriate responsible authority, and/or take such other emergency measures as the situation demands."

These passages do not state directly that information received in a counseling interview between a school counselor and a pupil has only limited confidentiality. It clearly may be inferred, however, that when a pupil is a minor with the attendant legal, moral, and other responsibilities of the parent and school such information must be shared with them in some form or manner, and therefore has only limited confidentiality. This inference indicates the position taken by the counselors in the sample group is not only incongruent with that of the administrators sampled but also is not supported by the official position of their own profession.

The following position is offered as a workable and ethical guide for the school counselor in regard to the confidentiality of the information received in a counseling interview with a pupil who is a minor. The degree of professional authority granted the counselor by the official spokesman (the administrator) of the sponsoring unit (the school) is the determinant of the amount of confidentiality delegated to the counselor in regard to information received in a counseling interview. The nature and confidentiality of the counselor's communications with pupils in counseling interviews, the form in which pertinent information from such interviews is to be transmitted, the method of transmission, and appropriate receivers of such information, should be defined by guidelines which are as clear and explicit as possible. These guidelines should be arrived at by mutual consent of the administrator and the counselor before the counselor is involved in counseling interviews. The counselor is responsible for communicating these conditions or limits on the confidentiality of information to pupils before the establishment of a counseling relationship.

The degree of confidentiality enjoyed by a specific set of information will depend upon the judgment of the counselor as to the manner in which the information may be used to the maximum advantage for the pupil and the school. The counselor's freedom to use his judgment is dependent upon the degree of professional authority delegated to him. If a rare instance should occur when the interests of the school and the pupil are in an irreconcilable conflict and the counselor must choose between them, the interests of the school should usually be given precedence. Even in such extreme cases the school counselor must strive to protect the welfare, privacy, and rights of the pupil against undue invasion.

COUNSELING WITH LIMITED CONFIDENTIALITY

Limited confidentiality, if agreed upon in advance by all of the people who are or may be concerned, provides an environment in which an effective counseling relationship may be developed in a public school setting. The child comes for counseling because of the anxiety engendered by inability to solve his problems or because he is referred by adults, but in any situation expecting the counselor to intervene in a manner which leads to a resolution of the problem. Rarely do such clients have expectancies of specific kinds of behavior on the part of the counselor, although they are most responsive in a climate of mutual respect, understanding, and integrity [5, 8]. This situation (institutional setting, working with children and adolescents, delegated professional authority, limited confidentiality, and expectancy of the client that the counselor will intervene in his life) gives the counselor latitude in allowing the client time to make his own decisions and act for himself, or permits the counselor to intercede actively in the case, if his professional judgment indicates this is the best course of action. This position places the responsibility for decisions in an individual case upon the professional judgment of the counselor and not upon predetermined solutions based on rules of ethics. The counselor in this situation may justifiably activate all of the therapeutic factors—home, school, and community—in a case. Usually of course, this should occur after consultation with the child, or parents, for the counselor has the responsibility of guarding the privacy and rights of the child against undue invasion [4]. In this situation information obtained during an interview will not usually be shared with other professional staff members in the school without the previous knowledge and consent of the client, but on occasion information may be shared for professional purposes without the knowledge or consent of the client and still be within the ethical limits of the situation. Sharing such information with people, even professional personnel, outside the school is not ethical without the expressed consent of the school and the child or his guardian. The ethics of the National Education Association [7], which are usually those of the school, expressly forbid such information being transmitted without the consent of the child or his guardian and therefore this is the usual limitation binding the school counselor.

REFERENCES

1. American Personnel and Guidance Association, Committee on Ethics. "Code of Ethics," *Personnel Guid., J.* (1961), *40*, 206–209.
2. American Psychological Association. *Ethical Standards of Psychologists.* Washington, D. C.: APA, 1962.

3. Bordin, E. S. *Psychological Counseling*. New York: Appleton-Century-Crofts, 1955.

4. Carter, T. M. "Professional Immunity for Guidance Counselors," *Personnel Guid. J.* 1954, *3*, 130–135.

5. Hobbs, N. "Sources of Pain in Psychotherapy," *Amer. Psychologist* (1962), *11*, 741–747.

6. McRae, B. S. "A Study of Administrators' Expectations of a Counselor in the High Schools of Texas." Unpublished master's thesis, Univ. Texas, Austin, 1963.

7. National Education Association. *Code of Ethics of the National Association of the United States*. Washington, D. C.: NEA, 1952.

8. Weitz, H. "Guidance as Behavior Change," *Personnel Guid. J.* (1961), *7*, 550–560.

9. Wrenn, C. G. "The Ethics of Counseling," *Educ. Psychol. Measmt.* (1952), *2*, 161–177.

34

Confidentiality: Where Is Our First Obligation?

Robert F. Cox, M.Ed.°

One concern of many writers in the guidance field has been with the subject of ethics in counseling. There is a general feeling that our desire to emerge as a profession should be matched by a greater desire to identify ourselves with a code of ethics. My concern in this paper is with the narrower area of confidentiality, and I would like to further limit the content to certain aspects of confidentiality as they apply to the counseling relationship.

There is much to be said about the proper confidential use of test results, student records, and transcript materials. But the basic area in guidance is still the counselor's office and the area of basic interest still centers in the activities that take place in this office between the counselor and the counselee. It is here that the distinction is made between the professional counselor and the teacher who asks questions. It is here that the student decides for himself whether he can find someone to accept him where he is and help him go where he wants to go, or whether he will find someone who is likely to look upon him as an object of curiosity and who will probably see to it that others share in approval or disapproval of what the student says. It is here he will decide whether this person is here to help, or to see to it that the school, which possibly may be the source of his troubles, is aware of his wrongdoing and that it has its will enforced. It is here he decides whether this is a fellow he can talk to. And if he decides this is not a fellow he can talk to, there is not much else in the guidance program, no matter how elaborate it may be, that justifies its existence.

Actually much of this student's decision has been made before he enters the office. He will have heard what happened to those who came before him. He will have noticed whether the teachers (by their words, their actions, or even by their looks) have had access to information his friends have confided to the counselor. He will have noticed an administrative action which could only have originated in the guidance office. He will know of the pregnant girl who took her troubles to the counselor and found

°Mr. Cox is a counselor at Susquehannock High School, Glen Rock, Pennsylvania. His article, in substantially similar form, appeared originally in *The School Counselor*, 12: 3: 153 (March 1965), and is reprinted with permission of the author and of the journal.

herself suddenly asked to leave school. He will know of the prank that was stopped before it happened and he will have some idea of the source of action that stopped it. He very often will have formed an idea of the reception the secret that so plagues him would receive if he were to share it with this man in the guidance office.

We say the student has formed an opinion based on what he has seen and heard. He hasn't heard everything. He hasn't heard of all the times the counselor kept a secret. He doesn't know that this particular counselor subscribes to the practice of confidentiality as outlined by Dr. Edward Bordin [2]: "The counselor's decision will depend upon such a characteristic of the situation as whether the client came to him voluntarily or at the request of the administrator who expects that the counselor will make a report or recommendation to him," or:

> Where the information requested is of a general sort that might easily be obtained from many sources, and where the counselor feels he is in no position to press upon the administration the distinction between a counselor's responsibility to an administrator and his responsibility to a client, the counselor would probably accede to the administrator's request even when it comes without the client's knowledge (p. 37).

In short, he doesn't know that the counselor has decided, in those cases the student has heard about, that, "it wasn't worth fighting city hall." He doesn't know that this counselor figures he must weigh each confidence and decide which to pass on and which to retain.

But what if the counselor felt that the student should know this? What if he made it his policy to do as Dr. C. Gilbert Wrenn said he would do [9]: "I will define my personal and ethical responsibility to my client as well as my legal and vocational responsibility to my organization and to society. I work for both the group to which I am responsible and for each individual that I serve as a client. This dual responsibility must be defined and understood by my employers and by myself." (p. 167) What if the student is made to realize that this counselor feels he must report *some* things, just as, as Dr. Frederick Thorne [8] points out, physicians must report tuberculosis, venereal disease, and gunshot wounds? Would our student go to the physician with his VD until the consequences of not going were greater than those of going? What purpose does it serve, other than to clear the counselor's conscience, to serve notice that you must repeat some things you hear, but that you are unable to tell before you hear them which ones you will have to repeat?

Or what if our student finds himself facing the counselor who has rationalized his actions by telling himself that he is dealing with a minor and thus knows better than he what must be done with this information? Wrenn [9] believes that, "A child's trust in a counselor may be betrayed as well as an adult's," and that "A child is very much a person and the integrity of his personality must be protected. . . " (p. 172) I quote Wrenn here with what seems a rather obvious statement mainly because I am continually surprised by the number of counselors who seem to think that being a child is very different from being a person.

So far we have sent our student to a counselor about whom he has heard tales of confidence violating, a counselor who makes it clear that he may have to violate confidence, and a counselor who considers him a child with little right of decision. Ethical considerations aside for the moment, how is our student likely to react to each of the three? There are, of course, all types of students and possibly all types of reactions. But is it not possible that, with the first type of counselor, no matter how justified the reasons for the broken confidences that the student has heard about, and no matter how much the counselor hastens to assure that, in this case, he will not repeat what he hears, our student will have no trust, and will relate nothing of his true feeling?

Is it not possible that, with the counselor who lays his cards on the table and admits he is going to be forced to repeat some of what he hears, the student will share what he knows to be harmless, but retain what he feels really threatens him? This, I would judge, is the most common reaction. It makes possible most of our present day vocational and educational counseling. It identifies the counselor as a likeable, well meaning, and rather harmless fellow, but it does not provide the troubled student with the setting of strength and security wherein he can emotionally undress and change his psychological clothing.

Is it possible that, while there are a considerable number of youngsters, depending on age and home background, who desire to be considered children and who want to place themselves in the hands of an authority figure who will take complete charge of them and their problems, doing with both as they please, the majority of the students we work with will avoid any contact with this type of counselor?

Here I would like to propose a fourth counselor, a counselor who can say to his client that he has never repeated a confidence without the consent of the client, and that he never intends to. I believe that it is possible to be a counselor in a public school and operate without repeating confidences. I intend to discuss the arguments against such a program of operation in their proper places later in this paper, but, in this section of the paper, I will limit myself to the statement that I believe we not only can, but must be ready to make this assurance to our counselees. If we are content to restrict ourselves to vocational and educational counseling our present approach is enough to serve the purpose. But if we are going to attempt to promote ourselves to junior-grade psychotherapy, we can no longer operate as school employed investigators. We can't ask the student to tell us all and refuse to assure him that we are not going to use this information against him or to effect a change in his life that he does not want. We can't go in to the interview as agents and protectors of the school and ask the student to have faith in our good will as he attacks the school. We must be prepared to tell him that, as far as the world beyond the closed door is concerned, what he has said has not been said.

We must, at the same time, make this so definite and so clear that he will not be tempted to test us to his own detriment. To take the extreme, you want to make sure the follow that threatens suicide is not going to be counting on you to thwart his attempt. You want to be sure that he understands that telling you about a future or past robbery does not relieve him of the responsibility of possessing the knowledge.

This, the fourth, counselor would be there for the sole purpose of counseling—of listening, of helping the student in his efforts to gather and organize a body of facts and ideas that will aid him in his attempt to solve, or at least deal with, his own problems. If this counselor is to be a manipulator, as most of us to some degree are, let him confine his manipulation to the counseling office, or to the outside only with the client's complete consent. To take the pregnant girl as an example: the counselor would first listen, and in listening try to guide the girl into her own working out of the problem. We will say here that it becomes apparent to the counselor that the girl really wants to go with the boy to face her parents, but that she is very much afraid. We will say also that the counselor, during the course of the session, comes to feel strongly that this would be the best thing to do. The counselor must first sit there patiently, maybe nudging a little in a subtle way here and there, while the girl tries to talk herself into the needed nerve. If the counselor sees this failing, he might start to manipulate within the counseling office by actively urging the girl to see the parents, or in suggesting that the girl invite the equally scared young man to come in with her to see the counselor. If the fear is still so great that action is impossible, the counselor may go so far in manipulating beyond the office door as to offer to go along with the pair if he feels this might accomplish the desired goal. But here he must stop. If the offer is rejected, he must realize that this is all he can do. He must realize that, no matter how tragic the outcome or how strong his feelings, if he manipulates without consent he is no longer a counselor. If he manipulates without consent the next pregnant girl will probably not give him a chance to offer to be of help.

This counselor can operate in this manner only if he subscribes to three basic principles: 1. That he, the counselor, will know in his mind how he will handle all confidential information before he asks the counselee to reveal that information. 2. That he will see to it by his actions and his words that client knows exactly how the counselor will deal with confidential information. And 3. That the counselor will under no circumstances depart from this policy, at whatever cost to himself or to his client.

THE COUNSELOR'S RESPONSIBILITY TO THE SCHOOL
AND SOCIETY

The fourth counselor that I have been advocating rather clearly places his obligation to the client above his obligation to school or society. Although I am traveling quite a bit farther from an allegiance to society than they would condone, I find the ethical principles outlined by the American Psychological Association [11] establish a rather firm base on which to build.

> The psychologist's ultimate allegiance is to society. . . . In nearly all circumstances, the welfare of the public, of the profession and of the individual psychologist can best be served by placing highest value on the immediate responsibility of the psychologist. . . In service, the responsibility of most weight is the welfare of the client with whom the psychologist is working (p. 2). When information received in confidences reveals clear and imminent danger that the client may do serious harm to himself or to others, intervention by the psychologist may be required. . . Otherwise, information obtained in professional work must be kept in confidence, recognizing that the clinical or consulting relationship can develop most fully only in an atmosphere of trust, and that the psychologist can serve society most effectively not by revealing confidences of antisocial events or intentions but by helping the individual realize himself as a socially competent and responsible person (p. 5).

The "clear and imminent danger" part must be discussed before I can justify my stand, but the rest of the statement goes far in establishing that I am best serving society by serving the individual.

The American School Counselor Association isn't as definite about the subject. I did find a suggested code of ethics published in May of 1961 in which Mary Flanagan [3] suggests, "The counselor is primarily responsible to the counselee, then to the school, and ultimately to society and its institutions, unless there is a conflict with the legal statutes or accepted mores of the community, or when the status or reputation of the school or its students is in question. . ." (p. 139).

It seems to me that the poor counselor would be so busy worrying about the "accepted mores" and the "status or reputation of the school" that he may have trouble bringing himself to listen to anything more threatening than an observation on the weather. If we must put in all of these unlesses and or whens we might as well not try to set up a code.

Going back to our brothers, the psychologists, who are not as concerned with the accepted mores as more than an environment in which to view their client, we must take some notice of their concern for the fellow who may harm himself or others. What do we do with the information he gives us and will not let us give to anyone else? Dr. Milton Schwebel [6] says we clear it with the administration and then go to the psychiatrist, physician or legal authority, but he acknowledges that the occasions when this is necessary are rare. Dr. Merle Ohlsen [4] says that the counselor who breaks confidence to protect others should refer his counselee to another counselor because, "When he turns against the pupil to protect others, he destroys the counseling relationship" (p. 288). Dr. C. H. Patterson [5] says each counselor must decide for himself in each case. I can't find anyone who says that the counselor should keep it to himself.

But what if the counselor is told by a girl that she is going to elope? We will say he feels this is wrong, but fails to talk the girl out of it. He calls the home and prevents the elopement. He feels he is justified because he has prevented her from doing harm to herself. But who asked him? The girl is carrying a problem around. She wants to think it through and has heard that the guidance office is a good place for this sort of activity. Unless this sort of thing happens often and she has heard that the counselor will take some action on what is said, she goes there looking for a place to talk and to think and maybe to even listen to what someone thinks of her elopement plans. She talks and listens to his arguments against her plan, and then she decided she will elope. She has asked for nothing more. She has brought a problem with her, examined it, gotten an opinion from the counselor and taken *her* problem on out of the office. What justification does the counselor have for listening? If she had chosen not to bring the problem to his office, he would never have heard about it. If she had not been led to believe that the counselor would not take any action she would probably not have brought the problem. So the problem is not his, but he makes it his. Now he assumes his God-playing role. He is so sure he is right he takes an action that can strongly alter the lives of at least two people, and he takes this action on the limited information he has heard in an interview. Are all elopements wrong? Is this one wrong for these two people? Are these parents right in this case? What is the right age to marry? What is the right age for these people to marry? Does he know enough to make a reasonable decision? Does he know enough to start fooling around with the lives of these two people uninvited?

He has called the parents, the elopement is off. The grateful parents tell their friends about the fine thing the counselor did. The friends discuss the affair over the supper table in front of the family. The family brings it back to school. Now who else is going to tell the counselor about their elopement plans. and who else is going to tell the counselor about the baby she is carrying? And how much help will this counselor be able to be to the others who might have been helped by the talking and the listening, but who now will not bring their problems to this adult who acts just like so many of the other adults and can be trusted no farther?

I see the counselor as one of a few with a very special job. There are many others in the school to enforce the school regulations. There are many others in society to enforce society's regulations and to see that right is done by society. Can we not afford a comparatively very small budgetary allotment for someone who will use a comparatively very small amount of school space to sit and concentrate his full allegiance on that most important institution, the individual?

While there is admittedly room for debate in the question of breaking confidence to prevent future harm, it seems only the more conservative educators still argue that the counselor must report harm that has been done. Most of our writers seem to feel pretty much as Ohlsen [4] does in the following passage: ". . . in his dealing with things which have already happened, which have no possibilities of dangerous future action . . . it is *not* the responsibility of the counselor to make sure that society's 'justice is done.' His first responsibility is to the person who seeks his help in achieving a better way of adjusting to life" (p. 289).

In summing up the section on responsibility to school and society with regard to confidentiality, we note the following points.: 1. While saying that the psychologist's ultimate allegiance is to society, the APA states that society is best served by honoring the confidence of the individual. 2. That it is generally agreed that reporting of past antisocial action is not the counselor's responsibility. 3. While there is some justification for believing the counselor might break confidence to prevent future harm to self and others, there is caution against rushing to assume a God playing role and there is the strong possibility that great damage will be done to the counselor's future ability to be of help because potential counselees will fear similar confidence breaking.

THE COUNSELOR'S RELATIONS WITH THE SCHOOL STAFF

Our question here has been stated by Wrenn [10]: "When fellow counselors, teachers, administrators inquire about a counselee, how does the counselor keep their good will while maintaining the integrity of his relationship with the student?" (p. 182)

We may first ask if we can ethically tell them anything. Flanagan [3] in her suggested code of ethics says, "The counselor will not discuss case matters or information obtained from a counselee with anyone outside or within his profession except as it is necessary to the welfare of the counselee or the ultimate solution of his problem" (p. 139).

It is noted that she does not say anything about consent. Our psychologist brothers give a little more respect to the client in their statement of principles [1]: "The psychologist should give clinical information about a client only to professional persons whom the client might reasonably be expected to consider a party to the psychologist's efforts to help him, and the client's concurrence should be obtained before there is any communication exceeding these customary limits" (p. 6).

Patterson [5] acknowledges a fact that most counselors feel when he cautions that most teachers are not to be considered "professional persons" and warns against giving information to them without the consent of the counselee.

While the general findings of counselors with regard to policies of the school and to education in general should certainly be given to the staff and administrators in the hope of improving the school, there is no need to associate this information to any particular student or incident. If the administrator must take some action with regard to the client and asks the counselor for his opinion, it would seem to me that the counselor could give his opinion only if it were based totally on facts gained outside of the interview. If his opinion is based on information from the interview the counselor must obtain the consent of the counselee to venture the opinion. Any discussion with fellow counselors should have the counselee's consent.

By now the reader is probably saying that this is all very professional and fine sounding, but what about that "good will' that Wrenn mentioned? This counselor must work with these teachers, this principal and these counselors. They are often his friends. Can he get away with being this secretive? He often depends on these same teachers for background information, upon this principal for support with the school board and in school policy, and upon his fellow counselors for advice and support to the general guidance program. How does he live with these people?

It is very interesting to see the number of books and articles [2, 3, 6, 7, 9, 10] which contain the suggestion that the counselor first look to himself in dealing with this problem. Is he really interested in the welfare of his client as he is in his own welfare? Doesn't he know any better? Schwebel [7] devotes an entire article to this topic and ends up with a list of reasons why counselors so often do the wrong thing. "Practices that are contrary to the best interests of the client appear to stem from (a) the overpowering self-interest of the professional worker as expressed in personal profit, self-enhancement, and the maintenance of security and status; (b) poor judgment, due in part at least to inexperience in problem solving in counseling, and (c) ignorance of technical knowledge and of one's own values" (p. 128).

The word "courage" comes up often. Sometimes it is courage of a special sort. Marshal Dillon, on the old radio version of "Gunsmoke" would open the program with, "It's a chancy job, and a little bit lonely." He, of course, was talking about his job as marshal, but he could just as easily be talking about the counselor's job. The counselor must be prepared to take chances in his protection of confidence. The student tells him he cheated on the last exam, the counselor keeps this information to himself, the student is later caught and announces that he had told the counselor all about it. The girl says she is going to run away, the counselor doesn't repeat the information, the girl runs away, and the counselor wonders what he should have done. It's a chancy job. And the counselor must have the courage to take some chances.

And it is a lonely job. How many people want to admit publicly that they ever had problems, much less point you out as the one who helped them solve these problems? Are the girls who invite you to their weddings the ones who knew you mainly as a nice person around school, or the ones who discussed their sexual problems with you? A good counselor is seldom a public hero. Might it then be natural that our counselor, after a rough day in the counseling office, wants to go to the faculty room and be accepted by his fellow faculty members. And is it not an easy way to draw attention to one's self by repeating something interesting you have just heard in the counseling office, while at the time rationalizing the repetition as a professional discussion with a fellow professional with the future good of the counselee as its aim?

As we must have the courage to take chances, we must also have the courage to be at least professionally lonely.

Often this matter of living with these co-workers successfully is one of gaining their respect for counseling as a profession. Wrenn [9] presents this argument rather concisely, "If people generally are to regard counseling with respect because counselors consider themselves to be professional men, then the members of this profession must have a clear understanding of its social purpose and obligation. So long as the counseling function is merely an arm or a projection of some institution there is little problem, for under these conditions it tacitly adopts the principles and procedures of its parent organization. If, however, counseling is to operate independently or is to have professional independence within an institution then its status as an independent profession demands a clear understanding of its ethical obligation" (p. 162–63). Thus, the counselor I have been advocating, who must have professional independence to operate as I have outlined, must identify himself as a professional, and make it clear to those around him that he is acting according to the principles of his profession, not by personal whim. The question of acceptance will then center on the professional and not on the counselor. Once the profession is accepted, the counselor's task is much easier, and his own acceptance becomes a matter of his own personality and not of his performance of his job.

In summing up the section on the counselor's relations with the school staff, we note the following points: 1. Although he may generalize the findings from a number of interviews in making suggestions with regard to school or educational policy, he may repeat actual contents of specific interviews only with the consent of the counselee. 2. The counselor must examine his own motives when tempted to reveal confidential material to a fellow worker and must have the courage to take chances in holding back information and the courage to experience the professional loneliness that often accompanies the keeping of confidence. 3. The counselor must identify himself as a professional, and make it clear that he is operating according to the principles of his profession.

SUMMARY

I have in this paper advocated a counselor that possibly doesn't exist in any school today. I know he doesn't exist in mine. But I believe that, if we are ever to do a really effective job of counseling and overcome some of the handicaps that have been set up for us and some of those that we have set up for ourselves, we must adopt and adapt the following points:

1. The counselor must know how he will handle all confidential interview information before the counselee enters his office, and he must be determined that under no circumstances will he depart from that policy.

2. The counselor must see to it that by his actions and his words the client will know exactly how the counselor will deal with confidential information.

3. The counselor best serves society by honoring the confidence of the individual.

4. The counselor has no responsibility to report past anti-social action.

5. The counselor should make every effort to avoid the breaking of confidence to prevent the client's harming of self or others, knowing that by the breaking of such confidence he is jeopardizing his future effectiveness.

6. The counselor's responsibility to the school administration and staff should include only the reporting of generalized conclusions from numbers of interviews as they affect school and educational policy.

7. The counselor must examine his own motives for revealing confidential information, and must have the courage to take chances and risk professional loneliness.

8. The counselor must identify himself as a professional, and make it clear that he is operating according to the principles of his profession.

REFERENCES

1. American Psychological Association. *Ethical Standards of Psychologists, a Summary of Ethical Principles*. Washington, D. C., 1953.

2. Bordin, Edward S. *Psychological Counseling*. New York: Appleton-Century-Crofts, Inc., 1955.

3. Flanagan, Mary M. and McGrew, David R. "A Suggested Code of Ethics for School Counselors," *The School Counselor*, Vol. 8 (May 1961), 136–141.

4. Ohlsen, Merle M. *Guidance, an Introduction*. New York: Harcourt, Brace and Company, 1955.

5. Patterson, C. H. *Counseling and Psychotherapy, Theory and Practice*. New York: Harper & Brothers, 1959.

6. Schwebel, Milton. "Some Ethical Problems in Counseling," *The Personnel and Guidance Journal*, Vol. 33 (January 1955), 254–259.

7. Schwebel, Milton. "Why-Unethical Practice?" *Journal of Counseling Psychology*, Vol. 2 (Summer 1955), 122–128.

8. Thorne, F. C. *Principles of Personality Counseling, Journal of Clinical Psychology*. Vermont: Brandon, 1950.

9. Wrenn, C. Gilbert. "The Ethics of Counseling," *Educational and Psychological Measurement*, Vol. 12 (Summer 1952), 161–177.

10. Wrenn, C. Gilbert. "Status and Role of the School Counselor," *The Personnel and Guidance Journal*, Vol. 36 (November, 1957), 175–183.

35

Confidentiality of Student Records: A Counselor's Point of View

Elizabeth A. Burianek, M.A.*

As a member of the American Personnel and Guidance Association, a counselor is bound by the statement of Ethical Standards, first published by the Association in 1961. Two of the APGA principles are especially applicable to the matter of confidentiality:

1. The counseling relationship and information resulting therefrom must be kept confidential consistent with the obligations of the member as a professional person.

2. Records of the counseling relationship including interview notes, test data, correspondence, tape recordings, and other documents are to be considered professional information for use in counseling, research, and teaching of counselors but always with full protection of the identity of the client and with precaution so that no harm will come to him.

Thus, for example, the counselor should not repeat the funny story the sophomore boy tells about the time when, as a seven-year-old, he stole a doll dress to costume his white rat for a pet show. The uniqueness of the story would easily identify it with the boy, and a repetition of it in his presence and the presence of others might destroy the boy's confidence in his counselor.

Indeed, the counselor who does not guard against retelling the "funny story I heard at school today" will find fewer and fewer students turning to him for counseling. They may still seek him out as a source of information about college placement or job openings, but they will be reluctant to confide in him the kind of information essential to a true counseling situation. No single item can be assumed to be insignificant.

The counselor must be a constant guardian of information divulged to him by the counselee. He must not discuss such information with others unless he receives permission from the student to do so, and then only when the discussion facilitates professional work with the student.

For example, what does the counselor do when his principal orders him to divulge information about a student to a third party who is not in

°Elizabeth T. Burianek is a counselor at Washington High School, Cedar Rapids, Iowa. Her article appeared originally in the *NEA Journal*, 55: 28 (January 1966), and is reprinted with permission of the author and of the journal.

any way connected with the school? In one such case of which I know, the principal sent to the counselor a private investigator who was gathering information about a boy. The investigator's clients, who were personal friends of the principal, did not want the young man to marry their daughter.

When the counselor refused to divulge information about the boy, the investigator complained to the principal, who subsequently ordered release of the information. In this case, the counselor was left with only one choice, as indicated by another principle in the APGA statement on ethics: "Within the member's own work setting, if, despite his efforts, he cannot reach agreement as to acceptable ethical standards of conduct with his superiors, he should end his affiliation with them."

In short, the counselor must resist pressure to release personal information, even pressure from superiors. Otherwise, he should resign.

What does a counselor do about employer inquiries?

In one such case, an employer seeking an "ideal" clerical worker called the school to inquire about a former student. He asked the counselor questions about what kind of family the applicant came from, whether she would be "meeting her boy friends for lunch," and how likely she would be to leave home to share an apartment with other girls.

The counselor limited his reply to the usual report on attendance and grades but refused any further information. Even though the interests of this businessman might have been served by divulging personal information about the applicant, they are not the primary concern of the school, at least so far as a counselor is concerned. Furthermore, the counselor has no business making the kind of value judgments the employer demanded of him.

No matter how strongly or frequently he is challenged to offer information, the counselor must check his actions against his primary obligation, which is, in the words of the APGA statement, "to respect the integrity and promote the welfare of the counselee or client with whom he is working."

Thus, the counselor must guard against not only those persons who serve their own interests by seeking information about a counselee but also some persons who seek to help the student.

For instance, not long ago a sympathetic woman called the school in her neighborhood to offer her home as a study hall for a girl whose parents were holding nightly and noisy fights. The woman felt that the bickering in the house might be interfering with the girl's school work and she wanted a report of the girl's grades. The counselor did not give the woman the grades and courteously declined to cooperate in any way with her.

The counselor was not judging the sincerity of the woman's offer; she was merely protecting the integrity of the girl. The girl might well have considered the woman's offer an intrusion on her privacy and on her right to help herself. If she had wanted her neighbor to know her grades, she herself could have shown the woman her report card.

The examples cited demonstrated the need for the counselor to be constantly on guard not only against others but also against himself. He must guard against his own inadvertent and inappropriate disclosures by exercising self-control, sound judgment, and discrimination. He must guard against others by resisting pressures, both public and private, from superiors, prospective employers, and unauthorized "helpers." The welfare and integrity of the counselee must always come first.

36

*Statement on Confidentiality of Student Records**

In the summer of 1966, the House Un-American Activities Committee issued subpoenas to obtain from two leading universities the membership lists of campus organizations known to oppose the present policies of the United States in southeast Asia. The institutions in question complied. Thus far, the information obtained by the Committee has not been publicly released.

Although educational institutions, like others, have an obligation to cooperate with committees of the Congress, they also have an obligation to protect their students from unwarranted intrusion into their lives and from hurtful or threatening interference in the exploration of ideas and their consequences that education entails. The American Council on Education therefore urges that colleges and universities adopt clear policies on the confidentiality of students' records, giving due attention to the educational significance their decisions may have.

For educational reasons, our colleges typically favor the forming by students of organizations for political activity and the consideration of politically relevant ideas. For instance, space is regularly provided such groups for offices and meetings. In such circumstances, it seems only appropriate for students to expect their institutions to resist intimidation and harassment. Where particular persons are suspected of violating the law or are thought to possess information of value to an investigatory body, they can be directly approached in properly authorized ways. There is no need to press the college or university into the doubtful role of informant.

The maintenance of student records of all kinds, but especially those bearing on matters of belief and affiliation, inevitably creates a highly personal and confidential relationship. The mutual trust that this relationship implies is deeply involved in the educational process. Colleges acquire from students and other sources a great deal of private information about their enrollees for the basic purpose of facilitating their development

°This "Statement on Confidentiality of Student Records" was formulated by staff members of the American Council on Education, and endorsed by the Board of Directors of the Council in June 1967. Although the statement focuses upon problems more typically encountered in the college setting than in the public school, its implications are clear for pupil personnel workers who practice their profession at other school levels—particularly in secondary schools. The Statement is reproduced with permission of the American Council on Education, Washington, D.C.

as educated persons. This purpose is contravened when the material is made available to investigatory bodies without the student's permission. Thus, although a student may not require that his record be withdrawn, improperly altered, or destroyed, he may appropriately expect his institution to release information about him only with his knowledge and consent. Without that consent, only irresistible legal compulsion justifies a college's indicating anything more about a student than his name, dates of registered attendance, the nature of any degrees granted, and the dates on which degrees were conferred.

The educational concept of a confidential relationship between the student and his college or university is supported here by the legal principles of freedom of association and the right of privacy. Like other citizens, students are entitled to engage in lawful assembly; if they are to learn true respect for the Constitution, they must learn from their own experience that that entitlement is never abridged without serious reflection, due cause, and profound reluctance. Similarly, at a time when every individual's privacy is subject to serious erosion, each new invasion should be strongly resisted. Except in the most extreme instances, a student's college or university should never be a source of information about his beliefs or his associations unless he has given clear consent to its serving this function.

Finally, requests for information about a student's beliefs and associations inevitably imply the spectre of reprisals. To the extent that they do, they put at hazard the intellectual freedom of the college and the university. This dampening of free inquiry and expression may affect faculty members and administrative officers as well as students. It is therefore in the interests of the entire academic community to protect vigilantly its traditions of free debate and investigation by safeguarding students and their records from pressures that may curtail their liberties. America cannot afford a recurrence of the incursions made on intellectual freedom in the 1950's.

In the light of these considerations, the American Council on Education offers four recommendations to institutions of higher learning:

1. Mindful of the principle that student records should be held in a relationship of confidentiality between the student and the institution, each college and university should formulate and firmly implement clear policies to protect the confidential nature of student records. Such policies should reflect a full understanding of the intimate connections between this relationship and the historic traditions of freedom of association, of the right of privacy, and of intellectual liberty.

2. When demands which challenge the fundamental principle of confidentiality are made for information about students' beliefs or associations, no response, beyond the reaffirmation of the principle, should be made without consultation with attorneys. Counsel for the institution

should be asked not merely to advise a prudent course, but to prepare every legal basis for resistance.

3. Institutional policy should pay proper respect to the interests of research and scholarship to insure that the freedom of inquiry is not abridged. Neither investigators seeking generalizable knowledge about the educational enterprise, historians examining the background of a deceased alumnus who became a publicly significant figure, nor other legitimate scholars should be unduly restricted in their pursuits. The confidentiality of the individual student's record is paramount, however. When there is any doubt about its being safeguarded, the person's consent to its use should be formally obtained, and the same general principles should be applied to the preservation of records as are recommended here with respect to the maintenance of records.

4. Colleges and universities should discontinue the maintenance of membership lists of student organizations, especially those related to matters of political belief or action. If rosters of this kind do not exist, they cannot be subpoenaed, and the institution is therefore freed of some major elements of conflict and from the risks of contempt proceedings or a suit. To communicate with a campus group, the institution needs only to know its officers, not its entire membership. Whatever may be the advantages of more comprehensive listings, they must be considered, in the determination of policy, against the disadvantages and dangers outlined here. In addition, it must be remembered that the surrender of membership rosters to investigative bodies carries no guarantee that they will not be reproduced and fall eventually into unfortunate hands. The use of blacklists, limited neither in time nor by honor, is a practice to which no college or university wishes to be, even inadvertently, an accessory.

Catharsis

27A. How might NEA's Code of Ethics be made operable and enforceable in public schools by counselors? What role should teachers play? Administrators?

27B. NEA's Code expresses the responsibility of the profession for the conduct of its members. What does this mean? How far does it go? What responsibilities do counselors have under this provision for the conduct of their counseling colleagues? Do counselors assume responsibility for the conduct of teachers? Of administrators?

27C. According to the NEA Code of Ethics, members must "Represent honestly our professional qualifications. . ." How does this relate to the suggestion that counselors place the initials of the highest degree after their names in correspondence and display framed diplomas and credentials on the walls of their offices? How about encouraging classroom teachers with masters' and doctors' degrees to do the same? Why not a shingle on each teacher's classroom door, giving full name and highest degree? Ours *is* the academic profession; why not let it be known that educators have succeeded at what we encourage others to accomplish?

28A. How might APGA's Code of Ethics be made operable and enforceable in public schools by counselors?

28B. It has been estimated that only about one-third of practicing counselors in the public schools are members of APGA. What effect might this have upon the question of ethical behavior? What influence might it have on other questions relating to professionalism?

28C. APGA's Code of Ethics holds members responsible for the conduct of other members, and of non-members as well. Can the reader see how this might create problems in the school setting? How might such problems be handled?

28D. The reader should select five principles from the APGA Code, indicate how each might cause problems for the counselor, and suggest how the solution to these problems might best be approached.

29A. With reference to Dr. Adams' paper, under specifically what conditions might the counselor's duty to society outweigh responsibilities to his client?

29B. Dr. Adams says, "Counselors in all areas of work should clearly recognize the limits of their competence and should not offer services which fail to meet the professional standards of recognized specialists in the fields in question." Do we also assert that members of other helping professions should not offer services in *our* area of special competence? How might we make such an assertion effective?

29C. Dr. Adams warns against injudicious referrals to other professionals, particularly when the question of competence is at issue. How might the counselor assess competency among members of other helping professions? What are the appropriate ways to refer clients to other professionals, i.e., psychologists in the community? What standards might the counselor employ in determining to what psychologist he would refer? What if there is more than one qualified psychologist in the community? What should the counselor's criteria be? (Would the readers consider an alphabetical list, revised annually, of APA-affiliated psychologists, to be handed out as necessary?)

29D. How does the question of ethics relate to the matter of counselors preparing college recommendations? Recommendations for employment personnel in business? Military recruiters? Should we obtain routinely blanket, signed consents for the release of such data and withhold all information in the absence of such release? If the client has signed away his privacy rights, what might this do to the counseling relationship? If he does not waive confidentiality, then how can we ethically reveal *anything* about him: to colleges, business, the FBI, etc., etc.?

29E. How does the reader react to Dr. Adams' suggestion that counselors don't really know enough to use "psychological jargon" (i.e., "professional language with specialized meaning"?) or to determine if a client is demonstrating schizophrenic tendencies, and should confine himself to such statements as, " 'I feel that the counselee has an emotional problem which needs attention' "? Should counselors, as front-line workers in mental health, be able by virtue of training to be more precise and meaningful than this?

29F. Dr. Adams raises the interesting suggestion that counselors operate on a fee-for-service basis with graduates for whom their publicly supported services have been terminated. The reader might react to this proposition. How about the notion of counselors maintaining evening hours once or twice a week to provide fee services for former clients?

29G. Why might it be, as Dr. Adams reports, that school counselors tend to focus more on society and college counselors focus more on the client?

29H. Dr. Adams quotes Dr. Carol Smith's standard that "A counselor should not intervene in a counselee's curriculum choice despite predictive evidence of academic or emotional outcomes." One of the counselor's functions in a school is to assist in educational planning. Is it not appropriate for counselors to make professional recommendations, based upon their unique expertise? Is the notion of counselor-as-educational-expert in-consistent with the notion of the non-judgmental-image many would want the counselor to convey? To what extent do readers feel the practicing counselor should ethically "intervene" in students' curriculum choices?

29I. Dr. Smith is quoted as suggesting that "It is ethical for a coun-selor to gather information about a counselee from other schools without the counselee's consent." But is it ethical for the *other* school to make such disclosures without consent? What are some of the implications here? Clearly, confidentialities are not violated if exchanged among professional people for the benefit of the client—but what if such confidential reports and statements pass through the hands of a clerk on the way from one professional to another? What if School A requests confidential informa-tion on a transfer student from School B, and the staff of School B know that counselors at School A are untrained, unqualified, uncertified, and unwilling to affiliate with professional associations? Would it be ethical for the people at School B to release information to such unproven re-cipients? What if Counselor X, known as one who entertains social guests with amusing stories of the strange and unhappy kids he deals with, re-quests confidential information from Counselor Z, who is taking a new position or leaving the community? Should Counselor Z release the in-formation to X?

30A. What reference to Dr. Schmidt's article, might the counselor's withholding of private information be justified on the Constitutional guar-antee to citizens of freedom from unreasonable searches and seizures?

30B. Would it be advisable for local guidance associations to employ attorneys on a retainer basis, to be available in the event information or legal assistance is needed? Might they share an attorney similarly em-ployed by the teachers' organization? What problems might this procedure raise?

30C. How might a counselor react to a parent's suit for damages against him on the basis that "derogatory material" concerning the parent's child is on file in the counselor's office?

30D. Dr. Schmidt says, "The unique social service the school counselor performs must be identified in a manner which will differentiate it from the services properly provided by all other staff in the school setting." How do we distinguish between "guidance" and "counseling," and what members of the school's professional staff are properly involved in which?

30E. What leadership are practitioners prepared to provide to meet Dr. Schmidt's suggestion that "Standards for the selection and training of school counselors must be developed and such standards must be accepta-ble to the corporate group of qualified school counselors as well as to those professional schools offering counselor preparation of high quality"? Are practitioners prepared to develop and enforce such standards?

30F. Dr. Schmidt says, "Neither do most trainees discover much about [the demands of the Real World of counseling] during the more or less didactic phases in the early part of their training. There one reads and listens and discusses what counseling is about but it does not seem to have much reality, even in the most interesting and inspiring moments of theoretical or philosophical discovery." What might practitioners do to assure themselves that trainees will be well prepared in the realities of school counseling? Is it of any importance to practitioners that persons preparing to work with them experience such training? What are the ethical issues here?

30G. Dr. Schmidt refers to the "personal demands that counseling can make on a counselor that will test his limits." How might trainees be exposed to these demands? Should training programs be toughened? Should features of harassment be introduced to test the trainees' limits? Would it be helpful for counselor educators to play very heavily loaded, emotional tapes of counseling interviews for students in the first introductory course? Should a deliberate effort be made to scare off the faint of heart?

31A. Referring to the article by Dr. Geiser and Mr. Rheingold, if the question is raised as to the need for psychologists to enjoy the rights and responsibilities of privileged communication, should we ask if school counselors should share these rights and responsibilities? Do counselors really need the protection of privileged communication?

31B. "Assumption of confidence" may be the crucial issue in any discussion of privileged communication. Do clients of the school counselor *assume* that their communications will be regarded as private, e.g., privileged?

31C. What of privileged communication in the case of the minor child *vis-a-vis* his parent? May not the parent legitimately and lawfully demand to know what his child tells the counselor? What effect might the counselor have under such a circumstance by asserting that while the child is in school, teachers (and counselors) stand *in loco parentis*, and, in law, *are* the parents during school hours?

31D. What should the counselor do, uphold his client's right to privacy and possibly face a contempt charge, or break the client's trust and reveal confidential information?

31E. What might be involved if counselors were to assert that society could place trust in their absolute competence to determine if revealing a confidence was in society's interest?

31F. Americans are protected so that they need not testify against themselves. Do they, in consulting a counselor, waive this Constitutional right—is the counselor potentially an agent of the court? If not, then isn't it true that the professional recipient of information freely given *also* may be assumed to have an extension of the Constitutional protection afforded his client?

31G. To *which* counselors might privileged communication be extended? Remember that in most states any third grade dropout can suspend a shingle from his front porch and go into business as a "counselor"— or as a "psychologist." Is the *counselor* privileged or is his *client*?

31H. The reader should react to the following proposition: "The good potentially derived from privileged communication for counselors is enough to outweigh any possible evils which might on occasion accompany the right."

31I. Several Supreme Court decisions of the middle 1960's dealt with rights of the accused. Might a defense attorney not properly challenge testimony from a counselor, and thus protect the confidential relationship, on the ground that the client, in divulging confidences, was not warned by the counselor that his statements might be used against him?

32A. Dr. Schwebel cites the case of a naval psychologist who refused to obey an order by his senior officer, who was making unqualified intrusions into the psychologist's area of specialization. To what extent is the counselor, as a specialist, prepared to refuse orders of administrative superiors which intrude into the counselor's particular area of expertise? Is the counselor ready to accept full responsibility for the conduct of his practice?

32B. Select any one of the cases of improper conduct cited by Dr. Schwebel, and indicate in some depth how similar problems might be avoided among counselors as a result of (a) modified training programs, (b) colleague evaluations, and (c) enforcement by counselors of ethical conduct among fellow practitioners.

33A. Referring to Dr. Clark's paper: many administrators, according to considerable research, simply don't know what counselors are around the building for. Naturally, this clouds several ethical questions. Specifically what might be done to correct this situation? What *specific* steps is the reader prepared to take, *right now*, to get *at* this issue?

33B. If "only limited confidentiality" may be inferred by the counselor from the APGA Code, then should he proceed on the assumption that he can guarantee *any* privacy about *anything* to his clientele? Why is privacy important, anyway?

33C. Must pupil needs *always* be evaluated in terms of *school* needs? Even when there's no conflict? What happens when the needs of Client A conflict with the needs of Clients B–Z?

33D. Dr. Clark says, "The counselor's freedom to use his judgment is dependent upon the degree of professional authority delegated to him." Do we wait for this delegation or simply assume that as highly trained professionals we should *assume* it? What do we do about the principal who imagines that the counselor should spend his time handing out occupational literature, lecturing home room classes on the virtues of promptness and diligence to studies, taking lunch money, and patrolling the corridors? To engage in conflict (or even reasoned discussion) with such a character might well cause the counselor to lose his position. While it's true that the counselor is ethically bound to resign when circumstances make professional practice impossible or unreasonably difficult, is it not also true that most counselors need to consider supporting their families and few are prepared to be martyrs to the cause and move from school to school?

33E. Must we assume that since our clients are, for the most part, minors that they have no rights to privacy? If they *have* rights to privacy, do we deny to them the right to share their privacy with a counselor? Do we then say to them that as counselors we must share what they say with parents, or others? What are some of the implications here?

34A. Mr. Cox suggests that if as counselors "we are going to attempt to promote ourselves to junior-grade psychotherapy, we can no longer operate as school employed investigators." Is the counselor properly conceived of as a "junior-grade psychotherapist"? What's the difference between a psychotherapist and a counselor working with personal-social problems? Is counseling therapeutic? If we are trained as counselors, and if counseling can be therapeutic, then what is there about our profession which is "junior-grade"? How might our work differ from that of the "senior-grade" psychotherapist?

34B. If the counselor comes into possession of information regarding a past robbery and does not reveal it, does he become, in law, an accessory? If he learns of a planned robbery and does nothing, could he be considered both an accessory and a conspirator to felony (in itself a felonious offense)? Does the Code of Ethics cover this situation?

34C. If "the accepted mores of the community" have any relationship whatever to the counselor's regard for private communications from his client, what might be done by the Unreconstructed Southern counselor, in possession of information that a Caucasian student believes in civil rights for Negroes? Are there broader implications?

34D. Suppose the girl planning to elope talks it over with her counselor. He says nothing. She elopes. Her father then comes raging around demanding the counselor's head on a platter. Would the counselor's colleagues back him up? What about the administration? Suppose Daddy is on the school board, or runs the local newspaper? Suppose the girl's under 18—could that make the counselor an accessory and conspirator to statutory rape?

34E. Mr. Cox quotes Dr. Schwebel to the effect that in the case of a client who we feel may harm himself or others, we should "clear it with the administration and then go to the psychiatrist, physician or legal authority . . ." Why on earth should we run to the physician when a client says he's going to harm someone? If hospitalization or sedation is required, the issue is fairly clear—but suppose it's a matter of pronounced hostility associated with adolescent jealousy? Aren't we capable of handling such eventualities? Under what conditions should the medical referral be made?

34F. How does the reader react to the apparent agreement Mr. Cox expresses toward the notion attributed to Dr. C. H. Patterson that "most teachers are not to be considered 'professional persons' "?

34G. What is our ethical responsibility when we hear continually from students and parents about a teacher or two whose behaviors as reported are clearly suggestive of malpractice or incompetence? Scuttle off to the administration? Deal directly with the teacher? Report to a Professional Practices and Standards Committee? Keep quiet? What are some of the implications of each approach?

35A. Miss Burianek suggests that there is "only one choice" when the principal orders release of confidential information, and that choice is to abide by ethical principles and resign. But another choice remains to be made—while still in the position, what must the counselor do about the information the principal has ordered released? If the counselor refused to reveal it, might he be branded "a troublemaker," "uncooperative," or "unprofessional" in administrative parlance? What effect might this have on his future employability? What protection do counselors have, or what protections can they develop, against the occasional administrative dud who has life or death powers over the careers of other specialists?

35B. What might the counselor do when the mother of the sweetest, most naive little thing in the sophomore class phones and asks if her daughter should accept a date to an upcoming dance with a senior boy who is known to the school staff as an amoral lout with a long juvenile court history, most of which relates to sexual offenses? Suppose that both students are the counselor's clients.

36A. The American Council on Education's statement was drawn with the university in mind. Identify some ways in which the statement might be equally applicable to the secondary school, and suggest various difficulties which might be anticipated by counselors in defending the principles enunciated.

Termination

Probably no one would quarrel with the proposition that first-rate service is the basis on which all considerations of professionalism must rest, and that professional problems in school counseling practice must, ultimately, get back to the basic question of just how good the service is as it is experienced by other educators, parents, students, and all the rest of those who are touched by the school counselor in his work.

Beyond that, however, other issues arise—and these are the issues which have perhaps received too little attention in the past and to which school counselors, as well as those who train them, must attend with increasing forcefulness if our young and vigorous art-science is to prosper internally and to be maximally effective externally. It is to these ancillary but vital issues that the reader has been exposed in the preceding pages, and it remains the editor's hope that the readings presented herein have contributed in some measure to facilitating the growth traumas of our special sort of work.

A book of this kind doesn't really start in one place and end at another. It doesn't reflect that kind of story, since counselors don't interact with fiction. Since the book deals in what one hopes to have been an ordered fashion with various matters of professional concern and significance, a beginning and end are implicit; however, the problems discussed within these covers are circular in nature, and will remain so, interwoven and overlapping, until those of us who teach and practice school counseling have resolved the questions presented. Thus, the book does not end here, but continues until the issues no longer exist. The readings will need to be studied and considered until their pertinence becomes a matter of historical curiosity.

Is counseling a unique profession, or is it a specialty within professional education?

Is teaching experience necessary for the school counselor?

What of our role? Who should define it?

What of the half-breed counselor—he who dabbles in teaching or administration?

Are there needs for improving counselor education, or of reshaping it? Are training programs as they should be for the school counseling practitioner?

What relationship should exist between senior practitioners and the training of candidates, their certification, evaluation, and retention?

What is the school counselor's professional identification? *Who* is his professional model?

What of the practitioner's autonomy within the practice of his profession (be it education or counseling), *vis-a-vis* lay control?

What of the workability of codes of ethics, and how do we enforce their provisions?

None of these are easy questions, nor are quick responses indicative of the serious attention each deserves.

If counseling is to come of age—as a unique profession or as a specialty within some existing profession—answers must be found to these questions and many more. We must be prepared to position ourselves and to defend actively the stances we have assumed, whatever they may be.

In hope that the papers collected here will assist the reader and his organizations in defining the positions which must be taken and held, all are left to what is hoped will be their more fortified devices to get on with the work which remains to be done.